HANDBOOK OF
DENOMINATIONS

IN THE UNITED STATES

HANDBOOK OF DENOMINATIONS

IN THE UNITED STATES

Second Revised Edition

Frank S. Mead

Abingdon Press

NEW YORK • NASHVILLE

7064

HANDBOOK OF DENOMINATIONS IN THE UNITED STATES

Library of Congress Catalog Card Number: 61-8412

SET UP, PRINTED, AND BOUND BY THE
PARTHENON PRESS, AT NASHVILLE,
TENNESSEE, UNITED STATES OF AMERICA

TO
THOSE IN THE CHURCH who see that the great truths we
hold in common are of more importance to God and
man than the little fences and barriers which divide us

This book is dedicated

ACKNOWLEDGMENTS

Many people, many books and sources contribute to the building of such a book as this; to them we would immediately admit our debt. The account of each religious body represented in these pages has been prepared from the latest and most authentic data available—from historical records, statistical reports, conference minutes and the official statements of innumerable boards, commissions, and committees supplied promptly and gratis by innumerable and most co-operative denominational officials and spokesmen. Without them the book would have been impossible. Most sections have been read, corrected, and often amended by authorities within the churches. The critics, both friendly and furious, have had their say—and often their way— except in those cases where propaganda seemed to outweigh accurate and objective information. Out of it has come, we trust, a book both accurate and fair. To these critics—our unspeakable gratitude.

Hundreds of books have been consulted; it would be impossible to list a complete bibliography. A dozen encyclopedias have been a very present help in time of need. In the field of American cults, minor religious movements, and the smaller sects, *The Small Sects in America,* by Elmer T. Clark (Abingdon Press, 1949), and *These Also Believe,* by Charles S. Braden (The Macmillan Company, 1949), have been invaluable. We are also indebted to *How We Got Our Denominations* (revised edition), by Stanley I. Stuber (Association Press, 1959); *Yearbook of American Churches,* edited by Benson Y. Landis (National Council of the Churches of Christ in the U.S.A.); *The Story of Religions in America,* by William Warren Sweet (Harper & Brothers, 1930); *Religion in America,* by Willard L. Sperry (Macmillan, 1946); *Protestantism, a Symposium,* edited by William K. Anderson (Commission on Courses of Study, The Methodist Church, 1944); *The March of Faith,* by Winfred Ernest Garrison (Harper & Brothers, 1933); *Primer for Protestants,* by James Hastings Nichols (Association Press, 1947); *The American Churches,* by William Warren Sweet (Abingdon Press, 1948); *What Americans Believe and How They Worship,* by J. Paul Williams (Harper & Brothers, 1952); *Churches and Sects of Christendom,* by J. L. Neve (Lutheran Publishing House, 1952); and *The Religious Bodies of America,* by F. E. Mayer (Concordia Publishing House, 1954).

Perhaps the reader should be warned: we have endeavored to produce not a popular "digest," nor a book of opinion, criticism, or value judgments, but a reference volume concerned only with factual truth as it is involved in the development of the religious bodies of the United States. In this second revised edition, we have checked and rechecked information which has appeared in earlier editions and added such other information as was deemed important and necessary by the various denominational authorities with whom we worked. Every effort has been made to include every body of importance; some which appeared in earlier editions have been dropped, thanks to mergers, the ravages of time, or our failure to secure replies

7

to repeated requests for information. If any have been slighted or omitted for any other reason, we offer our apologies. The book will continue to be revised; in future editions we hope to write with yet greater objectivity and in continued "malice toward none; with charity for all."

FRANK S. MEAD

CONTENTS

CONTENTS

ADVENTISTS

Adventism in general is a Christian faith based upon the conviction that the second advent of Christ is the sole hope of the world. It holds that the world is evil and will be destroyed by divine intervention, and that the wicked are to perish in this cataclysm while the righteous are to be saved. After this cataclysm Jesus Christ will reign in triumph through the 1,000-year period, or millennium, of Rev. 20:1-6. The whole Adventist thesis rests heavily upon the prophetic and apocalyptic texts of Daniel and Revelation.

As a religious movement it began with a widespread "awakening" on the question of the advent, which developed spontaneously in the Old World and in the New in the early decades of the nineteenth century. It became strongest and most clearly defined in the United States, at first under the leadership of William Miller (1782-1849), of Low Hampton, New York, a veteran of the war of 1812 and a man respected as a diligent student even though he did not have college or seminary training.

The movement under Miller was at first an interchurch (or, more accurately, *intra*church) development, with many Methodists, Christians, Baptists, Presbyterians, and Congregationalists among its adherents. It was thus a movement within the existing churches, and in the days of its beginnings there was no intention or attempt to organize a separate denomination.

So influential was William Miller that for years his followers were known as Millerites. Miller himself became a Baptist in 1816. He began at once a careful study of the Scriptures, concentrating on the prophecies of Daniel and Revelation. Using only the Bible, its marginal references, and Cruden's *Concordance* as his sources, he came to the conclusion that many Old and New World biblical scholars had already reached—namely, that the symbolic "day" of Bible prophecy really represents a year. He also concluded that the 2,300 "days" of Dan. 8:14 started concurrently with the 70 weeks of years of Dan. 9, or from 457 B.C., the year of the command to rebuild and restore Jerusalem; and he believed that the longer of the two periods would end in or about the Jewish sacred year "1843." Miller thought that the "sanctuary" mentioned in Dan. 8:14 was actually the earth, which would be cleansed by fire at the time of the Second Advent. He believed that this cleansing would occur sometime between March 21, 1843, and March 21, 1844.

When the great expectation failed to materialize by the spring of 1844, many left the movement. Miller's associates then set a second date, October 22, 1844, which they calculated would be the great antitypical Day of Atonement, confident that the "day of the Lord is near, even at the door." By 1844 there were between fifty thousand and one hundred thousand Adventists in this country. Hundreds of them, perhaps even thousands, disposed of their property as the day of expectation approached, gave away their goods, settled all their accounts, and waited prayerfully for the fateful day to come. October 22 came and passed with no Second Coming. Now vast numbers lost all interest in Adventism and went back to their former churches.

There were enough left, however, of

19

the main group to form several smaller bodies. At first a loose Adventist organization came into being at a conference in Albany, New York, in 1845. This group held generally to Miller's positions and theology, emphasizing the personal and premillennial character of the second advent of Christ, the resurrection of the dead—the faithful to be raised at Christ's coming, the rest 1,000 years later— and the renewal of the earth as the eternal abode of the redeemed. Known at first as the American Millennial Association, a portion of them later came to be called Evangelical Adventists, a church which has dwindled with the passing of the years to the point of obscurity. Another and larger group in 1861 became known as the Advent Christian Church.

Considering the nature of their doctrine and the opportunity for such wide divergence in the interpretation of the apocalyptic passages of the Bible upon which their conclusions are based, it was inevitable that the Adventists should become divided into different groups, maintaining different positions. Basically, nearly all Adventists were, and still are, agreed that the second advent of Christ will be premillennial—that is, that his return will *precede* the 1,000 year period foretold in Rev. 20. Only the Life and Advent Union among present-day Adventist bodies is postmillennial.

Beyond this their congregations were soon plagued with speculation and dissension over other questions. Just what is the state of the dead—conscious or unconscious—as they await the resurrection? Who are to arise—the righteous *and* the wicked, or only the righteous? Is there to be eternal punishment for the wicked, or ultimate annihilation? What is the nature of immortality? Does the cleansing of the sanctuary of Dan. 8 refer to a sanctuary in heaven or on earth? When should the Sabbath be celebrated —on the first day or on the seventh, on Sunday or on Saturday? Over these questions the Adventists, as organizations, became divided into 5 separate groups, in which we find them today.

Seventh-day Adventists

By far the largest single Adventist body in point of numbers, both in the United States and particularly throughout the world, is the Seventh-day Adventist Church, which traces its beginning back to the 1840's. They trace their convictions on the Sabbath back to the earlier Seventh Day Baptists of New England and the Old World.

Their first major point of disagreement with other Adventist bodies was not, however, over the seventh day but over the question of the "sanctuary" in Dan. 8:14 and over the true interpretation of that passage. A small group of Adventists were convinced that this sanctuary was in heaven and not on earth and that there would be a work of "investigative judgment" in this heavenly sanctuary prior to the Second Advent. Other Adventist bodies of the period still held that the sanctuary was on earth.

Coupled with the divergence came another, concerning the time of the Second Advent. The Seventh-day group claimed that the historical and prophetic evidence pointing to October 22, 1844, was correct, but that the error lay in a mistaken interpretation of Dan. 8:13-14— that Christ was not at that time to come out of, but was to *enter into*, the Most Holy Place in heaven to complete the second phase of his high priestly ministry before coming to this earth. The group holding these dissenting views also came to advocate the observance of the seventh day.

As early as 1844 a small group of these Adventists near Washington, New Hampshire, had begun observing the Sabbath on the seventh day. A pamphlet written by Joseph Bates in 1846 gave the question wide publicity and created great interest. Shortly after this, Bates, together with James White,

Ellen Harmon (later Mrs. James White), Hiram Edson, Frederick Wheeler, and S. W. Rhodes, set out definitely with the aid of regular publications to champion the seventh-day Sabbath, along with the imminence of the Advent. Hence their name—Seventh-day Adventists.

The growth of the group around these leaders was slow at first owing to the general derision in which Adventists were held and to their economic and social handicaps. By 1855, however, they were sufficiently prosperous and numerically strong enough to set up headquarters at Battle Creek, Michigan, with a publishing house called the Review and Herald Publishing Association. In 1860 they officially adopted the name Seventh-day Adventists, and in 1903 they moved their headquarters to its present location in Washington, D. C.

Doctrinally the Seventh-day Adventists are evangelical conservatives. Their standard statement of belief, appearing annually in their *Year Book*, reveals that they take the Bible as their sole rule of faith and practice; that they believe in God as revealed in the Father, the Son, and the Holy Spirit, each equally and uniquely divine, personal, and eternal. They believe in creation by divine fiat, and in the fall of man. Man is by nature not immortal, they hold, but only mortal; he is saved solely by grace and redeemed only through the atoning, substitutionary death of Jesus Christ.

They hold the Ten Commandments to be the standard of righteousness for men of all ages; and they base their observance of the seventh day as the Sabbath on the Fourth Commandment— "Six days shalt thou labour, . . . But the seventh day is the sabbath of the Lord thy God." They tithe their incomes; the support of the ministry in this church is entirely by the tithing system. Beyond the tithe they give toward missions, local church expenses, and other church enterprises in unusually generous

freewill offerings—their annual per capita giving being $216.09.

They believe in the gift of prophecy in the church; that the dead are awaiting the resurrection in an unconscious state; that the body will be resurrected in the last day, with immortality for the righteous and utter destruction by fire for the wicked. They stand stanchly for religious liberty for all men and for the complete separation of church and state. They consider the body of man to be the temple of the Holy Spirit and, in consequence, rigidly abstain from the use of alcoholic beverages and tobacco. They believe in the premillennial, personal, visible return of Christ "at a time unknown but close at hand," and in a new earth to be created out of the ruins of the old as the final abode of the redeemed. They practice immersion as the only true form of baptism, and they also practice foot washing as a preparatory service for Communion.

The over-all administrative body of the church is the executive committee of their general conference, which is chosen by delegates from the various church groups in the quadrennial sessions of the general conference of Seventh-day Adventists. Working under this general conference are 3 lesser governmental units: (1) the 13 division organizations, administering affairs in different continents; (2) 72 union conferences and missions, making up the divisional organizations; and (3) 127 local conferences and missions, the smallest administrative units.

Each unit has a large amount of autonomy. Local congregations elect lay elders, deacons, and other officers; the local conference office supervises all local pastoral and evangelistic work and relations and pays all pastors and other workers in its territory from a central fund. Theirs is a highly representative form of government.

Evangelism, publishing, educational, health, and welfare work are outstanding and highly successful among Seventh-day Adventists. Regarding themselves not as just another church but as a movement established in fulfillment of Bible prophecy to prepare man for the Second Advent and to revive and restore the neglected truths of the Reformation and of the apostolic church, they carry forward their work in 791 languages and dialects—218 with publications and 573 orally.

They have 44 publishing houses distributed over the world, with 6 in the United States. Literature is printed in 218 languages and dialects, and in Braille for the blind. Their colporteurs sold over $24,000,000 worth of literature in 1958. They publish 305 periodicals. In North America they have 3 junior colleges; 11 liberal arts colleges; a university with a theological seminary; and medical, dental, and physical therapy schools. In the United States and abroad they support 221 medical units with 34 accredited nurses' training schools. They operate 324 colleges and secondary schools and 4,568 elementary schools. Their welfare work operates from 400 metropolitan centers.

They now have 1,172 radio broadcasts weekly in 25 languages—637 in North America and 535 abroad; and 3,793,000 students have enrolled in their Bible correspondence schools, offered in 66 languages. An international broadcast, "The Voice of Prophecy," goes out over 823 stations in 25 languages and 52 countries. A television program, "Faith for Today," is released weekly over 150 outlets.

As they practice only adult immersion, no infants or children are included in the Seventh-day Adventist membership. Their world membership in 1958 was 1,149,256, representing 12,241 churches, and is limited to those who are faithful in upholding their church standards, including abstention from liquor and tobacco. There are 318,939 Seventh-day Adventists in the United States and Canada organized into 3,139 churches.

Advent Christian Church

William Miller was never active in the Advent Christian Association, which later became the Advent Christian Church. While his teachings of the imminent return of Christ were strongly influential in its founding, another doctrine was equally prominent; this related to the doctrine of the nature and mortality of man. Dissatisfied with the Platonic doctrine of the immortality of the human soul, early Adventist leaders such as Professor Charles F. Hudson and George Storrs rejected it completely and sought a more biblical emphasis. They preached a new doctrine of "conditional immortality," which declared the unconscious state of all the dead until the resurrection at Christ's return, the setting up of a divine tribunal for the determination of rewards and punishments, the ultimate extinction of all evil, and the establishment of the everlasting kingdom of God upon this earth as a restored paradise.

The first Advent Christian Association was established at Salem, Massachusetts, in 1860, and its members—those who in their allegiance to Adventism had been cut off from their own churches—publicly disclaimed any intent to form a separate denominational group. By 1900 2 colleges—Aurora College at Aurora, Illinois, and the New England School of Theology at Boston—had been established, and foreign missionary work was under way in Africa, India, China, and Mexico. The church now has additional mission stations in Japan and the Philippines. It maintains 2 publishing houses, 3 homes for the aged, and 1 orphanage.

Congregational in polity, local Advent Christian churches are organized into state conferences in 5 regional districts of the United States and Canada. These conferences, together with denominational institutions and co-operating societies, are associated under the Advent Christian General Conference of America, which holds biennial sessions.

The only creedal statement is a declaration of principles adopted by the General Conference of 1900. Two sacraments are observed—baptism by immersion and the Lord's Supper. Worship is held on the first day of the week.

There are 421 churches and 30,000 members.

Primitive Advent Christian Church

This is a recent development from the Advent Christian Church, with 553 members in 12 churches, all of them in West Virginia. As the name implies, it is an effort to recapture the principles and thought of primitive Adventism. No statements on doctrine, history, work, or organization are available.

Church of God (Abrahamic Faith)

This church is the outgrowth of several independent local groups of similar faith; some of them were in existence as early as 1800, and others date their beginnings with the arrival of British immigrants in this country around 1847. Many of them organized originally under the name of Church of God in Christ Jesus.

State and district conferences of these scattered groups were formed as an expression of mutual co-operation. A national organization was instituted at Philadelphia in 1888, and this met again in 1889; however, because of very strong convictions on questions of congregational rights and authority, the national organization ceased to function until 1921, when the present general conference was formed at Waterloo, Iowa.

The Bible is accepted here as the supreme standard of faith. Adventist in viewpoint, the second (premillennial) coming of Christ is strongly emphasized. The church teaches that the kingdom of God will be literal, beginning at Jerusalem at the time of the return of Christ and extending to all nations. It believes in the restoration of Israel, the times of

restitution, the mortality of man (a sleep in death until the resurrection), the literal resurrection of the dead, the reward of the righteous on earth, and the complete destruction of the wicked in second death. Membership is dependent upon acceptance of doctrinal faith, repentance, and baptism (for the remission of sins) by immersion.

Delegates from each church meet each year to determine church plans and policies and to elect officers, who serve as a board of directors. A general conference operates Oregon Bible College for the training of ministers; the printing and publishing of church literature; the Berean Youth Fellowship; the Department of Evangelism and Missions; and the Sunday-School Department. The work of the general conference is carried on under the direction of the board of directors, which meets as necessary throughout the year. The executive officer is a general manager who administers the work as a whole. The officers of the general conference are incorporated as the National Bible Institution, which is the operating agency of the general conference. Because of the congregational nature of the church's government the general conference exists primarily as a means of mutual co-operation and for the development of yearly projects and enterprises. There are 5,215 members in 102 churches, divided into 17 state and district conferences. The church periodical, *The Restitution Herald,* is published bimonthly.

Life and Advent Union

In 1848 John T. Walsh, an Adventist preacher and editor, advanced the doctrine that only the righteous dead will have a resurrection; all others will remain in their graves forever. Other Adventists who accepted his views organized the Life and Advent Union at Wilbraham, Massachusetts, in 1863.

With Adventists generally, they look

for the literal, personal return of Christ to this earth. They believe that the dead are unconscious and that eternal life will be bestowed upon the righteous when Christ returns, immortality being given by a resurrection of the dead and translation of the living who have been faithful to Christ. Life will begin again upon a purified earth.

Omens of Christ's return are seen in the loss of religious faith and the unrest and confusion of the modern world, but even an approximate date for the Second Advent cannot be set. The doctrine of a millennium in the future is rejected; the thousand years of Rev. 20 refer to a period already past.

Foreign missionary work in China has necessarily been discontinued; the denomination co-operates with the Advent Christian Church in missionary work in Japan. There are 2 annual camp meetings, in Connecticut and Maine; a biweekly periodical, *The Herald of Life*, is issued; there are 3 local churches with about 300 members.

THE AFRICAN ORTHODOX CHURCH

Believing that Negro Episcopalians should have churches of their own, a Protestant Episcopal rector, the Rev. George Alexander McGuire, withdrew from that church in 1919 to establish independent Negro churches in the United States, Cuba, and Canada. He called them Independent Episcopal churches, but in 1921 the first general synod of the new body changed the name to The African Orthodox Church and elected McGuire as its first bishop. He was consecrated by Archbishop Vilatte, who took his episcopal orders from the West Syrian Church of Antioch; this put McGuire in the traditional apostolic succession, which he valued highly.

The church still lays strong emphasis upon the apostolic succession and upon the historic sacraments and rituals. It has the original 7 sacraments of the Roman Catholic Church; its worship is a blending of Western and Eastern liturgy, creeds, and symbols. The liturgy is usually Western, a mingling of Anglican, Greek, and Roman patterns. Three creeds—Apostles', Nicene, and Athanasian—are used.

The denomination maintains the adamant position of the Protestant Episcopal Church on marriage: no priest may remarry the guilty party to a divorce, and innocent parties are remarried only after special permission by a bishop. The government is of course episcopal; bishops are in charge of dioceses or jurisdictions, and groups of dioceses form a province, each led by an archbishop and a primate, who in turn presides over the provincial synod. At the head stands the patriarch, McGuire, who is general overseer of all the work of the church, which now extends over the United States, Canada, Latin America, and the Union of South Africa. Membership, as in the Roman Catholic Church, is counted not by communicants but by the number of persons baptized; in the United States there were 24 churches and 6,000 members in 1957.

AMANA CHURCH SOCIETY

Officially named the Amana (Faithfulness) Church Society but more popularly known as the Amana Society, this group stems from the Pietistic movement in eighteenth-century Germany. In 1714 a small company under the leadership of Johann Rock and Ludwig Gruber stirred the Germans with their preaching that the days of true and direct inspiration from God had not ended. Both these leaders were said to have the "gift of inspiration." Under persecution from the German government the group came to America in 1842, settling near Buffalo, New York. There were 800 of them, organized as the Ebenezer Society.

Life was completely communistic in these first American settlements; all property was held and shared collectively; each person did the work for which he was fitted and shared equally in the reward; each village had a common school, meetinghouse, and store. Local government was in the hands of a group of elected elders. The society moved in 1855 to Iowa, where the villages of Amana, East, South, Middle, High, and West Amana, and Homestead were established. Here they became incorporated under their present name.

These Iowa villages still constitute an outstanding experiment in communal living. The society was reorganized in 1932, many of the communistic practices were abandoned, and it was organized as a corporation for profit and is managed as such. Members might now be called co-operative rather than communistic. They conduct 50 different businesses and farm 25,000 acres of land; they are stockholders in a $4,000,000 corporation.

Once pacifistic, they will now bear arms in military service; but they still refuse to take oaths. Stated wages are paid to all. The traditional garb of the old German peasant has been largely discarded, but women in church still dress as the women dressed a century ago. Amusements, formerly frowned upon, are now more generally tolerated.

The purpose of the society is purely religious; it is based upon the "salvation of souls, the service of God." They believe that "God can now as well as of old inspire men," but none seems to have been inspired in the old historic sense since the deaths of 2 early American leaders, Christian Metz and Barbara Landmann. They accept the teachings of a holy universal church, the remission of sins and the communion of the saints, the resurrection of the body, the punishment of the wicked, and life everlasting. They acknowledge no baptism with water but only "baptism by fire and the Spirit." Members are confirmed and admitted to the church at 15; all children are required to attend public schools. There is no ordained ministry; services consist of prayer, testimony, and readings from the writings of Metz and Landmann. The church as it exists at present is known as the Amana Church Society; it is separated from the temporal affairs of the community but still a dominant influence. Membership is put at 1,050, with 400 minors not yet admitted; and there are 7 congregations.

AMERICAN ETHICAL UNION (FEDERATION OF SOCIETIES FOR ETHICAL CULTURE)

The Ethical Movement in the United States builds its thought and program upon moral philosophy and the ethical traditions of the great religions of mankind. It has no formal creed but in a statement of principles declares that the search for ethical values and their progressive realization are inherently a religious enterprize. . . . All human beings, however different their abilities or backgrounds, have an equal right to such fulfillment as encourages the fulfillment of their fellow-men. Such a goal requires diversity in beliefs and practices, and therefore freedom of conscience, thought and expression. . . . Our attitude toward that which is beyond present knowledge, including questions about cosmic matters, is one of free and cooperative exploration, and respect for individual experience.

Stress is laid upon the development of conscience and a sense of responsibility as great creative forces among men.

There are 28 active ethical culture societies in the Ethical Union, the first of which was founded by Felix Adler in 1876. Abroad there are active societies in England and Vienna.

Meetings of the societies feature inspirational music, readings, and addresses. There are no ministers in the usual sense, but there are salaried Leaders who serve as counselors, officiate at weddings and funerals, name children, and per-

form in general the functions of ministers. There are Sunday schools, young people's groups, and study groups; perhaps the most effective work is found in educational, philanthropic, and social efforts and projects. The New York society must be given credit for the start of settlement work in this country; at the present time societies in New York, Chicago, and Philadelphia sponsor very effective settlement-house programs. Free kindergartens, visiting nurses, the Child Study Movement, the abolition of child labor, model tenements, and the inauguration of free public legal aid societies constitute ethical culture drives.

Within the movement outstanding schools have been developed at Central Park and Riverdale in New York City and in Brooklyn; these schools are models in their field, setting high standards in progressive education, and are very popular with many not identified with the movement.

There are approximately 5,000 members.

AMERICAN EVANGELICAL CHRISTIAN CHURCHES

Launched in 1944 and incorporated in Illinois, this is a fellowship or conference of clergymen described as being "of an associational character for business, educational, and benevolent purposes." It engages in home and foreign missionary work; licenses and ordains teachers, ministers, missionaries, and evangelists; publishes religious literature; and conducts religious schools, conventions, and institutes. Churches established under its charter are known as American Bible churches and are quite independent of one another and of supervision from headquarters, except that any church may be dropped for devia-

tion from the doctrinal standards of the national body.

Applicants for membership must subscribe to the following articles of faith: (1) the Bible as the written word of God; (2) the Virgin Birth; (3) the deity of Jesus Christ; (4) salvation through the Atonement; (5) the guidance of life through prayer; (6) the return of the Saviour; and (7) the establishment of the kingdom of God on earth. Licenses are issued to qualifying members, enabling them to perform all church functions and rites with the exception of that of officiating at marriages. Ministers are ordained on approval of national headquarters by 2 previously ordained A.E.C.C. ministers.

Chief officer of the group is the moderator; there are 5 trustees who act as an executive committee and who elect their own successors.

The organization operates the American Bible College at Pineland, Florida, for the training of its ministers and missionaries. It also supervises the work of the American Bible School in Chicago, which specializes in home-study courses.

Five regionals in the United States and one in Canada supervise the American churches in their respective areas and plan the annual conferences and conventions. All ordinations are performed by regional officers upon approval of national headquarters.

The present membership now stands at approximately 500, about 5 per cent of which are women.

AMERICAN MINISTERIAL ASSOCIATION

An alliance or union of churches and ministers, this body originated in the efforts of Grant T. Billett, who withdrew from his ecclesiastical connections in 1929 to become an independent evangelist. In September of 1929 the initial plans were laid to organize a group of independent ministers and churches, and the alliance was first known as the American Conference of Undenominational Ministers. It was formally organized in 1944 and the name changed to the American Ministerial Association.

The association is incorporated in a number of states, which enables it to give churches and ministers standing equivalent to that of a denomination. Men and women are admitted to the ministry and are ordained on the approval of national headquarters. The membership represents all parts of the United States and Canada and some foreign fields, showing a continual increase.

The association is unique in the fact that it is not a branch of, or a split from, any denomination, but rather a coming together of members from many denominations. It is described as

not a "come out" movement, but a "coming together" movement, recognizing all members of the One True Church, the Body of Christ; the membership is embracive, not exclusive; its ministry is not restricted by

tradition, knowing that dogmas and creeds have held sway for centuries, but that truth is a divine revelation.

The association prefers to be known not as a denomination but rather as an evangelistic and missionary movement; yet it has a familiar denominational organization with home and foreign mission boards, a department of education, and a publishing commission.

Dr. Billett heads the group as president, and a limited ecclesiastical authority is vested in the national headquarters office, which guides the associational work in business, education, and benevolence. Its main work lies in the establishing of independent, nonsectarian local churches and missions. Regional offices are maintained throughout the United States and Canada, and the ministers meet for mutual consultations and inspiration in conferences. A college and seminary are maintained at Springfield, Illinois.

Doctrine and teaching here might be described as middle-of-the-road, embracing the customary Christian position, "yet allowing its ministers to live the religious life unhampered by creedal obligations." The cosmopolitan complexion of its ministers and membership, including as it does representatives of many different schools of religious thought, would naturally produce such an emphasis. Approximately 222 ministers are in affiliation with this body. Statistical records on membership of the associated churches are unavailable because of the autonomous nature of the local churches.

AMERICAN RESCUE WORKERS

Incorporated in 1896 and with a name amended to the organizational charter in 1913, the American Rescue Workers engage in a typical rescue mission work in offering emergency aid (lodgings, clothing, food) and evangelism, yet have the status of a full-fledged nonsectarian church. The rites of baptism and Communion are administered by the officers and ministers in charge of local corps, and regular church and Sunday-school services are held in their chapels and mission halls. Ministers are ordained at annual councils.

Their articles of religion include subscription to the Trinity, the inspiration of the Scriptures and their use as the divine rule of faith and practice, the fall of man, redemption through the atoning sacrifice of Christ, restoration through repentance and belief in Christ, regeneration through the work of the Holy Spirit, and the immortality of the soul.

Government is by a board of managers elected by the members of the corporation. Organization is on a military pattern with General Richard H. Ives as commander in chief and with territorial commanders in charge of some 23 stations across the country. A periodical, *The Rescue Herald*, is published in Philadelphia. There are 3,500 members in twenty-eight churches.

APOSTOLIC OVERCOMING
HOLY CHURCH OF GOD

Bishop W. T. Phillips, founder and senior officer of this church, is a former member of the Methodist Church who became deeply concerned with the teaching of the doctrine of holiness and in 1916, after four years of study and preaching on the doctrine, organized the Ethiopian Overcoming Holy Church of God. The word "Ethiopian" was later changed to "Apostolic."

Active in 14 states and with missions in the West Indies and Africa, the ministers of the body are supported by tithe payments of the membership; the clergy are also required to tithe. Worship includes foot washing and divine healing. Services generally are free, emotional affairs bordering on the bizarre, with the participants speaking in tongues and engaging in ecstatic dances.

It is claimed that this church existed "even from the days of Enos," when Christianity was known to be in existence in Abyssinia. Marriage to unsaved men and women, the use of snuff, foolish talking, jesting, and the use of slang are forbidden. Bishop Phillips put the membership at 75,000 in three hundred churches in 1956.

ARMENIAN CHURCH, DIOCESE OF AMERICA

Armenia claims to be the first Christian nation. The apostles Thaddeus and Bartholomew (sometimes held to be the same person) were there during the time of Paul, and Christianity was adopted as the state faith in A.D. 301. Gregory the Enlightener, preaching in Armenia at that time, became the first bishop of this national church, with the title of Catholicos, or supreme patriarch.

The story of the Christian church in Armenia has been written in blood; it suffered both in the inevitable conflict between the Byzantine Empire and Persia and in numerous persecutions by the Turks. Thousands fled to America just before and after World War I to escape the bloodshed; previously, as early as 1889, they had already become known as the Armenian Apostolic Church in America. Headquarters for this church are in a monastery at the foot of Mount Ararat; but an American hierarchy of archbishops, priests, and deacons directs the work in the United States. Diocesan organization is under the spiritual jurisdiction of the Holy See of Etchmiadzin, Armenia, U.S.S.R.

Doctrine is based on the historic writings and declarations of the early church fathers. The saints and the Virgin Mary are venerated, and the Immaculate Conception is not denied. On the other hand, the feast of the assumption of the Virgin is celebrated, but is not accepted as a dogma. A translation of the Scriptures by Sahak and Mesrob and other fathers of the American Church is accepted as the only authoritative version of the Bible. There are 7 sacraments: baptism by immersion eight days after birth, confirmation immediately following baptism, Holy Communion even for infants, penance, marriage, ordination, and visitation of the sick.

Government of the church is democratic in that all candidates for holy orders are elected by the people and hierarchal in that they must be ordained by bishops in the apostolic succession. Every province and diocese throughout the world has a constitution adapted to its peculiar needs, but which must be approved by the Catholics. The principal services are the Holy Sacrifice, or liturgy, on Sunday, and various feast days are held during the week. The Bible is read in public in Armenian at these services. Language schools, Sunday schools and a number of libraries help to keep the classic native tongue alive. In 1959 there were 130,000 members in fifty-three churches in the United States.

ASSEMBLIES OF GOD, GENERAL COUNCIL

The largest of the Pentecostal bodies, with 505,552 members and 8,094 churches, the Assemblies of God, General Council, is actually an aggregation of Pentecostal churches and assemblies accomplished at Hot Springs, Arkansas, in 1914. The founders were former ministers and pastors of evangelical persuasion who wished to unite into one body in the interests of a more effective preaching and an enlarged missionary crusade.

Ardently fundamentalist, its theology is Arminian; there is strong belief in the infallibility and inspiration of the Bible, the fall and redemption of man, baptism in the Holy Ghost, entire sanctification, a life of holiness and separation from the world, divine healing, the second advent of Jesus and his millennial reign, eternal punishment for the wicked and eternal bliss for believers. Two ordinances, baptism and the Lord's Supper, are practiced. Members stand officially opposed to war, but large numbers of their youth accepted noncombatant and even combatant service in World War II. They are especially insistent that baptism in the Holy Spirit is evidenced by speaking in tongues. The Assemblies of God believe that all the gifts of the Spirit should be in operation in the normal New Testament church.

The government of the assemblies is an unusual mixture of Presbyterian and Congregational systems. Local churches are left quite independent in polity and in the conduct of local affairs. District officers have a pastoral ministry to all the churches and are responsible for the promotion of home missions. Work is divided into 44 districts in the United States, most of which follow state lines, each with a distinct presbytery which examines, licenses and ordains pastors. In

addition to these three are 9 foreign language branches. The General Council consists of all ordained (not licensed) ministers, and local churches are represented by one lay delegate each. This council elects all general officers, sets the doctrinal standards, and provides for church expansion and development. Missionary work is conducted under the guidance of a central missionary committee; there are 758 foreign missionaries at work on a total missionary budget of about $3,500,000—unusually high among Protestant churches. The Sunday schools of the group have an enrollment of 922,663. A weekly periodical, *The Pentecostal Evangel*, has a circulation of approximately 167,500; and a prosperous church press produces books, tracts, and other religious literature. There are 12 Bible institutes, or schools, maintained. The latest school to be established is Evangel College, a Liberal Arts School, now in its fifth year, with an enrollment for 1959-60 exceeding 500, located in Springfield, Missouri.

BAHA'I

The faith called Bahá'í aims at the universal brotherhood of man, the unity of all religions, and peace for the whole world. Its leader Bahá'u'lláh said, "The religion of God is for the sake of love and union; make it not the cause of enmity and conflict." To him the one universal spirit which is God spoke alike in Zoroaster, Mohammed, Buddha, Moses, and Jesus; their messages fulfilled and revealed themselves in Bahá'u'lláh.

Originating in Persia in 1844, Bahá'í still bears something of an exotic flavor, although recent translations of its writings in English equivalents of the original thought make that element less conspicuous than it was. The founder was Mirzá 'Ali Muhammad, called the Báb (Arabic for "gate" or "door"). The Báb suffered

fierce persecution at the hands of the Mohammedans and was executed in 1850. In the decade following his death over 10,000 of his followers were slain. His successor was Mirzá Husayn 'Ali, later called Bahá'u'lláh (Splendor of God). Imprisoned for 40 years, Bahá'u'lláh announced himself as the Promised One; he also announced a new day of God had come and that the age of brotherhood had arrived. The separate streams of Christian, Jewish, and Mohammedan faiths were to merge. He died in the Turkish penal colony of Akká in 1892; and his mantle fell upon his eldest son, Abbás Effendi, later known as 'Abdu'l-Bahá.

Like his father, the son spent 40 years in captivity. Released in 1908, he toured

Egypt, Europe, and the United States. At Wilmette, a suburb of Chicago, he broke ground for the first Bahá'í temple in the Occident; this is today the seat of all Bahá'í offices in the United States. He was knighted by the British for his services in Palestine during World War I and died there in 1921.

The Wilmette temple is one of our most unique religious structures—a combination of mosque, cathedral, and synagogue. In its structure the numeral 9, the number of perfection in Bahá'í, is repeatedly emphasized. There are 9 concrete piers, 9 pillars or pylons symbolizing the 9 living religions of the world, and 9 arches; it is set in a park with 9 sides, 9 avenues, 9 gateways, and 9 fountains. The building was dedicated in 1953 to the "unity of God, the unity of his prophets, the unity of mankind." Services of public worship are conducted weekly with vocal music and readings from the different scriptures. A Bahá'í Home for the Aged, accommodating twenty guests, was constructed in Wilmette in 1958.

Local groups are officially recognized only when they have 9 members or more. Supervision of these groups is vested in the National Spiritual Assembly, which consists of 9 members. Shoghi Rabbani, who succeeded 'Abdu'l-Bahá, was leader, spiritual head, and sole interpreter of Bahá'í writings until his passing on November 4, 1957, in London. The co-ordination and direction of international Bahá'í activities have been vested in the World Center.

American Bahá'ís have summer schools at Eliot, Maine; Geyserville, California; Davison, Michigan. There are centers in more than 200 different countries and territorial divisions. In the United States, Bahá'ís are found in more than 1,500 cities and towns. They use a calendar given by the Báb, consisting of 19 months of 19 days each, with New Year's Day falling on March 21. For the future they plan an International Spiritual Assembly to sit at Haifa; they also plan enlargement of their work at Wilmette, including schools, hospitals, and homes for the aged.

The Bahá'ís have no ecclesiastical organization; there are only teachers instructing and discussing with local groups. It is considered in error to sell religious instruction. Their doctrine may be summed up in the following statement:

Unfettered search after truth and the abandonment of all superstition and prejudice; the oneness of mankind—all are "leaves of one tree, flowers in one garden"; religion must be a cause of love and harmony, else it is no religion; all religions are one in their fundamental principles; religion must conform with science, bringing faith and reason into full accord; and recognition of the unity of God and obedience to His commands as revealed through His Divine Manifestations.

There should be no idle rich and no idle poor; every one should have an occupation, for "work in the spirit of service is worship." Compulsory education is advocated, especially for girls who will be the mothers and the first educators of the next generation. In all walks of life, both sexes should have equal opportunities for development and equal rights and privileges.

An auxiliary international language should be adopted and taught in all the schools in order to bring men into closer fellowship and better understanding. In the interest of universal peace, there should be established a universal league of nations, in which all nations and peoples should be included, and an International Parliament to arbitrate all international disputes.

A 10-year world crusade was launched in 1953, calling for the formation of additional United States assemblies and for the construction of houses of worship on all continents.

BAPTISTS

The Baptists constitute one of the major Protestant forces in the United States. Twenty-seven Baptist denominations reported an approximate membership of 20,493,371 in 1958; there are 91,786 local Baptist churches, each one independent of the others, with members also completely independent of one another yet bound together by an amazingly strong "rope of sand" in a great common allegiance to certain principles and doctrines based generally upon the competency of each individual in matters of faith.

It is often heard among them that they have no founder but Christ and that Baptists have been preaching and practicing from the days of John the Baptist. That is true in a limited sense; there were certainly men and women holding what have come to be considered distinctly Baptist principles all across the years. But as a church, or as organized churches, they began in Holland and England.

When the Reformation set the Bible and men free early in the sixteenth century, scattered groups appeared advocating the convictions of faith which are today the warp and woof of Baptist theology and ideology. We find the name Baptist in various forms in Germany and Switzerland: Pedobaptists, among whom, however, there were no "Baptists in the modern sense," inasmuch as they baptized infants and children; Anti-Pedobaptists, who opposed infant baptism; and Anabaptists, who rebaptized adults once baptized as children. The Anabaptists were the left wing of the Reformation and held to a literal application of the word of God in social matters; they were communistic and pacifistic, opposing capital punishment, oaths in court, the holding of public office, and the payment of taxes and interest. They rejected infant baptism as unscriptural, insisted upon the separation of church and state, and defended this belief heroically and to the point of fanaticism and martyrdom. Under persecution they spread all over Europe. Some fled to Norway, others to Italy, Poland, Holland and England.

In Holland a group of Mennonites, or followers of the former Anabaptist leader Menno Simons (see Mennonites, p. 146), taught Anabaptist principles: that the Scriptures were the sole authority for man's faith and practice, that baptism was a believer's privilege, that church and state should be completely and forever separated, and that church discipline should be rigidly enforced in business, family, and personal affairs. These Mennonites met and perhaps deeply influenced a little group of British Separatists who had taken refuge in Amsterdam from the religious persecutions under James I; many of them lived in Mennonite homes, and one of their leaders, John Smythe, was completely captured by the Mennonite argument. He rebaptized himself and his followers in the Anabaptist, or Baptist, faith and with them organized the first English Baptist Church in 1609. When he tried to make Mennonites of them, however, he went too far; Baptist they would be, but not Mennonite, for that meant a threat to their British heritage, and they were still good Englishmen and proposed to remain so. Smythe was excommunicated, and he died in 1612, leaving behind him, in a "confession," his conviction that

The magistrate, by virtue of his office, is not to meddle with religion, or matters of conscience, nor to compel men to this or that form of religion or doctrine, but to leave the Christian religion to the free conscience of every one, and to meddle only with political matters.

So died John Smythe, Baptist to the last. His people drifted back across the Channel and, with persecution waning, established yet another Baptist church in London.

These first 2 churches were General Baptist churches, believing in a general

BAPTISTS

atonement for all men. In the course of time there arose a Particular Baptist Church, holding to the predestinarian teachings of John Calvin and preaching a limited atonement. The first Particular (British) Church dates back to 1638. Three years after their founding, a third body, known as Immersion Baptists, broke away and in 1644 wrote a confession of faith which is still held by many modern Baptists. It was this confession that stamped these people popularly for the first time as Baptists.

These early British Baptists wielded a tremendous influence in their times and upon the future; it is claimed for them that "more than any king or Parliament, they set the heart and mind of England free." John Smythe's teaching that the "Magistrate . . . is not to meddle with religion, or in matters of conscience" has become one of mankind's great spiritual bulwarks. They sent William Carey to India in 1793, and Carey became the pioneer of modern missions. More than a century earlier, in 1631, they had sent Roger Williams to America; Williams was to be the first great champion of freedom for faith and conscience on this side of the Atlantic.

Williams was not a Baptist but a Separatist minister when he arrived. His story is well known: preaching "new and dangerous opinions against the authority of magistrates," he fled their courtly wrath and organized a Baptist church at Providence, Rhode Island. John Clarke established another Baptist church at Newport, Rhode Island, at about the same time. The Baptists are still arguing as to which church came first, many scholars put the Providence church in 1639, the Newport church in 1641.

These were Particular, or Calvinistic, Baptist churches. Their strength was challenged by the rise of interest in Arminian theology during the preaching of George Whitefield, but their Calvinism prevailed; it is the theological standard of many, if not most, Baptists in this country today. Their progress was slow; a bitter persecution of their church ennobled them and left one of the darkest blots on colonial history.

Following the tour of Whitefield through the colonies a dispute arose among the Baptists, dividing them into Old Lights, or Regulars, who distrusted revivals and emotionalism, and New Lights, or Separates, who demanded a reborn membership in their churches. Separate Baptists were outstanding in the fight for religious freedom in the new land. The friction died down with the signing of the Constitution, however, and a new unity was found in a foreign missions crusade. The first Protestant missionary board in America was the American Board made up of Baptists, Reformed, Congregational, and Presbyterian churchmen. In 1814 the Baptists organized their own separate General Missionary Convention of the Baptist Denomination in the United States of America.

This convention, representing a national Baptist fellowship, marked the first real denominational consciousness of American Baptists. It was followed eventually by other organizations which welded them firmly together; a general Baptist convention; a general tract society—later called the American Baptist Publication Society, various missionary societies for work at home and abroad; an education society; and the famous Baptist Young People's Union.

These organizations were on a national scale. Their unity was disrupted first by a feeling that home missions agencies within the body had failed to evangelize southern territory, and later by the question of slavery and the Civil War. The great division over slavery came in 1845, when the Southerners "seceded" to form their own Southern Baptist Convention in order to carry on more effectively the work of the Southern Baptist churches. From this point forward there was to be a Northern (now the Amer-

33

ican) and a Southern Baptist Convention. The split is still in effect.

Various other Baptist groups, following to the logical end their love of independence, established themselves from East to West. While they differ in certain minor details, they are generally agreed upon the following principles of faith: the inspiration and trustworthiness of the Bible as the sole rule of life; the lordship of Jesus Christ; the inherent freedom of the individual to approach God for himself; the granting of salvation through faith by way of grace and contact with the Holy Spirit; 2 ordinances—the Lord's Supper and baptism of believers by immersion; the independence of the local church; the church as a group of regenerated believers baptized upon confession of faith; infant baptism as unscriptural and not to be practiced; complete separation of church and state; the immortality of the soul; the brotherhood of man; the royal law of God; the need of redemption from sin; and the ultimate triumph of God's kingdom.

These over-all doctrines have never been written by the Baptists into any official Baptist creed for all their churches, but they have been incorporated in 2 very important confessions of faith for the denomination. The Baptist churches of London wrote a Philadelphia Confession in the year 1689, and this confession was enlarged by the Philadelphia Association in 1742. The New Hampshire State Baptist Convention drew up another famous confession in 1832. The older Philadelphia Confession is strongly Calvinistic in statement; the New Hampshire Confession, only moderately so.

Baptists have insisted upon freedom of thought and expression in pulpit and pew. This has made them one of the most democratic religious bodies in America—and one in which liberal and conservative doctrine is preached freely. They have insisted, too, upon the absolute autonomy of the local congregation;

each church arranges its own worship, examines and baptizes its own members. There is no age limit set on membership, but the candidate is usually of such an age that he can understand and accept the teachings of Christ. Candidates for the ministry are licensed by local churches and ordained upon recommendation of a group of sister churches.

Baptist churches are commonly found grouped into associations, local and state, for purposes of fellowship. National conventions are established among many of them to carry on educational and missionary work and to make pension plans. Most state conventions meet annually, with delegates representing all Baptist churches in the given area. They receive reports and make recommendations, but they have no authority to enforce their decisions.

While Baptists in general have a reputation for exclusiveness, there have been in recent years several moves in the direction of interdenominational union. The American and Southern conventions have been discussing reunion for some time; in 1948 definite steps were taken toward the formation of a Baptist Alliance of North America. It was to be a nonlegislative alliance, providing an opportunity for all recognized Baptist bodies to give a united expression to their faith. In Washington, D.C., there is a Baptist Joint Committee on Public Affairs for both American and Southern conventions and other Baptist groups; which committee serves mainly to spread the Baptist conviction on public morals and to safeguard their principle of separation of church and state. Finally, there is the growing Baptist World Alliance, organized in 1905 and now including over 22,000,000 Baptists all over the globe. The alliance meets every 5 years and is a purely advisory body, discussing the great themes and problems common to all Baptists. Headquarters of the alliance are now located in Washington, D. C.

American Baptist Convention

Up to the time of the Revolutionary War, Baptist work in the northern states was in the hands of the local churches, some few of which formed themselves into associations such as the Philadelphia Association or the Warren Association of Rhode Island. Beyond these associations, which were limited to Virginia, New Jersey, Pennsylvania, and Rhode Island, there was no central administrative body to bind the churches together. The association did well, building churches, colleges, schools, and libraries; by the time of the split with the Southern Baptists about 1844, plans for a national co-ordinating body were under way.

In the early years of the nineteenth century there were 3 Baptist organizations in the North mutually maintained: the American Baptist Home Mission Society; the American Baptist Missionary Union, later known as the American Baptist Foreign Mission Society; and the American Baptist Publication Society. The deflection of the Southern Baptists served to intensify the efforts of these 3 bodies; they were separate corporations, but they often called annual meetings at the same time and place.

The women of the northern churches formed their own home and foreign missionary societies in the 1860's and 1870's. Separate appeals for funds to support all these competing societies created confusion and dissatisfaction, and led eventually to the incorporation of the Northern Baptist Convention in 1907. This convention, actually a corporation with restricted powers in conducting religious work, receiving and expending money and affiliating itself with other bodies, changed its name in 1950 to the American Baptist Convention. The two women's missionary societies eventually joined the general societies already established in what are known as co-operating organizations within the convention, although they continue to work under their own charters and management. To these were added a board of education and a ministers' and missionaries' benefit board, the latter to give relief to needy clergymen and missionaries and pensions to retiring ministers and missionaries.

State conventions and city mission societies were drawn into closer unity by grouping them into affiliated organizations through which they raise and distribute funds under a co-operative plan with a unified budget. The Council on Missionary Co-operation supervises the collection of money for this unified budget. Numerous other councils and committees carry on the work of the convention under the supervision of the General Council, which functions between the annual gatherings of the convention. At the 1950 meeting, for the first time, a general secretary was elected.

The local church is still the basic and independent unit of American Baptist government and administration. There are 6,362 churches and 1,555,360 members, 37 state conventions and 15 Baptist city societies. The convention owns and controls 14 children's homes, 37 homes for the aging, 7 hospitals, 10 theological seminaries, 6 academies, 24 senior colleges and universities, 5 junior colleges, and 1 school for nursing education. The American Baptist Home Mission Society and the Woman's American Baptist Home Mission Society have workers in 40 states and 6 Latin-American countries; they support schools in those countries, and Bacone College for Indians in Oklahoma; do a widespread work among Negroes, Indians, and Orientals resident in the United States. The American Baptist Foreign Mission Society and the Woman's American Baptist Foreign Mission Society support 391 missionaries in Burma, Assam, India, Bengal, Thailand, Japan, Okinawa, Hong Kong, the Congo, and the Philippines, and maintain a co-operative relationship in 7 European countries.

In matters of faith every Baptist church of the convention speaks for itself, but there are certain Baptist doctrines held in common. The Bible is the foundation of their belief; the individual conscience, the interpreter of the Bible. There is the usual Baptist insistence upon the inspiration and validity of the Scriptures, the lordship of Christ, immortality and the future life, the brotherhood of man, and the need of man's redemption from sin. The ordinances of baptism and the Lord's Supper are considered more as aids than as necessities to the living of the Christian life.

By and large the Northern Baptists represented in the American Baptist Convention are more liberal in thought and theology than those in the Southern Baptist Convention. This gulf of theological difference, coupled with southern suspicion of northern social and economic liberalism, keeps the two larger Baptist conventions in the nation apart. Gestures at reunion are still frequent and still unsuccessful.

Independently Baptist as they are, there is still a clear trend among the Northerners toward co-operation if not organic union with other churches, both Baptist and non-Baptist. The American Baptist Convention is a constituent body of the National Council of the Churches of Christ in the U.S.A., with several members on the council's executive committee. Its leaders were prominent at the world gatherings at Edinburgh, Utrecht, and Oxford, and they are well represented in the World Council of Churches. Moves have been made toward union with the General Baptists, the Disciples of Christ, the Southern Baptist Convention, and the National Baptist Convention. The Free Baptists have been received into full fellowship.

Southern Baptist Convention

It was inevitable that Northern and Southern Baptists should split over the slavery question, even before the outbreak of the Civil War. The friction between the two sections began a quarter of a century before Bull Run. The acting board of foreign missions of the Baptists in the country had its headquarters in Boston. Being located there, it was naturally strongly influenced by the abolition movement. There was bitter debate among the board members, and in the early 1840's it became evident that this board would not accept slaveholders as missionaries. This question of missionaries and of missionary money was the immediate cause of the split. The "brethren of the North" first suggested separation; a month later, in May of 1845, the Southern Baptist Convention was organized, establishing at once its own boards for foreign and home missions.

Southern historians now recognize that in addition to the slavery issue there was a long-standing disagreement between Baptists in the North and Baptists in the South over the nature of denominational organization. Certainly the slave issue precipitated the break, but there was a very significant consequence to it. Baptists in the United States under northern leadership heretofore had no central denominational organization. Instead there were separate and independent organizations (usually designated as "societies") for various phases of co-operative effort, such as foreign and home missions and publication. Southerners had desired instead to have one organization controlling these varied activities. From the beginning the Southern Baptist Convention was such an organization. Northern Baptists, on the other hand, waited until 1907 to form a convention uniting their societies. This cohesion of centralized organization and co-operative societies has had much to do, Southern Baptists believe, with their growth.

In Maryland, Virginia, North Carolina, South Carolina, Georgia, Louisiana, Kentucky, and Alabama 300 churches entered the new organization. Up to the outbreak of the Civil War this convention met biennially; since 1869 it has met annually.

A hard struggle for existence lay immediately ahead. The new convention suffered badly in point of churches, membership, and finances during the war. Homes, schools, churches, the livelihood of citizens, and the very pattern of southern society were destroyed, with devastating effects among all the churches. An antimissionary movement decimated their ranks, and membership —not finances and leadership—was affected when the Negro Baptists withdrew to form their own convention. The recovery of the Southern Baptist Convention was amazing, however. In 1845 there were 351,951 members in the convention, of whom 130,000 were Negroes; by 1890 there were 1,235,908 members, all of them white; in 1959 there were 9,485,276 members in 31,906 churches.

There was not at the start, and there is not now, any serious difference in doctrine between the American and Southern Baptist conventions. As a rule Southern Baptists are more conservative and more Calvinistic, and it is one of the ironies of Baptist history that the Southern Baptist Convention adheres more firmly to the New Hampshire Confession of Faith than the American. Church polity and government are the same in both conventions; membership and ministry are exchanged in perfect harmony and understanding.

Five denominational agencies have charge of the work in home and foreign missions, Sunday schools, educational institutions, and ministerial retirement. The Home Mission Board, with 46 members, works throughout the South and in Cuba, Panama and the Panama Canal Zone, with more than 1,600 missionaries active in the field. It co-operates with Negro Baptists; works among migrants in the South and Indians in the West and Southwest and among several language groups and the deaf; operates several highly efficient mission schools in the Appalachians and the Ozarks; and provides loans for the erection of new church buildings.

Foreign missionary work is in 42 countries and on 4 continents. Their record is a proud one; yet in comparison with their huge membership Southern Baptists rank second among Protestant denominations in the number of missionaries sent overseas—with over 9,000,000 members they have more than 1,300 active missionaries in the field. There are 887 schools supported by the foreign missions program, 3,229 churches and 17 hospitals.

The Sunday School Board is one of the ablest in America; it provides the literature for and supervises the work of 7,276,502 students in 31,412 Sunday schools. The first chair of Sunday-school pedagogy was established in 1915 at the Southwestern Seminary in Fort Worth, Texas. There are 7 theological seminaries in the Southern Baptist Convention with 6,000 students, 30 senior colleges and universities, 21 junior colleges (several additional junior colleges are being established but are not yet operating), 8 academies and 4 Bible schools, 39 hospitals, 35 orphanages, and 13 homes for the aged.

The publishing work of this convention is one of the most prolific in Protestantism—circulation of its publications reached a figure of nearly 79,000,000 in 1959. A chain of 52 bookstores distributes this material across the nation.

Southern Baptists are said to be the fastest-growing large denominational group in the United States; new churches are being established not only in the South but in northern, eastern, and western states as well. Their annual convention is being held more and more in northern and western cities, and two reasons are given for this: one is that there are few southern cities with hotel accommodations adequate to care for the ever-increasing numbers of delegates attending conventions; and the other is that there are so many Southern Baptist churches in northern territory that northern cities from sheer force of numbers are entitled to national conventions within their own states. State and territorial lines are being crossed, and it is increasingly evident that the word "southern" is a misnomer. This is fast becoming a national Baptist body in every meaning of the word.

Negro Baptists

The first Negro Baptist church in America was organized at Silver Bluff across the Savannah River from Augusta, Georgia, in 1773; other churches followed in Petersburg, Virginia, in 1776; Richmond, Virginia, in 1780; Williamsburg, Virginia, in 1785; Savannah, Georgia, in 1785; and Lexington, Kentucky, in 1790. It is interesting that Andrew Bryan, a slave, was the first pastor of the First African Baptist Church of Savannah, Georgia, and that its organization came about through the efforts of the Rev. Abraham Marshall (white) and the Rev. Jesse Peter (Negro).

As early as 1700, white slaveholders in the South were providing religious teaching and places of worship for their slaves; at least most of them did little to prevent it. Usually, however, the Negro slave sat in the gallery of the white church, identified with the faith of his owner. White ministers, sometimes assisted by Negro helpers, moved from one plantation to another holding services more or less regularly; occasionally a Negro minister was liberated to give full time to religious work among his people. These ministers had great influence; they were consulted by the whites as the respected leaders of their people and where a real power up to the time of the slave rebellion of 1831 led by Nat Turner. For a period following this disturbance it was illegal in some sections of the South for Negroes to become Christians or to build meetinghouses.

The great majority of Negroes in pre-Civil War days were either Baptists or Methodists. When Bull Run was fought in 1861, there were 200,000 Negro members of the Methodist Episcopal Church, South, and 150,000 Negro Baptists. In 1793 there were 73,471 Baptists in the United States, and one fourth of them were Negroes; in 1806 one third of the Baptists of North Carolina were Negroes. The lack of formality in the Baptist churches, together with the absence of ritual and the freedom and democracy of the local congregation, appealed to the Negro more than the episcopal structure of the Methodists. This was accented at the end of the Civil War; a revival spirit swept the Negroes, creating thousands of new churches. Aided by the Freedman's Aid Society and various Baptist organizations, nearly 1,000,000 Negro Baptists worshipped in their own churches within 15 years.

The first Negro Baptist association, the Providence Baptist Association of Ohio, was formed in 1836; the first attempt at national organization came in 1880 with the creation of the Foreign Mission Baptist Convention at Montgomery, Alabama. In 1886 the American National Baptist Convention was organized at St. Louis, and in 1893 the Baptist National Educational Convention was organized in the District of Columbia. All three conventions were merged into the National Baptist Convention of the U.S.A. at Atlanta in 1895. In 1915 a division arose in this convention over the adoption of a charter and the ownership of a publishing house. The group rejecting the charter continued to function as The National Baptist Convention of America, while the group accepting the charter became known as The National Baptist Convention of the U.S.A., Incorporated (incorporated, that is, under the laws of the District of Columbia). The former is frequently referred to as the "unincorporated" and the latter as the "incorporated" convention, but both trace their beginning to the Foreign Mission Baptist Convention of 1880.

Today, out of approximately 15,000,-000 Negroes in the United States, better than 10,000,000 are in the South, and 44 per cent of the total Negro population are church members as compared with 42.4 per cent of the whites. They are grouped into a bewildering number of churches and denominations. There are more than 30 recognized and entirely different Negro denominations, some with less than 20 members, but seven eights of our total Negro population is either Methodist or Baptist. Nearly 8,000,000 Negro Baptists are found in the two major conventions: 5,000,000 in The National Baptist Convention of the U.S.A., Incorporated, and 2,668,799 in The National Baptist Convention of America.

Negro Baptist doctrine runs quite parallel to that of white Baptist churches; however, it is slightly more Calvinistic. The polity of the two larger white conventions prevails; local churches unite in associations, usually along state lines, for the purposes of fellowship and consultation. There are also state conventions concerned with missionary work and often extending beyond state boundaries.

Foreign missionary work is especially strong in Africa, and home missionary efforts are generally those expended in the direction of helping needy churches and schools, and in family support and relief. The National Baptist Convention, Inc., has several missionary stations in the Bahamas, has 5 colleges, 1 theological seminary, and 1 training school for women and girls. The National Baptist Convention of America has stations in Jamaica, Panama, and Africa, and gives support to 10 colleges.

The old enmities between the two conventions are disappearing, but no reunion is expected for some time to come. Moves have been made, however, toward the union of the National Baptist Convention of the U.S.A., Inc., with the American Baptist Convention.

American Baptist Association

Sometimes called Landmarkers because of their historic adherence to the old apostolic order of church polity, the American Baptist Association members deny that those Baptists organized in conventions are faithful to Bible precedent. Maintaining that their own is the only true New Testament form, they hold themselves separate from all other religious groups.

Starting in 1905 as the Baptist General Association, they organized under their present name in 1924 at Texarkana, Arkansas-Texas. Denying all denominationalism, they seem to be quite denominational in their attitude in refusing to affiliate with any other group. Teaching that the great commission of Christ (Matt. 28:18-20) was given to a local congregation, they believe that the local congregation or church is the only unit authorized to administer the ordinances and that it is an independent and autonomous body responsible only to Christ. Thus, every church is equal "with every other like church"; they are often called Church-Equality Baptists.

Their doctrine is strictly fundamentalist. Condemning "so-called modern science," they stand for the verbal inspiration of the Bible, the Triune God, the virgin birth and deity of Christ, the suffering and death of Christ as substitutionary, the bodily resurrection of Christ and all his saints. The second coming of Jesus, "physical and personal," is to be the crowning event of the "gospel age"; this second advent will be premillennial. There is eternal punishment for the wicked; salvation is solely by grace through faith and not by law or works. There must be absolute separation of church and state, and absolute religious freedom.

Government of both the local congregations and the annual messenger meetings of the association is congregational in nature. Missionary work is conducted on county, state, interstate, and foreign levels, with the program originating in the local church and the missionaries being supported by the cooperating churches. Educational work is pursued through the Sunday schools and several seminaries which are also established on the local church level. These seminaries are: Missionary Baptist Seminary, Little Rock, Arkansas; The Texas Baptist Seminary, Henderson, Texas; Oklahoma Missionary Baptist Institute, Marlow, Oklahoma; Eastern Baptist Institute, Somerset, Kentucky; Florida Baptist Institute, Lakeland, Florida; California Missionary Baptist Institute, Bellflower, California; Carolina Missionary Baptist Institute, Greenville, South Carolina; Louisiana Missionary Baptist Institute, Minden, Louisiana.

The greater strength of this group is found in the South, Southwest, and Southeast, but much new work has been started in recent years in the East, North, and West. Their 1959 statistics show 3,045 churches with a total combined membership of 630,000; 3,000 Sunday schools with an enrollment of 234,205; and 2,200 ordained clergy with charges. Their membership continues to shift from rural to urban.

Ten monthly and semimonthly periodicals are published as well as Sunday school and Young People's literature.

Baptist General Conference of America

The history of what is now known as the Baptist General Conference of America began at Rock Island, Illinois, in the summer of 1852. Gustaf Palmquist, a schoolteacher and lay preacher, had come from Sweden to Illinois the previous year to become the spiritual leader of a group of Swedish immigrants who had been influenced by the pietistic movement within the State Church (Lutheran) of Sweden. At Galesburg, Illinois, he came in contact with the Baptists and early in 1852 was baptized and ordained a Baptist minister. Visiting his countrymen at Rock Island, he won his first converts to the Baptist faith and baptized 3 in the Mississippi River on August 8, 1852. From this humble beginning has come a denomination of 65,000 members, 516 churches, and 18 state or district conferences. In 1879 a national conference—the Swedish Baptist General Conference of America— was organized.

For several decades the American Baptist Home Mission Society and the American Baptist Publication Society of the American (then the Northern) Baptist Convention aided the new work among the immigrant Swedes, but gradually the church became self-supporting. A theological seminary was founded in Chicago in 1871, and the first denominational paper was launched in the same year. From 1888 to 1944 foreign missionary activities were channeled through the American Baptist Foreign Mission Society; a separation came in 1944, caused largely by a desire on the part of the Swedes to become completely independent and also in protest against the foreign society's "inclusive policy" under which missionaries of both liberal and conservative theologies were sent out to the foreign field. The Swedish conference set up its own foreign board and today has more than 125 missionaries in India, Japan, the Philippine Islands, Ethiopia, Mexico, Argentina, and Brazil.

Following the First World War, with its intensified nationalistic conflicts, the transition from Swedish to English in church services was greatly accelerated and practically completed in three decades. In 1945 the word "Swedish" was dropped from the name of the conference; it had already been dropped largely by the local churches. With the language barrier removed, the growth of the conference has been rapid and far-reaching. Home missionaries are at work in all northern states, in some of the southern states, and Canada; one of their most effective organizations is

God's Invasion Army, made up of young lay volunteers who spend a year in concentrated home missions work.

The conference owns and controls Bethel College at St. Paul, Minnesota (a 4-year college and a 3-year theological seminary with 700 students). Affiliated are 2 children's homes, 7 homes for the aged, and a Hebrew mission. Six periodicals, including *The Standard*, official denominational organ, are issued by the Board of Publication. The Baptist Conference Press offers Bibles, books, and Sunday-school materials.

Basically their doctrine is that of "theological conservatives, with unqualified acceptance of the Word of God," holding the usual Baptist tenets. They are a strong fellowship of churches, insistent upon the major beliefs of conservative Christianity but with respect and room for individual differences on minor points.

The conference tends to become more and more inclusive and to appeal to people of all nationalities. Actually about 20 per cent of their pastors are not even of Swedish descent, and a large number of their churches contain very few Swedes. The transition has been fast because of the lack of Swedish immigrants and also because of the Swedes' quick assimilation into the American way of life.

Bethel Baptist Assembly

The Bethel Baptist Assembly is a small association of Baptist ministers in Indiana and Illinois, organized in the interests of fellowship and the mutual proclamation of the Baptist message and theology. The name was recently changed from The Bethel Ministerial Council. The Bethel Publishing House issues an official periodical, *Words With Power*. A summer camp for youth is an important feature of their work. No statements on membership or churches are available.

Christian Unity Baptist Association

The Christian Unity Baptist Association originated in a dispute over the question of open and close Communion in the Mount Union Baptist Association of Regular Baptists in North Carolina. The dissenters believed that all Christians in all denominations should be admitted to participation in the Lord's Supper. They are one of the smaller groups, numbering 620 members and 11 churches.

They believe in one God and the Trinity and in the Bible as the inspired word of God; that all mankind is fallen and helpless to save itself; in the redemption of the "bodies of the saints," infants, and idiots; that sinners reach God by way of repentance and faith; that the only 2 authorized ordinances are baptism of believers and the Lord's Supper; in foot washing; in the resurrection of the bodies of both the just and the unjust; in the everlasting reward of the righteous and the punishment of the wicked.

Government is strictly congregational; there is one association for advisory purposes only. Work centers largely in home missions, evangelism, revivals, prayer meetings, and Sunday schools.

Conservative Baptist Association of America

The Conservative Baptist Association of America is officially described as a

voluntary fellowship of sovereign, autonomous, independent and Bible-believing Baptist churches working together to extend the Baptist testimony. . . . The Association is wholly separated from all other organizations, Baptist as well as non-Baptist. The several churches are held together, not by elaborate machinery, but by a common abiding love for the work and person of Jesus Christ, and the World of God, as well as love for the confidence in one another.

The founders of the association were active in an earlier organization known as the Fundamentalist Fellowship which was founded in 1920 within the American (then the Northern) Baptist Convention. This was a group of conservative churchmen who opposed what they considered to be the infiltration of liberal and modernistic tendencies and teachings within that convention. The basic disagreement was doctrinal and had to do with fundamentally different views and interpretations of the Scriptures and of Baptistic theology. The dispute was aggravated by the "inclusive" policy of the American Baptist Foreign Mission Society under which missionaries of both conservative and liberal theologies were sent out to both home and foreign fields. In September, 1943, the executive committee of the Fundamentalist Fellowship presented a directive to the board of managers of the American Baptist Foreign Mission Society stating that they could no longer give funds to this society unless it appointed as missionaries only those of conservative belief and theology. The gulf widened; the Conservative Baptist Foreign Mission Society was legally incorporated on December 15, 1943, and the Conservative Baptist Home Mission Society in 1950. The name of the Fundamentalist Fellowship was changed to the Conservative Baptist Fellowship in 1946, a constitution for a Conservative Baptist Association was adopted in 1947, and the association was formally organized a year later. It ceased to function within the framework of the American Baptist Convention in 1951.

The Conservative Baptists were at this time definitely not a separate Baptist denomination and had no desire to be known as such. They are still not a denomination in the usual sense of the word, but a fellowship of independent churches. Their work and organization, however, have expanded to such a point that they are in reality a denomination with approximately 300,000 members in 1,321 churches affiliated with state and national C.B.A.; there are C.B.A. organizations in 29 states. There are 378 foreign missionaries at work in 88 mission stations in Argentina, Brazil, the Congo, French West Africa, the Arab Near East, Portugal, Italy, Ceylon, India, Pakistan, Borneo, Japan, Taiwan, and the Philippines. A total of more than $2,000,000 was contributed for foreign missionary work in 1959.

Beyond this, 93 home missionaries are now in 18 fields in the U. S. and the West Indies. The Conservative Baptist Association (formerly the Fundamentalist Fellowship) is engaged in publication work; and a monthly periodical, *C.B.A. Builders*, is published by the association in Chicago. They have 4 seminaries, 3 colleges, and 4 Bible institutes; Bible colleges are located in Calcutta, India, and Leiria, Portugal, Bible schools in Brazil, Taiwan, and the Congo. Financial aid is offered to build or support new or struggling Conservative Baptist churches, local and foreign radio programs are on the air, 52 summer camps for youth have been established, and chaplains are sent into the armed forces.

A series of regional fellowship meetings are held in the fall of each year, at which regional officials are elected. Representatives of the association meet with local boards to "counsel, advise, and recommend," and to help local pulpit committees find suitable pastors. National headquarters have been established at Chicago.

Duck River (and Kindred) Associations of Baptists (Baptist Church of Christ)

Confined to 4 southern states, the Duck River Baptists originated in a protest movement within the old Elk River Association, which was strongly Calvinistic. This came in 1825; in 1843 the ranks of the dissenters were broken by a dispute over the legitimacy of missions and the support of a publication society and of a denominational school.

Those who withdrew became known as Missionary Baptists and in a few instances as Separate Baptists or the Baptist Churches of Christ. The division persists; there are today 2 Duck River associations.

Doctrinally they are liberally Calvinistic; they hold that "Christ tasted death for every man"; that God will save those who come to him on gospel terms; that sinners are justified by faith; that the saints will "persevere in grace." They stand for believer's baptism by immersion and celebrate the Lord's Supper and foot washing as scriptural ordinances. As they admit their close gospel ties with Regular, United, and Separate Baptists, there are growing sentiments in favor of union.

They are congregational in government, with 5 associations for fellowship only: Duck River, Mount Zion, Union, and East Union in Tennessee; and Mount Pleasant in Alabama, Tennessee, and Georgia. There is a "correspondence" relation with other associations in Alabama, Tennessee, Mississippi, and Georgia. Membersip is by vote of local congregations; ministers are ordained by 2 or more ministers. There are 9,488 members and 96 churches.

Free Will Baptists

Free Will Baptists in this country have a Welsh background; they migrated from Wales in 1701, settling on a grant of land in Pennsylvania known as the Welsh Tract. They were organized in the South in 1727 by Paul Palmer and in the North in 1787 by Benjamin Randall. Their churches today number 4,200, and are found in 42 states and in Cuba, Africa, Japan, Mexico, India, and Spain. They list 425,000 members. The organization in the United States is known officially as the National Association of Free Will Baptists with national headquarters in Nashville, Tennessee, where the Executive Department, Home and Foreign Mission Departments, Sunday School Department, League (Youth) Department, Master's Men (laymen's organization), and Woman's Auxiliary are located. The official publication is *Contact*, edited and published monthly in Nashville, Tennessee.

Distinguished by their adherence to Arminian (freewill) doctrine rather than to the usual Calvinistic (predestinarian) tenets, they suffered badly during the early growth of Calvinism in this country. At one time in the United States they had only four churches left; however, their growth since that time has been phenomenal.

They hold that Christ gave himself as a ransom for the many, not for the few; that God calls all to repentance; and that all may be saved who believe in Jesus Christ and trust him as personal Saviour. Baptism is by immersion. This is one of the Baptist churches practicing open Communion; they also practice foot washing. Their government is strictly congregational; there are quarterly conferences, which are grouped into state associations, and an annual Convention representing the entire denomination. The Woman's Auxiliary Convention and a laymen's organization meet with the annual convention, and in alternate years there are also meetings of the Free Will Baptist League Conference for the youth and the Free Will Baptist Sunday School Convention. A Bible college, owned and operated by the National Association, is located in Nashville, Tennessee.

General Baptists

The General Baptists claim their name and origin in John Smythe and Thomas Helwys and the group of Baptists organized in England and Holland in 1611 (see general article on the Baptists, pp. 32 ff.). They hold Roger Williams to be their first minister in the American colonies.

The General Baptists in the colonies along the Atlantic coast were at first overwhelmed by the influence of Calvinism (General Baptists have always been Arminian), but their work was reopened by Benoni Stinson with the establishment of the Liberty Baptist Church in what is now Evansville, Indiana, in 1823. They spread into Illinois and Kentucky, and a general association of General Baptists was organized in 1870. Since that time they have grown steadily; today they are strong in Kentucky, Tennessee, Indiana, Michigan, Illinois, Missouri, and Arkansas, and have located churches in Oklahoma, Nebraska, Kansas, Iowa, Ohio, Arizona, and California.

Their confession of faith is similar to that of the Free Will Baptists; it is their belief that Christ died for all men; that failure to achieve salvation lies completely with the individual; that man is depraved and fallen and unable to save himself; that regeneration is necessary for salvation except in the case of infants and idiots, who are not responsible for sin; that salvation comes by repentance and faith in Christ; that the Christian who perseveres to the end is saved; that the wicked are punished eternally. The dead, just and unjust, will be raised at the judgment; the Lord's Supper and believer's baptism by immersion only are the only authorized Christian ordinances and should be open to all believers. Some of the General Baptist churches practice foot washing.

Church polity is about the same as that found in all Baptist churches. The denomination is congregational in church government. Churches of a common area are organized into local associations, which are in turn organized into a general association. Both local and general associations are representative bodies and advisory in power. A peculiar feature of the General Baptists lies in their use of a presbytery, into which the ordained members of local associations are grouped; they examine candidates for the ministry and for deacons. Ministers and deacons are responsible to this presbytery, which exists only on the local level.

Current statistics show 737 churches with a total membership of 54,596. They maintain at Oakland City, Indiana, a liberal arts college with a theological department. A publishing house is operated at Poplar Bluff, Missouri, where their weekly paper, the *General Baptist Messenger*, is issued together with Sunday-school literature.

Foreign missionary work is supported in Guam, Saipan, Chichi Jima, and the Philippines. They have an active home missionary work in various states.

The General Association of Regular Baptist Churches

Twenty-two Baptist churches of the American Baptist Convention left that convention in May of 1932 to found The General Association of Regular Baptist Churches. The protest was against what they considered to be modernist tendencies and teachings in the American Convention, the denial of the historic Baptist principle of the independence and autonomy of the local congregation, the inequality of representation in the assemblies of the convention, the control of missionary work by convention assessment and budget, and the whole convention principle in general.

Any Baptist church coming into this association is required to "withdraw all fellowship and cooperation from any convention or group which permits modernists or modernism within its ranks." Dual fellowship or membership is not permitted, nor is participation in union evangelical campaigns, union Thanksgiving services or membership in local ministerial associations where modernists are involved or present.

Missionary work is conducted through 5 approved Baptist agencies completely independent of any convention and completely orthodox; a close watch is maintained upon these agencies before annual approval is granted. Likewise, only 6 schools are approved; these, too, are "guarded" against any deflection from approved practice or doctrine.

The association subscribes to the New Hampshire Confession of Faith with a premillennial interpretation of the final article of that confession. They hold to the infallibility of the Bible, the Trinity, the personality of Satan as the author of all evil, man as the creation of God and man born in sin. There are doctrines dealing with the virgin birth and the deity of Jesus and faith in Christ as the way of salvation through grace. The saved are in everlasting felicity, and the lost are lost forever. There is a bodily resurrection; Christ rose and ascended and will return premillennially to reign in the millennium. Civil government is by divine appointment. There are only 2 approved ordinances: baptism by immersion and the Lord's Supper.

Church government is strictly congregational. Member churches have the privilege of sending 6 voting messengers to an annual convention; thus a church with 50 members has the same power as a church with 2,500 members. A Council of Fourteen is elected—7 each year— to serve for 2 years. It makes recommendations to the association for the furtherance of its work and implements and puts into operation all actions and policies of the association, and its authority depends completely upon the will and direction of the association.

In 1959, there were 690 fellowshiping churches with 130,612 members. The six approved schools had a total student body of over 1,200, and 1,100 missionaries were at work in the 5 missionary agencies. State and regional associations have been established across the country; these are supplied with literature published by the Regular Baptist Press, including *The Baptist Bulletin*, a 32-page monthly magazine.

General Conference of the Evangelical Baptist Church, Inc.

The Evangelical Baptists were organized among the members of several Free Will Baptist Churches in 1935; they were formerly known as The Church of the Full Gospel, Incorporated.

Their doctrine and organization are naturally similar to that of the Free Will Baptists, with whom they are still in close fellowship. They exchange pastors regularly with the Wilmington Conference of the Free Will Baptist Church. As of 1952, there were about 2,200 members in 31 churches.

General Six-Principle Baptists

There are 2 Six-Principle Baptist Associations in the United States, one in Rhode Island and the other in Pennsylvania. The former claims to have been founded by Roger Williams in 1638; the latter was founded in 1813. Both claim as their charter the 6 foundation principles laid down in Heb. 6:1-2—namely, repentance, faith, baptism, the laying on of hands (a custom evidently disappearing, at least in Rhode Island), the resurrection of the dead, and eternal judgment.

Broadly speaking, they are Arminian in doctrine and congregational in polity. The conferences they hold are primarily for fellowship, but there is an increasing interest in foreign missions and in the support of students in Christian colleges. Rhode Island lists 96 members in 3 churches; Pennsylvania has 7 churches, with membership not reported.

Independent Baptist Church of America

This is a church of Swedish origin, founded in 1893 at Dassel, Minnesota, by a group of Swedish Free Baptist immigrants. A series of disagreements within the body brought about several changes in name and a split into two churches, which were united under the present name in 1927.

The Independent Baptist Church of America teaches faith in the Resurrection, that repentance and baptism by immersion are prerequisite to membership and participation in the Lord's Supper. They practice the laying on of hands at the time of admission into church membership. They are generally pacifists, but in all other matters they pledge obedience to the civil government.

No record of the work or organization of this church is available; there were 106 members and 2 churches in 1956.

Landmark Baptists

"Landmarkism," among Baptists, is not a denomination; it is a position (called by many Baptists a heretical position) concerning the nature of the church and certain matters of church practice. The name is borrowed from a tract written by James Madison Pendleton entitled "An Old Landmark Re-set." Pendleton and James Robinson Graves are generally credited with inauguration of the Landmark movement; they were the leaders of the "Cotton Grove Convention" organized among Southern Baptists in 1851. (Southern Baptists are vigorously opposed to Landmarkism.)

There are four main tenets to Landmarkism:

1. The church is only local and visible; there is no such thing as "the Church," but only churches in the local sense. The kingdom of God is equal to the sum of all true (Landmark-thinking Baptist) churches.
2. Valid baptism calls for a proper administrator (a properly ordained Baptist clergyman). Any baptism performed by any other person is worthless.
3. Members of other denominations or churches are not recognized as Christians; they are not "saved" in "the true Gospel sense." Other churches are called "societies," and their ministers are not to be recognized as such.
4. There is a direct, historic "succession" of Baptist churches back to New Testament times; true Baptist churches have existed in every century.

This "succession" has been called "Apostolic succession" and "succession of believers Baptistism." As one of the main principles of Landmarkism, it is an idea held by few Baptists today outside the American Baptist Association (which see), as part of that groups' extreme separatism.

National Baptist Evangelical Life and Soul Saving Assembly of the U.S.A.

This assembly was founded in 1920 at Kansas City, Missouri, not as another denomination, but as an evangelical group working within the National Baptist Convention (Unincorporated). It had the endorsement of the parent body for 17 years but became an independent group in 1937.

No new doctrine is set forth by this group; it has no doctrine except the "Bible doctrine as announced by the Founder of the Church, Jesus Christ." Concentration is mainly upon evangelical and relief efforts. The assembly maintains an automatic correspondence school, offering courses in evangelology, deaconology, missionology, pastorology, and laymanology; degrees are granted in 60, 90, and 120 days.

In 1951, 57,674 members and 264 churches were reported.

National Primitive Baptist Convention of the U.S.A.
(Formerly Colored Primitive Baptists)

The Negro population of the South all through the years of slavery and the Civil War worshiped with the white population in their various churches.

This was true of Colored Primitive Baptists, who attended white Primitive Baptist churches until the time of the emancipation, when their white brethren helped them to establish their own churches, granting them letters of fellowship and character, ordaining their deacons and ministers, and helping in other ways.

Their doctrine and polity are quite the same as in the white Primitive Baptist organization, except that they are "opposed to all forms of church organization"; yet there are local associations and a national convention, organized in 1907. Each church is independent, receiving and controlling its own membership; there is no appeal from a decision of the officers of the local church.

In 1957 they had a membership of 80,983 in 1,100 churches. Unlike the white Primitive Baptists, they have since 1900 been establishing aid societies, conventions, and Sunday schools over the opposition of the older and more orthodox members.

North American Baptist Association

Organized at Little Rock, Arkansas, on May 25, 1950, for the purpose of encouraging and fostering missionary co-operation, this body has had a phenomenal growth, enrolling nearly 2,000 churches and 300,000 members in 23 states. They have 7 workers in the home missions field and missionary work abroad in Mexico, Japan, Brazil, Formosa, Portugal, and Cape Verde Islands. A strong publications department publishes literature for Sunday-school and training classes, pamphlets, books, tracts, and magazines. They also own and operate a printing business in Brazil, where literature is printed in Portuguese for use in Africa and Europe.

They are militant fundamentalists, claiming to hold the historic Baptist faith and placing strong emphasis upon the verbal inspiration and accuracy of the Scriptures, direct creation, the virgin birth and deity of Jesus, his blood atonement, justification by faith, salvation by grace alone, and the imminent, personal return of Christ to the earth. They brand as unscriptural open Communion, alien baptism, pulpit affiliation with heretical ministers, unionism, modernism, modern conventionism, one-church dictatorship, and "all the kindred evils arising from these practices." The Lord's Supper and baptism are accepted as ordinances; baptism is considered "alien" unless administered to believers only and by "divine authority as given to the Missionary Baptist churches."

Churches are completely autonomous in the Baptist tradition and have an equal voice in the co-operative missionary, publication, evangelical, and educational efforts of the association regardless of size or membership. Member churches must, however, conform to the doctrinal standards of the association and deny alien baptism and modernism in all its forms.

There are one college—Jacksonville—and several junior colleges, maintained on a state level, and several orphan's homes. Two theological seminaries are located at Jacksonville, Texas, and Campinas, Brazil.

North American Baptist General Conference

The churches in this conference began in German Baptist churches established on our soil by German Baptist immigrants of more than a century ago. The first of them settled in New Jersey and Pennsylvania—where Penn's Quakers offered them the perfect chance at the religious freedom they sought in flight from the mother country. Some of these Germans became members of the United Brethren group (established here in 1800), or of the Church of God (Winebrennarians, established in 1830), or of the scattered German Baptist churches which later became the North American Baptist General Conference

47

and which organized their first local churches during 1840-51.

The prosperity of these German Baptist churches followed the rise and fall of German immigration. By 1851 they had 8 churches and 405 members, and in that year they organized their churches into an eastern conference for fellowship and mutual consideration of common problems.

The local conference idea was enlarged as their churches increased. As their membership moved across the nation they organized a total of 9 such conferences, following geographical lines. In 1865 they held a joint meeting of eastern and western conferences and called it a general conference. The General Conference is now their chief administrative unit.

Local conferences meet annually, elect their own officers and missionary committees, and guide their own work. The General Conference meets triennially and is made up of all churches in the 9 local conferences and has clerical and lay representation from all of them. It superintends the work in publication, education, missions, and homes for children and the aged. A general council acts for the General Conference between its sessions.

German Baptists have been active in the development of what is now Colgate-Rochester Divinity School and they have a seminary of their own, the North American Baptist Seminary, at Sioux Falls, South Dakota. A Christian Training Institute is located at Edmonton, Alberta, Canada. There are 6 homes for the aged, a children's home at St. Joseph, Michigan, and a publishing house, the Roger Williams Press, at Cleveland, Ohio. Home missions are conducted among the Indians of Canada and among Spanish-Americans in the United States; foreign missionaries are located in Cameroons, West Africa, Austria, and Japan.

Theologically there is little variance here from the usual Baptist position;

German Baptists in general follow the New Hampshire Confession, stressing the authority of the Scriptures, the revelation of God in Christ, regeneration, immersion, separation of church and state, the congregational form of government, and with very strong emphasis on missions. There are 50,455 members and 292 churches.

Primitive Baptists

The Primitive Baptists have the reputation of being the most strictly orthodox and exclusive of all Baptists. Unique in that they have never been organized as a denomination and have no administrative bodies of any kind (they believe that each church should "govern itself according to the laws of Christ as found in the New Testament, and that no minister, association, or convention has any authority"), they represent a protest against "money-based" missions and benevolent societies and against "assessing" the churches to support missions, missionaries, and Sunday schools. The position taken was that there were no missionary societies in the days of the apostles, and therefore there should be none now. Apart from this, there was objection to the centralization of authority in these societies. Sunday schools also were unauthorized by Scripture; they believed in the religious training of children but not in Sunday schools. They stood for evangelism as a missionary effort, but on individual responsibility and at individual expense, and not under the sponsorship of a money-based society. Spearheading the protest, the Kehukee Association in North Carolina in 1827 condemned all such money-based and authoritarian societies as contrary to Christ's teachings. Within a decade, several other Baptist associations across the country made similar statements and withdrew from other Baptist churches.

The various associations adopted the custom of printing in their annual minutes a statement of their articles of faith, their constitution, and their rules of order. These statements were examined by every other association and if they were approved, there were fellowship and exchange of messengers and correspondence between them; any association not so approved was dropped from the fellowship. Added to this was the difficulty of communication in many parts of the South. The result was confusion; there was no chance under such conditions for growth as a denomination and little chance even for fellowship or quasi unity. This is apparent in the variety of names, some friendly and some derisive, which have been applied to them, such as "Primitive," "Old School," "Regular," "Antimission" and "Hard Shell." In general, the term "Primitive" has been widely accepted and used.

A strong Calvinism runs through their doctrine. In general they believe that by Adam's fall all his posterity became sinners; that human nature is completely corrupt; and that man cannot by his own efforts regain favor with God. God elected his own people in Christ before the world began, and none of these saints will be finally lost. The 2 biblically authorized ordinances are the Lord's Supper and baptism of believers by immersion. All church societies are the invention of men and are to be denied fellowship; Christ will come a second time to raise the dead, judge all men, punish forever the wicked and reward forever the righteous; the Old and New Testaments are verbally and infallibly inspired.

Ministers must be called of God, come under the laying on of hands, and be in fellowship with the local church of which they are members before they can administer the 2 ordinances; they are to deny to any other clergyman lacking these qualifications the right to administer such ordinances. No theological training is demanded of ministers among Primitive Baptists; while there is no opposition to such education, the position is that the Lord will call an educated

man if he wants one, but that lack of education should not bar a man from the ministry. Some Primitive Baptists still practice foot washing, but not all do. In spite of their opposition to money-based missionary societies they are intensely evangelistic, and their preachers travel widely and serve without charge, except when their hearers wish to contribute to their support.

Membership is granted only after careful examination and vote of the congregation. Membership is estimated at about 72,000 in 1,000 churches, but probably the figure is larger. Factionalism, divisiveness, and politics prevent an accurate report on membership.

Regular Baptists

The term "Regular" as applied to Baptists has been the cause of some confusion. Originally it was applied to the Baptists of the Northern, Southern, and National conventions. That usage ended about 1890, and the expression is now applied only to the denomination bearing that name, centering in North Carolina, Virginia, West Virginia, and Kentucky. These Regular Baptists claim to be the modern representatives of the original English Baptists before the divisions into Particular (Calvinistic) and General (Arminian) Baptists were established. They are in close sympathy with the United Baptists and the Duck River (and Kindred) Associations of Baptists.

Regular Baptists believe that men are responsible to all the commands of God, compliance always being by enabling grace; that with such grace all men may meet the conditions of salvation; that man through sin is completely depraved with neither the power nor the will to save himself; that salvation is by grace alone as a result of God's mercy and love; that on the basis of the sacrifice of Christ for all sin the gospel of God's grace must be preached to all men; that the lost are lost because of their unbelief. In general they hold a middle-of-the-road position on the Atonement, but a few of their churches are sympathetic with the views of the Primitive Baptists.

Each association has its own confession of faith; there is no over-all confession for all. Most of them are Arminian; a few lean toward Calvinism. They practice close Communion and foot washing. The governmental policy is strictly congregational with associations meeting for fellowship only. Regular Baptists in 1936 numbered 17,186; there were 266 churches. A noticeable decline in both churches and membership is evident.

Separate Baptists in Christ

The first Separate Baptists arrived in the United States in 1695 as one refugee section of the separatist movement in England. They were especially active during the days of the blazing preaching of Whitefield in the early eighteenth century and in the conflict between the Old Light and New Light sects. Separate Baptist churches of this period were marked by their milder Calvinism and by an occasional use of infant baptism.

In 1787 Separate and Regular Baptist churches merged in Virginia in the United Baptist Churches of Christ in Virginia. There were other mergers and gestures toward union in New England and other states, but a few Separate Baptist churches maintained their independence. In 1959 they had 90 churches and 7,215 members.

All creeds and confessions of faith are rejected by Separate Baptists; however, there is an annual statement of articles of belief by the several associations. These include statements of faith in the infallibility of the Scriptures and in the Trinity; 3 ordinances—baptism of believers by immersion only, the Lord's Supper, and foot washing; regeneration, justification, and sanctification through faith in Christ; the appearance of Christ on Judgment Day to deal with the just and the unjust. The election, reprobation, and fatality of Calvinism are rejected.

Separate Baptists are congregational in government with associations for advisory purposes only. The associations carry on a limited home missions work; there are no foreign missions and no colleges, but there are good Sunday schools throughout the denomination. A magazine called *The Messenger* is published at Kokomo, Indiana.

Seventh Day Baptists

Differing from other Baptists in their adherence to the seventh day as the Sabbath, Seventh Day Baptists (or Sabbatarian Baptists, as they were called in England) first organized themselves as a separate body on this side of the Atlantic in 1672 at Newport, Rhode Island. Stephen Mumford, a member of the Bell Lane Seventh Day Baptist Church in London, had come there knowing well the perils of religious nonconformity and had entered into covenant relation with those who withdrew from "Doctor John Clarke's (Baptist) Church" under the Sabbath persuasion. Other churches were organized in Philadelphia and in New Jersey. From these 3 centers Seventh Day Baptists went west with the frontier; they now have 6,200 members in 66 churches and fellowships.

Belief in salvation through faith in Christ, believer's baptism by immersion, insistence upon intellectual and civil liberty and in the right of every man to interpret the Bible for himself have characterized this people. They hold baptism and the Lord's Supper only as ordinances, practice open Communion, and have fostered one university and two colleges. The Alfred University School of Theology is located at Alfred, New York.

Local churches enjoy complete independence, although all of them support the united benevolence of the denomination known as Our World Mission. For fellowship and service the churches are organized into 9 regional associations and these often assist local church councils in the ordination of deacons and ministerial candidates. The highest administrative body is the General Conference, which meets annually and delegates interim responsibilities to its president, executive secretary, and commission. The conference promotes World Mission giving and channels it through mission, publishing, and educational agencies. It also accredits ministers certified to it by ordaining councils and local churches. The denomination participates in the ecumenical movement at local, regional, national, and world levels. Foreign missions are carried on in China, Germany, the Netherlands, Nyasaland, British Guiana, and Jamaica, British West Indies.

Seventh Day Baptists (German, 1728)

The Seventh Day Baptists (German, 1728) are not to be confused with the original Seventh Day Baptist Church organized earlier in Rhode Island; this group was established by John Conrad Beissel, a Palatinate German, in 1728. Beissel worked for a while with Peter Becker, the Germantown mystic who founded the German Baptist Brethren, or Dunkards. He left Becker in 1732 to set up a monastic, communistic religious community at Ephrata, Pennsylvania. Goods were held in common, and men and women lived in separate houses under a regulation requiring celibacy.

The community declined late in the nineteenth century; the church last reported only 150 members in 3 churches in 1951. Generally they hold the usual Dunker doctrines: the inspiration of the Bible; one God, the Father, and Jesus Christ, his Son, the mediator; the Ten Commandments as the sole rule of righteousness for all men; baptism by trine forward immersion—the candidate is immersed 3 times, for Father, Son, and Holy Ghost. They practice foot washing, anointing of the sick, and the

blessing of infants; observe Saturday as the Sabbath; and induct ministers by personal request rather than by congregational election.

A general conference meets annually; there is a small home missions program but no educational or philanthropic work.

Two-Seed-in-the-Spirit Predestinarian Baptists

Tracing their thought back to the Waldenses, the Two-Seed-in-the-Spirit Predestinarian Baptists in this country began in the late eighteenth century with the protests of Elder Daniel Parker against missions and Sunday schools. Parker opposed the Arminian doctrine of the Methodists and based his dislike of the missionary effort and church schools on what he called his Two-Seed Doctrine. This, briefly, is the conviction that two seeds entered the life stream of humanity in the Garden of Eden. One seed was good, planted by God; the other was evil, from the devil. The two seeds have been in conflict in humanity ever since. Every baby is predestined, born with one seed or the other. Nothing can be done for him one way or another. Inasmuch as nothing can be done, missions are useless; they are, moreover, an institution which "usurps the privileges of God."

The seed is in the spirit, not the flesh; this is the cardinal point in the theology of the group. Other points include belief in the resurrection of the body of Christ, which is the Church, and salvation by grace alone. The church observes the Lord's Supper and practices foot washing. There is no paid ministry "inasmuch as Christ came to save sinners, and He finished his work." Government is congregational; there are associations for fellowship only. There are no home missions or benevolences. The membership is decreasing; there were 201 members and 16 churches in 1945.

United Baptists

The United Baptists represent a merging of several groups of Separate and Regular Baptists mainly in the states of Virginia, Kentucky, and the Carolinas. While these groups were bodies holding both Arminian and Calvinistic theologies, they maintained a perfect freedom in preaching and polity after their union. As the years passed many of their members found their way into either the Northern or Southern Baptist conventions; but they are still recognized as a separate denomination with 63,641 members in 568 churches. Their first organization was in Richmond, Virginia, in 1787; a second group organized in Kentucky in 1801. Two associations —Salem and Elkhorn (Regular Baptists) and South Kentucky (Separate Baptists)—joined to form the United Baptists.

Doctrinally there are still traces of both Arminianism and Calvinism. Generally they hold that salvation is by grace rather than by works and conditional upon gospel requirements. All men are in a state of general depravity and are commanded to repent; they are led either to repentance through the goodness of God or to rebellion by the devil. It is a matter of individual choice.

There are 26 associations for fellowship and counsel quite independent of one another, yet working together closely. A general association is probable in the near future. They practice close Communion in some associations and churches, open Communion in others. There are three ordinances—baptism, the Lord's Supper, and (in most churches) foot washing.

The United Free Will Baptist Church

While they trace their history back to the same original sources of the white Free Will Baptist Church, the United Free Will Baptists (Colored) have been independent since their official organization in 1901. Their members are found largely in North Carolina, Georgia, Florida, Mississippi, Louisiana, and Texas.

Although in general agreement with the congregational polity of other Baptist bodies, this church grants a rather limited autonomy to the local church. There is a system of quarterly, annual, and general conferences, with graded authority. Doctrinal disputes may be carried up to the general conferences; district conferences may exclude members from fellowship.

Doctrinally they are in agreement with white churches of the same faith. There is one institution of higher learning— Kinston College at Kinston, North Carolina. There were 100,000 members in 836 churches in 1952.

BIBLE PROTESTANT CHURCH

The churches in this body represent a break in the Eastern Conference of the Methodist Protestant Church in 1939, when about 50 delegates (approximately one third of the conference) withdrew in protest against the union of the Methodist Protestant Church with the Methodist Episcopal Church and the Methodist Episcopal Church, South, and what the withdrawing group considered to be the modernistic tendencies of the leaders of those churches. They operated for about a year under the original charter of the Eastern Conference and subsequently were incorporated under the name of the Bible Protestant Church (the Continuing Eastern Conference of the Methodist Protestant Church).

Doctrine here is conservative; this

church is a member of the fundamentalist American and International Councils of Christian Churches. Cardinal points in their belief emphasize the verbal inspiration of the Bible; the Trinity; the deity, virgin birth, resurrection, and ascension of Jesus; salvation by faith in his blood and sacrifice, death and resurrection. There is a strong faith in premillennialism with eternal punishment for the wicked and eternal joy for the righteous believer. Baptism and the Lord's Supper are practiced as divine institutions.

Their churches are confined to New Jersey, New York, Pennsylvania, Connecticut, Virginia, and Michigan. Actually they are a fellowship of self-governing churches, organized in a conference which meets annually with lay and clerical representation. The chief officer is the president, who holds office for not more than 3 years. All local churches own and control their own property, all contributions to the conference are voluntary and not by assessment, and call their own ministers from the conference roll of ministers or from other churches approved by the Committee on Ministerial Qualifications; formal assignment of the pastor is by a pastoral relations committee of the conference. Candidates for ordination must be graduates of high school and an approved seminary or Bible school. Missionary work is conducted in the Philippines, Japan, and South America; and Bible Protestant missionaries are serving in Mexico and Africa under the mission boards of other churches. The church publishing house issues a monthly periodical, *The Bible Protestant Messenger*. There are 41 churches, 2,498 members.

BLACK MUSLIMS

Franklin Williams, former director of the National Association for the Advancement of the Colored People, says that this movement "combines the emotional religious drive of Father Divine and Daddy Grace with the legal and political protest of the N.A.A.C.P., and on top of that it offers the hope of a black Utopia on this earth." More of a protest against social and economic discrimination than a religious faith, it nevertheless claims to be an authentic offshoot of Islam—a claim denied by Middle East Moslems in the United States. They reject the term "Negro"; consider the white man as their natural enemy; require that their adherents sever all ties with other churches; abstain from the use of alcohol, tobacco, cosmetics, and fancy clothing; and customarily demand that male members shave their heads. They eat but one meal a day, and face the East when they pray. Their leader is known as Messenger Elijah Muhammad; he claims to have made the Moslem pilgrimage to Mecca. Temples are located in 7 American cities—Chicago, Detroit, Boston, Pittsburgh, Newark (N. J.), Los Angeles, and New York. There are no membership statistics, but it is estimated that there are approximately 1,000 in each of the temples. Considerable literature is published; and there is widespread picketing activity in protest against white discrimination, and much calling upon Negroes to spend their money only in Negro stores. A school for children (the University of Islam), grocery stores, restaurants, garment manufacturing plants, and a department store are maintained in Chicago. The ultimate aim of the group is "to build our own society in the U. S.," and "to have our own Black State."

BRETHREN (DUNKERS)

The terms Brethren and Dunkers have been the cause of much confusion; they call for careful definition. Dunker is a direct derivation of the German word *tunken*, "to dip or immerse." It is a word to be identified with the peculiar method of immersion employed by this group of churches: trine immersion, in which the believer on his knees in the water is immersed not once but 3 times, in the name of the Father, Son, and Holy Ghost. Variously through their long history the Dunkers have been called Tunkers, Taufers, or Dompelaars. They were first called Brethren when their first church organization was established at Schwarzenau, Germany, in 1708.

It might be said generally that these Dunker or Brethren bodies are former German Baptists who took their theology and much of their practice from the Pietists of the seventeenth and eighteenth centuries in Germany. The Pietists, who were mostly Lutherans, became unhappy with the formalism of worship and ritual in their state church and with the general "barrenness" of German Protestantism. They took the New Testament literally and endeavored to put its teachings into practice in the least detail of their living. They spurned the idea of apostolic succession, and at the heart of their practice they had a love feast or agape, which was the serving of the Lord's Supper preceded by a ceremony of foot washing. They saluted one another with a "kiss of peace," dressed in the plainest clothing, covered the heads of women at services, anointed their sick with oil for healing and consecration, refrained from worldly amusements, refused to take oaths, go to war, or engage in lawsuits. These doctrines and practices are held today by many Brethren with certain modifications.

From these German Pietists came the Church of the Brethren (Conservative Dunkers), the Brethren Church (Pro-gressive Dunkers), the Old German Baptist Brethren (Old Order Dunkers), and the Church of God (New Dunkers). Another Brethren group, unrelated historically to these and known as the River Brethren, also took its ideology from the German Pietists. This group includes the Brethren in Christ, the Old Order, or Yorker, Brethren, and United Zion Church (formerly United Zion's Children). A third Brethren body, known as the Plymouth Brethren, has a British rather than a German background.

The Brethren bodies beginning in Germany were known for years simply as German Baptist Brethren; that title has largely disappeared except in the case of the Old German Baptist Brethren (Old Order Dunkers).

Church of the Brethren

The Church of the Brethren began in 1708 with a church of 8 persons in Schwarzenau, Germany. Persecuted and driven from Germany into Holland and Switzerland, one group of the church in Crefeld, Germany, under the leadership of Peter Becker came to America in 1719 to take up free lands offered them by William Penn. They settled in Germantown, near Philadelphia, where they were joined in 1729 by 59 families brought across the Atlantic by Alexander Mack. From Pennsylvania they spread across the country.

Their German speech, their opposition to war, and their insistence upon the inner Christian life as more important than church organization made them a suspected group from the start. Morally they opposed the Revolution; in the Civil War they opposed slavery. The suspicion and misunderstanding waned as time went on; today historians are generous in their praise of the contributions of the Brethren to American democracy. In our own day the work of their pacifists in World War II and

54

their outstanding efforts in relief to Europe following that war have made them one of the most honored bodies in American Protestantism. In their early days at Germantown they printed the first German Bible in America and circulated the first American religious magazine.

In 1728 a group under Conrad Beissel left the Church of the Brethren to found the famous Ephrata Community and the Seventh Day Baptists (German); and in 1848 another break resulted in the establishment of the Church of God (New Dunkers). In 1881 a third group withdrew to organize the Old German Baptist Brethren (Old Order Dunkers); and in 1882 came the worst split of all in the organizing of the Brethren Church (Progressive Dunkers). The original body is known today as the Church of the Brethren and has 214,316 members in 1,116 churches in the United States, Canada, India, Nigeria, and Ecuador.

Generally in doctrine this church follows the mainstream of Protestant theology with considerable freedom of thought for its members and the clergy and great emphasis to practical biblical piety. Its teaching is summarized in the following 5 divisions: (1) the doctrine of peace, including refusal to go to war and a positive peacemaking program which makes them more than mere war resisters; (2) the doctrine of temperance, under which total abstinence is practiced; (3) the doctrine of the simple life, under which worldly amusements and luxuries are shunned, and a practical, wholesome, temperate, clean way of personal and family life is stressed; they seek to develop a "concerned stewardship of life rather than prohibition of amusements and overindulgence in luxuries"; (4) the doctrine of brotherhood, under which all class distinctions are opposed as unchristian; and (5) that religion means obedience to Christ rather than obedience to creeds and cults. Christian living rather than forms

is stressed. Baptism is by trine immersion; the love feast is observed, following the pattern of John 13:1-7. There is a waning adherence to the Brethren traditions of plainness in dress and the veiling of women in worship, as "commanded" in I Corinthians. They take no oaths and do not generally participate in lawsuits.

Moderators (lay or clerical, men or women, either resident or nonresident) are in charge of local congregations, which enjoy a great deal of autonomy. Ministers are chosen by the ballot of the local congregation. Above the local group stands the annual conference, a legislative body composed of delegates from the churches and an "upper house" known as the Standing Committee, made up of delegates elected from the 51 districts into which the churches are grouped. The annual conference is an over-all, unifying body.

A general brotherhood board, composed of 25 members elected by the annual conference, supervises the general church program. The board administers missions in India, Africa, and South America. It represents the church in the field of social education, social action, relief and rehabilitation, and carries on a world-wide program of peace and human welfare. The program includes a volunteer service in America and abroad for hundreds of young Brethren men and women, including conscientious objectors to war. Through Christian education it supervises church schools, weekday religious education, higher education in 6 colleges, and 40 summer camps. The board provides leadership and education in the ministry, in locating and supporting new churches, and in evangelism, and carries responsibility and the printing and merchandizing interests of the denomination.

The Church of the Brethren co-operates fully with the World Council of Churches, the National Council of the Churches of Christ in the U.S.A., and with local church councils; it is thoroughly ecumenical in outlook.

Brethren Church
(Progressive Dunkers)

The first Brethren in Pennsylvania were largely farmers with little education. While there were a few men of real learning among them, they were for the most part earnest Christians who had been denied the benefit of schools. They experienced a growing dissatisfaction with this situation and with the failure of the church to provide schools of higher learning for clergy and laity. Dissatisfaction arose also over the strict enforcement of the traditions of plain dress, worship, and especially over the transfer of authority from the local congregations to the several conferences. The dissent swelled into a rebellion, the progressive leaders were at last expelled, and a considerable number followed them out to establish the Brethren Church (Progressive Dunkers) in 1882.

This body is quite specific in its doctrine, which is set forth in a *Message of the Brethren Ministry*, written about 1917. The message includes statements of belief in the infallibility of the Scriptures; the pre-existence, deity, and incarnation by virgin birth of Jesus Christ; the vicarious atonement of Jesus Christ and his resurrection; the fall of man and the necessity of salvation; justification by personal faith in Christ; the resurrection of the dead; the judgment of the world and the life everlasting; the second coming of Christ; nonconformity with the world; believer's baptism by trine immersion; the ordinances of baptism, confirmation, the Lord's Supper, foot washing, and anointing the sick with oil.

In 1939 a split occurred in the Brethren Church which divided it into what came to be known as the Ashland Group and the Grace Group. There is no formal division here; both groups still carry the name of the Brethren Church, but each group has its own annual conference—the Ashland body at Ashland, Ohio, and the Grace body at Winona Lake, Indiana. Each conference has its own executives; and since the government of the Brethren Church is congregational, it is possible for a congregation to support either one group or the other and still remain in good standing in the Brethren Church. Each group has its own seminary and missions boards. There has been no change in general doctrinal statement, but it is generally true that the Grace Group represents the Calvinistic viewpoint and the Ashland Group the Arminian viewpoint. A dispute over the necessity of baptism to salvation is still unsettled.

Polity in the Brethren Church is more congregational than in the Church of the Brethren (Conservative Dunkers). Each church is completely autonomous; there are ministers, elders, deacons, evangelists, and deaconesses. Deaconesses may become ministers. Churches are grouped geographically into 9 district conferences. The Grace Group has 24,660 members and the Ashland Group 18,697.

Church of God (New Dunkards)

Disagreement concerning the practice of trine immersion, the love feast, the veiling of women, and nonconformity in taking oaths brought about a schism among the first Dunkers in this country. A group led by George Patton and Peter Eyman withdrew to organize the Church of God (New Dunkards) in 1848. They held that "Bible things should be called by Bible names," and that the only name for a church authorized by Scripture was the Church of God.

This church accepts no human creed of confession of faith; it holds the Bible as the only infallible guide to Christian living. Members lay strong emphasis upon the second coming of Christ, future rewards and punishments, on holiness of heart and life not as a second work of grace but as one definite work of cleansing and filling, and on being born again in order to become a true child of God. They practice anointing of the sick with oil and foot washing at

Communion. They do not believe in wars of aggression but will take part in wars for defense. Baptism is in the name of Father, Son, and Holy Ghost; but there is only one immersion.

The 8 churches of this body are grouped in an annual conference, which is the governing authority. Each church is equally represented in the conference. There are 622 members.

Old German Baptist Brethren (Old Order Dunkers)

While the Brethren Church (Progressive Dunkers) left the Church of the Brethren (Conservative Dunkers) because the latter body seemed too conservative, the Old German Baptist Brethren (Old Order Dunkers) left it because they considered it not conservative enough. The dissenters stood literally for the old order and traditions. The salient point in their opposition lay in their suspicion of Sunday schools, missions, higher education, and church societies. They withdrew in 1881.

Their basic objections still hold, but with certain modifications. Children are not enrolled in Sunday schools, but they are encouraged to attend the regular services of the church and to join the church at a very early age—anywhere from 10 to 20. Many congregations list a majority of members between 15 and 40 years of age. The church today is not completely opposed even to higher education; many of their youth enter high school and college; many teach in colleges or are training in college or professional schools for various professions.

They stand for a literal interpretation of the Scriptures in regard to the Lord's Supper and practice close Communion, which excludes all but their own membership. They favor non-co-operation in war, but at the same time they advocate compliance with the ordinary demands of government; they leave conscientious objection to military service to the individual conscience. Non-co-operation in political and secret societies is stressed; their dress is the severely plain garb of the Quakers, and they frown on all worldly amusements. They follow other Brethren bodies in refusing to take oaths or to engage in lawsuits, have no salaried ministry, enforce complete abstinence from alcoholic liquors, anoint the sick with oil, veil the heads of their women at worship, and refuse to perform a wedding ceremony for any divorced person. They have no Sunday schools, missions, or educational work, and report 4,092 members in 57 churches.

PLYMOUTH BRETHREN

Restless under the close connection of church and state in nineteenth-century England and Ireland, and opposing the stereotyped forms of worship in the Established Church, groups of Brethren began to meet for quiet fellowship and prayer. They had no connection whatever with the sects of Brethren in Germany but took their name from the Scriptures; at one time or another they were also called Christians, Believers, or Saints. The largest and most important meeting was held at Plymouth, England—hence the name Plymouth Brethren, which has never been officially accepted by any of the group.

These Plymouth Brethren set up their meetings on strictly New Testament lines. They had no ordained ministers, inasmuch as they held to the "priesthood of all believers." They put strong emphasis upon the second coming of Jesus—to be expected momentarily—and upon his deity; and they denied fellowship with all who were "not fundamentally sound as to doctrine and godly in walk." Differences arose over divergent views on the effects of unsound teaching in the Plymouth Assembly, and in 1848 there came a division into Exclusive and Open Brethren. The Open Brethren held that they should receive all persons personally sound in faith, even though they came from an assembly where error was taught, if they personally rejected the error. The Exclusive Brethren held that such reception disqualified the assemblies from participation in the Circle of Fellowship, which was, and is, a joint body of approved assemblies holding a corporate unity and responsibility made up of leaders who make decisions for all constituent assemblies.

The tendencies toward division followed the Plymouth Brethren to America when they came here in the late nineteenth century. Today there are 8 bodies of Plymouth Brethren in this country, distinguished only by the Roman numerals I to VIII. Plymouth Brethren I and II, the two largest bodies, have practically dropped their differences and are in practice one body.

In doctrine the various bodies are in substantial agreement; the separation of these groups is caused mainly by conflicts in church discipline. Generally they acknowledge no creeds; they take the Bible as their only original guide, believing it verbally inspired of God and inerrant. They are Trinitarians; they hold that Christ was begotten of the Holy Spirit and born of the Virgin Mary, and is true God and true man; that man is created in God's image; that by sin he has incurred physical and spiritual death, which is separation from God; that all men are sinners; that salvation and justification come through faith in Christ's shed blood, apart from works; that Christ was resurrected and ascended into heaven to abide there as high priest and advocate for the redeemed. Christ's return will be premillennial; it is imminent

and personal, and he will return in glory with all his saints to rule and judge the world. All who receive him by faith are born again and thereby become the children of God. There is a bodily resurrection for the just and the unjust, eternal reward for the righteous and everlasting punishment for the wicked.

Plymouth Brethren hold that the true church includes all regenerated believers. There are not specific requirements for membership, but all candidates are expected to give "satisfactory evidence of the new birth." They are received as "members of Christ" and do not join any organization. There are no ordained or salaried ministers in the usual sense; "personal gift and spiritual power" from the Holy Spirit are sufficient evidence of a call to ministry (I Cor. 12:4-11). Hence they do recognize in certain men certain gifts of preaching and teaching, and those who devote their time to such work are supported by voluntary contributions. Gifted and godly men are acknowledged as elders and overseers who hold no official position but who care for the spiritual needs of the saints.

Government among Brethren I and II is by individual assembly or congregation; these bodies hold that each assembly is responsible to the Lord alone as head of the church. Brethren III to VIII, on the other hand, are joined in Circles of Fellowship, as already described.

The idea of the "priesthood of all believers" is practiced in their meeting, service, and ministry. There is no ritual. The larger assemblies own church buildings, or gospel halls; smaller assemblies meet in rented halls or rooms, or in private residences. Baptism and the Lord's Supper are observed as ordinances; the Supper is celebrated each Sunday, usually in the morning, and the gospel preached at night. There are other meetings for prayer and Bible study, young people's meetings, missionary activities supported by voluntary subscription, tent meetings, evangelistic services, and the like.

Plymouth Brethren I follows closely the teachings of the English leader John Darby of the original Plymouth congregation. It puts special emphasis upon the teaching that "eternal life in Christ is the common blessing of all believers of every age," in distinction to other Plymouth Brethren, who restrict that blessing. There are about 5,000 members.

Plymouth Brethren II is "open," having some fellowship with Christians beyond its own membership. Uniquely its members hold that ecclesiastical position in itself does not disqualify anyone. There is actually a variety of teaching here, some holding that an open ministry is obligatory, others that it is optional, and some others not tolerating it at all. This is the largest Plymouth body, claiming some 15,000 members.

Plymouth Brethren III had 1,000 members and 22 assemblies as of 1936. This might be called the high church group inasmuch as they believe that "absolute power of a judicial kind" has been assigned by Christ to the Christian assembly. They refuse fellowship with all of differing doctrine.

Plymouth Brethren IV refuses to be designated by any name, for this would make it a sect, and the Bible (I Cor. 1:10-15) forbids all sects. Its differences with other Plymouth bodies are largely concerning government and discipline. There were 1,909 members and 56 assemblies as of 1936.

Plymouth Brethren V clings closely to the doctrinal position of the original British (Plymouth) body. They do a widespread work in jails, hospitals, and so on, and distribute a large number of tracts and pamphlets. There were 1,776 members and 67 assemblies as of 1936.

Plymouth Brethren VI is the smallest of all with only 2 assemblies and 34 members in 1936. Their existence as a separate body goes back to the failure of an attempt to join all Plymouth Brethren bodies in England.

Plymouth Brethren VII and *VIII* are comparatively new organizations. Both were part of Plymouth Brethren I up to 1936. They have about 2,000 members and 100 assemblies.

Thus together all 8 groups had an approximate membership in this country of over 25,000 in 664 churches in 1936. They are also found in Canada, Great Britain, and in various other countries. There is no unifying international bond or body.

RIVER BRETHREN

A considerable number of post-Reformation Anabaptist and Pietists, fleeing Europe, settled in Lancaster County, Pennsylvania, near the middle of the seventeenth century. They were grouped in a chain of brotherhoods, one of which became known as the Brotherhood by the River (the Susquehanna River) and later as the Brethren in Christ Church.

Various disputes, many of which would seem quite unimportant today, brought about the establishment of 2 smaller bodies—the Old Order, or Yorker, Brethren in 1843, and the Brinsers or United Zion's Children in 1855. The others remained in the original Brethren in Christ group. They are today the largest of the 3 churches, which altogether number about 20,000 communicant members. This church at present ministers to about 150,000 in United States of America and other countries.

Brethren in Christ

With the outbreak of the Civil War the draft reached into the ranks of the Brethren, and it became necessary for them to obtain legal recognition as an established religious organization in order to protect their objectors. Nonresistance has always been one of their principles. A council meeting in Lancaster County, Pennsylvania, in 1863 officially adopted the name Brethren in Christ Church. The church was not incorporated until 1904.

The Brethren in Christ Church pledges loyalty to the following doctrines: the inspiration of the Holy Scriptures; the self-existent, triune God—Father, Son, and Holy Spirit; the deity and virgin birth of Christ; Christ's death as atonement for our sins, and his resurrection from the dead; the Holy Spirit who convicts the sinner, regenerates the penitent, and empowers the believer; justification as forgiveness for committed sins, and sanctification as heart cleansing and empowerment by the Holy Spirit; observance of the ordinances of God's house; temperance, and modesty of apparel as taught in the Scriptures; the personal, visible, and imminent return of Christ; the resurrection of the dead, with punishment for the unbeliever and reward for the believer; the supreme duty of the church as world-wide evangelism.

The government is in the hands of the local churches, 6 regional conferences, and a general conference. There is a board of directors consisting of the regional conference bishops, the General Conference Secretary, and the treasurer of the Board of Administration. Church boards include those on benevolence, administration, Christian education, missions, the ministry, publications, and schools and colleges; there are commissions on home, Sunday school, and youth.

The church has three institutions of learning: Messiah College, Grantham, Pennsylvania; Upland College, Upland, California; and Niagara Christian College, Fort Erie, Ontario, Canada. Missionaries are at work in Africa, India, Japan, and Cuba.

Old Order, or Yorker, Brethren

The Old Order, or Yorker, Brethren is the smallest of all Brethren in Christ Church groups in the United States; they reported only 291 members and 7 churches in 1936. The primary reason for their existence as a separate body lay in their feeling that the Brethren in Christ had became lax in their enforcement of nonresistance and nonconformity to the world. They left the original body in 1843. Old Order in their name refers to their desire to keep the old traditions alive; Yorker resulted from the fact that most of them at the time of withdrawal lived in York County, Pennsylvania.

Their doctrine is no longer identical with that of Brethren in Christ Church. They refuse to build or meet in church edifices; lacking these, they meet usually in the homes of the members.

United Zion Church

Bishop Matthias Brinser was expelled from the Brethren of Christ Church in 1855, together with about 50 others, for building and holding services in a meetinghouse. They organized under the name United Zion's Children; this was changed in 1954 when the body incorporated under the name United Zion Church.

They are essentially the same in doctrine as the Brethren in Christ. They baptize by trine immersion, observe foot washing as an ordinance along with the Lord's Supper. They encourage the veiling of women and are opposed to divorce and immodest attire.

Located almost exclusively in Dauphin, Lebanon, and Lancaster counties in Pennsylvania, they list a few less than 1,000 members and 23 churches. Church officers are bishops, ministers, and deacons; the top administrative body is a general conference composed of a representation of the various district conferences; the basic unit of government is the district conference.

No foreign missionary work of their own is reported, but they support 3 missionaries working under the Brethren in Christ Church. There is some interest in reunion with the Brethren in Christ Church with whom ministers are interchanged. One home for the aged is maintained.

BUDDHIST CHURCHES OF AMERICA

Buddhism is found in real strength in this country in Utah, Arizona, Washington, Oregon, and California; and it represents the transplanting of the Buddhism of the East. Most of the Buddhists in the United States are Japanese or Japanese-Americans; however, there are "English" departments in San Francisco, Los Angeles, and Tacoma.

The faith is built upon the teachings of the founder, Buddha—Siddartha Gautama, the Enlightened One (566 B.C.)—who attained his enlightenment in India and whose teachings have spread all over the Far East. Often challenged as a system of religious faith, it remains a most complex and involved pattern of thought and action. It is divided into 2 schools—Hinayana, or Theravada, Buddhism, or the Lesser Vehicle; and Mahayana Buddhism, or the Greater Vehicle. These offer, on the one hand, a path of escape from suffering and, on the other, a thorough preparation for entry upon that path. Hinayana seems devised for those among its disciples who are satisfied with a comparatively modest attainment of Buddhist virtue, while Mahayana is for those who would practice a more exacting discipleship. Buddha himself put the essence of his system in these words: "One thing only I teach. Sorrow [or pain], the cause of sorrow, the cessation of sorrow, and the path which leads to the cessation of sorrow." These are the Four Truths of Buddhism, the latter of which includes the actual means of arriving at these truths by way of the "noble eightfold path"—"right views, right intention, right speech, right action, right livelihood, right effort, right mindfulness, right concentration." This description of the 8 paths covers the whole training of the disciple who seeks nirvana, which means literally "blown out" or "extinguished." He strives to extinguish in his living all desire, hatred, and ignorance, and thus attain a nobler life.

There are no theories of creation, no miracles, and no divine being in Buddhism. Supreme reality is neither affirmed nor denied; it is only said to be beyond the comprehension of the human mind. It is actually a system of self-education in the conquering, or forgetting, of pain, sorrow, and suffering. Recognizing that this is a long process, the Buddha taught that man has an indefinite number of lives, or reincarnations, in which to accomplish it.

The titular head of American Buddhism bears the title of bishop; he is in charge of all religious activities, and he is authorized to transfer or dismiss the clergy under his jurisdiction. The first Buddhist church or temple in the United States was consecrated in San Francisco in 1905; the Buddhist Mission of North America was started in San Francisco in 1898 and incorporated in 1942 as the Buddhist Churches of America. There are 80 ministers and 2 deans and about 20,000 members. They represent the Jodo Shinshu Sect of Buddhism in this country, a faith based on "the anatman doctrine, supplemented by the idea of karma, and nirvana, the holy ease or a blissful mental state of absolute freedom from evil." Each church, of which there are 52, is autonomous, holding complete control of its own property. Weekly services are held, and Japanese language schools are maintained by many of the churches. Because of Buddhism's introspective nature and its lack of social outlook or endeavor, there are no hospitals or other philanthropic institutions; but a very active National Young Buddhist Co-ordinating Council has established district leagues in San Francisco, Seattle, Salt Lake City, Denver, and New York. A home for the aged was established at Fresno, California, in 1952.

CATHOLIC APOSTOLIC CHURCH

The founders of the Catholic Apostolic Church never intended to establish a separate denomination. They were British millenarians who believed in the bestowal of the gifts of the Holy Spirit, their meetings characterized by speaking in tongues and prophetic revelations.

They also believed that a twelvefold apostleship was the only form of church government or supreme ecclesiastical authority authorized by Scripture and that church officials should follow the order laid down in Eph. 4:11. Accordingly they "set aside" 12 apostles who, being divinely called and not elected by the church, were "superior . . . to all other ministry." The movement began in England in 1830; their first church in America was established in 1851.

Their doctrine, based upon the Nicene, Apostolic, and Athanasian creeds, affirms belief in the authority and inspiration of the Bible, baptism, the Lord's Supper, the indissolubility of marriage short of death, the ordination of ministers (priests), the laying on of hands, the gift of tongues, the tithe—by which all their ministers are supported—and a strong insistence upon the premillennial appearance of Christ, who will raise the dead, translate the living, and establish peace on earth.

Church government, following the pattern of Ephesians, is in the hands of apostles, prophets, bishops (commonly called angels), evangelists, priests, and deacons. Only deacons are elected by the church; all others are chosen of God but under the authority of the apostles. There are approximately 2,500 members in 7 churches in the United States. Inasmuch as the last divinely chosen apostle died in 1901, there have been no ordinations of any sort since that year. There are no home or foreign missions, educational or institutional efforts; but there are a few Sunday schools. Worship and ritual are highly liturgical, laying great emphasis upon symbolism; their forms are borrowed from the great historic churches.

CHRISTADELPHIANS

John Thomas came to the United States from England in 1844. He joined the Disciples of Christ but later became convinced that their doctrine made them the apostate church predicted by Scripture and that many other more important Bible doctrines were being neglected. He left the Disciples to organize a number of societies which under his leadership began preaching the need of a return to primitive Christianity. Loosely organized, these societies bore no name until the outbreak of the Civil War, when their doctrine of nonresistance forced them to adopt a name, and Christadelphians (or Brethren of Christ) was the name chosen.

Christadelphians are both Unitarian and Adventist in theology. They reject the Trinity and belief in a personal devil, maintaining the Scriptures teach that Christ is not God the Son, but the Son of God; not pre-existent, but born of Mary by the Holy Spirit. Man is mortal by nature with Christ as his only means of salvation. Eternal life comes only to the righteous. Strong millenarians, they believe that Christ will come shortly to reward the saints with immortality and to destroy the wicked; that he will take David's throne in Jerusalem, the faithful will be gathered, and the world will be ruled from the land of Canaan for a thousand years.

The church is congregational in polity; local organizations are known not as churches but as ecclesias. Membership is by profession of faith and immersion. There are no paid or ordained ministers in the usual sense; each ecclesia elects serving brethren, among whom are included managing brethren, presiding brethren, and lecturing brethren. Women take no part in public speech or prayer, though all vote equally. Christadelphians do not vote in civil elections or participate in war, and they refuse to accept public office. There are no associations or conventions, but there are fraternal gatherings for spiritual inspiration. Meetings are generally held in rented halls, schoolhouses, or private homes; there are few church edifices.

Home missions work is local, usually in the form of lectures and instruction in Christadelphian doctrine and righteous living. There are no foreign missions, but ecclesias are found in several countries. There is no educational work with the exception of summer Bible schools in several states. Found in 26 states from coast to coast, they reported 3,755 members in 115 ecclesias in 1950. Larger numbers are located in Great Britain, New Zealand, and Australia.

THE CHRISTIAN AND MISSIONARY ALLIANCE

The Christian and Missionary Alliance, which prefers to be known not as a denomination but as an evangelistic and missionary movement, originated in 1881 under the leadership of the Rev. A. B. Simpson, a Presbyterian minister in New York City who left that church to carry on independent evangelistic work among the unchurched. It was at first divided into 2 societies, the Christian Alliance for home missions work and the International Missionary Alliance for work abroad. The two bodies were merged in 1897 in the present Christian and Missionary Alliance.

Strongly evangelical and fundamentalist, the alliance stands for the literal inspiration of the Bible, the atonement wrought by Christ, the reality of supernatural religious experience, separation from the world, the premillennial return of Jesus Christ, Spirit baptism, and practical holiness. While there is no creed as such, there is a formula of belief built upon a fourfold gospel of Christ as Saviour, Sanctifier, Healer, and coming Lord.

Work is carried on in 14 organized districts in the United States and Canada, with 1,142 churches fully or partially organized. Each of these churches or groups is a self-maintaining and self-governing unit engaged in missionary and evangelical activities. There is an over-all conference, called the General Council, which meets annually in various parts of the United States and Canada.

Foreign missionary work is carried on in South America, Africa, the Near East, India, Viet-Nam, Thailand, Japan, New Guinea, among overseas Chinese, the Philippines, and Indonesia. In 22 different mission fields are found 832 missionaries from the United States and 2,702 indigenous workers and there are 1,213 organized churches with 114,904 members.

In addition to the organized church work in North America missionary work is carried on among Indians and Negroes, as well as in Mexico and the West Indies, and in certain other areas where there has not yet been full development. Bible training colleges are maintained at Nyack, New York; St. Paul, Minnesota; San Francisco, California; and Regina, Saskatchewan, Canada. In 1958 there were 64,153 members in North America in 1,142 churches. Thus the alliance has a larger constituency abroad than at home.

CHRISTIAN CATHOLIC CHURCH

John Alexander Dowie, a Congregational preacher educated in Scotland and ordained in Australia, founded this movement in Chicago in 1896. In 1901 he established his organization at Zion City, forty miles north of Chicago. Here it became a sect and a colony with communal businesses and industries, governed by a theocracy of which Dowie was general overseer. Dowie had extensive plans for educational and cultural projects; he criticized both the injustices of capitalism and the excesses of labor leaders, alcoholic beverages, tobacco, medicine and the medical profession, secret lodges, and the press.

Theologically, Dowie was firmly rooted in orthodoxy, but he refused to be bound by what he felt was a cut-and-dried orthodox scholasticism; he objected strenuously to the doctrine of eternal punishment, contending that a God of love must provide an ultimate universal redemption for all men. He emphasized the healing of disease through prayer, and his success in healing led to the establishment of a tabernacle and "divine healing rooms" first in Chicago and later in Zion City. Several years after the organization of the Christian Catholic Church at Zion, he claimed to be Elijah the Restorer and maintained his leadership of the group until 1906,

when he was deposed and Wilbur Glenn Voliva became his successor. At first an exclusively religious community with one church, Zion has changed considerably since Dowie's day; the Christian Catholic Church is still strong, but independent businesses have been welcomed, and several other churches are at work in the city.

The Scriptures are accepted as the rule of faith and practice by the group; other doctrines call for belief in the necessity of repentance for sin and trust in Christ for salvation, trine immersion, and tithing as a Christian obligation. The bases of belief and teaching have been broadened in recent years. The Presbyterian (Westminster) Curriculum is used in the junior-and senior-high departments of the church school; the ministers are trained in Bethany, Gordon, and Fuller theological seminaries, Moody Bible Institute, Biblical Seminary (New York), and Garrett Biblical Institute. The Zion Conservatory of Music attracts many students unaffiliated with the church, and a Passion Play, started in 1935, annually attracts thousands of visitors. There are branches of the church in Chicago, Michigan City (Indiana), and Phoenix (Arizona). Missionary work is conducted in Japan, Australia, the Philippines, British Guiana, Jamaica, Palestine,

India, Nigeria, and the British Isles. An official monthly publication, *Leaves of* *Healing,* has a world-wide circulation. No report on membership is available.

CHRISTIAN CHURCH OF NORTH AMERICA

This church represents a merger of 2 former Italian denominations: the Italian Christian Churches of North America and the General Council of the Italian Pentecostal Assemblies of God. The former group—and the largest—was founded in 1907 by Louis Francescon in Chicago as a nondenominational and nonsectarian union of independent Italian congregations. Its work spread across this country and into Italy, Brazil, and Argentina. The Pentecostal Assemblies Group was founded—also in Chicago— in 1904 by Rocco Santamaria and his father, John Santamaria, gathering together some 200 Italian missions and congregations. First named "The Unorganized Italian Christian Churches of North America," it dropped the word "Unorganized" in 1939 and the word "Italian" in 1942, as the use of the English language was gradually being adopted in the member churches. The church was incorporated under its present name in Pittsburgh, Pennsylvania, in 1948.

There are today 20,000 members listed in 217 churches, and 233 ordained clergymen. Individual churches exist as separate religious corporations under various state laws. The first general council was held in Niagara Falls, New York, in 1927; since that time each church has sent delegates to an annual conference of the entire society. A board of general overseers, a general superintendent, and a missionary board constitute an executive board. Mission stations are found in Canada, Italy, Africa, Belgium, Brazil, and Argentina.

CHRISTIAN CHURCHES (DISCIPLES OF CHRIST), INTERNATIONAL CONVENTION

The revival movements of the early nineteenth century in the United States had both positive and negative results and influence: while inspiring new consecration and zeal in the established churches, they also resulted indirectly in the creation of new communions, separating from the larger bodies. One of these was the Disciples of Christ.

Thomas Campbell, a clergyman of the Seceder branch of the Presbyterian Church in Ireland, settled in western Pennsylvania in 1807 and started preaching on a Presbyterian circuit. Almost immediately he was in trouble. Finding many Presbyterians and others with no pastoral oversight, he invited them to attend his service, opposed all exclusiveness in the church—and Presbyterian exclusiveness, so evident in the restrictions placed on the Communion service, in particular. He advocated closer relations with Christians in other churches than the Seceders permitted; he preached that acceptance of the creed, or of any creed, should not be a condition of church communion or fellowship, and he appealed from the creed to the Bible. He was restive under the domination of the church by the clergy, and he taught that all men who believed were saved by Christ. All this challenged ecclesiastical authority and the Calvinistic doctrine of the Presbyterian Church, and Campbell was censured for his departure from the paths of orthodoxy. Appealing from his presbytery to the higher Associate Synod of North America, he succeeded in 1808 in having the censure removed; but so severe was his criticism of the whole idea of sectarianism and denominationalism that further service with the Presbyterians was impossible. With his son, Alexander Campbell, he withdrew in 1809 to establish the Christian Association of Washington, Pennsylvania. His "declaration and address" on this occasion has become an ecclesiastical document of historic importance.

Campbell made it plain that what was sought in this move was not so much reformation as restoration—restoration of New Testament polity and ideal. There ought to be, Campbell declared, "no schisms, or uncharitable divisions" among the churches; such divisions were "anti-Christian, anti-Scriptural, anti-natural," and "productive of confusion and every evil work"; they were a "horrid evil, fraught with many evils." The church and membership in the church should be based solely upon the beliefs and practices of primitive New Testament Christianity. The articles of faith and holiness "expressly revealed and enjoined in the Word of God" were quite enough without the addition of human opinions or the creedal inventions of men.

As the Campbells insisted thus upon the unity of believers, the last thing in their minds was the founding of still another Protestant church. To avoid it, overtures were made to the Presbyterian Synod of Pittsburgh in the hope that the 2 groups could work together. This gesture failed, and the Brush Run Church was organized in May, 1810, in Washington County, Pennsylvania. A working unity with the Redstone Baptist Association was established and lasted

nearly 10 years, but eventually points of disagreement arose and the 2 groups drifted apart. The separation was gradual, becoming complete about 1830, after which time the followers of the Campbells were known as Christians, or Disciples of Christ.

The name Christian was used by Barton W. Stone, a Presbyterian minister in Kentucky (see Christian Churches, p. 218). Stone's followers entered into a union with the Campbells in 1832. Stone felt that the whole church should be called simply "Christians," and Campbell favored the name "Disciples." No final decision was reached; both names were used intermittently; a church was generally called a "Christian Church" or a "Church of Christ."

The first national convention of the Disciples and the first missionary society, the American Christian Missionary Society, were organized in 1849; state conventions and societies also began meeting in that year. The church developed rapidly through and after the Civil War period; unlike Methodists, Baptists, and Presbyterians, the Disciples did not divide on the issue of slavery. Especially in the Midwest, in Ohio, Indiana, Illinois, Tennessee, and Missouri, the church gathered impressive strength in membership in spite of the persistent inherent objection toward any emphasis on denominationalism or ecclesiastical organization. This objection became acute in differences between Conservatives and Progressives over the development of missionary societies and the use of instrumental music in the churches. Out of this long debate came the Churches of Christ.

The Disciples believe that the Bible is divinely inspired, and they accept it as their only rule of faith and life; neither Trinitarian nor Unitarian, they urge a simple usage of New Testament phraseology as to the Godhead. They believe that Christ is the Son of God, that the Holy Spirit is at work in the present world, that sin has alienated every soul from its maker. They feel that baptism and the Lord's Supper are divine ordinances and that it is a sacred duty to observe the Lord's Day. They believe that holiness is a necessity for every believer and that there is a final judgment with reward for the righteous and punishment for the wicked.

In detail their characteristic beliefs are set forth as follows:

1. Feeling that "to believe and to do none other things than those enjoined by our Lord and His Apostles must be infallibly safe," they aim "to restore in faith and spirit and practice the Christianity of Christ and His Apostles as found on the pages of the New Testament."

2. Affirming that "the sacred Scriptures as given by God answer all purposes of a rule of faith and practice, and a law for the government of the church, and that human creeds and confessions of faith spring out of controversy and, instead of being bonds of union, tend to division and strife," they reject all such creeds and confessions.

3. They place special emphasis upon "the Divine Sonship of Jesus, as the fundamental fact of the Holy Scripture, the essential creed of Christianity, and the one article of faith in order to receive baptism and church membership."

4. Believing that in the Scriptures "a clear distinction is made between the law and the gospel," they "do not regard the Old and New Testaments as of equally binding authority upon Christians," but that "the New Testament is as perfect a constitution for the worship, government, and discipline of the New Testament church as the Old was for the Old Testament church."

5. While claiming for themselves the New Testament names of "Christians," or "Disciples," "they do not deny that others are Christians or that other churches are Churches of Christ."

6. Accepting the divine personality of the Holy Spirit, through whose agency regeneration is begun, they hold that men "must hear, believe, repent, and obey the gospel to be saved."

7. Repudiating any doctrine of "baptismal regeneration," and insisting that there is no other prerequisite to regeneration than confession of faith with the whole heart in the personal living Christ, they regard baptism by immersion as "one of the items of the original divine system," and as "commanded in order to the remission of sins."

8. Following the apostolic model, the Disciples celebrate the Lord's Supper on each Lord's day, "not as a sacrament, but as a memorial feast," from which no sincere follower of Christ of whatever creed or church connection is excluded.

9. The Lord's day with the Disciples is not a Sabbath, but a New Testament institution, commemorating our Lord's resurrection, and consecrated by apostolic example.

10. The Church of Christ is a divine institution; sects are unscriptural and unapostolic. The sect name, spirit, and life should give place to the union and co-operation that distinguished the church of the New Testament.

Strictly congregational in polity, each church of the Disciples of Christ elects its own officers—pastors, elders, and deacons—and acknowledges no outside ecclesiastical authority. Baptism by immersion follows the reception of candidates for church membership who are received on profession of faith in Christ. Ministers are ordained usually by the local church and sometimes by a committee from neighboring churches. The minister is a member of the church in which he serves as pastor or evangelist. Ministerial associations are organized for fellowship and mutual help on a country-wide and also a state level, but they have no authority.

Churches are grouped into district and state conventions, which, like all others, have no final authority. There is no national ecclesiastical organization of the churches, but there is an International Convention of Disciples of Christ, meeting annually with advisory powers only and composed of individual members of the churches.

The supervision of denominational activities is placed with the usual boards, which, however, are more unified than in most Protestant bodies. The American Christian Missionary Society was formed at Cincinnati in 1849 to "promote the preaching of the Gospel in this and other lands." The Christian Woman's Board of Missions was organized in 1874. Other boards, organized to supervise ministerial relief, social action, benevolences, higher education, and church extension, were grouped together with the missionary societies in a new United Christian Missionary Society at the international convention at Cincinnati in 1919. A small percentage of the churches of the Disciples of Christ, generally called Independents, conduct an independent foreign missions work and do not report to denominational boards or societies.

The Board of Higher Education has under its supervision about 34 colleges, universities, Bible schools, and foundations. There are 6 homes for children, 6 homes for the aged, and Valparaiso Christian Hospital at Valparaiso, Indiana.

In 1959 there were 8,060 congregations and 1,801,414 church members in the United States. In Canada in 1959 there were 80 congregations and 7,533 church members. The total for these two countries, which for the most part are affiliated with the International Convention of Disciples of Christ, is therefore 8,140 congregations and 1,808,947 church members. In these two countries there are 8,142 Sunday schools with an enrollment of 1,193,676 as of 1959.

The global work of the Disciples was further co-ordinated in the organization of their World Convention of Churches (Disciples) in October of 1930 at Washington, D.C. The second convention was held in Leicester, England, in 1935; the third in Buffalo, New York, in 1947; and the fourth in Melbourne, Australia, in 1952. The fifth convention was held at Toronto, Canada, in August, 1954. There are 30 countries represented in the world convention with churches having a total membership of 2,005,003. World convention headquarters are located at 475 Riverside Drive, New York City.

Moves toward union have been made by the Disciples with the American Baptist Convention and with the United Church of Christ.

THE CHRISTIAN CONGREGATION

The philosophy and work of the Christian Congregation, formed in Indiana in 1887, revolve about the "new commandment" of John 13:34-45. It is a fellowship of ministers, laymen, and congregations seeking a noncreedal, nondenominational basis for union. It opposes all sectarian strife, insisting that according to the new commandment "the household of faith is not founded upon doctrinal agreement, creeds, church claims, names or rites," but solely upon the relationship of the individual to God. The basis of Christian fellowship is love toward one another, the actual relations of Christians to one another transcending in importance all individual belief or personal opinions. Free Bible study is encouraged, and the Bible Colportage Service of the Congregation circulates the *Christian Indicator* quarterly publication series, Bibles, and Bible helps and literature for field workers.

Churches and pastorates are now located in every state in the union; they still remain strongest, however, in the areas in which Barton Stone preached and in which the original Christian Congregation groups were located—Kentucky, the Carolinas, Virginia, Pensylvania, Ohio, Indiana, and Texas; for the greater part, the work is done in rural, mountain, and neglected areas. In many respects the work of the Christian Congregation is identical with that of the Stone movement and with his original Christian Church, although Christian Congregations were established and at work when the Christian Church was organized.

Polity is that of "a centralized congregational assembly"; congregational assemblies and a general assembly are held annually. Ministerial titles and forms of worship common to Presbyterian and Episcopal churches are employed. All political and sectarian controversies are avoided, and members refuse to contract debts of any kind.

Membership, as last reported from local areas of pastoral service, now exceeds 26,000.

CHRISTIAN NATION CHURCH

Originating in a band of independent evangelists called "equality evangelists," the Christian Nation Church was incorporated at Marion, Ohio, in 1895. Membership today stands at 450, and there are 25 churches.

The church teaches a fourfold gospel: justification, entire sanctification, divine healing, and the second coming of Christ. Two ordinances, baptism and the Lord's Supper, are celebrated. Needless ornaments on clothing, worldly organizations and amusements, tobacco and liquor, Sabbath breaking, the remarriage of the divorced, jesting, foolish talking, and the singing of worldly songs are forbidden; and marriage to the unsaved is discouraged. Each family is encouraged to "raise just so large a family of children as God will be pleased to give them," tithing is practiced, and love for friend and enemy is emphasized. Days of fasting and prayer are observed, the sick and needy are assisted, and camp meetings are strongly supported.

Government is by local churches, which are grouped into districts and which meet in annual conferences. The licenses of all pastors expire at the end of each conference year.

CHRISTIAN UNION

Christian Union represents an attempt to unite all Christians on a scriptural basis and to offer a larger unity in thought and worship. Organized in 1864 at Columbus, Ohio, its announced purpose is "to promote fellowship among God's people, to put forth every effort to proclaim God's saving grace to the lost . . . and to declare the whole counsel of God for the edification of believers."

There is no one creed binding upon members of the Union, but 7 principles are stressed: the oneness of the Church of Christ, Christ as the only head of the church, the Bible as the only rule of faith and practice, good fruits as the one condition of fellowship, Christian union without controversy, complete autonomy for the local church, and avoidance of all partisan political preaching. Men and women are ordained ministers; ordinances include baptism—by any method, at the choice of the individual —and the Lord's Supper.

While church government is congregational, a series of councils meet for fellowship and to conduct such business as concerns the entire church. State councils meet once a year and a general council meets every 3 years with both lay and ministerial delegates.

Local missionary work is largely evangelistic and is carried on by state missionary boards; a general mission board administers home and foreign missionary work; twelve missionaries are located in Africa, Japan, the Dominican Republic, and Ethiopia. There are no colleges, but a Christian Union Extension School is established at Excelsior Springs, Missouri.

One periodical, *The Christian Union Witness,* is published monthly in Indianola, Iowa. There are 119 churches in Oklahoma, Missouri, Arkansas, Iowa, Indiana, and Ohio; 124 ministers; and something over 8,000 members.

CHRIST'S SANCTIFIED HOLY CHURCH

This church began with the preaching of holiness and sanctification in the Colored Methodist Church in Louisiana by a small body of white evangelists; it was organized in 1904 as the Colored Church South. Its central theme is sanctification by faith "as a distinct experience from justification by faith in Christ, which is not brought about by a growth in grace but is wrought instantaneously." There is emphasis on "one Lord, one faith, one baptism"; unequal persons, holy and unholy, should not marry; both men and women are ordained to the ministry; the strict observance of all church rules is required; no member using or selling tobacco or alcoholic liquors is acceptable; and members pledge that they will "expose all evil" to church officials.

The governing body is a 5-member Board No. 1, which ordains all deacons, deaconesses, and ministers and which supervises boards of extension, investigation, managers, ministers, and others. An annual conference meets in September, a district conference in June, a Sunday-school convention in March. The church, listing 600 members in 30 churches in 1957, is too small to maintain any sizable missionary, philanthropic, or educational work. A summer Bible school, organized in 1940, meets at headquarters during the month of July.

CHURCH OF CHRIST (HOLINESS) U.S.A.

C. P. Jones, a Baptist preacher in Selma, Alabama, and Jackson, Mississippi, left that denomination in 1894 to seek a faith which would make him "one of wisdom's true sons and, like Abraham, 'a friend of God.'" He called a convention at Jackson, enlisting the aid of men who like himself were interested in holiness, and founded there a holiness movement, which was at first completely interdenominational. By 1898, however, it had become a full-fledged denomination; it now reports 9,018 members in 151 churches.

Doctrine in this church emphasizes original sin, Christ's atonement, and his second coming; sacraments include the gift of the Holy Ghost, baptism by immersion, the Lord's Supper, foot washing, and divine healing. Episcopal in government, the church is led by bishops, one of whom is named senior bishop. The final authority in doctrine and church law is vested in the biennial annual convention.

The church is divided into 7 dioceses, each under the charge of a bishop. A district convention made up of elders, ministers, and local church representatives, meets semi-annually. A small missionary work is supported at home and abroad; there is a college, Christ Missionary and Industrial College, at Jackson, Mississippi; Boydton Institute at Boydton, Virginia; and a publishing house at Los Angeles, California.

CHURCH OF CHRIST, SCIENTIST

At Lynn, Massachusetts, in 1866 Mary Baker Eddy recovered almost instantly from a severe injury after reading in Matt. 9:1-8 the account of Christ's healing of the man sick of the palsy. Profoundly religious and a lifelong student of mental and spiritual causation, she came to attribtute causation to God and to regard him as divine Mind. From these roots came Christian Science and the Church of Christ, Scientist.

Generally described as "a religious teaching and practice based on the words and works of Christ Jesus," Christian Science was regarded by Mrs. Eddy as "divine metaphysics," as "the scientific system of divine healing," and as the "law of God, the law of good, interpreting and demonstrating the divine Principle and rule of universal harmony." She believed "the Principle of all harmonious Mind-action to be God"; she wrote most of these definitions and descriptions of her faith in *Science and Health with Key to the Scriptures*, a famous volume which together with the Bible has become the twofold textbook of Christian Science.

Like many other religious leaders and pioneers, Mrs. Eddy hoped to work through existing churches. She did not plan another denomination; but organization became necessary as interest in the movement spread, and under her direction the Church of Christ, Scientist, a local church, was established at Boston in 1879. In 1892 she established the present world-wide organization, the First Church of Christ, Scientist, in Boston, Massachusetts, and its branch churches and societies. This church in Boston is frequently referred to as the Mother Church.

Applied not only to the healing of sickness but to the problems of life generally, the tenets and doctrines of Christian Science are often confusing to the non-Scientist, and call for careful explanation. They start with the conviction that God is the only might or Mind; he is "All-in-all," the "divine Principle of all that really is," "the all-knowing, all-seeing, all-acting, all-wise, all-loving, and eternal; Principle; Mind; Soul; Spirit; Life; Truth; Love; all substance; intelligence." The inspired word of the Bible is accepted as "sufficient guide to eternal Life." The tenets state: "We acknowledge and adore one supreme and infinite God. We acknowledge His Son, one Christ; the Holy Ghost or divine Comforter; and man in God's image and likeness." Jesus is known to Christian Scientists as Master or Way-shower. His chief work lies in the atonement, "the evidence of divine, efficacious Love, unfolding man's unity with God through Christ Jesus the Way-shower." Man, made in the image of God, "is saved through Christ, through Truth, Life, and Love as demonstrated by the Galilean Prophet in healing the sick and overcoming sin and death." The crucifixion and resurrection of Jesus are held as serving "to uplift faith to understand eternal Life, even the allness of Soul, Spirit, and the nothingness of matter."

This "nothingness of matter" involves the basic teaching of Christian Science concerning what is real and unreal. Says Mrs. Eddy.

All reality is in God and His creation, harmonious and eternal. That which He creates is good, and He makes all that is made. Therefore the only reality of sin, sickness, or death is the awful fact that unrealities seem real to human, erring belief, until God strips off their disguise. They are not true, because they are not of God.

God forgives sin in destroying sin with "the spiritual understanding that casts out evil as unreal." The punishment for sin, however, lasts as long as the belief in sin endures.

It is a mistake to believe that the followers of Christian Science *ignore* that which they consider unreal; rather, they seek to forsake and overcome

71

error and evil by demonstrating the true idea of reality with the help of spiritual law and spiritual power. Error is simply "a supposition that pleasure and pain, that intelligence, substance, life, are existent in matter. . . . It is that which seemeth to be and is not."

Certain terms are important in the exposition of Christian Science. Animal magnetism is the mesmeric action of erroneous belief; Christian Science is its antithesis. Healing is not miraculous but divinely natural; disease is a mental concept dispelled by the introduction of spiritual truth. Heaven is not a locality but "harmony; the reign of Spirit; government by divine Principle; spirituality; bliss; the atmosphere of Soul." Hell is "mortal belief; error; lust; remorse; hatred; revenge; sin; sickness; death; suffering and self-destruction; self-imposed agony; effects of sin; that which 'worketh abomination or maketh a lie.'" Mortal mind is "the flesh opposed to Spirit, the human mind and evil in contradistinction to the divine Mind." Prayer is "an absolute faith that all things are possible to God—a spiritual understanding of Him, an unselfed love." Baptism is not a ceremony in this church but an individual spiritual experience, a "purification from all error."

All local Churches of Christ, Scientist, of which there are more than 3,200, as branches of the Mother Church are organized under the laws of the states or countries in which they exist. They enjoy their own forms of democratic government, but they are still subject to the bylaws laid down in the *Manual of the Mother Church* by Mrs. Eddy. Reading rooms open to the general public are maintained by all churches. The affairs of the Mother Church are administered by the Christian Science Board of Directors, which elects a president, the first and second readers, a clerk, and a treasurer. The board of directors is a self-perpetuating body electing all other officers of the church annually with the exception of the readers, who are elected by the board for a term of 3 years.

Important in the Christian Science movement are the reader, teacher, and practitioner. There are 2 readers in each church, usually a man and a woman; in all Christian Science services on Sunday and Thanksgiving Day they read alternately from the Bible and from *Science and Health;* the lesson-sermon of the Sunday service is prepared by a committee of Scientists and issued quarterly by the Christian Science Publishing Society. This system is followed by all Christian Science churches throughout the world. A midweek meeting, which is conducted by the first reader alone, features testimonies of healing from sin and sickness.

Practitioners devote their full time to healing and are authorized to practice by the board of directors. There is a board of education consisting of 3 members—a president, a vice-president, and a teacher of Christian Science. Under the supervision of this board a normal class is held once in 3 years. Teachers are duly authorized by certificates granted by the Board of Education to form classes of pupils in Christian Science. One class of not more than 30 pupils is instructed by each teacher annually.

There is a board of lectureship consisting of nearly 30 members. These members are appointed annually by the Board of Directors. At the invitation of branch churches free lectures are given by these members all over the world. A committee on publication works to correct impositions or misstatements concerning Christian Science in the public press. The Christian Science Publishing Society is one of the most effective units within the church; it publishes very much and very well-written literature, including the *Christian Science Sentinel,* the *Christian Science Journal,* the *Christian Science Quarterly,* the *Herald of Christian Science* in 9 languages and in Braille, and the *Christian Science Monitor*. The *Monitor* is acknowledged in all journalism to be one of the finest newspapers in the world. There are 2 Christian Science Benevolent Association sanatoria and a home for elderly Christian Scientists, which are maintained by the Christian Science Church.

The bylaws written by Mrs. Eddy prohibit the publishing of membership statistics; no comprehensive, accurate, or up-to-date figures are available. The government census of 1936 reported 268,915 members, but this figure has since been held inaccurate and not at all indicative of the total membership strength of the Mother Church and its branches. Actually today the figure would be much larger than this; in deference to the wishes of the officials of the church no estimate will be given here. It is enough to remark upon a strange situation, found here and probably in no other church in America: the number of people studying Christian Science and attending its services but not yet admitted to full membership exceeds the number who have been so admitted.

CHURCH OF GOD

At least 200 independent religious bodies in the United States bear the name Church of God in one form or another. Of these, 3 have their headquarters in Cleveland, Tennessee, where the name was first applied in the later years of the last century, and where important developments have taken place.

The Cleveland bodies began on August 19, 1886, in Monroe County, Tennessee, as a Christian fellowship, first known as The Christian Union, with 8 members led by Richard G. Spurling. The Union was reorganized under the name of "The Holiness Church" in May of 1902, and a simple form of government was introduced. A. J. Tomlinson, an American Bible Society colporteur, joined them in 1903 and was elected general overseer in 1909; he was impeached in 1923, and withdrew to form a rival group known as the Tomlinson Church of God; this name was changed to The Church of God of Prophecy in 1953. When Tomlinson died in 1943 his group was divided between his two sons, Milton A. Tomlinson, who remained in Cleveland as head of the Church of God of Prophecy, and Homer A. Tomlinson, who organized his followers under the name Church of God and established headquarters in Queens Village, New York. A small splinter group left the Church of God of Prophecy in February of 1957 under the leadership of Grandy R. Kent to form the Church of God of All Nations in Cleveland.

Still another body, known as The (Original) Church of God (see p. 74), was organized in 1917 following a split among the followers of Richard G. Spurling; it claims to be the first church to use the name Church of God and has' headquarters in Chattanooga.

Today, the Church of God (Cleveland, Tenn.) claims 162,589 members and 6,071 ministers in 3,156 churches in the United States and Canada; the Church of God of Prophecy claims 32,526 members and 1,150 ministers in 1,214 churches in the U. S.; the Church of God (Queens Village, New York) claims 71,777 members and 1,555 ministers in 1,829 United States churches; the Kent group makes no report on membership.

The Tomlinson groups are not recognized as a part of the Church of God by the Church of God (Cleveland). The Cleveland Church is the only one of the four thus far admitted to the National Association of Evangelicals, the National

Sunday School Association, the Pentecostal Fellowship of North America, and the World Pentecostal Fellowship.

In spite of the differences between these bodies, they hold in common doctrines of justification by faith, sanctification, baptism of the Holy Spirit, speaking in tongues, being born again, fruitfulness in Christian living, and a strong interest in the premillennial second coming of Christ. The Cleveland Church of God, especially, while "relying upon the Bible as a whole rightly divided rather than upon any written creed," is thoroughly Arminian, stressing Pentecostal and holiness tenets; practicing divine healing and condemning the use of alcohol, tobacco, and jewelry; opposing membership in secret societies; and accepting baptism, the Lord's Supper, and foot washing as ordinances. The Queens Village group puts strong emphasis upon the fulfillment of scripture "for the last days" and upon preparation now for the return of Christ.

The Cleveland churches elect their officers; the Queens Village church appoints them. There are differences in licensing and ordaining ministers. The ministry includes 3 orders: minister of the gospel, evangelist, and exhorter,.

The Cleveland Church of God holds state assemblies and an annual general assembly; operates Lee College at Cleveland; maintains 3 Bible schools and 1 preparatory school plus a number of schools abroad, 2 orphanages, and a publishing house. Foreign missions are directed by a missions board, but home missions are in charge of a state superintendent and his council.

The (Original) Church of God, Inc.

This church was organized in Tennessee in 1886 under the name The Church of God after a difference of opinion in regard to doctrine and teaching brought about a split among the followers of the Rev. Richard G. Spurling. The faction adhering to the original doctrines added the word Original to the name and incorporated in 1922.

The church believes in the "whole Bible, rightly divided"; in repentance, justification, and regeneration as defined by Martin Luther; in sanctification as defined by John Wesley; in divine healing; in the second coming of Christ; in eternal life for the righteous and eternal punishment for the wicked. Christian fruits alone stand as evidence of faithful Christian living; creeds that bind the conscience are considered unscriptural. Pentecostal experience and speaking with tongues are accepted; ordinances include baptism by immersion, the Lord's tithing, freewill offerings, the Lord's Supper, and foot washing.

Local churches, following the apostolic pattern, take local names such as the Church of God at Corinth. Each local church is self-governing. The church recognizes the New Testament orders of ministers, apostles, deacons, exhorters, evangelists, bishops, and teachers, as given in Eph. 4:11-14. A general convention meets annually; there are a general office and publishing house, and denominational headquarters are at Chattanooga, Tennessee; a correspondence Bible school offers courses leading to a Doctor of Divinity degree. There were 6,000 members and 75 churches in 1952.

Church of God (Anderson, Indiana)

The Church of God with headquarters at Anderson, Indiana, started about 1880 as a movement within existing churches. It prefers to have its name accepted in an inclusive rather than in a denominational sense and is actually a movement in the direction of Christian unity and the re-establishment of the New Testament standard of faith and life by realizing the identity of the visible and invisible church in the free fellowship of believers. The founders believed that the church at large was too much restricted and overburdened with organization and ecclesiasticism; it should be "more directly under the rule of God."

Doctrine in this church includes belief in the divine inspiration of the Scriptures; the forgiveness of sin through the atonement of Christ and repentance of the believer; the experience of holiness; the personal return of Christ, which is not connected with any millennial reign; the kingdom of God as established here and now; the final judgment; the resurrection of the dead; the reward of the righteous and the punishment of the wicked.

Baptism is by immersion. Members of this church also practice foot washing and observe the Lord's Supper, but not as conditions of fellowship. They believe the church to be the body of Christ, made up of all Christians, and that all Christians are one in Christ. The confusion of sects and denominations, however, is an obstacle to this unity; being unscriptural it should be removed. God desires this restoration of the New Testament ideal in his church; it is a restoration based upon spiritual experience and not on creedal agreement.

There were 136,254 members reported in this church at the end of 1958, along with 52,265 adherents in home and foreign mission stations. They are governed by a congregational system; while they preach the idea of God governing his church, they agree that the aid of human personalities is quite necessary. Membership is not on a formal basis, and hence no formal membership is kept. Ministers meet in voluntary state and regional conventions, which are chiefly advisory. The General Ministerial Assembly meets annually in connection with the annual convention and camp meeting held at Anderson, Indiana. With an unusually large Sunday-school enrollment of 239,077, this is said to be one of the few Protestant groups in which Sunday-school attendance exceeds church membership.

The Church of God (Seventh Day), Denver, Colorado

At the time of the Puritan migration to Massachusetts there were 7 churches in London bearing the name Church of God; members of these congregations settled in Massachusetts, Pennsylvania, Rhode Island, and New Jersey between 1664 and 1800. Many drifted West and South after the Revolution. The Church of God at Shrewsbury, New Jersey, moved to Salem, West Virginia, in 1789; another group became strong in Missouri. Formal organization of these scattered churches was effected in Michigan in 1865; the first general conference was held in 1883, and the body was incorporated in Gentry County, Missouri, in 1899. Headquarters were established at Stanberry, Missouri.

These people constituted a Church of God that was Sabbatarian, observing the seventh day as the true Sabbath. A large number of their membership joined the Adventist movement led by Ellen Harmon White and changed the names of their churches accordingly; those who could not become Adventists reorganized under the old name, Church of God. A second withdrawal from their membership resulted in the organization, in 1933, of the Church of God (Seventh Day) with headquarters at Salem, West Virginia. These 2 bodies were reunited in August, 1949, under the present name, The Church of God (Seventh Day). A small group, however, refused to accept the merger and still operates under the same name, Church of God (Seventh Day), with headquarters at Salem. This body (2,000 members) since 1949 is reported to have split into at least 3 groups.

Fundamentalist doctrine and theology prevail here. The church believes in the infallibility of the Scriptures; the natural sinfulness of man; the blood atonement of Christ on the cross for all men; the remission of sin by baptism; premillennialism; annihilation of the wicked and

75

the reward of the righteous at the final judgment; the observation of the seventh day as the Sabbath; holiness in living; abstinence from tobacco, alcohol, and narcotics; and the use of only such foods as are classified as clean by the Scriptures.

A general conference meets every 2 years; an executive board of 12 ministers accredited by the general conference is the direct administrative body, and state conferences with executive boards of 7 members each have been organized.

This church is one of the few in this country with more members abroad than at home. In the continental United States they have 4,300 members in 130 churches; abroad the total is estimated as high as 45,000. They have 80 foreign workers in 6 foreign countries, not including Canada and Mexico; 2 grade schools have been established in Nigeria. Their foreign work is so heavy that it is supported with real difficulty by the church at home.

Church of God and Saints of Christ

The Church of God and Saints of Christ was founded in Lawrence, Kansas, in 1896 by William S. Crowdy, a Negro cook on the Santa Fe Railroad who claimed visions from God, a divine commission to lead his people, and a prophetic endowment. He became the first bishop of the church and is still known as the Prophet.

The members of the church, 36,041 in 216 churches, believe that the Negro people are descendants of the lost tribes of Israel. Sometimes called Black Jews, they observe the Old Testament Sabbath and feast days, and use Hebrew names for the months of the year. Following the teachings of the Prophet, they call for literal interpretation and practice of the Ten Commandments. A pamphlet entitled *The Seven Keys* is published, explaining to the faithful just which commandments are to be thus

followed and why. Members are admitted by confessing belief in Christ, repenting of sin, being baptized by immersion, taking Communion, having their feet washed and head breathed on by an elder, being saluted with a holy kiss, being instructed in prayer, and promising to obey the Ten Commandments.

An executive board or council of 12 ordained elders or evangelists, usually called a presbytery, administers the general business of the church. A prophet, or successor to Crowdy, still stands at the head of the organization; he holds his position not by election but by divine call, and he is said to be in direct communication with God to utter inspired prophecies and to perform miracles. Upon his death, his office remains vacant until another vision is given.

Other officers include ministers not fully ordained, elders fully ordained, evangelists, and bishops. Deacons supervise the temporal affairs of the church under the direction of annual district and general assemblies. Tithes are collected for the support of the ministry and the Prophet; storehouses are established by the district assemblies to receive the tithes and to distribute groceries and other necessities to the members. There is strong emphasis on temperance; marriage is permissible only between members of the church. The Belleville Industrial School and Widows and Orphans Home is located at Belleville, Virginia.

The Church of God in Christ

C. H. Mason and C. P. Jones, rejected by Baptist groups in Arkansas for what the Baptists considered overemphasis on holiness, founded the Church of God in Christ in 1897. The name was divinely revealed to Mason, who now heads the church. He put strong emphasis upon entire sanctification and in a revival received the baptism of the Holy Spirit together with "signs of speaking with tongues"; his ardent preaching on these gifts and subjects aroused resentment and subsequent division among his followers.

Doctrine is Trinitarian, stressing repentance, regeneration, justification, sanctification, speaking in tongues, and the gift of healing as evidence of the baptism of the Spirit. Holiness is considered a prerequisite to salvation; ordinances include baptism by immersion, the Lord's Supper, and foot washing.

Church organization is held to have its authority in Scripture; there are 8 bishops, or commissioners, apostles, prophets, evangelists, pastors, elders, overseers, teachers, deacons, deaconesses, and missionaries. Each local church has an overseer; a state overseer supervises the churches within the various states and holds state and district conferences annually. A national convocation meets each year.

Missionaries are found in South Africa, Thailand, Jamaica, Haiti, Liberia, and West Coast, Africa. Saints Junior College is maintained at Lexington, Mississippi; there is a department of publications and a Sunday-school publishing house furnishing the denomination with literature. There are 380,428 members in 3,800 churches.

THE CHURCH OF ILLUMINATION

Described as a "church at large rather than a church of congregations," this body was organized in 1908 under the inspiration of the Rev. R. Swinburne Clymer. Its stated purpose is to harmonize the teachings of philosophy with the truths of religion, thus offering a spiritual, esoteric, and philosophical interpretation of basic Bible teachings to those in search of spiritual truth. Membership is by written request and does not require severance of membership in any other church.

Much is made of the "priesthood of Melchizedek," which dates from "beyond the year 4255 B.C. and includes all that small body of chosen seekers initiated into the mysteries of the divine law"; this priesthood has come down from the days of Genesis through Jesus, the Gnostics, the early Egyptians, Greeks, Indians, and Persians to the present time, where it is to be found in the Church of Illumination.

The essence of religion here is found in the simple biblical statement that "whatsoever a man soweth, that shall he also reap." This is interpreted as being a matter of inevitable compensation rather than of rewards and punishments at the hands of God. Furthermore:

Religion teaches the Law—the way of Life—a way which makes man aware of the all-important truth that he is, in fact, a child of God, and that within him, buried by much debris, is a spark of the Divine. This Divine Spark is the *Christos*—the unconscious Soul—which may be awakened and brought into consciousness—a second or Rebirth. This is the "talent" entrusted to man and for which he is responsible to his Creator. Neglected, it remains just as it is— a tiny spark. Recognized, aroused, awakened and brought into consciousness, it becomes an inexhaustible source of wisdom and power, lifting man to the heights of Illumination and achievement. The process that makes all this possible is, in reality, the Second Birth. It is the process of Regeneration—mortality taking on immortality—the means whereby the son of man actually and literally becomes the Son of God.

Enlarging upon this, four great fundamentals are taught: (1) the law of action and reaction (sowing and reaping), (2) the indebtedness of man to God for his talents and his obligation to use them well, (3) the practice of the Golden Rule, and (4) the practice of the law of honesty. All this is the means to the fulfillment of man's destiny. It is also taught that we are now in a "manistic" age (*manisis*, the recognition of the equality of man and woman), which will last 2,000 years and in which Revelation will become the "unsealed book of the Bible," and that the world right now is the scene of the final battle of Armageddon. There is also some emphasis upon reincarnation, although belief in this is not required of adherents.

Yearly conferences of ministers and leaders are held in various parts of the country. Officially there were 7 established churches with 5,000 members in 1945, but the bulk of the membership is made up of those who are members only in correspondence and not members of any specific church.

CHURCH OF OUR LORD JESUS CHRIST OF THE APOSTOLIC FAITH, INC.

Confident that it is a "continuation of the great revival begun at Jerusalem on the day of Pentecost in A.D. 33," this church was organized in Columbus, Ohio, in 1919 by its present bishop, R. C. Lawson. Doctrine is stated to be that of the apostles and prophets with Christ as the cornerstone. Creed, discipline, and rules of order are found in the Bible only. Perhaps the basic emphases are those laid upon Christ's resurrection and premillennial second coming, the resurrection and translation of the saints, the priesthood of all believers, and the final judgment of mankind. Baptism is by immersion, and the baptism of the Holy Spirit is held necessary to the second birth. The Lord's Supper and foot washing are practiced as ordinances.

Found in 27 states, the British West Indies, West Africa, and the Philippines, the group reported 155 churches and a membership of 45,000 in 1954. Two elementary schools, a Bible institute, and 1 hospital are maintained. A national convocation meets annually at the headquarters church, Refuge Temple, in New York City. Officers of the denomination consist of 1 bishop (Lawson), 3 secretaries, and a treasurer.

CHURCH OF THE NAZARENE

The theological and doctrinal foundations of the Church of the Nazarene lie in the preaching of the doctrines of holiness and sanctification as taught by John Wesley in the eighteenth-century revival in England. Its physical structure is the result not so much of schism as of the merging of 3 independent holiness groups already in existence in the United States. An eastern holiness body, located principally in New York and New England and known as the Association of Pentecostal Churches in America, joined at Chicago in 1907 with a western (California) body called the Church of the Nazarene; the 2 merging churches agreed on the name "Pentecostal Church of the Nazarene." The southern group, known as the Holiness Church of Christ, united with this Pentecostal Church of the Nazarene at Pilot Point, Texas, in 1908. In 1919 the word Pentecostal was dropped from the name, leaving it as we know it today, the Church of the Nazarene. This was primarily a move to disassociate in the public mind any connection with the other more radical Pentecostal groups which taught or practiced speaking in tongues, a teaching and practice always opposed by the Church of the Nazarene.

The background of the Nazarenes is definitely Methodist; they adhere closely to the original Wesleyan ideology. Most of the early holiness groups in this country came out of the Methodist Episcopal Church; 2 of the original 7 general superintendents of the Church of the Nazarene were ex-Methodist ministers, and the Nazarene *Manual* has been called a "rewritten and modified Methodist *Discipline*."

The doctrine of the church is built around sanctification as a second definite work of grace subsequent to regeneration; all ministers and local church officials must have undergone this experience. Other doctrines include belief in the plenary inspiration of the Scriptures as containing all truth necessary to Christian faith and living; in the atonement of Christ for the whole human race; in the justification, regeneration, and adoption of all penitent believers in Christ; in the second coming of Christ, the resurrection of the dead, and the final judgment. Members of this church believe in divine healing but never to the exclusion of medical agencies. The use of tobacco and alcoholic beverages is denounced. Two ordinances—baptism by sprinkling, pouring, or most often immersion and the Lord's Supper—are accepted as "instituted by Christ." Members are admitted on confession of faith and on agreement "to observe the rules and regulations . . . of the Church." It is a middle-of-the-road church, neither extremely ritualistic on the one hand nor extremely informal on the other; one church historian calls it the "right wing of the holiness movement."

There are 4,696 local congregations grouped into 74 districts. Local pastors are elected by local churches; each district is supervised by a district superintendent elected annually by the members of the district assembly. Quadrennially the various districts elect delegates to a general assembly, at which general superintendents are elected for a term of 4 years to supervise the work of the entire denomination. All this closely resembles the Methodist system of administration; in general it may be said that the Nazarenes have the more democratic form and procedure.

The general assembly also elects a general board, consisting of an equal number of lay and ministerial members, which is in turn divided into 7 administrative departments: foreign missions, home missions, evangelism, publication, ministerial benevolence, education, and church schools. Foreign missionary work is conducted in 33 fields with 411 missionaries and 1,466 native members at work. Home mission activities are carried on in all 74 districts and in 7 areas outside the continental United States; strong emphasis is laid upon evangelism. Six liberal arts colleges are maintained; there are a theological seminary in Kansas City, a Bible institute (Negro) at Institute, West Virginia, and Bible colleges in Canada and the British Isles.

The books and periodicals of the church are produced at the Nazarene Publishing House in Kansas City, Missouri; 40 periodicals are published, and the annual volume of business exceeds $3,000,000.

Membership in the United States is reported at 311,300, in Canada and the British Isles 9,385, in overseas home mission areas 1,612, with an additional 50,350 abroad. There are 6,208 churches at home and overseas, 6,101 ordained ministers, 4,631 Sunday schools, and 3,614 young people's societies with a membership of 97,080.

CHURCHES OF CHRIST

Twenty thousand independent congregations with a total membership of about 2,000,000 constitute the Churches of Christ. They are located in 50 states with greatest concentrations in the South and West, have congregations in 65 foreign countries, and in the past 20 years have emerged as one of the top ten non-Catholic bodies in North America.

There is a distinctive plea for unity at the heart of the Churches of Christ—a unity that is Bible-based. It is believed here that the Bible is "the beginning place" in and through which God-fearing people can achieve spiritual oneness; it is an appeal to "speak where the Bible speaks and to be silent where the Bible is silent" in all matters pertaining to faith and morals; consequently members recognize no other written creed or confession of faith than the Scriptures. In all religious matters, there must be a "thus saith the Lord."

Historically, the churches have their roots in the movements which inspired the founding of the Christian Church and the Disciples of Christ—in the work and ideology of James O'Kelley in Virginia, Abner Jones and Elias Smith in New England, Barton Stone in Kentucky, and Thomas and Alexander Campbell in West Virginia. (For a detailed discussion of these men and their contributions, see Christian Church (p. 218) and Disciples of Christ (p. 65.) These 4 movements, all contending that "nothing should be bound upon Christians as a matter of doctrine which is not as old as the New Testament," and all completely independent at the start, eventually became one strong religious stream because of their common purpose and plea.

Those who founded the Church of Christ were originally members of the Disciples of Christ; they were a conservative group who came into conflict with the more progressive Disciples over questions of pastoral power developing among the preachers, the use of the title "Reverend" instead of "Elder," the government of the local church by the pastor instead of the elders, the introduction of instrumental music in the services of the church and the establishment of missionary societies supported by annual membership dues—all of which seemed to the conservatives to be in violation of New Testament patterns and procedure. It is impossible to set a date of actual division, for no formal division has ever been declared, but such division was apparent early in the twentieth century. In the 1906 Census of Religious Bodies, the Churches of Christ were for the first time listed as separate from the Disciples, yet neither Disciples nor Churches of Christ wish to be considered as a denomination, and hence there can be said to have been no *denominational* division between them. The Disciples remain true to their polity; the Churches of Christ are more a group of unattached, completely autonomous local congregations, practicing a more extreme form of congregationalist government than is the case among the Disciples.

Today, one of the outstanding features of the Churches of Christ lies in their acceptance of the Bible as a true and completely adequate revelation. This basic concept has resulted in such characteristic practices as weekly observance of the Lord's Supper, baptism by immersion, *a cappella* singing without instrumental aids, a vigorous prayer life, support of church needs through voluntary giving, and a program of preaching and teaching the Bible. This concept also explains the autonomy of local churches, governed by elders and deacons appointed under New Testament qualifications, dignified worship services, enthusiastic mission campaigns, and far-flung benevolent programs all financed by the local churches.

The great scriptural doctrines usually classified as "conservative" are received in the Churches of Christ, including the concept of the Father, the Son, and the Holy Ghost as members of one Godhead; the incarnation, virgin birth, and bodily resurrection of Christ; and the universality of sin after the age of accountability and its only remedy in the vicarious atonement of the Lord Jesus Christ. Strong emphasis is also laid on the church as the body and bride of Christ. A figurative rather than a literal view is prevalent with reference to the book of Revelation. Membership is contingent upon the faith of the individual in Jesus Christ as the only begotten Son of God, repentance, confession of faith and baptism by immersion into Christ for the remission of sins. Church attendance is stressed.

While professing identity with the original church established by Christ and the apostles at Pentecost, the Churches of Christ maintain that the final judgment of all religious groups is reserved unto the Lord himself. Members believe they are "Christians only, but not the only Christians." They see themselves as "Christ's Church, but not *all* of Christ's Church." This view, however, still allows for a vigorous evangelism which finds unacceptable the doctrines, practices, names, titles, and creeds which have been grafted onto the original Christianity in the long post-apostolic period.

Ministers are ordained rather than licensed, and they hold tenure in their pulpits under mutual agreement with the elders of churches where they preach. Their authority is moral rather than arbitrary, the actual government of the church being vested in its eldership.

A vigorous missionary program is carried on in 65 nations outside the United States, and in recent years a strong movement to extend the influence of the group in the northeastern United States has developed. Counting native workers in the foreign field and mission activities within the United States, there are over 500 missionaries, or evangelists, supported by others than the groups where they preach. A full quota of chaplains is maintained in the Air Force and the Army.

Properties owned by the group probably exceed $75,000,000 in value. There are 16 colleges, including one in Japan; 41 secondary and elementary schools; 20 homes for orphans or the aged; and 65 periodicals, newspapers, and magazines published throughout the country. The strongest periodicals, however, are issued from Nashville, Tennessee (*The Gospel Advocate*), Austin, Texas (*The Firm Foundation*), and Abilene, Texas (*The Christian Chronicle*). All of these are church-related, privately owned and controlled institutions. Since all official status in these institutions is lacking, none of them being authorized to speak for the entire church, their conformity in ideas and teachings is all the more remarkable.

Another medium of evangelism has been put to use in the publication of articles in a number of big national magazines (*Coronet, Harpers, Atlantic Monthly, American Weekly*). This is the work of the Gospel Press of Dallas, Texas, and is supported entirely by voluntary contributions from individual members throughout the country, just as the missionary program is supported. Many churches offer correspondence courses in connection with this advertising. (The advertising program is similar in purpose and method to that of the Knights of Columbus for the Roman Catholic Church.) A "Herald of Truth" radio and television program had nationwide coverage; it is sponsored by the Highland Church of Christ in Abilene, Texas, and support is found in hundreds of other churches and individuals throughout the country.

CHURCHES OF CHRIST
IN CHRISTIAN UNION

A difference of opinion in the council of the Christian Union Churches concerning holiness as a second definite work of grace subsequent to regeneration brought about the organization of the Churches of Christ in Christian Union of Ohio at Washington Court House, Ohio, in 1909. When the majority of the council decided against those holding the second-blessing view, the minority withdrew. The words "of Ohio" have since been dropped from the name. The Reformed Methodist Church in New York united in 1952 with this body.

Aside from the second-blessing doctrine, these churches have the usual fundamentalist theology; there is strong emphasis on divine healing and the second coming of Christ. Church administration is congregational; pastors with the aid of first, second, and third elders guide the spiritual affairs of the churches, while trustees administer all business

matters. Each local church is a member of a district council and is subject to the council's rulings; each district council is a member of a general council. All ministers are ordained by the district council examining committee. Members are admitted on evidence of good fruits and a "personal experience of the new birth."

Foreign missionary work is conducted in India, Africa, South and Central America, Mexico, and Dominica; there is a widespread work in home missions, welfare, and publishing. The church publishing plant and a Bible college are located at Circleville, Ohio; the college offers a 4-year course, majoring in religious education and liberal arts, and a shorter 2-year missionary and gospel workers' course is offered. Headquarters are located at the Mount of Praise Bible School in Circleville. There are 11,500 members and 205 churches.

CHURCHES OF GOD, HOLINESS

The Churches of God, Holiness, began in 1914 with a group of 8 people in Atlanta, Georgia, under the preaching of K. H. Burruss. Large churches were founded in Atlanta and in Norfolk, Virginia, in 1916; and by 1922 there were 22 churches in 11 states, Cuba, the Canal Zone, and the British West Indies. In 1922 these churches were incorporated into what is currently known as the National Convention of the Churches of God, Holiness.

All doctrine within this group is tested strictly by New Testament standards; the Scriptures are accepted as inspired, and the New Testament "gives safe and clearly applied instructions on all methods of labor, sacred and secular," and on the conduct of the whole of life.

The churches believe in the Trinity, in justification, entire sanctification, and regeneration, and hold that the gift of the Holy Spirit is an act subsequent to conversion. Perfection is both *present* and *ultimate*. One must believe in divine healing to be acceptable as a member, but medicines and doctors are approved for those who desire them, not being expressly denounced by Scripture. Two ordinances, baptism and the Lord's Supper, are observed. The washing of feet is approved but not regularly practiced.

Pastors of all churches are assigned by the one bishop of the denomination; they are assisted in the local congregation by deacons. In direct supervision over the pastors is the state overseer, also appointed by the bishop. State conventions are held annually. The highest administrative body is the national convention, a delegated body that elects the national president, or bishop, who from the start has been the founder, K. H. Burruss. The church reports 25,600 members and 42 churches.

CHURCHES OF GOD IN NORTH AMERICA (GENERAL ELDERSHIP)

The Methodist, Presbyterian, Baptist, and German Reformed churches among the Germans of Pennsylvania were active in the religious revival which swept this country in the early years of the nineteenth century. John Winebrenner, a German Reformed pastor in Harrisburg, aroused criticism and finally determined opposition by his ardent evangelical preaching during this period; and he severed his connections with his Reformed brethren about 1823. As early as 1825 he had organized an independent congregation, which he called the Church of God. Six other preachers joined with him in 1830 to organize the General Eldership of the Church of God, using the word "General" to distinguish it from local church eldership. The words "in North America" were added in 1845, and "Church" became "Churches" in 1903.

Arminian in theology, these churches have no written creed; the Bible is considered the sole rule of faith and practice. "Bible things, as church offices and customs, should be known by Bible names, and a Bible name should not be applied to anything not mentioned in the Bible." Sectarianism is held to be antiscriptural; "each local church is a church of God and should be so called," and this church in a denominational sense is the only true church. Three ordinances are "perpetually obligatory"— baptism by immersion only, the Lord's Supper, and feet washing; the last 2 are companion ordinances, observed together and in the evening. There is a strong insistence upon the Trinity, human depravity, the sacrificial atonement of Christ, the office and work of the Holy Spirit, man's moral agency, justification by faith, repentance and regeneration, practical piety, Sabbath observance, the resurrection of the dead, the eternal nature of the soul, and final judgment.

The church is organized into 17 elderships, or conferences, in as many states; there is also an India-Pakistan Eldership. Over these is a General Eldership, composed of an equal number of lay and ministerial delegates and a proportionate number of youth delegates from the lower elderships, which meets triennially and has charge of the general interest of the church. In local affairs the churches are presbyterian in government, but the ministers are appointed to their churches by the annual elderships.

Home and foreign missionary work is under the supervision of the Board of Missions. Home missions are confined principally to the West and Southwest; foreign mission stations are found in India and other fields.

There is 1 college and a theological seminary (Winebrenner) at Findlay, Ohio, and a publishing house at Harrisburg, Pennsylvania, where headquarters are located. There were 401 churches and 37,647 members in this group in 1959.

CHURCHES OF THE LIVING GOD

Two churches of common origin, similar in type but differing in details, bear the title Church of the Living God. Both came out of an organization formed at Wrightsville, Arkansas, in 1889 by William Christian, who "by virtue of a divine call, created the office of chief." Christian held that "Freemason religion" is the true expression of religion and insisted that his "organism" be known as "operative Masonry and [that] its first three corporal degrees shall be baptism, Holy Supper and foot washing." Both groups are organized along fraternal lines; members tithe their incomes in support of the church and call their churches temples.

The first body, the larger, is known as The Church of the Living God (Motto: Christian Workers for Fellowship). It claims 25,000 members in 236 churches, stresses believer's baptism by immersion, foot washing, and the use of water and unleavened bread in the celebration of the Lord's Supper. A chief bishop is the presiding officer; an annual assembly meets every 4 years to elect other officers and to determine the laws for the Church. Membership is biracial.

The second body, called The House of God, Which is the Church of the Living God, the Pillar and Ground of the Truth, Inc., is also episcopal in polity and generally follows the form and thought of the Workers-for-Fellowship group. They have 2,350 members in 107 churches.

CHURCHES OF THE NEW JERUSALEM

Commonly called Swedenborgian, the Churches of the New Jerusalem are based on the teachings of Emmanuel Swedenborg and exist in 3 main bodies: the General Convention of the New Jerusalem in the U.S.A. (the older United States body); the General Church of the New Jerusalem, which broke from the parent group in 1890; and the General Conference in England.

Swedenborg, who was born in Stockholm in 1688 and died in London in 1772, was a Swedish scientist distinguished in the fields of mathematics, geology, cosmology, and anatomy before he turned seriously to theology. Interested in the relation of these sciences to the spiritual life of man, he experienced a series of dreams and visions which resulted in an illumination of the things and ways of the spiritual world. He claimed to have had communication with the other world and to have witnessed certain stages of the last judgment there. He taught that with this judgment a first dispensation of the Christian church had come to an end and a new dispensation, which he called the "New Jerusalem" or the "Descent of the Holy City," was beginning. While he said that he was "dead on this side of the world," he still continued his usual activities in the world, including participation in the Swedish Parliament of which he was a member.

Certain that he was divinely commissioned to teach the doctrines of the New Church, Swedenborg taught that God *is* man, meaning that the origin of all that is truly human is in God. The divine humanity is, however, Christ's glorified and risen humanity in which God is manifested and which is God's. These doctrines were accepted and preached by his followers, who considered him to be a divinely illuminated seer and revelator. Against the background of his concept of "correspondence" of the natural world with the spiritual world he expounded a deeper and additional sense of the Scriptures than was offered by most interpreters of his time. Swedenborg himself never preached, and he preferred to leave his followers in the churches of which they were already members; he never intended to found a new sect or church.

The New Church as an organization started in London in 1783 when Robert Hindmarsh, a printer, gathered a few friends together to discuss and read the writings of Swedenborg; they formed a general conference of their societies in 1815. The first Swedenborg Society in America was organized at Baltimore in 1792; in 1817 the General Convention of the New Jerusalem in the U.S.A. was established.

The doctrines of the General Convention as given in the *Liturgy* are as follows:

1. That there is one God, in whom there is a Divine Trinity; and that He is the Lord Jesus Christ.
2. That saving faith is to believe on Him.
3. That evils are to be shunned, because they are of the devil and from the devil.
4. That good actions are to be done, because they are of God and from God.
5. That these are to be done by a man as from himself; but that it ought to be believed that they are done from the Lord with him and by him.

The societies are grouped into a general convention meeting annually; there are also state associations. Each society is self-regulating. They have ministers and general pastors (in charge of state associations); the ministers, except for those retired or otherwise inactive, serve the local societies. Services are liturgical, using chants extensively but with wide latitude, and based on the *Book of Worship* issued by the General Convention.

The General Convention now has 5,709 members active in 74 societies; it carries on a home mission program in the United States and a foreign mission program in 14 countries abroad. A theological school is located at Cambridge, Massachusetts; and the Swedenborg Foundation in New York City distributes Swedenborg's writings. The church publishes a biweekly.

The General Church of the New Jerusalem holds the same doctrine, emphasizing the "original" teachings of Swedenborg. There is no fixed constitution in this church; polity is based on "practical unanimity" in council and assembly. There are ministers, pastors, and bishops, the latter being chosen by a general assembly; there are 1,832 members in 8 societies. There are a theological school, a college, an academy for boys, and a seminary for girls. Headquarters are at Bryn Athyn, Pennsylvania, where a cathedral church has been built.

CONGREGATIONAL HOLINESS CHURCH

Founded in 1921 by a group of ministers withdrawing from the Pentecostal Holiness Church in an effort to retain holiness doctrines and to establish a more democratic church polity, this church is Trinitarian, emphasizing the inspiration of the Scriptures, justification, sanctification, divine healing (without objection to medicine), the second coming of Christ, eternal punishment and rewards, the merits of the Atonement, and the salvation of the entire church.

The Bible is held as the sole rule of conduct; slang, tobacco, membership in oath-bound secret societies, and other forms of worldliness are condemned. Ordinances include baptism, foot washing, and the Lord's Supper. The crowning blessing of religious experience is held to be the baptism of the Holy Ghost and speaking with other tongues "as the Spirit (gives) utterance."

Church government is, as the name suggests, congregational. Local churches are grouped in annual associations from which delegates are elected to a general association. Local church officers, elected annually, consist of deacons, trustees, a secretary, and a treasurer. Pastors are called by a majority vote of the congregation; women are licensed to preach but are not ordained. There are 148 churches and 4,617 members in the United States; newer churches and conferences have recently been established in Cuba and Nigeria.

DIVINE SCIENCE CHURCH AND COLLEGE, INC.

Three sisters—Althea Brooks Small, Fannie Brooks James, and Nona Lovell Brooks—of Denver, Colorado, and Mrs. Malinda E. Cramer of San Francisco in the late years of the last century worked out independently of one another the principles and practice of Divine Science. They met and joined forces in 1898, incorporating the Divine Science College; their first church—the First Divine Science Church of Denver—was organized by the college in Denver.

The core of its teaching is the principle of the all-inclusive God-mind:

God [is] the Omnipresence, the Universal Presence, Substance, Life, and Intelligence; man, a child of God, is of God, is like God; knowledge of this truth used in our living frees us from sin, sickness, and death; the practice of right thinking, or thought training, results in the elimination of fear, doubt, anxiety, and other wrong mental habits, and the establishment of love, faith, joy, and power in the consciousness; evolution is God's method of accomplishing, and love, conscious unity, is the fulfilling of the law.

The founders had all had the experience of divine healing, and the emphasis upon healing naturally persists. Healing through thought training is described as the "cleansing of the inner man from all that is unlike God." Sickness, sin, and death persist because of man's ignorance of the truth; they vanish when man knows God and lives by that knowledge. Divine Science does not deny the existence of visible matter but interprets both form and substance as manifestations of God.

Divine Science further stands for: (1) the fatherhood of God as Omnipresent Life, Substance, Intelligence, and Power; (2) the brotherhood of man; (3) the unity of all life; (4) the highest thought in science, philosophy, and religion; (5) the power of right thinking to release into expression in each individual life man's divine inheritance—health, abundance, peace, and power; (6) the transcendence and immanence of God manifest in all created things.

For many years local churches and colleges of Divine Science were independent of one another. In 1957 some of the ministers and key workers of existing Divine Science Churches and Colleges met and organized the Divine Science Federation International. This new movement serves as the meeting ground and clearing house for determining standards of teaching and conduct for the workers and churches of the Divine Science Movement. The headquarters of the movement are in Denver, Colorado, where publications are printed and a monthly periodical called *Aspire to Better Living* is issued.

EASTERN CHURCHES

When, in A.D. 330, Constantine moved his capital from Rome to Byzantium and began to rule his vast empire from the new Constantinople, the most important split in the history of Christianity was under way. Up to this time the church in the West, centered in Rome, and the church in the East, with its headquarters in Byzantium, were one church. Both accepted the Nicene Creed; both were sacramental and apostolic. There were, however, certain basic differences which made for confusion; racially, socially, linguistically, mentally, morally, and philosophically there were deep gulfs between the two. The East was Greek in blood and speech; the West was Latin. The transference of the capital from West to East meant a shifting of the center of political, social, and intellectual influence. When the Goths swept down upon Rome that city turned for help, not to Constantinople, but to the Franks; in gratitude for his aid the pope crowned Charles the Great as emperor on Christmas Day in 800, and the die was cast.

Conflict deepened between the pope at Rome and the patriarch at Constantinople. In 857 Ignatius in Constantinople refused to administer the sacrament to Caesar Bardas on the ground that he was immoral. Tried and imprisoned, Ignatius was succeeded by Photius, an intellectual giant for whom the weaker pope was no match. Their increasing friction broke into flame at the Council of St. Sophia, where Photius bitterly condemned the Latin Church for adding the word "filioque" to the Nicene Creed. The Eastern Church held that the Holy Spirit proceeded directly from the Father; the Western Church had adopted the view that the Spirit proceeded from the Father *and* the Son —filioque. Political and ecclesiastical jealousies fanned the flame until, in 1054, the pope excommunicated the patriarch and the patriarch excommunicated the pope, the result being that there were finally two churches,

Eastern and Western, instead of one. The pope remained head of the Western Church; at the moment, in the East, there were 4 patriarchs, or heads, guiding the destinies of Eastern Orthodoxy. This is important to an understanding of the Eastern Orthodox Church. It is not a monarchy with one all-powerful ruler at the top; it is "an oligarchy of patriarchs." It is based on the body of bishops, holding power variously as metropolitans, primates, and exarchs, and is conducted finally through the sovereignty of the 4 patriarchal thrones. No one patriarch is responsible to any other patriarch, yet all are within the jurisdiction of an ecumenical council of all the churches in communion with the patriarch of Constantinople, who holds the title of Ecumenical Patriarch.

Today, Christendom remains divided into 3 principal sections: Roman Catholic, Eastern Orthodox, and Protestant. Eastern Orthodox churches consist of those churches which accept the decisions and decrees of the first 7 general church councils—2 at Nicaea, 3 at Constantinople, 1 at Ephesus, and 1 at Chalcedon—and of such other churches as have originated in the missionary activities of these parent churches and have grown to self-government but still maintain communion with them.

Claiming to be "the direct heir and true conservator" of the original, primitive Church, Eastern Orthodoxy has tended historically to divide into independent national and social groups— Russian, Serbian, Bulgarian, Romanian, Albanian, Greek, Georgian. These groups have had a bitter struggle for existence, caught as they have been between Arabian, Turkish, and Western armies in endless wars. Generally it may be said that Greek Christianity became the faith of the people of the Middle East and the Slavs in Europe, while Latin Christianity became the religion of Western Europe and the New World.

There are at present 5 large Eastern

patriarchates: Constantinople, Alexandria, Antioch, Jerusalem, and Moscow, while the lesser patriarchates of the Serbs, the Romanians and the Bulgarians, the Georgians, Mount Sinai, Cyprus, Athens, Japan, and Albania constitute autonomous archbishoprics, or national churches. The Turkish conquest of Constantinople greatly depleted the power of the mother church in that city; and the First World War and the Russian Revolution of 1917, with the attendant disruption of the Russian Empire, led the Eastern Orthodox churches in Poland, Finland, Estonia, Latvia, and Lithuania to assert their independence. After World War II, they were reintegrated into the Russian Orthodox Church; widely separated, they are all still in essential agreement in doctrine and worship, and together they make up what we know as The Holy Eastern Orthodox Churches. Nearly all of the European and Asiatic bodies of the Eastern Orthodox Church have branches in America; some of them are governed by one or another of the 5 major patriarchates, but others have become independent or self-governing.

In the United States today Albanian, Bulgarian, Greek, Romanian, Russian, Serbian, Ukranian, Carpatho-Russian, and Syrian churches are under the supervision of bishops of their respective nationalities. The Albanian, Greek, Serbian, and Syrian (Antioch) bishops serve under their respective patriarchs. The patriarch of Alexandria has jurisdiction over a few churches in the United States.

Doctrine in Eastern Orthodoxy is based on the Bible, on the holy tradition, and on the decrees of the 7 ecumenical councils. The Nicene Creed is recited in all liturgies and at vespers and matins, the Eastern churches holding that a "creed is an adoring confession of the church engaged in worship"; its faith is expressed more fully in its liturgy than in doctrinal statements. Actually the basis lies in the decisions and statements of the 7 councils which defined the ecumenical faith of the early undivided church, and in the later statements defining the position of the Orthodox Church of the East with regard to the doctrine and faith of the Roman Catholic and Protestant churches. The Niceno-Constantinopolitan Creed is still held in its original form without the "filioque" clause. The dogma of the pope as the sole "Vicar of Christ on earth" is rejected, together with the dogma of papal infallibility. Members of Orthodox churches accept the virgin birth but do not dogmatize on the Immaculate Conception, and they honor the saints and 9 orders of angels. They reject the teaching of the surplus merits of the saints and the doctrine of indulgences but reverence the saints, pictures (icons) of holy persons, and the cross. The use of carved images is forbidden. Bas-relief is permitted in some Orthodox groups.

They have 7 sacraments: baptism, anointing (confirmation or chrismation), Communion, penance, holy orders, marriage, and holy unction. Both infants and adults are baptized by threefold immersion. The sacrament of anointing with chrism, or holy oil (confirmation), is administered immediately after baptism. Holy unction is administered to the sick but not always as a last rite. The Holy Eucharist is the chief service on all Sundays and holy days, and all Orthodox churches believe and teach that the consecrated bread and wine are the body and blood of Christ. Purgatory is denied, but the dead are prayed for; and it is believed that the dead pray for those on earth. For justification both faith and works are considered necessary.

Government is episcopal. There is usually a council and a synod of bishops, over which a bishop presides. In a national church this synod is composed of bishops, and the presiding bishop is called archbishop or metropolitan. In certain instances he is called patriarch. There are 3 orders in the ministry:

deacons (who assist in parish work and in administering the sacraments), priests, and bishops. Deacons and priests may be either secular or monastic; candidates for the diaconate and the priesthood may marry before ordination, but they are forbidden to marry thereafter. Bishops are chosen from members of the monastic communities. All belong to the same monastic rule, that of St. Basil the Great, and are under lifelong vows of poverty, chastity, and obedience.

Church services are elaborately ritualistic. Of their worship Frank Gavin has said:

In the details of Eastern worship is a rough epitome of the history of Eastern Christendom: the *ikons*, about which a bitter controversy once raged; the service in the vernacular as against Latin; the existence of both a married and a celibate priesthood; the strong and passionate loyalty to the national allegiance evidenced by the provision of special prayers for the rulers by name—all these mark the characteristics, peculiarities, and contrasts with the customs of the West.

In the United States they pray for the president, Congress, the armed forces, and for all in places of lawful civil authority.

Membership statistics are confusing and often unreliable, inasmuch as membership seems to have different meanings in different Eastern churches. Infants are confirmed immediately after baptism and are given their first Communion, and are from that moment considered as communicant members of the church. *Parish* membership, however, is more frequently determined by the number of males over 21 than by communicants (the male head of each family is the voting member in the parish organization). There are probably well over 3,000,000 Orthodox church members in the United States.

It must be kept clear, however, that there are other members of other Eastern churches in the United States, who are not acknowledged as "Orthodox" at all. These are members and churches having no historic connection with valid, recognized, ancient Orthodoxy. To be Orthodox, a church must be under the jurisdiction of a historic patriarch or autocephalous synod. These irregular Eastern churches might be called autogenic, or self-starting, but they can never be called "Orthodox." There is frequently confusion in dealing with these irregular groups among the Eastern churches; almost any classification might be in error, at one point or another, but they can generally be classified in the following categories:

I. The Eastern Orthodox Churches which are in communion with the Patriarchate of Constantinople and with each other.

II. The ancient Eastern churches which are separated as a result of definitions reached during the first seven ecumenical councils.

III. The Uniat and the so-called Byzantine Catholic, or other churches in communion with Rome.

IV. The self-styled American Orthodox groups, which have no official connection, and which are not in communication, with either Roman or Eastern church authorities.

I.
Albanian Orthodox Diocese in America

The modern Albanian is the direct descendant of the ancient Illyrian who lived in the regions north of Greece bordering the Adriatic; the Albanian Orthodox Church in America is the spiritual descendant of the ancient ecclesiastical Western Illyricum or "sanctum Illyricum" (the Holy Illyria) of early Christianity and the early church, and it has suffered a bewildering series of persecutions and changes in the religio-political struggles of the area.

With the Peace of Constantine and the division of the Roman Empire, the Western Illyricum (the Western Balkans and the Adriatic Coast) were included in the Western Empire and the Western Church and patriarchate; it was ecclesiastically a part of the church of North Italy under the supervision of Ambrose, then bishop of Milan. Later the popes established exarchs (or primates) in Durazzo, the civil capital of Western Illyricum, and made them papal legates or "vicars" for the entire area. Then the East Roman, Byzantine (Greek) emperors, in A.D. 732, conquered the Illyrian provinces and placed their churches forcibly under the Patriarch of Constantinople. Much of the history of the Balkan region since then has been the history of their struggle to obtain religious independence and dignity.

Christianized by both Latin and Greek missionaries, Albania, as part of Illyricum, had both Latin and Greek Rite Christians—and still has, today. There were close ties with both Rome and Constantinople until the Moslem Arabs and Turks swept over the Eastern Empire; in 1478-79, the Turks became masters of Albania. Half of its people became Moslems, and a small minority remained divided between Latin Rite Christians in the North and Greek Rite Christians, subordinated to Constantinople, in the South. There followed four centuries of oppression, broken at last by the political and religious revolts of the nineteenth and twentieth centuries when Albania became independent and its people demanded a national church independent of Constantinople.

Meanwhile thousands of Albanians had emigrated to America. The Turkish rulers had long refused to allow the maintenance of Albanian language churches by the church authorities in Constantinople, and accordingly the Russian Greek Orthodox Catholic Church in America set up Albanian dioceses here under an Albanian archimandrite-administrator, the Right Rev. Theophan S. Noli, with a liturgy

translated into Albanian in 1908. With the outbreak of the Russian revolution these ties with the Russian church were severed, and Theophan Noli became the first bishop of a completely independent Albanian-Rite Church—a "mother church" which, strangely enough, spread its influence back into the motherland of Albania. Noli was consecrated in the Korche Cathedral in Albania as the Archbishop and Metropolitan of Durazzo, and Albanian candidates for the priesthood in America were ordained in Albania. He returned to America to establish a metropolitan throne, with its see in Boston. All Albanian Orthodox in the New World are under this see; it includes 13 organized territorial parishes and some thousands of unorganized, scattered communicants visited by priests on mission circuits. There are 45,000 to 50,000 Albanians in this country; perhaps half are Moslems, and most of the rest—from 12,000 to 15,000—are members of the Albanian Orthodox Church.

They have made outstanding contributions in liturgy, the most notable of which is the production of a liturgical literature in a language which has developed as a composite of ancient Pelasgo-Illyrian dialects, Latin, Greek, and Turkish. Their "Albanian Rite" liturgy actually preceded the liturgy of the Albanian Rite Church in Albania. Uniquely, this church has never depended upon the church of its native land. Thanks to Communism and the dropping of the Iron Curtain, communication between the two churches is no longer possible, but the influence of the American church remains.

A further liturgical contribution is found in the publication of liturgical books in English, including prayer books, Bible readings, and hymnals. Through this literature the traditional devotion to Christ and the Virgin, to prayer and the sacraments (especially the Eucharist and penance) has strengthened the faith and broadened the influence of this fiercely independent and deeply spiritual people.

The American Carpatho-Russian Orthodox Greek Catholic Church

The Carpatho-Russians are Carpatho in that their homeland is in the Carpathian Mountain regions of eastern Czechoslovakia; they are Russian because historically they and their homeland have been a part of the Russian nation, and their religious allegiances have been bound to the Russian and Orthodox churches. Their mother church endured for long years a strife between Eastern Orthodoxy and Roman Catholicism; under political pressure in the seventeenth century it became a Uniat church, with Eastern rites and customs but under the Uniat or "Union" plan, recognizing the supremacy of the Roman pope. The desperate struggle to separate from Rome and to become completely Eastern was transferred to the United States with the immigration of large numbers of their people, especially to our coal-mining and industrial areas. In 1891 the Rev. Dr. Alexis Toth, a Carpatho-Russian Uniat priest, led his church in Minneapolis back to the Orthodox Church, and with several other pastors and parishes was absorbed in the Russian Orthodox Church in America. In 1938 the new Carpatho-Russian Orthodox Greek Catholic Diocese was formed and the Rev. Orestes P. Chornock was elected bishop. The diocese was canonized by his Holiness Patriarch Benjamin I in Constantinople.

They now have 60 churches and an inclusive membership of approximately 80,000. Headquarters, a seminary, and a new cathedral have been established at Johnstown, Pennsylvania.

Bulgarian Eastern Orthodox Church

Before the outbreak of the Macedonian revolution in 1903 there was very little Bulgarian immigration to the United States; in 1940 there were only 9,000 Bulgarians resident here. Coming out of the Bulgarian Orthodox Church, which is the state church of the country, they brought with them memories of the long struggle for independence of that church from the domination of Constantinople. It was in 1872 that the Bulgarian Church won its freedom and self-government.

The church started in this country as the Bulgarian Orthodox Mission in 1909 and established a bishopric in 1938. It is attached directly to the Holy Synod of Bulgaria, with a membership made up of immigrants from Bulgaria, Macedonia, Thrace, Dobruja, and other parts of the Balkan peninsula. Services are in the Bulgarian language, and doctrine is in accord with that of other Eastern Orthodox churches.

Membership is reported at 75,389 members in 22 churches.

Greek Archdiocese of North and South America

Greeks arrived in the United States in increasing numbers between 1890 and 1914, coming from the Greek mainland, the Greek islands of the Aegean Sea, Dodecanese, Cyprus, Constantinople, Smyrna, and other sections of Asia Minor. They asked for and secured the services of Orthodox priests sent to them by the Holy Synod of Greece or the Ecumenical Patriarchate of Constantinople. Each priest maintained his relation with the synod or patriarchate from which he came; there was at first no central organization to unite them.

Following a period of confusion (1908-1922), during which jurisdiction of the American churches was shifted from the Ecumenical Patriarchate of Constantinople to the Holy Synod of Greece and then back again, an act known as The Founding Tome of 1922 established the Greek (Orthodox) Archdiocese of North and South America, consisting of 4 bishoprics under the supervision of the Archbishop Alexander and the

91

Patriarchate of Constantinople. Alexander's successor, Archbishop Athenagoras, was elected patriarch of Constantinople in 1948, and was succeeded in turn by Archbishop Michael and Archbishop Iakovos, the present incumbent.

Doctrine, polity, and worship are of the usual Eastern Orthodox patterns. There are 1,200,000 members in 325 churches, 250 parochial schools, 350 Sunday schools, a theological seminary at Brookline, Massachusetts, and a teacher's college for girls, known as St. Basil's Academy, at Garrison, New York.

The Romanian Orthodox Episcopate of America

There are about 150,000 Romanians in the United States, spread over 13 states and coming principally from the provinces of Transylvania, Banat, and Bucovina. Since April of 1929 the Romanian Orthodox parish churches of the United States and Canada have been united under the jurisdiction of the bishop of the Romanian Orthodox Episcopate (Diocese) of America, with headquarters in Jackson, Michigan. It has severed all relations with the Orthodox Church of Romania because of present political (Communist) conditions, but in matters of faith and doctrine this church recognizes the spiritual and canonical authority of the Holy Synod (House of Bishops) of the Orthodox Church of Romania, of which the titular bishop of the American diocese is a *de jure* member. In administrative matters the episcopate is an autonomous organization having the Church Congress, a yearly convention, as its supreme administrative body and a Council of the Episcopate as the executive body of the congress. The episcopate adheres to the same doctrine as all other Eastern Orthodox churches and respects the canon laws governing them all. There are 51 churches and 50,000 members.

Russian Orthodox Church

Eastern Orthodoxy came to what is now the Soviet Union with the baptism of Vladimir in A.D. 988. Government of the church at first was in the hands of metropolitans appointed or approved by the patriarch of Constantinople. About 500 years ago Job became the First Patriarch of All-Russia. This patriarchate was suppressed, and a Holy Synod was instituted during the reign of Peter the Great; the other Orthodox churches recognized this synod as being patriarchal in effect. From 1721 to 1917 the Holy Synod was made up of 3 metropolitans and other bishops from various parts of Russia, who sat in rotation at its sessions. A civil officer of the czar, known as the Chief Procurator of the Holy Synod, attended its sessions as the czar's representative, sitting at a small side desk. This pre-1917 church, like every public organization in Russia, was dominated by the czarist regime.

In 1917 dramatic changes were instituted by the Great Sobor, or church council. Administration was changed, the office of chief procurator was abolished, and plans were made to return to the old patriarchal form of government. The reforms were put into effect. As the Great Sobor held its sessions, however, the gunfire of the revolution was heard in the streets, and once the followers of Lenin had taken over the state, they immediately applied their Communist principles: separation of church from state, school from church; and restriction of church activity to worship alone. The patriarch and the synod resisted, but the government found some priests and a few bishops who were ready to support the new regime. These held a rigged assembly which deposed the patriarch, endorsed communism, and declared itself the governing body of the Russian church. Calling themselves the Renovated or Living Church, they changed the ancient disciplinary rules of the church and instituted liturgical reforms. With the support of the Soviet authorities who hoped thus to divide and weaken the church, they held control for several years. Although they misled some of the Russian people, they were never recognized by the great body of clergy or people. The government considered opposition to the Living Church a civil offense, and on this basis banished thousands of bishops, clergy, and laymen to hard-labor camps.

When the Germans invaded Russia, it was the aged metropolitan, later Patriarch Sergius who, in spite of the years of cruel persecution, called on his people to support the Soviet government in the defense of their country. This marked a turning point in the Soviet government's policy toward the church. Persecution gradually ceased; the patriarch's authority was recognized by the state. Many surviving clergy and bishops who had been banished to Siberia were permitted to return, and gradually the patriarchal administration became again the sole authority in the Orthodox Church of Russia.

The main missionary efforts of Russian Orthodoxy were directed toward the Moslem, Buddhist, animistic populations of Central Asia and Siberia. In the late nineteenth century an Orthodox mission was begun in Japan. Eight Russian Orthodox monks entered Alaska in 1792; they established headquarters at Kodiak and built there the first Eastern Orthodox Church in America. Twelve thousand natives were baptized within two years' time. Orthodox monks and bishops created an alphabet and printed a grammar in the Aleutian language, translated portions of the Bible, and built a cathedral at Sitka.

A chapel was built in the early years of the century at a Russian trading post near present-day San Francisco, in California. An episcopal see was established in San Francisco in 1872 and moved in 1905 to New York City, as Russian immigration brought thousands of Ortho- dox to the eastern states. Immigrants from other countries with Orthodox churches—Serbia, Syria, Greece—were for many years cared for by the Russian hierarchy in America. Many Orthodox from the old Austro-Hungarian empire, where a Uniat church had grown to impressive numbers, came to this country and found themselves in an embarrassing situation, being placed under the direction of Irish and German Roman Catholic bishops. (Uniat churches are described on pp. 97-98.) Torn between conflicting demands and loyalties, many of these Uniat parishes returned to the jurisdiction of the Russian Orthodox Church.

Hard days were ahead, however. The Russian revolution of 1917 cut off the financial support that had come from the mother church, which was now fighting for its life. The Living Church faction in Russia, supported by the Communist government, sent an emissary to secure control of the church property in the United States, and he succeeded by action in the civil courts in securing possession of the Russian cathedral in New York City. Further seizures were prevented by the declaration of the Russian Orthodox in America at a Sobor (church assembly) at Detroit in 1924 asserting its administrative, legislative, and judicial independence of Moscow. Since then this church has been an autonomous Orthodox church and has made great progress in the support and loyalty of its people. It now has 9 archbishops and bishops, and reports 755,000 members in 352 churches. Its official title is The Russian Orthodox Greek Catholic Church of America.

In addition to this Russian Orthodox jurisdiction (or administrative units), with its continuous history in this country since 1792, there are now 2 other Orthodox jurisdictions that have come to America within recent years. No doctrinal differences separate these 3 groups; their disagreement is exclusively on the question of recognizing the authority of the patriarch of Moscow. The Russian Orthodox Greek Catholic Church of America has declared itself ready to affirm its spiritual loyalty to the patriarch provided he will recognize its administrative and legislative autonomy, which he has refused thus far to do. The Russian Orthodox Church Outside Russia holds that the Moscow patriarchate has forfeited its right to be considered a true Orthodox Church because it accepts the authority of the atheist Soviet government. The Russian Orthodox Catholic Church, Archdiocese of the Aleutian Islands and North America, accepts the full authority of the patriarchate and is its representative in America.

This last church is comparatively small (no statistics are available) though it holds *de facto* occupancy of the old Russian cathedral in New York City, which passed into its hands when the former emissary of the Living Church faction made his submission to the patriarch's representative. It is governed by an exarch appointed by the patriarch; but its 2 latest appointees, coming from the Soviet Union, have been denied permanent residence by the United States government.

The third body, known as the Russian Orthodox Church Outside Russia, has a membership of Russian exiles. When armed resistance to the Soviet revolution was finally put down, many sought refuge abroad. A number of bishops and clergy gathered at Sremski Karlovici in Yugoslavia and there set up a synod to give spiritual leadership to these refugees. After World War II the immense increase in the numbers of Russian refugees (including the bishops of this synod) gathered in displaced persons camps led this synod to move its headquarters to Munich. Relief programs of the churches brought great numbers of these displaced persons to America, and the headquarters of the synod (now called the Russian Orthodox Church Outside Russia) was moved to New York City in 1952. Its complete rejection of the Moscow patriarchate conformed to the attitude of many of these new arrivals and kept them from uniting with the Russian church already established there. It is still growing as more displaced persons arrive, and it claims (as of 1951) some 55,000 members and (as of 1955) 81 churches. In addition, this church maintains bishops and clergy wherever Russian refugees are resettled —in Canada, South America, Australia, Africa, as well as in Europe. The synod president is Metropolitan Anastassy Gribanovski, who has his headquarters in New York City.

Serbian Eastern Orthodox Church

The church in Serbia from the seventh century to the thirteenth was under the jurisdiction of the Greek Patriarchate of Constantinople and became the independent National Serbian Church in 1219. It made notable contributions to art and architecture and played an important part in the Serbian struggle for independence all through the long period of Turkish invasion and domination (1389-1876), during which it suffered an unbelievable persecution.

Serbian immigrants to the United States, coming here more for political than economic reasons, began to arrive in large numbers about 1890. They worshiped at first in Russian churches, accepting the ministrations of Russian priests and the supervision of Russian bishops. The Serbian Patriarchate of Yugoslavia approved the organization of the Diocese of the United States and Canada in 1921, and sent its first bishop in 1926. Headquarters were established and still remain at St. Sava's Serbian Monastery at Libertyville, Illinois. There are today 61 parishes and 150,000 members. Doctrine and polity are in harmony with other branches of the Orthodox Church.

Syrian Antiochian Orthodox Church

Under the jurisdiction of the Patriarch of Antioch, this church is made up of former residents of Syria, Lebanon, Palestine, Egypt, and Iraq now living in the United States. At first they were under the supervision of a Syrian bishop appointed by the Russian archbishop in America. In September of 1934 the Patriarch of Antioch appointed the Very Rev. Archimandrite Antony Bashir as patriarchal vicar for all Syrian Orthodox people in North America, with authority to unite all parishes in America in one organization, to be known as the Syrian Antiochian Orthodox Archdiocese of New York and All North America. In February of 1936, at the request of both people and clergy, he was elected; and on April 19, 1936, he was consecrated at the Cathedral of St. Nicholas in Brooklyn as the Metropolitan-Archbishop of the Archdiocese.

Work is maintained in the United States, Canada, Mexico, and Central America; and there are 110,000 members enrolled in 80 churches in this country. Doctrine and polity are typically Eastern Orthodox.

Ukrainian Orthodox Churches

Eastern Orthodoxy was established as the state religion in the Ukraine by a unique procedure. In the tenth century Vladimir the Great, ruler of Kiev, sent investigators abroad to study the doctrines and rituals of Islam and Judaism as well as those of Christianity. They came back to report that the Eastern Orthodox faith seemed best suited to the needs of their people. Vladimir was immediately baptized in that faith, and by 988 the entire Ukraine population had become Orthodox Christian.

For more than 600 years the Ukrainian Church was under the jurisdiction of the Ecumenical Patriarchate of Constantinople. In 1686 it was placed under the supervision of the Russian Patriarch of Moscow. Rejecting the authority of Moscow after the 1917 revolution. Ukrainians in the United States are still engaged in a bitter dispute among themselves; attempts at union have been made, but to date have been unsuccessful. Three groups are in competition. The first, known as the Ukrainian Orthodox Church of the U.S.A., was formally organized in this country in 1919; Archbishop John Theodorovich arrived from the Ukraine in 1924. This group has 90 churches and 84,000 members. The second body is known as the Ukrainian Orthodox Church of America (Ecumenical Patriarchate), was organized in 1928, and had 36 churches and 44,350 members in 1951. The Rev. Joseph Zuk was consecrated as first bishop in 1932. His successor was the Most Rev. Archbishop Bohdan, who was consecrated by the order of the Ecumenical Patriarchate of Constantinople in 1937 in New York City. The third body is known as the Holy Ukrainian Autocephalic Orthodox Church in Exile. It broke from the Ukrainian Church in the U.S.A. in 1951 in a dispute over administrative matters and is made up largely of Ukrainian laymen and clergy who came to America after World War II. Two bishops came from Europe in 1954 to organize and administer the work of the church, which reports 4,500 members in 10 local churches.

Holy Orthodox Church in America (Eastern Catholic and Apostolic)

An interchurch movement rather than a denomination, this body was instituted in 1927-28 to present the Eastern liturgies in the English language, to offset the disadvantages of the use of foreign languages in America, and to establish an autocephalous Orthodox church in America for English-speaking people with American customs and traditions.

The movement stems from the authorization of the late Patriarch Tikhon of the Russian Orthodox Church and the acts of his successors to propagate

Orthodoxy among English-speaking people around the world. For its first 15 years in this country it was a program of translating, lectures, classes, and writings.

Services are based on the original liturgy composed by James, first bishop of Jerusalem, as abbreviated and arranged in the fourth century by John Chrysostom into the local usage it has today in all Orthodox bodies, varying only in local custom and language. This liturgy is used throughout the year with the exception of the weekdays of the Great Feast (Lent). The liturgy of Basil the Great is used 10 days of the year.

The faith and order of the Holy Orthodox Church in America rest on the Holy Scripture, holy tradition, the canons of the 7 councils, and the teachings of the anti-Nicene Fathers. Concessions have been made to Western custom in the installation of seats in its churches, in the use of organs and mixed choirs, and in conformity to the Western calendar with the single exception of Easter, which is celebrated according to the Julian calendar. It wishes to be known as an independent unit of the Holy Eastern Orthodox Greek Catholic Church, following strictly, however, the ancient traditional doctrines and dogmas of that church. In 1944 there were 211 members in 3 churches.

II.
The American Catholic Church (Syro-Antiochean)

Deriving its orders from the Syrian Patriarch of Antioch, this church is better known as the Jacobite Apostolic Church. It was organized in the United States in 1915 and is a Monophysitic body. Armenian Coptic and Jacobite Syrian churches are all Monophysitic. The word "Jacobite" was borrowed from the name of Jacobus Baradeus (died in 578), the Syrian monk who founded the movement. Historically, a bitter quarrel has raged between the Jacobites and the Orthodox Christians.

Syrian Jacobites are found in Mesopotamia, Iran, Syria, India, and Kurdistan, where they claim something over 80,000 members. It is from this section of the Middle East that they have migrated to America, where today they are found in 1 of 2 churches—the Assyrian Jacobite Apostolic Church with about 1,400 members and 4 churches, and the American Catholic Church (Syro-Antiochean), with 4,471 members in 39 churches. They use Eastern rites.

III.
Assyrian Orthodox Church

Fleeing the persecutions of the Moslem Turks, large numbers of Syrians came to the United States in 1893 and during the years immediately following. They were Christians belonging to the Assyrian Uniat Church, the Assyrian Protestant Church, the Assyrian Nestorian or Chaldean Church, and the Assyrian Jacobite Apostolic Church.

In 1907 one of the Assyrian groups raised the necessary funds to send Deacon Hanna Koorie of Paterson, New Jersey, to Jerusalem for ordination as priest and bishop. He returned to supervise the establishment of the Assyrian Jacobite Apostolic Church in Massachusetts, Rhode Island, New Jersey, and Michigan. This body is now known as the Assyrian Orthodox Church. It differs in liturgy from the Eastern Orthodox churches, but doctrine is based upon the Nicene Creed; it accepts the findings of only the first 3 ecumenical councils. It has 7 sacraments: baptism, confirmation, the Eucharist, penance, extreme unction, orders, and matrimony. Baptism is administered by pouring or immersion, and in the course of the baptismal ceremony, which comes several days after the birth of the child, the priest breathes upon the water and the child. The bread and wine at Holy Communion are considered to be the actual body and blood

96

of Christ. The Virgin Mary is venerated, as are the saints of the church.

The membership totaled 3,300 as of 1951, concentrated in 4 local churches. The Assyrian Jacobite Patriarch of Antioch stands at the head of the church government; he resides at Homs, Syria, and his word is final on all church matters. Under him serve the metropolitan, or mifrian; numerous iskiffs and mitrans; bishops, rhahibs, priests, and deacons. Every officer is elected to his office by vote of the people, which gives the body a democratic flavor.

Holy Apostolic and Catholic Church of the East (Nestorian)

The Holy Apostolic and Catholic Church of the East is the ancient Church of Persia, usually known in the West as the Nestorian Church. Its patriarch originally resided in Chaldea, near the Persian Gulf. From the fourth to the twelfth centuries it spread throughout most of Asia, and was confined to Asia until the days of its recent spread to the New World. It is estimated that at its peak this church had 10,000,000 members, but except for the church that still exists in India, this membership was almost completely exterminated by Genghis Khan and later by Tamerlane. Only a small remnant escaped to the mountains of Anatolia, to be driven from there by the Turks in 1916 and scattered in Iraq, Syria, and Persia.

This church claims as founders Thomas, Thaddeus, and Simon Peter from the Apostles, and Mari and Addai from the Seventy. Its theology stresses the two natures (or the duality) of Christ, holding that he was "man and God, two natures and two substances united in one person and will," and insists that Mary should not be granted the status or name of "Mother of God." ("Mary did not give birth to the divinity, but to the humanity, the temple of divinity.") Accordingly, she is not the mother of God, but the mother of

Christ. They hold that it was the man in Christ that died, not the God in Christ. It was for these beliefs that Nestorius was condemned by the Council of Ephesus in A.D. 431; however, he is still revered as a saint by his followers.

The American branch of this church began during the immigration wave of 1911, and nearly all its adherents have come to America during the last half century. In 1940 the head of the church, exiled in Iraq, also came to this country; he is Mar Eshai Shimun XXIII, Catholicos Patriarch of the Church of the East and of the Assyrians CXIX. In 1952 3,200 members were reported in 10 churches.

Eastern Rite (Catholic) Churches

Known both as Eastern Rite and Eastern Catholic churches, these churches recognize the pope as the supreme head of the church, but they differ from the Roman Catholic Church in their liturgies, rites, laws, and customs. They follow any one of 5 principle Eastern rites: Byzantine, Alexandrian, Antiochan, Armenian, or Chaldean—and are usually specified by the Eastern jurisdiction to which they are subject (Alexandria, Antioch, Jerusalem, or Constantinople). There are 3 Eastern Rite jurisdictions in the United States: Philadelphia, Stamford, and Pittsburgh, with a startling total of 685,746 members subject to one or another of the Eastern patriarchs appointed by Rome in Eastern homelands. There are an estimated 11,698,035 Eastern Rite Catholics throughout the world.

Uniat Churches

Uniat is a Russian-Polish word meaning "union"; the background and structure of the Uniat churches fulfill the intent of the word inasmuch as they are a union of Eastern and Western, Latin and Greek. Eastern in both thought and rite, they accept the authority of the Roman pope. Abroad, these churches are found in Russia, Romania, Armenia, Syria, and Abyssinia under the leadership of 9 Uniat patriarchs. A group of Carpatho-Russians in 1938 severed all connections with Rome, and the Uniat churches of Russia left Rome in 1946 to go over completely to the Russian Orthodox church. The Communist regime in the Balkan states has almost destroyed the influence and control of Rome in that area.

In the United States, Uniat churches are largely Ukrainian in membership; known as the Ukrainian (Roman) Catholic Church, they are separated from and independent of the churches abroad and seem increasingly restless of any Roman control. A dictate of the pope, forbidding the appointment of married priests, has not found acceptance here among either clergy or laity. The Roman Catholic Directory of 1948 reported 2 Uniat dioceses with 335 parishes.

IV.
The American Orthodox Church

In 1927 the Orthodox mother church in Russia, which at that time held precedence in the Americas, sought a federation of the various racial groups in the church here and the extension of the Orthodox faith among non-Orthodox Americans. The federation has still to be realized, but the second objective has been, at least in part, committed to the Society of St. Basil, organized in 1932 as the Orthodox Mission to the Americas. The archbishop-president, Aftimios Ofiesh, consecrated the late Ignatius Nichols as Titular Bishop of Washington and placed him in charge of the American work. For reasons of clarity the Basilian Fathers adopted the denominational title of the American Orthodox Church in 1940 and incorporated that year by act of the New York State legislature.

The Western rite is used in the vernacular according to the authorization of the Moscow Synod of 1870. It is claimed by this church that "American Orthodoxy is . . . not a derivative or imitative Orthodoxy, but is the latest local aspect of that eternal dispensation which began at Pentecost," and that while they are the smallest and youngest of American Orthodox organizations, they are nevertheless the "right-believing, right-teaching, and right-worshiping church as Christ left it in A.D. 33 . . . unchanged in faith and practice though considerably developed in its cultural and intellectual dimensions."

No statistics on work or membership are available.

The American Holy Orthodox Catholic Apostolic Eastern Church
(in Association with The Orthodox Catholic Patriarchate of America)

Instituted in 1932 and incorporated in 1933, this church is self-governing, "maintaining the Eastern Orthodox faith and rite for all men indiscriminately." Spiritually it "owns no head but the head of the Christian faith, Jesus Christ our Lord," but considers itself "inseparably joined in faith with the great church of Constantinople and with every other orthodox eastern church of the same profession." The Greek rite is used in all worship services, but it receives into Communion and affiliates with other churches of Eastern Orthodox persuasion and belief which desire to retain their national and individual characteristics.

Government is autocephalous; the archbishop does not acknowledge the authority or jurisdiction of any other church or bishop. He is responsible to the National Council, the supreme legislative, administrative, and judicial authority, which is made up of bishops, clergy, and laity. It meets every third year. Two lower ecclesiastical bodies, the Holy Synod and the Supreme Ecclesiastical Council, manage the affairs of the church between councils.

The work of the church is not only

religious but social and educational. It represents an effort, fairly successful, to draw together those of Eastern Orthodox faith into one group regardless of race, nationality, or language. A provisional synod was set up in 1935 to encourage co-ordination between the national groups in the various Eastern Orthodox churches, and the Patriarchal Holy Synod was fully established in March, 1951, in the state of New York. The church and patriarchate has 10 bishops, 25 clergy, 30 churches, and an inclusive membership of approximately 9,000 members.

EVANGELICAL CONGREGATIONAL CHURCH

Objecting to the "usurpation of powers in violation of the discipline" by bishops and district superintendents, 7 annual conferences and from 60- to 70,000 members of the Evangelical Association—later known as the Evangelical Church—withdrew from that body in 1894 to organize the United Evangelical Church. The two churches were reunited in 1922, but again a minority objected and remained aloof from the merger. The East Pennsylvania Conference, together with several churches in the Central, Pittsburgh, Ohio, and Illinois Conferences, continued their separate existence under the old name. This was later changed to the Evangelical Congregational Church.

Today the boundaries of the East Pennsylvania Conference are somewhat larger than at the time of the merger; the Midwest churches are joined in a Western Conference. They are, like their parent Evangelical Church, "Methodists in polity, Arminian in doctrine." There is emphasis upon the inspiration and integrity of the Bible and the "fellowship of all followers of Christ." There are annual and general conferences with equal lay and clerical representation, bishops and district superintendents, and an itinerant ministry. Pastors are appointed yearly by the annual conferences. Local congregations, as the name implies, have more freedom—especially in temporal matters—than congregations in either Evangelical or Methodist churches. The Board of Missions with two women's auxiliaries and two conference missionary societies supervise the home and foreign missionary programs. There are 34 missionaries abroad and 45 at home, and 156 nationals at work in various lands.

Large summer assemblies are held in 5 parks strategically located in the conferences. Church headquarters, the publishing house, the infirmary, the home for the aging, and the school of theology are located at Myerstown, Pennsylvania. There are nearly 30,000 members and approximately 170 churches.

EVANGELICAL COVENANT CHURCH OF AMERICA

Known until 1957 as The Evangelical Mission Covenant Church of America, this church traces its roots to the Protestant Reformation, to the biblical instruction of the Lutheran State Church of Sweden, and to the great spiritual awakenings of the nineteenth century. These three influences have in large measure shaped its development and are to be borne in mind in seeking to understand its distinctive spirit.

The Covenant Church adheres to the affirmations of the Protestant Reformation regarding the Holy Scriptures as the word of God and the only perfect rule for faith, doctrine, and conduct. It has traditionally valued the historic confessions of the Christian church, particularly the Apostles' Creed, while at the same time it has emphasized the sovereignty of the Word over all creedal interpretations. It has especially cherished the pietistic restatement of the doctrine of justification by faith as basic to its dual task of evangelism and Christian nurture, the New Testament emphasis upon personal faith in Jesus Christ as Saviour and Lord, the reality of a fellowship of believers which recognizes but transcends theological differences, and the belief in baptism and the Lord's Supper as divinely ordained sacraments of the church. While the denomination has traditionally practiced the baptism of infants, in conformity with its principle of freedom it has given room to divergent views. The principle of personal freedom, so highly esteemed by the Covenant, is to be distinguished from the individualism that disregards the centrality of the word of God and the mutual responsibilities and disciplines of the spiritual community.

The local church is administered by a board of laymen elected by the membership; it calls its ministers (ordained by the denomination) with the aid and guidance of the denomination's pastoral relations commission and the conference superintendent. There are 12 geographical districts known as regional conferences, each of which elects its own superintendent. The highest authority is vested in an annual meeting, which is composed of ministers and laymen elected by the constituent churches. An executive board, elected by the annual meeting, implements its decisions.

Missionaries are found in Africa (Belgian Congo), China (Formosa), Ecuador, Indonesia, and Japan. There are a number of educational institutions: the Canadian Bible Institute at Prince Albert, Saskatchewan, Canada; Minnehaha Academy at Minneapolis, Minnesota; Swedish Covenant Hospital School of Nursing and North Park College and Theological Seminary at Chicago, Illinois. There are also 2 homes for orphaned children, 2 sailors' homes, 2 hospitals, 10 homes for the aged. There are 58,371 adult members in 536 churches.

THE EVANGELICAL FREE CHURCH OF AMERICA

This church is composed of two bodies of Scandinavian background which united in 1950: the Free Church of America and the Evangelical Free Church Association. The Evangelical Free Church of America began with a number of small congregations which refused to join the merger in 1885 of the old Swedish Ansgarii Synod and the Mission Synod into the Swedish Evangelical Mission Covenant of America. It was a body of self-governing congregations, each free to establish its own doctrine; the several churches elected delegates to an annual conference, purely advisory in character. A society of ministers and missionaries was organized in 1894 to guide the denomination generally in doctrine and practice. This church brought 12,000 members and 200 churches into the 1950 merger.

The Evangelical Free Church Association was but slightly smaller at the time of the union, with 10,033 members and

51 churches. It was a Norwegian and Danish body which had grown out of the free-church movement in Norway in the nineteenth century. The increase of immigration from Scandinavia resulted in the organization of a number of Norwegian and Danish Free churches that were eventually brought together in eastern and western districts that were united in Chicago in 1910, still maintaining their identity in their work. The churches in these 2 districts elected delegates to an annual conference, which was the chief administrative body. No notice-able changes in either polity or doctrine —still left to the individual congregations—have been brought about by the union, which gives the new Evangelical Free Church of America a total strength of 32,480 members and 452 churches. There are today 13 district organizations (11 in the United States, 2 in Canada). Mission stations are established in Japan, the Philippines, Hong Kong, Belgian Congo, Singapore, Germany, and Venezuela. The denomination's Trinity Bible College and Seminary is located in Chicago.

THE EVANGELICAL UNITED BRETHREN CHURCH

The Evangelical United Brethren Church was born in a union at Johnstown, Pennsylvania, in 1946, merging bodies previously known as the Church of the United Brethren in Christ and the Evangelical Church. Both churches originated in Pennsylvania and were much alike in doctrine and polity.

Jacob Albright (1759-1808), founder of the Evangelical Church, was reared and confirmed a Lutheran and later became a Methodist exhorter. He began to preach in 1796 among the German people of Pennsylvania; while he had no intention of forming a new church, his work was so successful that an ecclesiastical organization was effected in 1803, and he was ordained as an elder. He brought his Methodist ideas and ideals to this organization—the circuit system was adopted and an itinerant ministry instituted. At the first annual conference held in 1807 Albright was elected bishop, and articles of faith and a book of discipline were adopted. The name Evangelical Association was approved by the first general conference in 1816.

Gradually, as the church spread, the German language was displaced by English. Missionary work under a society organized in 1839 was developed in the United States and Canada, Germany, Switzerland, Russia, Poland, Latvia, Africa, China, Japan, and Brazil. A division rent the church in 1891, resulting in the organization of the United Evangelical Church. It was not healed until 1922, when the 2 churches were reunited under the name of the Evangelical Church.

The body was Arminian in doctrine, closely resembling that of the Methodists. The deity of Jesus and his perfect humanity and the divinity of the Holy Ghost were stressed. There was strong emphasis laid upon the personal experience of salvation and Christian perfection; entire sanctification was based upon this perfection.

The polity of the church was connectional, democratic, and Methodistic. The quadrennial general conference elected the bishops of the church, who, however, were not ordained or consecrated as such; they presided at the general conference, which was a delegated body.

The Church of the United Brethren in Christ had a similar development. It began in the work of Philip William Otterbein, a German Reformed pastor who reached Pennsylvania in 1752 at the invitation of Michael Schlatter, a minister of the Reformed Church of Holland. Otterbein, already an ardent evangelist, joined with Martin Boehm, a Mennonite preacher, in an evangelistic work among the German settlers of Pennsylvania, Maryland, and Virginia. They held 2-day "great meetings" which produced thousands of converts but which seemed so irregular to Otterbein's fellow ministers that he left their fellowship to organize an independent congregation in Baltimore in 1774.

Neither Otterbein nor Boehm had any intention or desire to create a new denomination, but such a move became imperative. Other evangelistic preachers working with them held a conference in 1800 which resulted in the establishment of the United Brethren in Christ; Boehm and Otterbein were elected bishops. It was not so much a schism as a fellowship of evangelists; they held their first general conference in 1817 and in the conference ordered a confession of faith and a book of discipline printed in both German and English.

As had been the case in the Evangelical Church, doctrine followed Methodist and Arminian patterns, with stress upon the Trinity, the authority of the Scriptures, justification, regeneration, the Sabbath, and the future state. Modes in baptism and the Lord's Supper, accepted as sacraments, were left to local preference. There were the same Methodist quarterly, annual, and general conferences; but the ministry had only one order—that of elder. The defection of the Church of the United Brethren in Christ (Old Constitution) in 1889 constituted the only serious break in the ranks of this church up to the time of its union with the Evangelical Church.

The Evangelical United Brethren Church in 1959 had 763,380 members in 4,438 churches in the United States and Canada plus 39,584 members in European and Sierra Leone Conferences. The total membership is 802,964. They work and worship as one body and with no changes in basic doctrines or polities of either of the two merged churches. They believe in the sinful state of man and the saving grace of God—which gives them a firm basic doctrine long common to both groups. The sacrament of baptism is obligatory for membership, and the Lord's Supper is conceived "in a Calvinistic sense to provide the spiritual, yet nevertheless real, presence of Christ for the believer." It is usually celebrated quarterly. Liturgically, the church belongs to the free tradition; orders of worship are optional, but the *Book of Ritual* suggests forms, aids to worship, and liturgical material. The new hymnal also provides a wide selection of worship materials.

The church is divided into 34 annual conferences in North America, under which are local conferences supervised by conference superintendents. There are 7 bishops, who serve as general overseers in their respective areas and in the general church. The General Conference meets every 4 years and is the final authority in all matters pertaining to the work of the church. Laymen have equal representation in the annual and general conferences, and there is parity among the clergy—no ecclesiastical power is granted to anyone beyond the authority of ordination. All general church officers are elected quadrennially by the General Conference.

The General Council of Administration acts as a co-ordinating body, recommends benevolence budgets and appropriations, assembles and prints the reports and memorials of the General Conference. Various boards—publication, missions, pensions, education, and evangelism—function under the General Conference.

There are also commissions on church federation and union and Christian social action. The 2 denominational publishing

102

plants are the Otterbein Press at Dayton, Ohio, and the Evangelical Press at Harrisburg, Pennsylvania; there are also publishing establishments in Stuttgart, Germany, and Bern, Switzerland. Special home missions work is carried on in the Cumberland mountains of Kentucky; and Spanish-speaking missions are maintained in Florida and New Mexico. Foreign missionaries are stationed in Sierra Leone, West Africa, Nigeria, the Sudan, the Philippines, Brazil, Japan, Puerto Rico, Santo Domingo, and Ecuador. There are 18 Bethesda Deaconess hospitals in Germany, France, and Switzerland, with 1,000 deaconesses in residence.

The church supports 7 colleges and 2 theological seminaries, 3 children's homes, and 9 homes for the aged in the United States. There is also a seminary in Germany. The church maintains hospitals, clinics, schools, and agricultural work on the mission fields. The women of the church are organized in the Women's Society of World Service, composed of 3,220 societies and 110,000 members, who contribute over $1,000,000 a year to missionary work; the laymen are banded in a brotherhood, which supports the denomination's program; and the Youth Fellowship is unusually active. Overseas there are 4 conferences in Europe, and one each in Puerto Rico and West Africa.

EVANGELISTIC ASSOCIATIONS

Many religious bodies in the United States are of such a nature as almost to defy classification. Some are called churches which are not churches at all in the accepted sense of the word. Some known as associations or bands or societies should be called churches, yet for all practical purposes they are denominations. Nine of these have been grouped in this section as evangelical associations, inasmuch as they are, while separate and distinct from the churches, to be recognized by their common evangelistic nature and effort rather than by any ecclesiastical or doctrinal distinction. They are small groups, variously organized and supported, engaged primarily in evangelistic or missionary work.

Apostolic Christian Church (Nazarean)

The Apostolic Christian Church (Nazarean) began in this country with the arrival of a Swiss, S. H. Froehlich, about the year 1850. Froehlich went to work immediately among Swiss and German immigrants, founding a number of small churches among those nationalities in the Midwest. Many of the early members were former Mennonites.

Distinguished in doctrine chiefly by their insistence upon entire sanctification, the local churches are independent in polity but united in a loose organization. Nearly half the membership is found in Illinois; small bodies are found in nearly all the northern states from New England to the West Coast. They report 43 churches and 2,259 members.

Apostolic Christian Churches of America

The Apostolic Christian Church of America began with the labors of Benedict Weyeneth, a Swiss who came to America about 1847 and organized a number of Swiss-German churches. Its doctrine is based largely on the teaching of entire sanctification, aiming "solely at the saving of souls, a change of heart through regeneration, and a life of godliness guided and directed by the Holy Spirit." Members are noted for their pacifism; they will not bear arms but will engage in any service in support of the government "which is compatible with the teachings of Christ and the Apostles."

There are 8,345 members and 64 congregations, each of which is directed by an unpaid minister. There is currently a widespread interest in a closer unity and a more definite organization.

Church of Daniel's Band

One of the smaller sects of American Protestantism, the Church of Daniel's Band had 200 members in 4 churches in 1951. Incorporated at Marine City, Michigan, in 1893, it stresses evangelism, Christian fellowship, abstinence from all worldly excess, and religious liberty. It is quite similar to The Methodist Church in form and organization, and is generally believed to have grown out of the Methodist class meeting. It strives to revive primitive Wesleyanism, and the preaching of the church is strongly perfectionist. Sunday-school work is carried on in union schools with other churches. There is a small missionary work in Canada.

Church of God (Apostolic)

Organized in 1896 at Danville, Kentucky, by Elder Thomas J. Cox, this body was first known as the Christian Faith Band and was incorporated under its present name in 1919. Its members believe that admission to the church must be only after repentance for sin, confession, and baptism; they teach holiness and sanctification, practice foot washing, and observe the Lord's Supper with unfermented grape juice and unleavened bread.

The general assembly is the governing body; under it serve officers known as the apostle or general overseer, the assistant overseer, district elders, pastors, evangelists, and local preachers. The church is divided into districts, each with an annual ministerial conference. There are 600 members in 22 churches.

Church of God as Organized by Christ

A Mennonite preacher, P. J. Kaufman, withdrew from the Mennonite body in 1886 to protest against the ecclesiasticism of Protestantism and the lack of scriptural authority in Protestant organizations, and to found the Church of God as Organized by Christ. Kaufman and his followers held that membership in the church is not dependent on human choice but that all true Christians "have equal rights with all in the services and are members of His church." A spirit birth constitutes church membership; there is no formal joining of the church as other denominations know it. Ordination for church service is by Christ alone; but the ministry may, if it desires, be licensed and ordained for the purposes of public recognition.

Positively, members of this church teach repentance and "restitution so far as restitution is possible," nonresistance and complete obedience to Christ; they practice the sacraments of baptism, the Lord's Supper, and foot washing. Negatively, they stand opposed to "denominationalism, churchianity, or sectism," union meetings and interdenominational co-operation, tobacco, secret societies, going to courts of law, church schools and Sunday schools, revivals, emotionalism, theaters, amusements, fine clothing, jewelry, human traditions and creeds, and a "hireling ministry." There were 14 congregations and 2,192 members in 1938.

Hepzibah Faith Missionary Association

This is a loosely bound group of churches founded at Glenwood, Iowa, in 1892 for the purpose of preaching holiness and developing missionary and philanthropic work at home and abroad, and advocating the "establishing of independent, nonsectarian, full-salvation local churches and missions." It was reorganized in 1935 and again in 1948.

While there is a central executive

committee with headquarters at Tabor, Iowa, to supervise general activities, each church, called an assembly, maintains its own work, establishes its own polity, and keeps its own records. There is no formal statement of creed or belief; but the group as a whole is strongly conservative and evangelical, emphasizing the emotional aspects of the influence and power of the Holy Ghost. Members, known as communicants, are required to give evidence of a new birth and of acceptance of the teachings of Scripture, and must be amenable to group discipline. Many of them retain their affiliations with other churches. Ministers receive no salaries; they engage in other occupations and are in part supported by freewill offerings. Approximately 100 ministers, evangelists, and deaconesses are at work. Foreign missionary work, begun in 1894, is maintained in Japan, China, Africa, and India. There were 700 members and 20 assemblies in 1946.

Metropolitan Church Association

Springing from a revival in the Metropolitan Methodist Church of Chicago in 1894, this association was originated primarily to carry on a local evangelistic work in the poorer and more densely populated sections of the city. It has since grown into a widespread work in this country and abroad.

Foreign missionaries are now stationed in the central provinces of India, South India, the Union of South Africa, and Swaziland. Home missions efforts are found in Mexico and the Virgin Islands. A Bible school for the training of both home and foreign missionaries is located at Dundee, Illinois.

The founders of the association sought a return to the teaching of primitive Wesleyan holiness, and that emphasis is still strong. There is no creed "except such as may be found in the Scriptures themselves." Inasmuch as this is an offshoot of Methodism, its government closely resembles the Methodist pattern.

The association was chartered under the laws of Wisconsin in 1918 and has headquarters at Dundee, Illinois. There are 443 members in 15 churches.

Missionary Church Association

Evangelical and conservative, giving strong emphasis to foreign missions, this association was founded at Berne, Indiana, in 1898. Stressing the Person of Jesus Christ as the center of all Christian experience and life, its members believe that they have in the Acts and in the New Testament epistles the ideal patterns of Christian faith, evangelism; and church organization.

Prominent in their beliefs are the doctrines of the plenary inspiration of the Bible, the virgin birth and the deity of Jesus, the Atonement, the bodily resurrection of Christ, divine healing, premillenarianism, the eternal life of the just, and the everlasting punishment of the wicked. Baptism by immersion and open communion are practiced.

Local churches are quite independent in managing their own affairs, but they recognize the authority of a general conference made up of ministers, missionaries, and appointed lay delegates, which is held biennially. Administrative authority is vested in 4 department boards: home, foreign, publications, and Bible college. A general board of 15 supervises the work of the whole church. The association operates the Fort Wayne Bible College which offers degree courses in preparation for the ministry and the mission field. The majority of its missionaries abroad serve in the Dominican Republic, Ecuador, Haiti, Hawaii, Jamaica, and Sierra Leone, under its own board; the remainder serve under various boards, chiefly that of the Christian and Missionary Alliance. There are 7,577 members and 118 churches.

Pillar of Fire

The Pillar of Fire originated from the evangelistic efforts of its founder, Mrs.

Alma White. The wife of a Methodist minister in Colorado, Mrs. White often preached from her husband's pulpit. Her fervent exhortations on regeneration and holiness—and especially her habit of organizing missions and camp meetings on her own authority—brought her into sharp conflict with the bishops and other leaders of Methodism, and she withdrew to become an evangelistic free lance. She established the Pentecostal Union in 1901 and changed the name to Pillar of Fire in 1917.

Mrs. White's first headquarters were located at Denver; they were later moved to Zarephath, near Bound Brook, New Jersey. In both Denver and Zarephath the body has a college, preparatory school, Bible seminary, radio station, and publishing plant. Other schools are located in Cincinnati, Los Angeles, Jacksonville, and London.

Modernism in theology is condemned by Pillar of Fire; its teaching is based upon primitive Wesleyanism, with doc-trines on the inspiration and inerrancy of the Scriptures, repentance, justification, second blessing holiness, premillennialism, and future judgment. Sacraments include baptism and the Lord's Supper; marriage is a "divine institution."

Mrs. White was the first bishop of Pillar of Fire; on her death authority passed to her 2 sons. The membership is divided into 4 classes: probationary, associate, regular, and full, with only regular and full members being allowed to vote on administrative matters. There are deacons and deaconesses, and both men and women are ordained as ministers; there are also consecrated deaconesses, licensed preachers, and missionaries, and as in Methodism, presiding elders (district superintendents) and bishops. Considerable literature is printed and distributed in the United States, and there are regular broadcasts from WAWZ, Zarephath, and KPOF, Denver. There were approximately 5,000 members and 61 branches as of 1948.

FEDERATED CHURCHES

Federated churches in the United States are largely a rural or village phenomenon, strongest in New England and the West. They are churches, 2 or more in number and representing different denominations, which unite for mutual conduct of their work while continuing their connections with the denominations involved. The first federated church of which we have any record was formed in Massachusetts in 1887; another was founded in Vermont in 1899. By 1936 there were 508 federated churches in 42 states, with 88,411 members. There may be double that number now; further statistics are unavailable because of the lack of any national organization or office. Dr. Ralph Williamson, conducting a survey for Cornell University, listed over 800 federated churches in 1952.

Economic pressure, conviction that the community is overchurched, flow of population, the inspiring example of the consolidated school, and the increased cost of church maintenance have been influential in forcing such federations. Ralph A. Felton in *Local Church Co-operation in Rural Communities* (Home Missions Council, 1944) describes the usual circumstances under which the average federated church is created:

Two churches in the same locality begin to have financial difficulties. Their memberships are too small to carry on thriving individual churches. They feel that if they could unite into one local congregation they could provide a more efficient religious program. Neither church wants to give up its affiliation with its denomination. For years they have been saying. "We should unite, but who's going to give up?" Finally they unite locally, hire one minister instead of two, but continue their separate "overhead" or denominational affiliations. The two or more separate churches thus become a federated church.

Usually there are joint religious services and a common Sunday school, and policy is determined by a joint official board. In some cases one minister is chosen to serve continuously; in others the minister is chosen alternately from the denominations represented. In approximately half the federated churches in this country all the Protestant churches in the community have entered the federation. Presbyterians seem to have the highest percentage of co-operation, with Congregationalists and Christians, Methodists, and Baptists following in that order. There is still a real conflict of loyalties in the federated churches; its conclusion depends upon a slow educational process. There is a noticeable trend toward eventual denominationalization. Majority groups have a way of absorbing minorities; and usually when denominationalization comes, people go to the denomination that continues to provide a minister. It is also clear that if a federated church lasts 5 years, it is seldom abandoned.

Doctrine, polity, and membership requirements correspond in some cases to the standards of the denominations included; in other instances they are completely independent. No blanket statement is possible in these matters.

FIRE BAPTIZED HOLINESS CHURCH

A Negro Pentecostal sect, this church was for the first 10 years of its existence a part of the white Fire Baptized Holiness Association of America; the Negro membership separated in 1908. In 1922 it became the Fire Baptized Holiness Church of God.

This church teaches the standard Pentecostal and holiness doctrines of repentance, regeneration, justification, sanctification, Pentecostal baptism, speaking with other tongues, divine healing, and the premillennial Second Coming. It stands opposed to the "so-called Christian Scientists, Spiritualists, Unitarians, Universalists and Mormons." Adventism, immorality, antinomianism, the annihilation of the wicked, the glorification of the body, and "many other modern teachings of the day" are denounced as false, wicked, and unscriptural. Government is by a bishop, 2 overseers, a general secretary, treasurer, and a board of trustees. Ruling elders, ordained ministers, and pastors are in charge of local churches; and a general convention is held yearly. In 1940 6,000 members were reported in 300 churches. Headquarters are in Atlanta, Georgia.

THE FIRE BAPTIZED HOLINESS CHURCH (WESLEYAN)

Preaching on the doctrine of holiness inspired the organization of this church about the year 1890; its first members were dissenters within the Methodist churches of southeastern Kansas. They called themselves at first the Southeast Kansas Fire Baptized Holiness Association; the present name was adopted in 1945.

Doctrine is primitive Wesleyan, emphasizing sanctification and complete holiness. The church government and organization follow the Methodist epis-copal pattern, and there is strong emphasis upon evangelism. There are 968 members in 53 churches.

FREE CHRISTIAN ZION CHURCH OF CHRIST

Led by E. D. Brown, a local Methodist missionary, a small group of Methodist and Baptist Negro ministers formed this church in 1905 at Redemption, Arkansas. They objected to the taxing of any church membership to provide support for any ecclesiastical organization, feeling that the care and relief of the needy and the poor were the first responsibility of the church. Such relief activities characterize their local churches today.

Doctrine is completely Methodist, and so is government except for minor titles and details. Chiefs or superintendents perform the functions of bishops; a chief pastor is chosen as top administrative officer, making all assignments to pastorates and appointing all church officers. Pastors and deacons head local churches and are responsible for the aid of the poor in their congregations. Laymen share in the conduct of the churches and in the annual General Assembly. The latest membership report (1957) listed 18,989 members in 728 churches.

FRIENDS

With a membership in the United States and Canada of only 120,492 and with 193,481 around the world, the Religious Society of Friends, better known as Quakers, has had a deep and lasting influence upon Western society. Contributions in both religious and humanitarian spheres have won the Quakers universal respect and admiration, and their amazing history and loyalty to their quiet faith offer a challenge and inspiration seldom paralleled among the churches.

Their vicissitudes and victories began with George Fox (1624-91), a British "seeker" after spiritual truth and peace. Failing to find such in the churches of his time, Fox found them in a new, intimate, personal relationship with Christ. He said: "When all my hopes in [churches and churchmen] were gone . . . then I heard a voice which said, 'There is one, even Christ Jesus, that can speak to thy condition.'" This is the Inner Voice or Inner Light of Quakerism, based upon the description of John 1:9—"the true Light, which lighteth every man that cometh into the world"—a voice available to all men, having nothing to do with outward forms or ceremonies, rituals or creeds. Every man to the Quaker is a walking church; every heart is God's altar and shrine.

Quakerism was revolutionary, and it was treated as revolution by the state Church of England. To tell this united state and church that they were both wrong, that their theology and dogma meant nothing, that men need not attend the "steeple houses" to find God, and that it was equally wrong to pay taxes in support of state church clergymen—this was rebellion.

Fox and his early followers went even further. They not only refused to go to church but insisted upon freedom of speech, assembly, and worship; they would not take oaths in court; they refused to go to war; they doffed their hats to no man, king or commoner; they made no distinction among people in sexes or social classes; they condemned slavery and England's treatment of the prisoner and the insane. The very names they took—Children of Truth, Children of Light, Friends of Truth, and finally the Religious Society of Friends—roused ridicule and fierce opposition. Fox, haled into court, advised one judge to "tremble at the Word of the Lord," and heard the judge call him "Quaker." It was derision, but it was not enough to stop them. Persecution unsheathed its sword.

The Quakers were whipped, jailed, tortured, mutilated, murdered. Fox spent 6 years in jail; others spent decades, dying there. From 1650 to 1689 more than 3,000 suffered for conscience' sake, and 300 to 400 died in prison. Thanks to that persecution they prospered, founding the society in 1666. When Fox died, there were 50,000 Quakers.

Some were already in America. Ann Austin and Mary Fisher arrived in Massachusetts from Barbados in 1656, were promptly accused of being witches and deported. Two days later 8 more came from England. Laws were passed hastily to keep them out; the whipping post worked overtime and failed. Four were hanged in Boston. Quakers kept coming into New England, New York, New Jersey, Maryland, Virginia, and Pennsylvania. Rhode Island and Pennsylvania welcomed them from the start. The long horror in the communities that did not welcome them ended with the passage of the Toleration Act of 1689.

With Fox's death and the Act a new phase began; persecution waned and died—and so did a great deal of Quaker zeal. They settled down, looked within rather than without, and began enforcing discipline on their membership so strictly that they became in fact a "peculiar people." Members were disowned or dismissed for even minor infractions of the discipline; thousands were cut off for "marrying out of Meeting." Pleasure, music, and art were taboo; sobriety, punctuality, and honesty were demanded in all directions; dress was painfully plain, and speech was biblical. They were different and dour; they gained few new converts and lost many old members.

Yet there were lights in this period of quiet. The meeting organization and community life became well organized. Closely knit family life was emphasized. It was a time of cultural creativeness and mystical inwardness. The period of withdrawal was one in which Quaker philanthropy became widely respected and even admired; their ideas on prison reform began to take effect. Quaker schools increased; as early as 1691 there were 15 Quaker boarding schools in England.

In 1682 William Penn came to Philadelphia. He sat under an elm at Shackamaxon and made a treaty with the Indians—the "only treaty never sworn to and never broken." Treated like human beings, the Indians reacted in kind. If all our cities had been Philadelphias and all our states Pennsylvanias, our national history would have been vastly different.

But even here the holy experiment had to end. Quakers controlled the Pennsylvania legislature until 1756, when they refused to vote a tax to pay for a war against the Shawnees and the Delawares and consequently stepped down and out of power.

Some few "fighting Quakers" went to battle in the American Revolution, but they were few; most of them remained pacifists. They worked quietly for peace, popular education, temperance, democracy, and against slavery. In 1688 the Friends of Germantown, Pennsylvania, said that Negro slavery violated the Golden Rule and encouraged adultery; they protested against the "traffic in the bodies of men" and called it unlawful. Their first attitude of toleration changed slowly to one of outright opposition; it took nearly a century for the Quakers to rid their society of slavery, but they did it years in advance of any other religious body in America. Sellers or purchasers of slaves were forbidden membership in the society by the close of the eighteenth century. Persistently all across the years the Quakers dropped their seeds of antislavery agitation into the body politic. First John Woolman and then the poet Whittier wielded tremendous influence in the fight; and once the Civil War was over, they threw their strength into such organizations as the Freedman's Aid Society. Ever since, they have been active in education and legislative protection for the free Negro.

Divisions arose within their ranks during these years: the Hicksites separated in 1827, the Wilburites in 1845, and the Primitives (a small group now extinct) in 1861. Other Wilburite separations came many years later, among them Iowa in 1887 and North Carolina in 1904.

The twentieth century thus far has been a century of Quaker unity and outreach. A Five Years Meeting was organized in 1902, merging a large portion of the pastoral yearly meetings. The 2 Philadelphia meetings, separated since 1827, were united in 1955. In the same year the two New York Yearly Meetings were merged, and the three Canada Yearly Meetings came together to form one body. Nine Quaker colleges have been built and strengthened; all but 2 of them are coeducational. On all levels Quaker schools have drawn students from other communions; their ideal of education for character is becoming increasingly popular.

In 1917, before the guns of World War I had stopped firing, Friends from all branches of the society were at work in the American Friends Service Committee in relief and reconstruction efforts abroad. The A.F.S.C. remains today one of the most effective of such agencies in

the world. Its volunteers erected demountable houses, staffed hospitals, plowed fields, reared domestic animals, and drove ambulances. Famine relief and child-feeding programs were instituted in Serbia, Poland, Austria, Russia, and Germany; at one time the Friends were feeding more than 1,000,000 German children every day; Greek refugees, earthquake victims in Japan, needy miners' families in Pennsylvania, West Virginia, and Kentucky were helped. Thousands would have perished but for the A.F.S.C.

Quakers drove ambulances and served in the medical corps of both world wars, and some were in combat; probably more young Quakers volunteered or accepted military service in these conflicts than resisted on grounds of religious principle. They also worked to relieve our displaced Japanese-Americans, and they co-operated with the Brethren and Mennonites in locating our conscientious objectors in work of real importance on farms, in reformatories, hospitals, and insane asylums. They were in Spain soon after the outbreak of the Spanish Civil War and later fed the child victims in Spain, southern France, Italy, Austria, Holland, North Africa, and Finland. In one year, 1945, they sent 282 tons of clothes, shoes, bedding, and soap to Europe and still more to China and India. Counting gifts, both of cash and materials, the income of the A.F.S.C. is apt to exceed $4,000,000 annually. At home and abroad summer camps of young volunteers have inspired an incalculable good will among nations and minority groups within nations.

Nor have they been satisfied with work merely in relief. Peace conferences have been a prominent part of their work, conferences ranging from local to international and covering all age groups. Lake Mohonk in New York was founded by a Friend. Scores of youth conferences and camps at home and in foreign fields testify to their devotion to the way of Christ; it is little wonder that they are known as a "peace church."

Worship and business in the society are conducted in monthly, quarterly, and yearly meetings. The monthly meeting is the basic unit, made up of one or more meetings in a neighborhood. It convenes each week for worship and once a month for business. It keeps records of membership, births, deaths, and marriages; appoints committees; considers queries on spiritual welfare; and transacts all business of the group. Monthly meetings in a district join 4 times a year in the quarterly meeting to stimulate spiritual life and to pass on whatever business they feel should be brought to the attention of the yearly meeting. The yearly meeting corresponds to a diocese in an episcopal system; there are 25 of them in the United States and Canada. They are in touch with Friends all over the world and have standing committees on such subjects as publications, education, the social order, missions, peace, charities, and national legislation; they allocate trust-fund incomes and generally supervise the work of the society.

Group decisions await the "sense of the meeting." Lacking any unity of opinion, the meeting may have a "quiet time" for a few minutes until unity is found, or it may postpone consideration of the matter or refer it to a committee for study. Minorities are not outvoted but convinced. Every man, woman, and child is free to speak in any meeting; delegates are appointed at quarterly and yearly meetings to ensure adequate representation, but they enjoy no unusual position or prerogatives. Women have as much power as men and hold a position of absolute equality in Quaker polity.

There are, contrary to popular misunderstanding, church officers—elders and ministers—among the Quakers; they are chosen for recognized ability in spiritual leadership, and they, too, stand on equal footing with the rest of the membership. All members are ministers to the Quaker. A few full-time workers are paid a modest salary, and "recorded" ministers serving as pastors in those meetings having programed worship also receive salaries.

Quaker worship is of two kinds: programed and unprogramed. The two, however, are not always distinct. The former more nearly resembles a simple Protestant service, but there are no rites or outward sacraments. While believing in spiritual communion, partaking of the elements is thought unnecessary. In the unprogramed meetings there is no choir, collection, singing, or pulpit; the service is devoted to quiet mediation, prayer, and communion. Any vocal contributions are spontaneous. There is no uniform practice; some of the so-called "churches" greatly prefer to be called "meetings."

In business sessions there is often frank inquiry into the conduct of business, treatment of others, use of narcotics or intoxicants, reading habits, and recreation. No true Quaker gambles, plays the stock market, bets, owns race horses, or engages in raffles, lotteries, or the liquor business. All controversy is avoided. Some follow conservative religious or theological patterns and others are liberal; all are guided by the Inner Light.

The Inner Light is highly important in Quaker belief. Grace, power from God to help man resist evil, is to Quakers universal among all men. They seek not holiness but perfection—a higher, more spiritual standard of life for both society and the individual—and they believe that the truth is unfolding and continuing. They place high evaluation on the Bible but try to rely on individual fresh guidance from the Spirit of God which produced the Bible, rather than to follow only what has been revealed to others. Some modern groups accept the Bible as the final authority in all religious matters.

Rufus Jones says:

They believe supremely in the nearness of God to the human soul, in direct intercourse and immediate communion, in mystical experience in a firsthand discovery of God. . . . It means and involves a sensitiveness to the wider spiritual Life above us, around us, and within us, a dedication to duty, a passion for truth, and an appreciation of goodness, an eagerness to let love and the grace of God come freely through one's own life, a reverence for the will of God wherever it is revealed in past or present, and a high faith that Christ is a living presence and a life-giving energy always within reach of the receptive soul.

Quakers are pacifist-minded, and many oppose all forms of war; many still refuse to take oaths. (The Quaker passion for peace persists, though the pacifist sentiment seems to be declining; there were 9,000 Quakers in uniform in World War II, many of them assigned, however, to alternative or noncombatant service.)

Marriage is not necessarily a ceremony to be performed by a minister; in cases where the traditional Quaker marriage is observed, the bride and groom simply stand before a meeting and make mutual vows of love and faithfulness and are thereby married. In certain sections of the country the pastor of the meeting officiates.

The Friends have never been great proselytizers; they depend almost entirely upon birthright membership and membership by "convincement." In many of their bodies, though not in all of them, every child born of Quaker parents is declared a member of the society. This has resulted in a large number of nominal or paper members who contribute little; efforts are being made to correct this custom by establishing a junior or associate membership for children. This reliance upon birthright membership, plus the "purges" of membership which expelled hundreds for offenses against their discipline, has seriously depleted their numbers. In the United States and Canada they now

have 120,492 members; abroad, scattered from Great Britain to the Far East, there are 72,989 Quakers. There are 25 yearly meetings in America, including one in Canada, one in Cuba, one in Jamaica, and a small group in Mexico. There are also 25 yearly meetings overseas.

If the Friends were ever "exclusive" they are not now; a world outreach has been evident and growing in recent years. The Five Years Meeting and the Friends' General Conference are members of the World Council of Churches. The Five Years Meeting and Philadelphia Yearly Meeting belong to the National Council of Churches. The General Conference has membership in this body under advisement. A Friends World Committee for Consultation, organized at Swarthmore, Pennsylvania, following the Second World Conference of Friends in 1937, functions as an agent or clearinghouse for the interchange of Quaker aspirations and experiences by way of regional, national, and international intervisitation, person-to-person consultations, conferences, correspondence, and a variety of publications. The committee has headquarters in Birmingham, England, and offices in Oslo, Norway, Philadelphia, Pennsylvania, and Wilmington, Ohio. The American section has helped some 50 small Friends groups in the United States to monthly meeting status. The F.W.C.C. is a nongovernmental agency under the Economic and Social Council of the United Nations and through co-operation with the A.F.S.C. helps to operate a program at the U.N. Headquarters to forward world peace and human brotherhood. Something of a world brotherhood, or "Franciscan Third Order," has been set up in the organization of the Wider Quaker Fellowship, in which non-Quakers in sympathy with the Quaker spirit and program may participate in the work of the Friends without leaving their own churches or coming into full Quaker membership. This is not so much an organization as it is a "fellowship of kindred minds—a way of life, a contagion of spirit"; it has 4,200 members, 360 of whom live abroad.

Religious Society of Friends (General Conference)

This is a national organization of 7 yearly meetings (Baltimore, Canada, New England, Illinois, Indiana, New York, and Philadelphia). It was established in 1868 as a Sunday-school conference and matured in 1900 as a general conference for fellowship across yearly meeting boundaries and as an instrument for implementing the social testimonies of the society. One of its main features is a biennial conference; in 1958 there was a registration of 2,800 at this conference, about one third of whom were children and young people. There are currently over 29,000 members in the General Conference, a fraction of whom also belong to the Five Years Meeting described below; this is explained by the fact that Canada, New York, and New England carry dual membership in the General Conference and the Five Years Meeting.

Known in the early days as Hicksites, these people had Elias Hicks as their leader; Hicks was a rural Long Island Quaker whose liberal and rational theological views brought him into conflict with those of more orthodox and evangelical persuasion. The division came in 1827; basically, while it had personal emphases, the split was due to the widespread nineteenth-century conflict between liberalism and rationalism on the one hand and an orthodoxy based on Methodist ideas of evangelism and salvation on the other. Two thirds of the Philadelphia Yearly Meeting withdrew with the Hicksites (a nickname never officially adopted by any Quaker group) and similar divisions followed in New York, Ohio, Indiana, and Baltimore

yearly meetings. A second series of separations resulted from the Wesleyan-Methodist influence, led by Joseph John Gurney and John Wilbur (see Religious Society of Friends [Conservative], below).

Important steps are being taken toward reunion among these groups, and there are indications that they may be successful. Yet, as the old differences heal in one direction, another division seems imminent: an Association of Evangelical Friends now claims about 20,000 members, or about one sixth of American Quaker membership, advocating fundamentalism and an emphasis on primitive Christianity which is not shared by all Quakers. How serious this movement is remains to be seen, but the Quaker witness and action remains as vital as ever. There are currently in the General Conference, 28,617 members in 229 churches.

Society of Friends (Five Years Meeting)

With 66,914 members in 1959, this is the largest single Quaker body in the United States. (The largest yearly meetings in the world are East Africa, with over 29,022 members, and London, with 21,643.) Of the 25 yearly meetings 13 were united in the Five Years Meeting in 1902; two of them—Kansas and Oregon—later withdrew, and Ohio and Philadelphia never joined. Constituent member meetings are Baltimore, California, Indiana, Iowa, Nebraska, New England, New York, North Carolina, Western (Indiana), Wilmington, Ohio, and Canada and 3 yearly meetings abroad —East Africa, Cuba, and Jamaica—with a somewhat different status. They work together in many departments—such as missionary service and in the production of Sunday-school materials—and while each yearly meeting in the body is autonomous, they come together for spiritual stimulation and conference every 5 years.

Religious Society of Friends (Conservative)

Known also as Wilburites, this group represents a second serious division. It resulted from the preaching of Joseph John Gurney, a British evangelical Quaker who came to America preaching doctrine which conservative John Wilbur of Rhode Island considered a menace to Quakerism, advocating the final authority of the Bible and acceptance of the doctrine of the Atonement, justification, and sanctification. Wilbur felt that this meant the substitution of a creed for the inner experience of the heart; with his followers he broke ranks to establish new yearly meetings in Kansas, Iowa, Canada, New England, Ohio, and North Carolina between 1845 and 1904.

Their doctrinal pattern was that "set forth by the Society in the beginning"; it was a movement back to the earliest and most conservative Quakerism. In New England in 1945 and in Canada in 1955, the Wilburite controversy was resolved at last in the reunion of all Friends in those areas, but elsewhere the division persists. There are 1,894 Wilburites in the United States.

HOUSE OF DAVID

Benjamin Purnell, who founded the House of David at Benton Harbor, Michigan, in 1903, claimed to be the seventh messenger prophesied by the book of Revelation; the other six, of whom Johanna Southcott (1792) was the first, had all been British. Purnell set up his Benton Harbor colony as a "commonwealth, according to apostolic plan" and was accepted there as the supreme ruler over all the community's spiritual and temporal matters. All who joined the colony put their earthly funds and possessions into the commonwealth treasury and contributed their work and services thenceforth to the cause. They lived in anticipation of the ultimate establishing of the kingdom of God on this earth; Purnell therefore called them "Israelites" and his movement an ingathering, because they were the direct lineal descendants of the 12 lost tribes of Israel, to be restored at the last days to their rightful places as judges and rulers in the kingdom of God.

Charges of dishonesty and immorality were brought against "King Benjamin" Purnell, and he died at the height of the scandal just before the supreme court of Michigan brought in a verdict in his favor; the movement, however, survived and continues on the original location. There are about 350 members at the immediate headquarters and other members in Australia, New Zealand, England, Ireland, Scotland, and in all states in the union. The colony is financed by the sale of produce from the farms, dairies, vineyards, greenhouses, cold-storage and fruit-preserving factories, and other industries and shops of the members. They are strict vegetarians, and they never shave their heads or faces. Their traveling baseball teams and band have brought them national publicity.

Immortality of the natural body is the bulwark of their belief, with certain interpretation of the Scriptures as proof. They find that automobiles, telephones, radios, and motion pictures are prophesied in the Bible as signs of the end of the evil powers and of Satan's kingdom, yet an elaborate picnic ground and entertainment area is maintained at Colony Park, east of Benton Harbor, offering everything from rodeos and dancing to billiards and midget auto rides. The custom of letting the hair grow long is based upon "what Jesus did" and also is done because in the Bible man is the head of the woman and the heads of women must never be

114

"uncovered" according to the Nazarene law.

The present church is controlled and directed by a board of directors with full authority. The community shows no signs of dwindling and disappearing as other such communities have and seems to enjoy a peaceful and prosperous existence.

INDEPENDENT ASSEMBLIES OF GOD

A holiness and Pentecostal group, this is more an unorganized association or fellowship of Pentecostal ministers than a denomination. Sometimes called "Philadelphia" churches, they have a Swedish background and work closely with the Swedish Pentecostal Movement, with which they conduct an extensive missionary program. No statistics have been available on their membership or work in the United States, but it is claimed that their missionary church in Brazil is the largest Protestant movement in that country, having "close to half a million followers [and] really converted people."

Doctrine is, of course, Pentecostalist, and government follows the loosely local autonomy of other Pentecostal churches and assemblies.

INDEPENDENT CHRISTIAN CHURCHES

The churches and members of the Independent Christian Churches make up not a denomination but a brotherhood; there is no formal organization other than that in the local congregations, and there are no denominational societies, officials, or boards. This is a group of churches allied usually with the Disciples of Christ, with a few congregations of the Churches of Christ, who preach and teach a conservative, fundamentalist theology which they feel is being neglected, especially among the Disciples. Their doctrine in general agrees with that of the Disciples and the Churches of Christ, stressing the divinity of Christ, the agency of the Holy Spirit in conversion, the Bible as the inspired word of God, future rewards and punishments and God as a prayer-answering deity. They maintain that "all ordinances should be observed as they were in the days of the apostles" and observe the Lord's Supper in open Communion every Sunday.

No official membership survey has ever been made, due to the unusual nature of the brotherhood, but various approximations have been made. These approximations are questionable in accuracy. There are said to be between 750,000 and 1,250,000 members in something over 3,000 independent congregations. (These congregations are still generally regarded as either Disciples of Christ or Churches of Christ.) The group supports at least 32 small Christian Bible colleges in different sections of the country; has over 450 missionaries at work operating dispensaries, hospitals, and Bible colleges; and circulates huge quantities of evangelical literature. Their publishing house—The Standard Publishing Foundation—is located at Cincinnati, Ohio.

INDEPENDENT CHURCHES

It is difficult, if not impossible, to classify properly all those churches in the United States calling themselves independent. Generally they may be identified as churches not controlled by any denominational or ecclesiastical organization, but even this does not hold in all cases. The following groupings are possible:

1. Churches called union, community, nondenominational, undenominational, or interdenominational. Community and nondenominational churches together constitute nearly one half of the number of so-called independent churches.

2. Churches using a denominational name but working without denominational supervision.

3. Churches organized by individuals: holiness, evangelistic churches or movements, gospel churches or halls, "storefront" churches, and so forth.

4. United churches of all types; Mark Dawber estimated a possible total of 2,500 such churches in 1940.

5. Federated churches (already discussed; see pp. 106-7).

Many of these churches shift from one classification to another; one listed as United one year may be listed as Community (Methodist) the next. Free as they are of denominational control, they are as widely different in doctrine and polity as the preferences of the individuals and groups involved are different.

While there are as yet no accurate or official reports or statistics on it, the community church movement is definitely growing; churches bearing this name, often adding the word "independent," are rapidly developing toward a United Church of the United States— if that name is appropriate. A National Council of Community Churches with 200 congregations was organized in 1946 under the leadership of Dr. Roy Burkhart of the Community Church of Columbus, Ohio. A Biennial Council of Community Churches, made up of more than 100 Negro congregations, merged in August, 1950, at Lake Forest, Illinois, with the national council in a new body known as the International Council of Community Churches. The international council thus claims 300 out of a possible 3,000 autonomous, nondenominational community churches in the United States, with a potential membership of more than 1,000,000. It is a movement of real proportions and importance.

INDEPENDENT FUNDAMENTAL CHURCHES OF AMERICA

Organized in 1930 at Cicero, Illinois, by representatives of various independent churches anxious to safeguard fundamentalist doctrine, this body has two types of membership—one for organizations, the other for ministers, missionaries, and evangelists. The organization membership accounts for 400 churches directly affiliated, with 357 other independent churches whose pastors are affiliated, 1 Bible camp, 3 Bible institutes, 1 Christian school, and 15 missionary agencies. More than 1,200 ministers, missionaries, and evangelists are members.

The president of the body presides over an annual conference in which the members have voting power. An executive committee of 12 serves for 3 years, acting between meetings of the annual convention, the ruling body. The constituent churches are completely independent but are required to subscribe to the statement of faith of the organization. Approximately 85,000 lay members are represented in this organization.

INTERNATIONAL CHURCH OF THE FOURSQUARE GOSPEL

Rising out of the evangelistic work of "Sister" Aimee Semple McPherson, this church is a tribute to the organizing genius and striking methods of its founder. Born in Ontario in 1890, Mrs. McPherson was converted under the preaching of her first husband, Robert Semple, an evangelist. He died in China, and she returned to the United States in 1911 to tour the country in a series of gospel meetings which were spectacular even in war years. She settled in Los Angeles in 1918, building the famous Angelus Temple which was opened January 1, 1923, and founding the Echo Park Evangelistic Association, the L.I.F.E. Bible College, and International Church of the Foursquare Gospel, religious corporations. The headquarters are still located at Angelus Temple in Los Angeles.

With her great speaking ability and her faith in praying for the healing of the sick, Mrs. McPherson attracted thousands to her meetings. Her more irreverent critics felt that her meetings were too spectacular but others appreciated her type of presentation. There was great interest in the sick and the poor; "more than a million" are said to have been fed by the Los Angeles organization.

The teaching of the sect is set forth in a 21-paragraph *Declaration of Faith* written by Mrs. McPherson. Strongly fundamentalistic, it is Adventist, perfectionist, and Trinitarian, advocating that the Bible is as "true, immutable, steadfast, unchangeable, as its author, the Lord Jehovah." The Holy Spirit baptism with the initial evidence of speaking in other tongues follows conversion, and there is the power to heal in answer to believing prayer. There are the usual doctrines on the Atonement, the second coming of Christ "in clouds of glory," reward for the righteous at the judgment, and eternal punishment for the wicked. Baptism and the Lord's Supper are observed.

Mrs. McPherson was president of the church during her lifetime and was the ruling power and voice of the organization; the office was conferred upon her son at her death. A general assembly is held annually, in which the officers of the corporation, the board of directors, ministers, evangelists, and lay delegates are entitled to vote. The board of directors, 5 in number, manages the business of the organization and appoints field supervisors in charge of the 9 districts into which the 723 branch churches in the United States and Canada are divided. There is a total net property and equipment valuation of $23,396,170. Each church is governed by a church council and contributes one offering a month to home and foreign missionary work. Eight hundred and six foreign missionary stations and meeting places are established in 28 different countries. There are 961 missionaries including children and nationalist pastors, 14 day schools, 24 Bible schools, and 3 orphanages on the foreign field. An ordination and missionary board examines, admits, and licenses all ministers, missionaries, evangelists, and other workers.

There are 122,907 members, and all are required to subscribe to the *Declaration of Faith*. The young people are organized into bands of Foursquare Crusaders. A church flag—red, yellow, blue, and purple with a red cross on a Bible background bearing a superimposed "4"—is prominently displayed in the churches and at rallies and assemblies; a radio station, KFSG, broadcasts from Los Angeles.

JEHOVAH'S WITNESSES

The people called Jehovah's Witnesses believe that they have in their movement the true realization of the "one faith" mentioned by the apostle Paul in Eph. 4:5. Their certainty of this and their zeal in proclaiming it have made them at least in point of public interest an outstanding religious phenomenon in modern America.

They were not known as Jehovah's Witnesses until 1931. Up to this time they had been called Millennial Dawnists, International Bible Students, and earlier Russellites, after the man who brought about their first incorporation in 1884. Pastor Charles Taze Russell, their first president, is acknowledged not as founder (there is no "human" founder) but as general organizer; Judge Rutherford, Russell's successor, claimed that the Witnesses had been on earth as an organization for more than 5,000 years and cited Isa. 43:10-12; Heb. 11; and John 18:37 to prove it.

Russell was deeply influenced by belief in Christ's second coming; he studied the Bible avidly and attracted huge crowds to hear him expound it. The first formal organization of his followers came in Pittsburgh in 1872; his books, of which 13,000,000 are said to have been circulated, laid the foundations of the movement. Russell was president; to assist him, a board of directors was elected by vote of all members subscribing ten dollars or more to the support of the work (a practice discontinued in 1944).

Under Russell's direction headquarters were moved to Brooklyn, New York, in 1909 and another corporation formed under the laws of the state of New York. In 1939 the name was changed to the Watchtower Bible and Tract Society, Inc. When Pastor Russell died in 1916, Joseph F. Rutherford was made president. Known widely as Judge Rutherford, he had been a Missouri lawyer who occasionally sat as a circuit court judge. He wrote tirelessly; his books, pamphlets, and tracts supplanted those of Russell; and his neglect of some aspects of the teaching of Russell brought dissension.

Government of the group became more theocratic in the days of Rutherford's presidency; the governing body of the Witnesses today is in the hands of older and more "spiritually qualified" men who base their judgments upon the authority of the Scriptures. This is considered not a governing hierarchy by the Witnesses but a true imitation of early apostolic Christian organization. Under this governmental system, 3 corporations eventually came to control the society: the Watchtower Bible and Tract Society of New York, Inc.; the Watchtower Bible and Tract Society of Pennsylvania; and the International Bible Students Association of England. Judge Rutherford as president was a moving power in all of them.

Under the direction of these leaders at headquarters local congregations of Witnesses (they are always called congregations and never churches) are arranged into circuits with a traveling minister visiting the congregations, spending a week with each. Approximately 20 congregations are included in each circuit. Circuits are grouped into districts, of which there are 16 in the United States. District and circuit organizations are now found in 175 countries and islands across the world.

Meeting in kingdom halls and not in churches, they witness and "publish" their faith not only in testimony in their halls, but in a remarkably comprehensive missionary effort. All of them are ministers; they do not believe in any separation into clergy or laity for the simple reason that "Christ Jesus did not make such a separation." They never use titles such as "Reverend" or "Rabbi" or "Father"; this, they feel, is not in accordance with the words of Jesus in Matt. 23:6-10. Every member is a minister, and all of them give generously of their time in proclaiming their faith and teaching in private homes. Called "Publishers of the Kingdom," most of them devote an average of 15 hours a month in kingdom preaching work, preaching only from the Bible. Pioneers are required to give at least 100 hours per month; special pioneers and missionaries devote a minimum of 140 hours per month and are sent out to isolated areas and foreign lands where new congregations can be formed. All pioneers provide for their own support, but the society gives a small allowance to the special pioneers in view of their special needs. The headquarters staff, including the president of the society, are housed at the Bethel Home in Brooklyn, engage primarily in editorial and printing work, and receive an allowance of 14 dollars a month in addition to room and board. The literature they write, print, and distribute is of almost astronomical proportions. The official journal, *The Watchtower*, has a circulation of 3,700,000; more than 700,000,000 Bibles, books and booklets have been distributed since 1920; Bibles, books, booklets, and leaflets are available in more than 125 languages. In 1959 more than 870,000 Witnesses were active in this work throughout the world.

In this literature (all of which is circulated without an author's by-line or signature) is contained the teaching of the society. It all rests firmly upon the idea of the theocracy, or rule of God. The world in the beginning, according to the Witnesses, was under the theocratic rule of the Almighty; all then was "happiness, peace, and blessedness." But Satan rebelled and became the ruler of the world, and from that moment on mankind has followed his evil leading. Then came Jesus, "the beginning of the creation by God," as the prophets had predicted, to end Satan's rule; Jesus' rule began in 1914. In 1918 Christ "came to the temple of Jehovah"; and in 1919 when Rutherford reorganized the movement shattered by the war, Jesus, enthroned in the temple, began illuminating the prophecies and sending out his followers to preach.

God, in Witness thinking, will take vengeance upon wicked man in our times; at the same time he is now showing his great love by "gathering out" multitudes of people of good will whom he will give life in his new world which is to come after the imminent battle of Armageddon is fought. This is to be a universal battle; Christ will lead the army of the righteous, composed of the "host of heaven, the holy angels," and will completely annihilate the army of Satan. The righteous of the earth will watch this battle but will not participate. After the battle a great crowd of people will remain on the earth; these will be believers in God and will be his servants. Those who have proved their integrity under test in this old world will multiply and populate the new earth with righteous people. A resurrection will also take place and will be an additional means of filling the cleansed earth with better inhabitants. After the holocaust, "righteous princes" are to rule the earth under Christ as "King of the Great Theocracy." The willfully wicked, being incorrigible, shall not be resurrected at all; once dead, they never awake. One special group—the 144,000 Christians mentioned in Rev. 7 and 14—will make up the "bride of Christ" and rule with him in heaven.

Judge Rutherford said often that "millions now living will never die"— which meant that Armageddon was close and that the Kingdom was at hand. He died in 1942, leaving guidance of the movement in the hands of the present president, Nathan H. Knorr; and Armageddon had not yet been fought. But the certainty of its imminence persists.

All this is based upon the Bible; Witnesses quote elaborately from the Scriptures, using the proof-text method in verifying their beliefs. All other teachings and interpretations are to them suspect and unreliable. They oppose and attack the teachings of the various churches as false and unscriptural, insisting as they do so that they are attacking or denouncing not churches or church members as such but only doctrines and interpretations of scripture which they consider false. They have been especially active in opposing what they consider to be 3 allies of Satan: the false teachings of the churches, the tyranny of human governments, and the oppressions of business. This "triple alliance" of ecclesiastical, political, and commercial powers has misled and all but destroyed humanity, the Witnesses claim, and must be destroyed at Armageddon before the new world can be born. They refuse, for instance, to salute the flag or to bear arms in war or to participate in the affairs of government not because of any pacifist convictions but because they consider these to be expressions of Satan's power over men. This attitude has brought them into

conflict with law-enforcing agencies; and they have endured jailing, whippings, assault by mobs, even stonings and tar-and-featherings and the burning of their homes. This they have accepted in a very submissive spirit; their position is that they will obey the laws of men when those laws are not in conflict with the laws of God, and they base their behavior on Acts 5:29.

The ranks of active "publishers" across the world has grown to 871,737, of which approximately 230,000 are in the United States. There are 4,020 congregations in the United States and 19,982 throughout the world. Branch offices are maintained in 85 countries, and work is reported in 175 lands. There are 261 established missions (including boats) and 3,395 specially trained foreign missionaries. The Bible School of Gilead was established at South Lansing, New York, in 1943 to train their missionaries.

JEWISH CONGREGATIONS

Jews arrived early in the American colonies; some were here before 1650. A small group of Portuguese Jews found safety if not complete understanding in Peter Stuyvesant's New Amsterdam, where they established the first official congregation in North America, Shearth Israel (Remnant of Israel) in 1654. Three years later there was a small group of Jews at Newport, Rhode Island. Jews came to Georgia with Oglethorpe and in 1733 organized a synagogue at Savannah. By 1850 there were 77 Jewish congregations in 21 states and at the end of the century more than 600 congregations of over 1,000,000 Jews. Today 5,367,000 American Jews have a widely varying synagogue membership estimated at anywhere from a minimum of 2,000,000 upward in 3,990 congregations.

The historic sense of unity among the Jewish people soon demonstrated itself here as it had abroad. That unity had

defied centuries of dispersion and persecution, and it now welded the followers of Judaism into one of the best-organized religious groups in America. This is especially impressive when we consider the fact that Judaism has no dogmatic creed and no articles of faith. In *The Truth About the Pharisees* it has been described by R. T. Herford as a "detailed system of ethical practices by which its adherents consecrated their daily lives to the service of God. The cornerstone of Judaism was the deed, not the dogma."

There are, however, 2 pillars upon which Judaism rests. One is the teaching of the Old Testament, particularly of the Pentateuch, the 5 books of Moses. This is known in Judaism as the Torah. It is the revelation of God, divine in origin and containing the earliest written laws and traditions of the Jewish people. The other is the Talmud, which is a rabbinical commentary and enlargement of the Torah, an elaborate, discursive compendium containing the written and the oral law which guides the Jew in every phase of his living.

In Torah and Talmud are the Judaistic foundation principles of justice, purity, hope, thanksgiving, righteousness, love, freedom of the will, divine providence and human responsibility, repentance, prayer, and the resurrection of the dead. At the heart of it all lies the Hebrew concept of the oneness of God. Every day of his life the good Jew repeats the ancient biblical verse, "Hear, oh Israel, the Lord is our God, the Lord is one." All other gods are to be shunned; there is but one Creator of man and the world, holding the destiny of both in his almighty hands.

Man, created by this one God, is inherently good. There is no original sin, no instinctive evil or fundamental impurity, in him; he is made in God's image and endowed with an intelligence which enables him to choose for himself between good and evil. He has and needs no mediator such as the Christians have in Christ; he approaches God directly. Men—Jews and Gentiles alike—attain immortality as the reward for righteous living.

Judaism looks forward to the perfection of man and to the establishment of a perfect divine kingdom of truth and righteousness upon this earth, the messianic era, in which all will be peace and bliss. To work toward this kingdom, the Jews have been established of God as a deathless, unique people, a "kingdom of priests and a holy nation," and as the "Servant of the Lord."

Some of their laws provide for the great festivals of the Jewish year: Pesach, or Passover, in late March or early April, a memorial of the Jewish liberation from Egypt; Shabuoth, the Feast of Weeks, or Pentecost, in late May or early June, commemorating the giving of the Ten Commandments to Moses; Sukkoth, or the Feast of Tabernacles, or Booths, in October, marking the years of Jewish wandering in the wilderness; the Feast of Lights, or Hanukkah, in late November or December, celebrating the purification of the Temple by the Maccabees after its defilement by Antiochus Epiphanes; the Feast of Lots, or Purim, in February or March, honoring the heroine Esther. Three principal minor fasts are observed: the Fast of Tebeth in January, commemorating the siege of Jerusalem; the Fast of Tammuz in July, observing the breach of Jerusalem's walls; and the Fast of Ab also in July, memorializing the fall of the city and the destruction of the Temple. The most important days in the Jewish religious calendar are the great fast of Yom Kippur, the Day of Atonement, in September or early October, closing the Ten Days of Penitence, which begin with Rosh Hashana, or New Year's Day.

Other laws are kept as reminders of God's covenant with Israel; these include the laws of circumcision and Sabbath observance. Still others are held as marks of divine distinction and are kept to preserve the ideal of Israel as a chosen, separate people.

Within the local congregation there is full independence. There are no synods, assemblies, or hierarchies of leaders to control anything whatsoever in the synagogue. The Jews are loosely bound by the "rope of sand" of Jewish unity, with wide variation in custom and procedure. They have been influenced deeply by the many peoples and cultures with which they have come in contact and have made adjustments accordingly. Because of differences in historical background over the centuries some congregations use a German-version Hebrew prayer book; others use a Spanish version. Some use English at various points in their services, such as the sermon; but all use Hebrew in their prayers. Sermons may be heard in English or Yiddish, a German dialect influenced by Hebrew. Traditional Orthodox synagogues have no instrumental music in their services;

the congregation worships with covered head; and the men and women sit separately. In Reform temples these traditions are not observed.

At the head of the congregation stands the rabbi, trained in college and seminary and fully ordained. He is preacher and pastor. He officiates at marriages and grants divorce decrees in accordance with Jewish law after civil divorce has been granted by the state. He conducts funerals and generally supervises the burial of Jews as Jewish law requires. Congregations usually own their own cemeteries or organize cemetery societies; there are also many private cemetery or burial associations owned and controlled by Jewish benevolent groups. Orthodox rabbis are also charged with the supervision of slaughtering animals for food and with the distribution of kosher meat products in accordance with the Levitical dietary laws. Many congregations engage readers or cantors, but it is the rabbi who is the leader and authority on Jewish law and ritual.

There is no examination for synagogue membership, all Jews being readily accepted as congregants. However, married women and unmarried children are not usually recognized as voting members. Men are almost always the corporate members. There are sometimes also pewholders, who contribute to and engage in the work of the synagogue but without the authority of corporate members. A third class of synagogue membership consists of those who merely pay for the use of a synagogue seat during the high holidays. Corporate members are supposed to control all synagogue property and to guide congregational policy and activity, but the other members often participate on almost equal footing.

There are 4 divisions in American Judaism: Orthodox Judaism, represented nationally by the Union of Orthodox Jewish Congregations of America, the Rabbinical Council of America, and the Union of Orthodox Rabbis of the United States and Canada, numerically by far the largest Jewish body in the United States; Reform Judaism, with the Central Conference of American Rabbis and the Union of American Hebrew Congregations—the first national organization of synagogues in America, established in 1873—as spokesmen; Conservative Judaism, organized in the United Synagogue of America and the Rabbinical Assembly of America; and Reconstruction Judaism, sponsored by the Jewish Reconstructionist Foundation, organized in 1940. The first 3 of these national Jewish organizations are constituent members of the Synagogue Council of America.

No accurate survey of membership in these American Jewish congregations has ever been taken, and one probably cannot be taken. Estimates differ widely depending upon the methods and classifications employed. Those who hold that all members of the race are by nature and spiritual necessity also members of the synagogue identify the number of American Jews, 5,260,000, with American synagogue membership. Others estimate total synagogue membership as low as 2,000,000. It is impossible to estimate the number of either members or synagogues with any accuracy at all inasmuch as many of them never report to any national Jewish organization.

The multiplicity of Jewish national organizations is bewildering. The American Jewish Yearbook for 1960 lists them in the following categories: community relations and political, 14; overseas aid, 11; religious and educational, 116; social and mutual benefit, 26; cultural, 27; social welfare, 32; Zionist and pro-Israel, 66. American Jews live in more than 700 communities. In over 225 of the larger cities and towns, the Jewish population maintains at least one central local organization: a federation, welfare fund, or community council. There are more than 200 Jewish periodicals and newspapers in 28 states and the District of Columbia, and three Jewish news syndicates. *American Judaism* is the quarterly Reform organ, the bimonthly *Jewish Life* speaks for the Orthodox Branch, *Conservative Judaism* is a quarterly for the Conservatives, and fortnightly *Reconstructionist* speaks for Reconstructionism. Among the magazines of general interest are *Commentary, Midstream, Menorah Journal, Jewish Frontier, Jewish Spectator,* and *National Jewish Post and Opinion.*

Education on all levels is a major Jewish concern. Children are enrolled in Sunday schools, weekday schools, all-day schools, Yiddish schools, and released-time schools. In 1958 there was a total of 553,600 children in all weekday and Sunday schools, but it was still estimated that not more than 75 per cent of available Jewish children were enrolled in Jewish schools.

Institutions of higher learning are limited to schools for the training of rabbis. The most important of these schools are the Rabbi Isaac Elchanan Theological Seminary of Yeshiva University in New York City (Orthodox); the Hebrew Union College in Cincinnati and the Jewish Institute of Religion in New York City (Reform institutions that were merged in 1948 into what is now called H.U.C.-J.I.R.); and the Jewish Theological Seminary in New York City (Conservative). The Jewish Theological Seminary has a branch in Los Angeles called the University of Judaism. Dropsie College, "a postgraduate, nonsectarian institution of Semitic learning," in Philadelphia and the Yivo Institute for Jewish Research in New York City are the only two institutions of higher learning working independently of Jewish seminaries; Yeshiva University in New York City and Brandeis University in Waltham, Massachusetts, are the only Jewish colleges awarding a B.A. degree.

Jewish charity is amazingly efficient. Jewish federations and welfare boards raised $123,000,000 in 1958; this money was divided among local agencies (health, welfare, education, and recreation), national agencies (civic defense, cultural, religious, and service), and overseas (mainly to help settle refugees in Israel and other countries).

The American Jewish Committee is organized to protect the civil and religious rights of all Jews around the world. It offers legal assistance; seeks equality for Jews in economic, social, and educational opportunities; and gives protection from persecution and intolerance through the Joint Defense Appeal, in which it co-operates with the Anti-Defamation League of B'nai B'rith.

Among the Zionist societies the Zionist Organization of America is one of the largest and most powerful; it is in the United States the acknowledged spokesman in politics and public relations for the whole movement. Zionism is limited to no one of the 4 major religious groups; it has crossed the line everywhere. The only organized opposition to Zionism within American Jewry is found in the comparatively small Council for Judaism.

Two trends are noticeable in American Judaism. One is the trend toward a relaxation of strict or letter observance of the time-honored Jewish law; the other, in seeming opposition, is the tendency to consider the inner spiritual strength of Judaism as its only hope for the future. Under this latter drive American Jews know fewer and fewer divisions, more and more co-operation and unity.

Orthodox Judaism

Orthodox Judaism has been called "Torah-True" Judaism; it is the branch which preserves the theology and traditions of Old World Jewry in the New World. It assigns equal authority to the written and oral law and to the ancient Jewish codes embodied in the Torah and the Talmud and their commentaries. The Torah is all-important and basic to all the rest: the Torah is of God, given to Moses, and there is no way to God except through obedience to the laws of the Torah; Torah is a revelation of the Fatherhood of God and the brotherhood of man, and it explains the place of the Jews as the chosen people of God. Everything a Jew needs to know is in the Torah; it governs every moment of his life. Moses is believed to have transmitted orally this great body of teaching to his successors, who in turn transmitted it down to the time when it was first committed to writing. There are, however, two slightly variant emphases in Orthodoxy; the Orthodoxy stemming from Hungary opposes resolutely *all* change or innovation in speech, dress, and education; that coming from Germany and western Europe is a bit less severe, attempting to preserve the more important elements of traditional Jewish life, but accepting modern changes and ideas in these three areas.

Orthodox Jews believe in the political rebirth of their nation, in the return of the Jew to Palestine to rebuild his Temple on Mount Zion and to re-establish his ancient sacrificial ritual. They look forward to the coming of the Messiah, who is to be a descendant of David. The biblical dietary laws are strictly observed, and the traditional holy days and festivals are faithfully kept. The Hebrew language is used in their synagogue prayers; English, in their sermons. They are the fundamentalists of Judaism.

Reform Judaism

Reform Judaism is liberal Judaism. It began in Germany just after the Napoleonic emancipation, when "reformers" within Judaism shortened the synagogue services, made use of the vernacular and of organs in those services, and established group in place of individual confirmation. Some reformers at that time advocated a complete break with Judaistic traditional forms, but that did not come.

Isaac Mayer Wise, one of their outstanding leaders in the United States, founded here the Union of American Congregations (1873), the Hebrew Union College (1875), and the Central Conference of American Rabbis (1889); these important groups sum up the aim of Reform Judaism in their conviction that Judaism should "alter its externals to strengthen its eternals."

Reform holds that there is divine authority only in the written law of the Old Testament; this is its main distinction from Orthodox Judaism. But revelation in Reform is not confined to the Old Testament; it is progressive. The Reform Jew limits himself to the practice of the ceremonial laws of the Pentateuch, with the exception of those laws which, like the law of sacrifice, he regards as having no application or purpose in the present day. The sacrifices of the Mosaic era, he insists, were merely concessions to the customs of the times. Claiming that the mission of Judaism is the spiritualization of mankind, he sees such practices as covering the head at worship, dietary laws, the wearing of phylacteries as anachronisms which isolate the Jew from the rest of mankind and make such spiritualizing impossible, and hence should be abolished. In other words, the Orthodox Jew accepts the entire body of oral and written law as sanctified by tradition; the Reform Jew has simplified the ritual and adapted it to modern needs.

Unlike his Orthodox brothers, he does not believe in the Messianic restoration of the Jewish state and return to Jerusalem; he is abandoning belief in a personal Messiah, but he still holds to his faith in the coming of a Messianic age. He does, however, support the return to Palestine under the Zionist movement, not so much on spiritual or Talmudic grounds as on the ground that Palestine offers a place of refuge for persecuted Jews of the world. He advocates the preservation in the new state of Israel of such Jewish values, customs, and traditions as have inspirational value.

Reform Judaism has doubled its membership in the last 10 years; it now claims 1,000,000 adherents (there are approximately 2,000,000 in Orthodox and 2,000,000 in Conservative Judaism).

Conservative Judaism

Conservative Judaism holds middle ground between Orthodox and Reform, and seeks preservation of the values and ideals of both. From Orthodoxy it takes its belief in the Torah, observance of dietary laws, and use of the Hebrew language; from Reform comes its tendency to reconcile the old beliefs and practices with the cultures in which it finds itself at work. To the Conservative, Judaism is not static but the deepening, growing, widening faith of a people who take into their culture many different influences from other cultures, and yet retain their own racial and religious aspects. Extreme changes in Jewish tradition are opposed, but some notable innovations are evident: the English language is often used in synagogue prayers, men and women sit together in family pews, and modern methods of education are applied in their development schools for children and youth. Adult education is a primary interest here; there has been a marked increase in adult schools and studies across the last two decades.

Reconstructionism

Reconstructionism, under the sponsorship of the Jewish Reconstructionist Foundation, Inc., is a new Jewish group, originated in 1934, whose aggressive leader is Mordecai M. Kaplan, a member of the faculty of the Jewish Theological Seminary. It calls for a reorganization of all Jewish life. It is active in the struggle to establish a Jewish national home in Palestine; in the broadening of Jewish education beyond instruction in language, ritual, and catechism; in the reinterpretation of Judaism to bring it into harmony with modern thought; and in the establishment of a world-wide co-operative Jewish society. There is respect here for the ceremonies and traditions of historic Judaism, but there is also a call for divergence and expansion to include ethical culture, ritual enrichment, and esthetic creativity.

Judaism, to these Jews, is a civilization more than a faith; it has religion as a central element, but only as one of many elements. Dr. Kaplan rejects belief in miracles, the personal Messiah, the resurrection; and he denies the divine origin of the Torah. He accepts Jewish ceremonial law as "folkways," valuable, but not necessarily binding. He also denies the concept of Israel as a "chosen" people.

Reconstructionists are found in Orthodox, Conservative, and Reform groups, but as yet they have no organization similar to that found in these three major groups.

Commandment Keepers, or Black Jews

This is a Negro Jewish sect in New York's Harlem founded in 1919 by Rabbi Wentworth David Matthew, who claims more than 3,000 members in Harlem and an equal number in other congregations beyond that section. They teach that the Negroes are actually Hebrews originating in Ethiopia. They maintain a home for the aged and co-operate in various business enterprises with the white Jews of Harlem. Two other Jewish Negro groups, the House of Israel and the Moorish Science Temple, also operate in and around Harlem. They wear full beards and teach that Adam was a Negro and that Negroes are the real Hebrews.

There are other Negro synagogues in Brooklyn and Cleveland, some claiming the Ethiopian (or "Falasha") origin, but most of whom are descendants of slaves who lived on Jewish-owned plantations in the American South. While their worship forms generally follow the Orthodox, they have little if any contact with other American Jewish communities or organizations.

KODESH CHURCH OF IMMANUEL

Formed in 1929 and incorporated in April, 1930, by the Rev. Frank Russell Killingsworth and 120 laymen, some of whom were former members of the African Methodist Episcopal Zion Church, this is an interracial body of 1,500 members, most of whom are Negroes. The 7 churches of the denomination are located in Pennsylvania, Virginia, and the District of Columbia; a missionary station has recently been established in Liberia, West Africa. Teachings are Wesleyan and Arminian, stressing entire sanctification, or the baptism of the Holy Spirit, and premillennialism. Divine healing is practiced, but not to the exclusion of medicine.

As the church was founded for the purpose of "conserving and propagating Bible holiness," the use of alcoholic liquors and tobacco is forbidden; pride in dress and behavior, Sabbath desecration, secret societies, dissolute dancing, and attendance at inferior and obscene theaters are denounced. Divorce is recognized only on the biblical ground of adultery. Water baptism is by the optional modes of sprinkling, pouring, or immersion.

The churches are under the charge of ministers and oversight of supervising elders. Ministers are elected and ordained by annual assemblies, to which they report. Supervising elders are elected and consecrated by general assemblies, which meet quadrennially to enact all the laws of the church. The work of the entire church, including the support of foreign missionaries, is maintained by freewill offerings and tithes.

LATTER-DAY SAINTS, OR MORMONS

Better known as Mormons, the Latter-Day Saints have had one of the most tempestuous histories of any church body in the United States. Attacked by mobs and once invaded by United States Army troops, they built a religious community in what was once a desert and established themselves as one of the outstanding religious groups of the nation.

Essentially a laymen's movement in its origin, their church is rooted in the visions of Joseph Smith, who organized the movement in 1830 at Fayette, New York. Smith claimed to have experienced a series of heavenly visitations in which he was informed that all existing churches were in error, that the true gospel was yet to be restored, that it would be revealed to him, and that he was to re-establish the true church on earth. He was led by an angel to discover, buried in a hill called Cumorah near Manchester Village, New York, certain golden plates or tablets left there by an ancient prophet and containing the sacred records of the ancient inhabitants of America and the true word of God. According to the Mormons America was originally settled by the Jaredites, one of the groups dispersed during the confusion of tongues at the Tower of Babel; the American Indians were direct descendants of the Hebrews who came from Jerusalem in 600 B.C. Jesus himself visited this country after his resurrection.

Smith translated the hieroglyphics on the golden tablets into the *Book of Mormon*, from which the name "Mormon" comes. Oliver Cowdery acted as his scribe. This *Book of Mormon* is considered by the saints as being equal with and "supporting but not supplanting" the Bible, and as being equal with 2 other writings of Joseph Smith, the *Book of Doctrines and Covenants* and the *Pearl of Great Price*, which contain the foundation teachings of the church. The golden plates were said to have been returned to the angel by Joseph Smith; their authenticity has been challenged by non-Mormon scholars and as ardently defended by the Mormons, who offer the names of 11 other persons beside Smith who saw them. Smith and Cowdery had the "priesthood of Aaron" conferred upon them by a heavenly messenger, John the Baptist, who instructed them to baptize each other. Later 3 other divine visitants, Peter, James, and John, bestowed upon them the "priesthood of Melchizedek" and gave them the keys of apostleship. This was in 1829, a year before the founding of the church with 6 charter members.

Opposition arose as the church gained strength, and the Mormons left New York in 1831 for Ohio, where headquarters were established at Kirtland. Another large Mormon center developed at Independence, Missouri, where they planned to build the ideal community with a temple at its heart. Friction with other settlers became so acute that the Mormons were expelled from Missouri; they settled at Nauvoo, Illinois. Violence followed them there and reached its peak with the murder of Joseph Smith and Hyrum Smith, the prophet and the patriarch of the church, in jail at Carthage.

With Smith's death Brigham Young, who was the president of the Quorum of the Twelve Apostles, was sustained president. A group of the defeated minority refused to accept his election or leadership and withdrew to form other Mormon churches. They objected on the ground that Young was not the legal successor to Smith, that control of the church belonged properly to the 12 apostles appointed by Smith, and that Young approved of the practice of polygamy, which had been responsible for much of their persecution. But Young held his office; he had the vote of the majority, and he also had the courage and the administrative ability necessary at that crucial period to save the church from extinction.

The saints were driven from Nauvoo in February, 1846, and began their epic march to what is now Utah. In the valley of the Great Salt Lake they finally found safety, building there the famous tabernacle and temple at the heart of what was to become a world-wide Mormonism, and creating a self-existent community. Their community became the state of Utah in 1896.

Based upon the *Book of Mormon* and the Bible, which is accepted "as far as it is translated correctly," the faith of the Mormons is in some respects the faith to be found in any number of conservative, fundamentalist Protestant churches, plus the revelations of Joseph Smith. They believe that the three persons comprising the Godhead are the Father, the Son, and the Holy Ghost; that the Father and the Son have bodies of flesh and bones as tangible as man's, and that the Holy Ghost is a personage of Spirit; that men will be punished for their own individual sins and not for Adam's transgression. All mankind may be saved through the atonement of Christ and by obedience to the laws and ordinances of the gospel; these laws and ordinances include faith in Christ, repentance, baptism by immersion for the remission of sins, and the laying on of hands for the gift of the Holy Ghost, and also in observing the Lord's Supper each Sunday. The believe in the gift of tongues and interpretation of tongues, visions, revelation, prophecy, and healing. There is a strong Adventism in this church. Christ will return to rule the earth from his capitals in Zion and Jerusalem, following the restoration of the 10 tribes of Israel.

Revelation is not regarded as confined to either the Bible or the *Book of Mormon;* it continues today—in the living apostles, prophets, pastors, teachers, and evangelists of the modern Mormon Church. Baptism is necessary to salvation; and obedience to the priesthood is of first importance. Subjection to civil laws and rules is advocated, together with an insistence upon the right of the individual to worship according to the dictates of his conscience.

Two Mormon practices, baptism for the dead and sealing in marriage for eternity, are exclusive with this church. Baptism and salvation for the dead are based upon the conviction that those who died without a chance to hear or accept the gospel cannot possibly be condemned by a just and merciful God. The gospel must be preached to them after death; authority for this is found in I Pet. 4:6: "For this cause was the gospel preached also to them that are dead, that they might be judged according to men in the flesh, but live according to God in the spirit." Baptism is considered as essential to the dead as to the living, though the rite will not finally save them; there must be faith and repentance for salvation. The ceremony is performed with a living person standing proxy for the dead.

Marriage in Mormonism has 2 forms: marriage for time and marriage for eternity (or celestial marriage). Marriage for time is for those who prefer it. Mormon men and women are sure that there is no exaltation to be had unless they are married for time and eternity. Mormon women believed that there could be no salvation for them unless they were married. Thus plural marriages were accepted and encouraged. Some plural marriages were for both time and eternity, and they had been practiced for some time before Joseph Smith's revelation on the practice was announced publicly by Brigham Young in 1852.

Polygamy was abolished to comply with the constitutional law in 1890, but some of the plural marriages contracted before that date were allowed to continue. Some of the dissenting Mormon churches held that it was never widely practiced or accepted and that Joseph Smith never approved or practiced it himself. As late as 1941, 20 excommunicated Mormons, breaking the law of both church and state, were convicted of polygamy and sentenced to prison; but generally the practice of polygamy has been abandoned.

Organization and government of the church differ in detail among 6 Mormon denominations but agree in essentials. They are based upon the 2 priesthoods: the higher priesthood of Melchizedek, which holds power of presidency and authority over the offices of the church and whose officers include apostles, patriarchs, high priests, seventies, and elders; and the lesser priesthood of Aaron, which guides the temporal affairs of the church through its bishops, priests, teachers, and deacons. The presiding council of the church is the First Presidency, made up of 3 high priests—the president and 2 counselors. Its authority is final and universal in both spiritual and temporal affairs. The president of the church is the "mouthpiece of God"; through him come the laws of the church by direct revelation.

Next to the presidency stands the Council of the Twelve Apostles, chosen by revelation to supervise under the direction of the First Presidency the whole work of the church and to ordain all ministers.

The church is divided into stakes (geographical divisions) which are composed of a number of wards corresponding to local churches or parishes. High priests, assisted by elders, are in charge of the stakes. Members of the Melchizedek priesthood hold authority under the direction of the presidency to officiate in all ordinances of the gospel. Seventies work under the direction of the twelve apostles; they are organized into quorums of 70 each, with 7 presidents of equal rank presiding over each quorum. The duties of the twelve apostles and the seventies carry them into all the stakes, wards, and missions throughout the entire church. The duties of the stake presidents, the ward bishops, the patriarchs, high priests, and elders are to supervise the work within the stakes and wards of the church.

The Aaronic Priesthood is presided over by the Presiding Bishopric who also supervises all work done in the stakes and wards by the members of the Aaronic Priesthood.

The church influences every phase of the living of every member; it supplies relief in illness or poverty, provides education, recreation, and employment. Such a program has inevitably resulted in deep loyalty in its membership. More than 4,000 young Mormons go out 2 by 2 each year as missionaries without compensation, giving a year or more to the work of spreading the teaching of their church at home and abroad. In fact less than 35 persons in leadership positions in the church receive salaries. They do not win converts in any great numbers, but their missionary experience strengthens both them and their church and offers a model of church service and zeal equaled in very few of the other larger churches in America.

Church of Jesus Christ of Latter-Day Saints

With headquarters at Salt Lake City this church is by far the largest Mormon body numerically with 1,555,799 members and 2,513 congregations. It follows the governmental pattern already described. A general conference is held twice a year. The church is supported by the tithes of the membership; each member who earns money is expected to give one tenth of his income.

The missionary effort of this church is one of the most consistent and vigor-

ous to be found anywhere in America; at its centennial celebration in 1947 it was reported that in the preceding 100 years 51,622 missionaries had been sent out, each at his own expense and most of them serving a full 2 years. About 67,615 missionaries have been at work in the years 1930-53. There were 12,823 missionaries at work in home and foreign fields in 1958. Active missionary service is also had among the American Indians and also serving abroad in 38 countries. There were 27 mission stations in North and South America, 11 in Europe, and 9 in the islands of the sea.

In education the Mormons have lifted Utah high among the states. They have 4 senior colleges and 3 junior colleges in Utah, which has the highest percentage of males and females in school among all the states. It stands fourth among the states in the percentage of income devoted to education. Utah's educational achievement is second to none in America and probably in the world.

The death rate among Mormons is lower than that of any group of people of the same size anywhere else in the world; it is the direct result of Mormon abstinence from liquor and tobacco and of their welfare efforts. This church has 105 storehouses for community food and clothing, with an asset value of about $2,289,408; members maintain vegetable, seed, and wheat farms; orchards; a cotton plantation; dairies; sewing centers; fish canneries; soap factories; cattle, sheep, and hog farms; food processing plants; a vitamin pill factory; and several grain elevators. Most of the products of these industries are consumed at home, but hundreds of thousands of relief packages have been forwarded under a plan of European relief.

Reorganized Church of Jesus Christ of Latter Day Saints

This church claims to be the continuation of the original church which was organized by Joseph Smith, Jr., on April

6, 1830. It has 174,000 members and 1,100 branches. It bases its claim to be the legal continuation of the original church on obedience to the rule of succession in its presidency as found in the *Book of Doctrine and Covenants.* Court action on two occasions, in Ohio in 1880 and in Missouri in 1894, named this church the legal continuation of the original church. The son of Joseph Smith, Jr., was designated by his father to succeed him when 12 years old, and he became president in 1860.

The Reorganized Church rejected the claims of the Mormons led by Brigham Young because of this rule, and also because of their adoption of the doctrine of polygamy in 1852, which, it is claimed, is contrary to the teachings of the *Book of Mormon* and the *Book of Doctrine and Covenants* endorsed by the original organization in 1835. It also differs from the Utah church on the doctrine of the Godhead.

At the death of Joseph Smith, Jr. in 1844, the church entered a period of confusion due to several claims to leadership. Those holding to the principle of "succession" eventually "reorganized," the first collective expression of this movement being at a conference in Beloit, Wisconsin, in 1852. Joseph Smith, the son of the founder, was chosen president in 1860 at Amboy, Illinois. His successors have all been descendants of the founder.

Basic principles of the Reorganized Church include: (1) The continuity of divine revelation, and the open canon of Scripture; (2) The restoration of Christ's church on the New Testament pattern; (3) The principles of doctrine as listed in Heb. 6:1, 2; (4) The doctrine of stewardship in personal and economic life; (5) The gathering together at Independence, Missouri, as a place of preparation and demonstration of the Christian way of life. This place was designated "Zion" by the prophet Joseph Smith in 1831; (6) The return of Christ and the millennial reign.

The work of the church is supported by "tithes" and "free-will offerings." This is regarded as a divine principle, and the tithe is calculated upon a tenth of each member's annual increase over and above just needs and wants.

The church has adherents in Canada, Australia, England, Europe, Hawaii, New Zealand, French Oceania, Japan, Korea, India, and Pakistan. It maintains a 4-year accredited college at Lamoni, Iowa (Graceland College) and a leadership and ministerial seminary at Independence, Missouri (School of the Restoration). It operates a 182-bed hospital and a home for the aged at Independence, Missouri.

The administration of the church is by a First Presidency of 3 high priests, a Quorum of Twelve Apostles who represent the presidency in the field, and a pastoral arm under the high priests and elders. Missionary activity is directed by the apostles who have the assistance of Quorums of the seventy. These are traveling elders and with the apostles they are traveling representatives of the general church. Bishops care for the financial needs of the church and a presiding bishopric of three, at headquarters in Independence, Missouri, is closely associated with the first presidency.

Doctrines, policies, and all matters of legislation must have the approval and action of a delegate conference which is usually held biennially at Independence, Missouri, headquarters of the church.

Church of Christ, Temple Lot

This church had 3,000 members in 12 churches in 1956; it was founded at Bloomington, Illinois, at the time of Joseph Smith's death. This dissenting body rejected the teachings of baptism for the dead, the elevation of men to the estate of gods following death, the doctrine of lineal right to office in the church, and the practice of polygamy. The group returned to Independence,

Missouri, in 1867 and began raising funds for the purchase of a temple lot upon which was to be erected the temple of the Lord for the day of his return and the gathering of the 10 lost tribes of Israel. The temple lot will be the center of the New Jerusalem, which will be a "movement of brotherhood and the turning point when the fullness of the gospel goes from the Gentiles to the Jews." The lot was lost to the Reorganized Church in a lawsuit in 1891-95, but the Temple Lot Church still believes that it is commissioned to build the temple there, and in this generation.

A general bishopric under the guidance of a general conference administers the work of the church; the highest officers are found in the Quorum of the Twelve, and local bishops direct the temporal affairs of the local church "under supervision of the congregation."

Church of Jesus Christ

This group was organized under the leadership of Sidney Rigdon, one of the pioneers of Mormonism. His followers refused to join the march to Utah under Brigham Young, denounced him and the twelve apostles for general wickedness (polygamy) and condemned the teachings of plurality of gods and baptism for the dead. They organized in 1862 at Green Oak, Pennsylvania, under the guidance of William Bickerton (they have been called "Bickertonites"), who claimed clear and divine succession of priesthood and authority. The president of the group today is W. H. Cadman.

Foot washing is practiced, and they salute one another with the holy kiss. Monogamy is required, "except in case of death." Members are required to obey all state and civil laws, but there is strong opposition to participation in war. They have their own edition of the *Book of Mormon*, and a monthly periodical, *The Gospel News*, is published at headquarters in Monongahela, Pennsylvania, where a general conference meets an-

nually. A missionary work is conducted in Italy, Nigeria, and among the Indians in the United States and Canada. There are approximately 2,000 members in 45 churches.

Church of Jesus Christ (Cutlerites)

This has always been the smallest Mormon group; today it is down to 8 members in 1 church. It was organized in 1853 by Alpheus Cutler, who was seventh in line of the original 7 elders of the church under Joseph Smith. Cutler ordained new elders "to act in the lesser offices of the church." Community of property is practiced in this church, which consists of the one congregation at Clitherall, Minnesota.

Church of Jesus Christ of Latter Day Saints (Strangites)

This group claims that it is "the one and original Church of Jesus Christ of Latter-day Saints" and that its founder, James J. Strang, is the only legal successor to church leadership with written credentials from Joseph Smith. Strang translated portions of the Plates of Laban; they, together with certain other revelations, are found in "The Book of the Law of the Lord." Strang also translated what is called "The Voree Record" —a record found under an oak tree near Voree, Wisconsin, dealing in hieroglyphic-like characters with "an ancient people . . . who no longer exist." He was crowned "king" of this church in 1850 and was murdered in 1856 during a wave of anti-Mormonism in the Great Lakes region.

Organized at Burlington, Wisconsin, in 1844, the church denies the virgin-birth theory, holds that Adam fell by a law of natural consequences rather than in the breaking of a divine law, and that the corruption thus caused could be removed only by the resurrection of Christ. They deny the Trinity and the plurality of gods, celebrate Saturday as the Sabbath

Day, and believe that baptism is essential for salvation. Due to "lack of prophetic leadership at the present time" they do not practice baptism for the dead.

Chief officer of the church is a high priest in the Melchizedek Priesthood, chosen by the General Church Conference. Membership is given at about 250 in 6 churches or branches.

LIBERAL CATHOLIC CHURCH

Tracing its beginnings back to the Old Catholic Church movement in Great Britain, which began in Holland, and its orders to an apostolic succession running back to the Roman Catholic Church under the reign of Pope Urban VIII, and even to the 12 apostles, the Liberal Catholic Church is still liberal in the extreme. It aims at a combination of traditional Catholic forms of worship with the utmost freedom of individual conscience and thought. It claims to be neither Roman Catholic nor Protestant, but still "catholic" in the broadest sense of the word. It was established during the reorganization of the British Old Catholic movement in 1915-16.

Members of the Liberal Catholic Church in the United States number about 4,000 in 8 churches. They use the Nicene Creed in most of their churches but do not require subscription to any interpretation of creeds, scriptures, or tradition; they aim not at profession of a common belief but at corporate worship in a common ritual. They draw their central inspiration from faith in the living Christ, based on the promises of Matt. 28:20 and 18:20. These promises are regarded as "validating all Christian worship," but special channels of Christ's power are found in the sacraments of the church, of which there are 7: baptism, confirmation, the Holy Eucharist, absolution, holy unction, holy matrimony, and holy orders.

The liturgy for the Holy Eucharist in this church is a free translation of the Latin rite of the Roman Catholic Missal and Church, with modifications which have been drawn from other liturgies; other services have been similarly translated and modified. No images of the dead Christ are permitted in Liberal Catholic churches. Priests and bishops may or may not marry, and they exact no fee for the administration of the sacraments. Divine healing is stressed through the "revivifying power of the Holy Spirit, the grace of Absolution, the Sacred Oil for the Sick and the Sacrament of Holy Unction," but not to the exclusion of physicians and medicine.

Bishops are in charge of regional areas, and the General Episcopal Synod is the chief administrative and legislative body.

LIFE MESSENGERS

Life Messengers can hardly be called a denomination; they describe themselves as "an Evangelical Interdenominational Witness." Their purpose seems to be to refute the teachings of Jehovah's Witnesses (pp. 118-20), and to that end they circulate a flood of pamphlets and the book, *Thirty Years a Watchtower Slave,* by W. J. Schnell, among the preachers and laymen of all denominations. No statement on membership is available, due to the peculiar nature of the organization. Headquarters are located at 3530 Bagley Avenue, Seattle 11, Washington.

LITHUANIAN NATIONAL CATHOLIC CHURCH

Organized at Scranton, Pennsylvania, in 1914 with the assistance of Bishop Francis Hodur, head of the Polish National Catholic Church of America, this is a small group of 3,940 members in Pennsylvania, Massachusetts, and Illinois. The Illinois (Chicago) churches were established under the jurisdiction of Archbishop Carmel Henry Carfora of the North American Old Roman Catholic Church, but have since become independent.

Doctrine in this church is based upon the first 4 general councils of the church, and the Niceno-Constantinopolitan Creed is used. Liturgy is in the Lithuanian tongue; a synod exercises ecclesiastical authority over the local churches, of which there were 4 in 1957.

LUTHERANS

"Lutheran" was a nickname fastened upon the followers of Martin Luther by their enemies in the days of the Protestant Reformation; today it stands for something far more comprehensive. "It is clear," says Abdel R. Wentz, "that 'Lutheran' is a very inadequate name to give to a movement that is not limited to a person or an era but is as ecumenical and abiding as Christianity itself." Luther's teachings of justification by faith and of the universal priesthood of believers might be called the cornerstone of Protestantism.

The story of Luther's rebellion against the Roman Catholic Church is well-known history. His position was, briefly, that the Roman Catholic Church and papacy had no divine right in things spiritual; that the Scriptures, and not the Roman Catholic priest or church, had final authority over conscience. "Whatever is not against Scripture is for Scripture," said Luther, "and Scripture is for it." Men were forgiven and absolved of their sins, he believed, not by good works or by imposition of church rite—and especially not through the purchase of indulgences offered for sale by the Roman Catholic Church—but by man's Holy-Spirit-empowered action in turning from sin directly to God. Justification came through faith and not through ceremony, and faith was not subscription to the dictates of the church but "by the heart's utter trust in Christ." "The just shall live by faith" was the beginning and the end of his thought. He held the individual conscience to be responsible to God alone; he also held that the Bible was the clear, perfect, inspired, and authoritative word of God and guide of man. God, conscience, and the Book—on these were Lutheranism founded.

In 1529 Luther wrote his Longer and Shorter Catechisms. A year later a statement of faith known as the Augsburg Confession was authored by his scholarly associate Philip Melanchthon; 1537 brought the Smalcald Articles of Faith written by Luther, Melanchthon, and other German reformers. In 1577 the Formula of Concord was drawn up. These documents in explanation of Luther's ideology and theology form the doctrinal basis of Lutheranism.

The Reformation resulted, not in a united Protestantism, but in a Protestantism with 2 branches: Evangelical Lutheranism with Luther and Melanchthon as leaders; and the Reformed Church, or branch, led by Calvin, Zwingli, and John Knox. Evangelical Lutheranism spread from its birthplace in Germany to Poland, Russia, Lithuania, Czechoslovakia, Austria, Hungary, Yugoslavia, France, and Holland; it became in time the state church of Denmark, Norway, Sweden, Finland, Iceland, Estonia, and Latvia. It was mainly from Germany and Scandinavia that Lutheranism came to the United States.

A Lutheran Christmas service was held on Hudson Bay in 1619; the first European Lutherans to come here and stay permanently arrived on Manhattan Island from Holland in 1623. They had a congregation worshiping in New Amsterdam in 1649, but they did not enjoy full freedom in their worship until the English took over control of "New York" in 1664. The first independent colony of Lutherans was established by Swedes along the Delaware at Fort Christiana in the colony of New Sweden in 1638.

The New York Lutherans were largely Germans. German exiles from Salzburg also settled in Georgia, where in 1736 they built the first orphanage in America. Lutherans from Württemberg settled in South Carolina. The great influx, however, came to Pennsylvania, where by the middle of the eighteenth century there were 30,000 Lutherans, four fifths of them being German and one fifth Swedes. From Philadelphia they swept over into New Jersey, Maryland, Virginia, and North Carolina.

Their first churches were small, often without pastors; and because only a minority of the immigrants joined the church, they were poor churches. The situation was relieved with the coming of Henry Melchior Muhlenberg from the University of Halle to effect the first real organization of American Lutherans; in 1748 he organized pastors and congregations in Pennsylvania, New Jersey, New York, and Maryland into what came to be called the Ministerium of Pennsylvania; it was the first of many Lutheran synods in America. Other synods followed slowly: New York in 1786; North Carolina in 1803; Maryland in 1820; and Ohio in 1836. Each synod adjusted itself to its peculiar conditions

of language, national background, previous ecclesiastical relationship with Lutheran authorities abroad, and geographical location. The need for even further organization, aggravated by the ever-increasing immigration of Lutherans from Europe, resulted in the formation of the General Synod in 1820; with that the last real bonds with European Lutheranism began to break, and American Lutheranism was increasingly on its own.

The General Synod was obliged to extend its efforts farther and farther west as German, Swedish, Norwegian, Danish, Icelandic, and Finnish Lutherans came pouring into the new country. The Missouri Synod was formed in 1847. From 1850 to 1860 1,000,000 Germans arrived, and the majority of them were Lutherans; the German Iowa Synod was organized in 1854, and in the same year the Norwegian Lutheran Church was established. The Augustana Synod was created in 1860 to care for the Swedes in the new West. By 1870 the Lutherans had the fourth largest Protestant group in the country, with approximately 400,-000 members.

The Civil War brought the first serious break in the Lutheran ranks with the organization of the United Synod of the South in 1863; three years later a number of other synods led by the Ministerium of Pennsylvania withdrew from the General Synod to form the General Council. To increase the complexity, Lutheran immigrants arrived in larger and larger numbers; from 1870 to 1910 approximately 1,750,000 came from Sweden, Norway, and Denmark; and in those years the Lutheran church membership leaped from less than 500,000 to nearly 2,250,000 New Lutheran churches, colleges, seminaries, and publications were established from coast to coast.

Since 1910 there has been an almost constant effort toward the unification of Lutheran churches and agencies. Three of the large Norwegian bodies united in

1917 in the Norwegian Lutheran Church of America; some of the Midwest German synods merged in the Joint Synod of Wisconsin in 1918; the synods of Iowa, Ohio, and Buffalo merged in the American Lutheran Church in 1930. The General Synod, the General Council, and the United Synod of the South merged into the United Lutheran Church in 1918, and no less than seven Lutheran churches were included in mergers in 1960-61. In addition to these, 2 groupings were created for the sake of closer co-operation in the work of the churches: the Synodical Conference (1872), and the National Lutheran Council (1918). These are purely co-operative bodies with no legislative or administrative authority over the synods or congregations involved. The National Lutheran Council is especially effective in co-ordinating the work in welfare service to refugees, American missions, student service, public relations, and ministry to the armed forces of 6 participating church bodies: The United Lutheran Church in America; the American Lutheran Church; the Augustana Evangelical Lutheran church; the Lutheran Free Church; the American Evangelical Lutheran Church; and the Suomi Synod. Perhaps the most co-operative effort in the history of American Lutheranism is found in Lutheran World Action, through which over $165,000,000 in goods and cash (inclusive of $59,000,000 worth of U.S. government-donated commodities) have been distributed across the world.

In spite of their organizational division there is real unity among American Lutherans; it is a unity based more upon faith than upon organization. All Lutheran churches represent a single type of Protestant Christianity. Their faith is built upon Luther's principle of justification by faith alone in Jesus Christ; it centers in the gospel for fallen men. The Bible is the inspired word of God and the infallible rule and standard of faith and practice. Lutherans confess their faith through the 3 general creeds of Christendom, the Apostles', the Nicene, and the Athanasian, which they believe to be in accordance with the Scriptures. They also believe that the Unaltered Augsburg Confession is a correct exposition of the faith and doctrine of Evangelical Lutheranism. The Apology of the Augsburg Confession, the 2 catechisms of Luther, the Smalcald Articles, and the Formula of Concord are held to be a faithful interpretation of Evangelical Lutheranism and of the Bible.

The 2 sacraments of baptism and the Lord's Supper are not merely signs or memorials to the Lutheran but channels through which God bestows his forgiving and empowering grace upon men. The body and blood of Christ are believed to be present "in, with, and under" the bread and wine of the Lord's Supper, and are received sacramentally and supernaturally. Consubstantiation, transubstantiation, and impanation are rejected. Infants are baptized, and baptized persons are believed to receive the gift of regeneration from Holy Ghost.

The congregation is the basic unit of Lutheran government, which is usually administered by a church council consisting of the pastor and a number of elected lay officers, some of whom are called elders, some deacons, and some trustees. There is a growing tendency to call all lay officials deacons. Pastors are elected, called, or recalled by the voting members of the congregation, but a congregation itself may never depose a pastor from the ministry. As a rule ministers are ordained at the annual meetings of the synods; they are practically all trained in college and seminary.

Congregations are united in synods; these are composed of the pastors and lay representatives elected by the congregations and have only such authority as is granted by the synod constitution. In some other instances there are territorial districts or conferences instead of a synod, operating in the same manner and under the same restrictions; some of these may legislate, while others are for advisory or consultative purposes only.

Synods (conferences or districts) are united in a general body which may be national or even international and which is called variously "church," "synod," or "conference." Some of these general bodies are legislative in nature, some consultative; they supervise the work in worship, education, publications, charity, and missions. Congregations have business meetings at least annually; constituent synods, districts, and conferences hold yearly conventions, and the general bodies meet annually, biennially, or triennially.

Worship is liturgical, centering on the altar. "No sect in Western Christendom outside the Church of Rome," said the late Lutheran Archbishop Nathan Söderblom of Sweden, "has accentuated in its doctrine the Real Presence and the mysterious communion of the sacrament as has our Evangelic Lutheran sect, although our faith repudiates any quasi-rational magical explanation of the virtue of the sacrament."

Non-Lutherans are often critical of the divisions among American Lutherans, but actually they are not so divided as they seem. At one time there were 150 Lutheran bodies in this country; but consolidation, unification, and federation have now reduced the number to 17. Six of the bodies in the United States account for about 96.6 per cent of all Lutherans of North America. With the old barriers of speech and nationality disappearing, the tendency toward union becomes constantly stronger. Even on the international front united efforts are noticeable; groups of lay and ministerial delegates from major Lutheran churches in 22 countries in 1923 formed a Lutheran World Convention, which became the Lutheran World Federation in 1947, for the purposes of relief and rehabilitation among Lutherans on a global scale. That agency now serves 61 church bodies in 32 countries, having 50,000,000 members.

Historically the Lutherans have shown a tendency to remain apart from the rest of Protestantism. In the United States they have consisted of churches founded by immigrant groups deeply conscious of their national and linguistic origins, conservative, confessional, nonrevivalistic, and suspicious of anything that might tend to modify their Old World faith and traditions. These traits seem to be vanishing, however, as the older membership passes and an English-speaking generation takes over. The mother tongues of Lutheranism are still used occasionally, but English is predominant. One Lutheran body, the United Lutheran Church, was a consultative member of the Federal Council of the Churches of Christ in America; and 3 bodies—The United Lutheran Church in America, the Augustana Evangelical Lutheran Church, and the American Evangelical Lutheran Church—are charter members of the National Council of the Churches of Christ in the U.S.A. Four bodies—the United Lutheran Church, the American Lutheran Church, the Augustana Evangelical Lutheran Church, and the American Evangelical Lutheran Church—participated in the organization of the World Council of Churches. A fifth body, The Evangelical Lutheran Church, united with the World Council in 1957. Lutheran groups participating in interdenominational organizations have always insisted upon the operation of two principles within those organizations: the evangelical principle that the churches in the association should be those confessing the deity and saviorhood of Jesus Christ, and the representative principle that the organizations shall be made up of officially chosen representatives of the churches.

The American Lutheran Church

On April 22, 1960, 3 American Lutheran bodies merged into a new American Lutheran Church; they were The American Lutheran Church, the

136

Evangelical Lutheran Church, and the United Evangelical Lutheran Church. Active operation of The American Lutheran Church starts on January 1, 1961. In the following account, we trace first their history and doctrine as separate bodies, then as a unit in the new church.

AMERICAN LUTHERAN CHURCH (ORIGINAL)

The original American Lutheran Church was, at the momentt of merger, the fourth largest Lutheran body in this country, with 1,034,377 baptized and 652,278 confirmed members in 2,086 churches. It is of German background and heritage; its American history begins in the formation of the Ohio Synod in 1818. Germans fleeing persecution in the homeland organized the Buffalo Synod in 1845, and missionary effort produced the Texas Synod in 1851 and the Iowa Synod in 1854. An affiliation between Texas and Iowa came in 1896, under which the Texas group became a "district synod" of the Iowa body. The 3 bodies merged into the American Lutheran Church at Toledo, Ohio, in 1930.

Faith was based upon the Bible as the inspired and infallible word of God; in addition to this the church accepted the 3 ecumenical creeds (Apostles', Nicene, and Athanasian), the Unaltered Augsburg Confession, the Smalcald Articles, Luther's Large and Small catechisms, the Formula of Concord, and all the symbolical books of the Evangelical Lutheran Church.

To the merger this church brought 2 theological seminaries, 3 colleges, 1 university, 1 junior college, 90 parochial schools with 4,963 pupils, 2 homes for children, 2 homes for the aged, and 2 hospitals. Missionaries working in South India, New Guinea and Ethiopia will now work under the united board.

EVANGELICAL LUTHERAN CHURCH

The Evangelical Lutheran Church was the result of a merger in 1917 of 3 Lutheran bodies: the United Norwegian Church, the Norwegian Synod, and the Hague Synod. It adopted the name Evangelical Lutheran Church in 1946. At the time of the merger with the American Lutheran Church and the United Evangelical Lutheran Church, this was the third largest Lutheran body in America, with 1,153,566 baptized and 754,431 confirmed members, and more than 2,000 churches.

Theologically, the Bible was accepted as the only true source of faith, doctrine, and life, and the 3 ecumenical creeds, the Unaltered Augsburg Confession and Luther's Small Catechism. The body is noted for its emphasis upon evangelism at the local church level.

To the new American Lutheran Church, the Evangelical Lutheran Church brought 5 colleges, 1 junior college, a Bible institute and theological seminary in Canada, 3 academies and one theological seminary in the U.S., 1 family-service agency, 4 rescue homes, 2 deaconess homes and hospitals, 8 children's homes or placing agencies, and 22 homes for the aged. Missionaries served in South Africa, Japan, Madagascar, Latin America, Formosa and Hong Kong.

UNITED EVANGELICAL LUTHERAN CHURCH

The United Evangelical Lutheran Church was founded in 1896 by immigrants from Denmark. Actually it was a union of 2 former Danish synods—the Danish Evangelical Lutheran Association (organized in 1884 by a small group of pastors and congregations that had seceded from the Norwegian-Danish Conference of 1870) and the Danish Evangelical Lutheran Church in North America (created in 1894 by pastors and congregations separated from the Danish Evangelical Lutheran Church of America in 1872). At the time of its organization this merged church had 63 ordained pastors, 75 member congregations, and

52 associated congregations. By 1960 the number had increased to nearly 200 active pastors and 185 member congregations with 70,149 baptized and 42,000 confirmed members. The Danish language was generally used in the churches until World War I; all services were in English after 1930 and the "Danish" was deleted from the name in 1946.

Liturgy was based on the Altarbook of the Church of Denmark until the new joint Service Book and Hymnal for Lutheran Churches in America was adopted generally by the larger Lutheran bodies in 1958. The Confession of Faith of the church was based on the Augsburg Confession and on Luther's Small Catechism. As an evangelical and conservative church, the Bible was—and is—regarded as the inspired word of God.

Home missionaries worked in 22 congregations; foreign missionaries were stationed in Japan, South America, India, and the Sudan (Africa). There was 1 theological seminary (Trinity), at Dubuque, Iowa, 1 college (Dana) at Blair, Nebraska. There was also a publishing house, founded in 1893, located at Blair.

The new American Lutheran Church, the first in this century to merge across ethnic lines (Norwegian, German, Danish), will have a membership strength of about 2,200,000 and more than 5,000 congregations. Headquarters have been established at Minneapolis.

In government, the highest constitutional authority is the General Convention, which meets every two years in October; it is made up of approximately 1,000 delegates (500 lay, 500 clergy) elected from the 19 districts into which the church is (geographically) divided. There are 3 national officers—a president, vice-president, and secretary. A church council composed of the president of the church (as chairman), the vice president, the presidents of the 19 districts, 1 layman elected from each district, and 3 pastors and 3 lay representatives at large, meets once a year to generally direct and supervise the church in spiritual matters, to appoint the members and determine the policies of the two commissions of the church (Evangelism, and Research and Social Action) and of the Standing Committee on Worship and Music. It also makes recommendations to the General Convention in all matters of extrachurch and intersynodical relationships. The members of the church Council, together with the secretary of the church and the board of trustees, are also members of the Joint Council, which meets once a year to function as the legislative agency of the church in the interim between general conventions, to deal with emergency situations and to interpret the constitution and bylaws of the denomination. The Board of Trustees (6 laymen, 3 clergymen) controls the business affairs of the church; twelve other boards work in 6 divisions: American Missions, World Missions, Education, Publication, Charities, and Pensions. All boards have 9 members except the Theological and College boards with 12 each and Research and Social Action with 10.

Few, if any, compromises are evident in the statement of faith of the new body: the Confession of Faith accepts the Bible as divinely inspired, revealed, and inerrant; the 3 ancient ecumenical creeds (Apostles', Nicene, and Athanasian); the unaltered Augsburg Confession; Luther's Large and Small Catechisms; the Book of Concord of 1580; the Apology; the Smalcald Articles; and the Formula of Concord.

In the field of education, there will be a single theological seminary with 4 units, 10 senior colleges, 2 junior colleges, and 4 academies. There will be 8 children's homes, 37 homes for the aged, 6 homes for both children and the aged, 4 specialized institutions (sanitarium, infirmary, etc.), and 3 hospitals. Foreign missionaries will be supported in 13 countries overseas, and home missionaries in all 50 states and in Canada and Mexico.

Lutheran Church in America

As we go to press, 4 other Lutheran bodies in the United States are looking toward a merger. They are the United Lutheran Church in America, The American Evangelical Lutheran Church, the Finnish Evangelical Lutheran Church (Suomi Synod), and the Augustana Evangelical Lutheran Church. Combined under the proposed name of the Lutheran Church in America, they would have a total membership of 3,000,000. The constituent churches are to vote finally by June, 1961, and it is hoped that the merger may be accomplished by June, 1962. Inasmuch as there still remain some points of difference in the discussions between the churches, we hesitate to list them as one church, under their new name, so each is considered separately. If and when the merger is consummated, fourteen of the twenty-two boards involved will establish headquarters in New York City.

UNITED LUTHERAN CHURCH IN AMERICA

As of 1960 the United Lutheran Church in America was the largest of all Lutheran bodies, with 2,439,792 members in 4,552 churches. Their church dates back to colonial times and the Ministerium of Pennsylvania. It was officially created in the 1918 merging of the General Synod, the General Council, and the United Synod of the South; actually, it has been in existence since the first Lutheran colonists arrived on these shores. While strongly devoted to the historic creeds and confessions of Lutheranism, it might be distinguished from other groups such as the Missouri Synod by its application of a more liberal and progressive interpretation and polity.

The *Common Service Book* of the Lutheran Church, arranged between 1877 and 1902, was adopted in 1918. This book was used throughout the United Lutheran Church until 1958, when it was succeeded by the *Service Book and Hymnal,* produced jointly by National Lutheran Council bodies. A president, secretary, and treasurer are elected for terms of six years; and the body was incorporated in 1918 under the laws of the state of New York. Conventions have met biennially since that year, and the 45 constituent synods merged in 1918 have been reduced to 32. The United Lutheran Church is a participating body of the National Lutheran Council.

Polity is less firm than might be expected; forms of government and worship are of secondary importance, and each church and synod is, for the most part, independent in these matters. Hence synodical and congregational polity varies slightly.

The 15 boards of the 3 merging bodies were in time reduced to 8: social missions, publications, pensions, parish education, foreign missions, education, deaconess work, and American missions. These agencies previous to 1954 were practically self-governing, but in that year the nineteenth biennial convention gave the 21-member executive board authority to review the actions and to exercise veto power over the 8 boards, and oversight of the work of (ULCA) officers, boards, agencies, auxiliaries, and committees.

There are also national supervisory boards or committees for the United Lutheran Church Women, the Luther League of America (the young people's work of the denomination), the United Lutheran Church Men, and the Lutheran Laymen's Movement for Stewardship. Other special work is conducted through commissions and committees or through participation in the National Lutheran Council and the Lutheran World Federation. The delegated national convention of the whole church, including 1 pastor and 1 layman for every 11 pastoral charges, meets biennially; and the Council of Synodical Presidents meets annually as an advisory body on questions of policy and procedure. The top judicial body is known as the Court of Adjudication and Interpretation.

The United Lutheran Church has 13 colleges, 13 theological seminaries, 1 junior college, 2 deaconess training schools, 944 home mission congregations, and 2,415 congregations on foreign missionary fields in Liberia, Argentina, British Guiana, Uruguay, India, Japan, Hong Kong, Formosa, and Malaya. There are 36 family service agencies, 38 homes for the aged and infirm, 30 child care and child-placing agencies and institutions, 13 hospitals in the United States, and 1 in the Virgin Islands. The church uses 17 languages in carrying on its work and worship.

AMERICAN EVANGELICAL LUTHERAN CHURCH

Ministers sent from Denmark in 1872 founded this church under the name *Kirkelig Missionsforening.* In 1894, 22 pastors and 3,000 members left the organization to form what is now the United Evangelical Lutheran Church; but 35 pastors, 53 congregations and about 5,000 members remained to organize what is now the American Evangelical Lutheran Church. The dispute was concerned with the place and meaning of the Bible as the word of God in Lutheran theology.

Worship is in accordance with the *Common Service Book and Hymnal,* subject to the decisions of the annual conventions of this church. Congregations meet in these conventions to discuss matters brought before it by a board of directors of 9 members—4 officers and 5 trustees; officers are elected for a term of 4 years, the trustees for 3. This board is authorized to carry out the resolutions of the convention. The church is a participating body in the National Lutheran Council. There are 3 homes for the aged, 1 hospital, 1 orphan's home. A seaman's mission in Brooklyn, New York, is conducted as a branch of the Seamen's Church in Foreign Ports, in co-operation with the Church of Denmark. There are 2 missionaries in India; a junior college

(Grand View) is maintained at Des Moines, and a theological seminary is being established at Maywood, Illinois. There are 23,591 baptized members and 80 churches.

FINNISH EVANGELICAL LUTHERAN CHURCH (SUOMI SYNOD)

Organized at Calumet, Michigan, in 1890, this is strictly a confessional church. It uses the 3 ecumenical creeds, and the unaltered Confession of Augsburg. In liturgy it uses the *Service Book and Hymnal.* In its Finnish services, the liturgy of the Church of Finland is used.

An annual synodical convention, composed of lay delegates, administers the work of the church, with each congregation maintaining residual sovereignty. The church constitution confers certain judicial and executive authority upon a permanent board of trustees called the Consistory, which is composed of the president, vice-president, secretary, and notary; its members are elected quadrennially. At the present time, the synod is composed of 155 congregations scattered throughout the United States; it supports a college in Hancock, Michigan, and affiliates with the Chicago Lutheran Seminary in Maywood, Illinois. The synod has among its agencies a board of home missions which has established new congregations in Florida, Ohio, and California in recent years, a board of foreign missions which maintains two separate mission fields in Japan, and a publishing house at Hancock, Michigan. The baptized membership (as of 1959) is 35,963.

AUGUSTANA EVANGELICAL LUTHERAN CHURCH

The Swedes who settled along the Delaware, beginning in 1638, remained as a part of the mother church in Sweden throughout the colonial period. After the Revolution they passed under the control of the Protestant Episcopal Church. Two of their old historic churches—Holy

Trinity (Old Swedes) Church in Wilmington, Delaware, built in 1699, and Gloria Dei Church in Philadelphia, built in 1700—still remain.

The great tide of Swedish immigration in the 1840's, however, produced a large number of Swedish Lutherans who remained "within the fold." The first congregation of these immigrants, which later became part of the Augustana Synod, was formed at New Sweden, Iowa, in 1848; the second was in Andover, Illinois, in 1850. The original synodical organization was called the Synod of Northern Illinois, organized in 1851; the Swedes and Norwegians left this synod to form the Scandinavian Augustana Synod of North America in 1860. The word "Scandinavian" was dropped in 1894. This Augustana Synod withdrew from the General Council, declining to enter the merger of the General Synod, the General Council, and the United Synod of the South in the United Lutheran Church in America in 1918; but later it joined the National Lutheran Council.

Coming as it does out of the eighteenth-century pietism of Sweden, the church is solidly confessional, accepting the 3 ecumenical creeds and the Augsburg Confession.

The synod meets annually as a general body and is presided over by a president chosen quadrennially. An executive council functions between synods. There are 13 conferences within the synod, one of which is in Canada; and each of them meets annually. The *Service Book and Hymnal* sponsored by the National Lutheran Council is used in all services.

Foreign missionary stations are found in Formosa, Hong Kong, North Borneo, Japan, Africa, India, and Latin America. The synod lists 4 colleges, 1 junior college, 1 theological seminary, 2 family service agencies, 24 homes for the aged, 10 child care and child-placing agencies and institutions, 11 hospitals and sanatoria. There was a baptized membership of 605,380 in 1960, and 1,248 churches, from coast to coast, but with the greatest membership concentrations in Minnesota, Iowa, and Illinois.

Church of the Lutheran Brethren of America

This is an independent church body, with churches located in Minnesota, Wisconsin, North and South Dakota, Iowa, Illinois, and on both East and West coasts. Organized in Milwaukee in 1900, they differ from other Lutheran churches in accepting as members only those who profess a personal experience of salvation, and in stressing nonliturgical worship and lay participation. Brethren congregations do not have confirmation; they instruct their children and wait until there is an individual experience and conversion before receiving them as communicant members. Communion is received in the pew; there are no altars in church buildings. Free prayer and personal testimony are stressed.

The church as a body is the supreme administrative unit, with a president, two vice-presidents, secretary, and treasurer. Foreign missions are supervised by a board of 9 members, and home missions by a board of 10. With a total membership of some 5,000 in 50 congregations, the church conducts foreign missionary work in Africa, Japan, and Formosa. There are 53 adult missionaries abroad. On an annual budget of about $225,000 (high among Lutherans in proportion to the membership), the church supports a 4-year high school, a 2-year Bible course, a 3-year seminary course—all operated by the Synod at Fergus Falls, Minnesota. Sarepta Home for the Aged and the Broen Memorial Home are also controlled by the church. Synodical headquarters are located at Fergus Falls.

Evangelical Lutheran Church in America (Eielsen Synod)

The first Norwegian synod in the United States was organized in 1846 under this name. Elling Eielsen was a preacher who had been active in the revival movement inspired by Hans Nielsen Hauge in Norway earlier in the century. A difference of opinion over questions of doctrine and admission of members in the Eielsen Synod in 1875 resulted in a revised constitution and a change of name to Hauge's Norwegian Evangelical Lutheran Synod. A small group with Eielsen clung to the old constitution and the old name and reorganized, electing him as president. The synod still insists upon proof of conversion as a prerequisite for admission to membership in the church.

It is one of the smaller existent Lutheran churches, with only an inclusive membership of 4,220 in 44 churches. All male members vote in the annual meeting of the synod, which acts through a board of trustees and a church council of 7 members each. The trustees have charge of all church property, while the council rules on doctrine and discipline. A home missions board under the guidance of the council supervises a work among the Indians of Wisconsin. There are no foreign missionaries, but members contribute to the foreign missionary programs of other Lutheran churches.

Evangelical Lutheran Synod (Formerly The Norwegian Synod of the American Evangelical Lutheran Church)

This synod was formed in 1918 by a minority group which declined to join the union of other Norwegian bodies in 1917; the merging groups are now known as the Evangelical Lutheran Church and the dissenters as the Evangelical Lutheran Synod, a name adopted in 1958. The cause of the separation was chiefly doctrinal—a dispute over the tenets of election and grace.

The jurisdiction of the synod is entirely advisory; all synod resolutions are accepted or rejected by the local congregations. The officers and boards of the synod, however, direct the work of common interest insofar as they do not interfere with congregational rights or prerogatives. It is a constituent part of the Synodical Conference.

The synod uses the facilities of the colleges and seminaries of the Missouri and Wisconsin synods; it co-operates in the foreign missions work of the Missouri Synod in India. It has 31 home mission stations in the United States, 1 preparatory school, and 14,004 baptized members in 80 churches.

The Evangelical Lutheran Synodical Conference

This is one of the more conservative Lutheran groups. It was organized in 1872 by a group of synods adhering firmly to the conservative doctrine of sixteenth-century Lutheranism, "to encourage and strengthen one another in faith and confession; to further unity in doctrine and practice and to remove whatever might threaten to disturb this unity; to co-operate in matters of mutual interest." The second largest Lutheran conference in the United States (the National Lutheran Council has 5,362,008 baptized members, and the Synodical Conference has 2,703,275), it is strongly opposed to co-operation with other churches wherever doctrinal compromise is involved. The conference includes the Lutheran Church—Missouri Synod, the Wisconsin Evangelical Lutheran Synod, the Synod of Evangelical Lutheran Churches (formerly the Slovak Evangelical Lutheran Church) and the Evangelical Lutheran Synod (formerly the Norwegian Synod of the Evangelical Lutheran Church). Each of these churches is completely independent in its programs of education, missions, and publications, but they do unite in the promotion of Negro missions and the building of Negro churches. The synodical conference now has charge of 51 Negro churches with 7,443 members.

Delegate meetings, or conventions, are held biennially.

The conference also supervises the work of 96 home mission stations, a mission in Nigeria (186 stations), and another in Ghana, begun in 1958. Within the conference there are now 24 high schools, 6 colleges, 9 junior colleges, 4 theological seminaries, 1 university, 20 homes for the aged, 33 hospitals and sanitoria, and 24 child care and child-placing agencies.

Finnish Apostolic Lutheran Church of America

Sometimes called the "Church of Laestadius," after Lars Levi Laestadius, a minister of the State Church of Sweden, this church originated with Finnish immigrants in and around Calumet, Michigan, in the middle years of the nineteenth century. They worshiped at first in the Lutheran Church of Calumet under a Norwegian minister; however, differences between the 2 national groups led to the forming, in 1872, of a separate Finnish congregation led by Solomon Korteniemi and called the Solomon Korteniemi Lutheran Society. The first incorporated church in Michigan was incorporated under the name of The Finnish Apostolic Lutheran Church of Calumet, in 1879. The national church was formed and incorporated under the name of The Finnish Apostolic Lutheran Church of America in 1929; this body was actually a merger of independent Apostolic Lutheran congregations into the one national body. Spreading over Michigan, Minnesota, the Dakotas, Massachusetts, Oregon, Washington, and California, the new church was divided into 2 districts—eastern and western.

A scriptural Christian experience is required as a condition for voting membership in spiritual matters; supporting members may vote on temporal matters only. The church accepts the 3 ecumenical creeds and puts strong emphasis upon the confession of sins, absolution, and regeneration; confession may be made to a Christian brother, but if someone has fallen into sin which is known to other people private confession is not sufficient, and "he should confess them publicly before the congregation and receive absolution."

The 60 local congregations of this church are quite free to govern themselves; at the annual church convention, where every congregation has 1 vote, 3 members are elected to an executive board for 3-year terms; the board elects a president, vice-president, secretary, and treasurer. Three members are also elected to the Eastern and Western mission boards and to the Elder's Home Board. There were 6,567 members in 1953.

The Lutheran Church—Missouri Synod

With 2,442,933 members and 5,948 churches (as of 1958) this is the second largest Lutheran church in the United States and the largest within the Synodical Conference. The "Missouri" in the name comes from the founding of the denomination in that state by Saxon immigrants; these were later joined by Hanoverians in Indiana and Franconians in Michigan. From the start all 3 of these groups were devoted to the maintenance of orthodox Lutheranism. They were Germans who had fought the trend toward rationalism in the old country and who came here for the sake of religious freedom and to establish a synod in which the sovereignty of the local congregation would be recognized.

This synod was organized in 1847 with 12 congregations and 22 ministers under the name German Evangelical Lutheran Synod of Missouri, Ohio, and Other States. Under the constitution adopted at the time all the symbolical books of the Lutheran Church were considered to be the "pure and uncorrupted explanation of the Divine Word," and doctrinal agreement was required for exchange of pulpits and altars with other churches.

The doctrinal standard of the Missouri Synod is strictly observed and enforced. That standard is found in the Bible "as it was interpreted by the Book of Concord," plus the 3 ecumenical creeds—the Apostles', the Nicene, and the Athanasian—and the 6 Lutheran confessions: the Augsburg Confession, the Apology of the Augsburg Confession, the Smalcald Articles, the Formula of Concord, and the 2 catechisms of Martin Luther. All across the years the synod has been unswerving in its allegiance to this conservative Lutheranism.

There are the usual Lutheran districts and district conventions, and the general convention meets triennially.

A startling work is done in education; the Missouri Synod has 1,430 parochial schools and 17 high schools, and 5,321 Sunday schools. It has 1,135 congregations in home mission fields and a total of 729 foreign mission stations in India, Japan, Formosa, New Guinea, Korea, Hong Kong, and the Philippines. The synod serves a total of 1,274 colleges and universities through its Student Service Commission, with 31 full-time pastors. It has 23 hospitals, 16 homes for the aged and 13 homes for children, 1 tuberculosis sanitarium and 3 convalescent homes, 9 junior colleges, 2 teachers' colleges, and 1 senior college. Concordia Seminary in St. Louis and Concordia Seminary in Springfield, Illinois, are the 2 largest Lutheran seminaries in America; and Valparaiso University at Valparaiso, Indiana, is the second largest Lutheran college in this country.

Affiliated with the Missouri Synod are the Walther League (a youth organization), the Lutheran Women's Missionary League, and the Lutheran Laymen's League. This synod carries on the most extensive work among the deaf in American Protestantism, with 37 full-time pastors serving 37 congregations for the deaf.

Lutheran Free Church

Organized in 1897 by seceders from the United Norwegian Lutheran Church of America, the Lutheran Free Church is remarkable for its emphasis upon the independence and autonomy of the local congregation, and it generally distrusts any higher governing body. While allowing wide freedom in doctrine, it has from the start adhered to the 3 ecumenical creeds and to the Lutheran confessions, with special emphasis on the unaltered Augsburg Confession and Luther's Small Catechism. Religious experience is regarded as more important than unity in doctrine, and there is constant effort to awaken and cultivate a deeper spiritual life within the congregation.

Each congregation is autonomous and "governs its own affairs subject to the authority of the Word of God and the Spirit." In harmony with this principle, the church body is not incorporated but the Board of Administration, its major executive board, is incorporated. Decisions of the annual conference are advisory only; this annual conference makes recommendations to the congregations of amounts necessary to carry on the several church activities. The activities connected with schools and missions are conducted by independently incorporated boards. The church operates two schools—Augsburg College and Theological Seminary in Minneapolis, and Oak Grove Lutheran High School in Fargo, North Dakota; it has 39 missionaries serving in Hong Kong, Formosa, Japan, and Madagascar. There are 3 homes for the aged, 1 deaconess home, and one hospital and nurses' training school.

The Lutheran Free Church is a member of the National Lutheran Council and an active participant in the Lutheran

144

World Federation. There are 80,248 members and 343 congregations.

National Evangelical Lutheran Church

Created by a dissenting group which withdrew from union with the Suomi Synod for fear that the synod was losing its congregational freedom and autonomy, this church was organized at Rock Springs, Wyoming, in 1898. It functioned for some years as the Finnish Evangelical Lutheran National Church of America. It resembles in polity and doctrine to the Missouri Synod.

Local churches send delegates to an annual meeting. A board of directors is elected, one member each year, for a 4-year term of office. The president is the executive officer of the church and acts as general representative of the denomination. Ordination of candidates is performed by the annual convention with the president as authorized officiant.

The work of the church is carried out by the Board for Missions and Evangelism, the Extension Board, the Board for Parish Education, the Pension and Disability Board, the Committee for Christian Stewardship, and the Committee on Doctrine and Practice.

The local congregations are autonomous and are aided by the synodical body which acts in an advisory and cohesive capacity. Geographically the church is divided into districts, each with its own executive and administrative boards and committees.

The church co-operates with The Lutheran Church—Missouri Synod in mission work in New Zealand and Finland, and with the Evangelical Lutheran Church of Australia in mission work among the Finnish immigrants in North Queensland, Australia. There are 9,195 members in 57 congregations in the U.S.A.

Orthodox Lutheran Conference

This body, like the Protestant Conference, is a small splinter body seeking fresh allegiance to the old doctrinal positions of orthodox Lutheranism. The objection here was to the "deviations" of the Missouri Synod from established belief—which would seem to make the Orthodox Lutheran Conference ultra-conservative. Organized in 1951 by former members of the Missouri Synod, there are as yet no statistics available on program, churches, or membership.

The Protestant Conference (Lutheran)

Dissatisfaction with alleged deviations from the original doctrinal positions of the Joint Synod of Wisconsin in 1928 led to the creation of the Protestant Conference (Lutheran). Members objected to "mistaken dogmas current in the church" and sought to correct the "spirit of self-righteousness and self-sufficiency" through a re-emphasis upon the "Gospel of Forgiveness of Sins through Our Blessed Saviour." The conference is reticent to release any statistical or organizational information; an inclusive membership of 3,000 in 11 churches was reported in 1959. A general conference meets semiannually; and one publication, *Faith-Life*, is issued from Manitowoc, Wisconsin.

Synod of Evangelical Lutheran Churches (Formerly the Slovak Evangelical Lutheran Church)

Established at Connellsville, Pennsylvania, in 1902, this church works in close co-operation with the Missouri Synod. The membership, 18,003, and the churches, 59, are grouped into 3 districts —eastern, central, and western. Synodical meetings are held every 2 years. Contributions are made by the membership to the home and foreign missionary programs of the Missouri Synod and the Synodical Conference, although the synod has its own board of missions.

Wisconsin Evangelical Lutheran Synod

Organized in 1850 under the name First German Lutheran Synod of Wisconsin, 3 synods—Wisconsin, Minnesota, and Michigan—united in an organic union in 1918 as The Evangelical Lutheran Joint Synod of Wisconsin and Other States. This name was changed in August of 1959 to The Wisconsin Evangelical Lutheran Synod. Very close to the theological pattern of the Missouri Synod, they stand for orthodox, confessional Lutheranism and are opposed to tendencies toward union *without doctrinal unity* among Lutheran groups.

The synod is divided into 9 districts, from Michigan, Ohio, and Florida to Arizona, California, and the Pacific Northwest. The districts meet in convention every even year, in joint synodical conference in odd years, with pastors, teachers, and laymen as delegates. With 346,790 baptized members and 233,357 communicant members in 853 congregations, it is a constituent member of the Synodical Conference, carrying on within the conference work among Negroes in America and among the natives of Nigeria and Ghana, in Africa. The synod conducts its own missions, from 195 mission stations, among the Apache Indians and Spanish-speaking people in Arizona (since 1893), Germany, Rhodesia, and Japan. There are 2 senior colleges, 5 junior colleges and academies, 1 theological seminary, 1 teachers' seminary, 8 area Lutheran high schools, some 22,616 children in 215 parochial schools, 3 homes for the aged, and 4 children's homes.

MAYAN TEMPLE

Incorporated in 1928 and reporting 3,312 members in 13 churches or groups in 1947, the Mayan Temple is a "restoration of the pristine faith catholic, practiced by the Mayas in prehistoric America and common to all North and South America, prior to the coming of the white man." Followers seek to preserve the ceremonials of various Indian tribes, to keep a record of all Americans with Indian blood, and to restore to religion certain values lost across the ages—music, the dance, healing, education, culture, interest in material as well as spiritual welfare, and so forth. They have as their aim the practice of scientific religion and the logical understanding of life and its purpose. They believe in one God and that reincarnation and the continuity of life are both reasonable and in accord with science and scientific discovery. The Ancient and Mystical Order of Po-ahtun, composed of both clergy and laity, is reported as the chief administrative body of the temple; a pontiff, abbot, and dean are also listed.

MENNONITES

The first Mennonite congregation of historical record was organized at Zurich, Switzerland, in 1525; it consisted of Swiss Brethren, or *Täufer*, who disagreed with Ulrich Zwingli in his readiness to consent to a union of church and state. They also denied the scriptural validity of infant baptism and hence were labeled Anabaptists, or Rebaptizers. Anabaptists congregations were organized in Holland by Obbe Philips as early as 1534; Philips baptized Menno Simons (*ca.* 1496-1561) in 1536.

Menno was a converted Roman Catholic priest; he organized more Anabaptist congregations in Holland, and his followers gave his name to the movement. Many of his Flemish adherents

146

crossed the channel on the invitation of Henry VIII. In England as well as in Germany, Holland, and Switzerland they met opposition largely because of their determined distrust of any union of church and state. An impressive martyr roll was created; it might have been much larger had it not been for the sudden haven offered in the American colony of William Penn. Thirteen families settled in Germantown, near Philadelphia, in 1683. Eventually they established a Mennonite congregation there, although many of them had left the Mennonite fold and united with the Quakers before they left Crefeld, Germany. Mennonite immigrants from Germany and Switzerland spread over Pennsylvania, Ohio, Virginia, Indiana, Illinois, farther west, and into Canada; these were later joined by others coming from Russia, Prussia, and Poland. Thanks to their historic insistence upon nonresistance their colonial settlements were comparatively peaceful and prosperous.

The faith of these Mennonites was based upon a confession of faith signed at Dordrecht, Holland, in 1632. In 18 articles the following doctrines were laid down: faith in God as creator; man's fall and restoration at the coming of Christ; Christ as the Son of God, redeeming men on the cross; obedience to Christ's law in the gospel; the necessity of repentance and conversion for salvation; baptism as a public testimony of faith; the Lord's Supper as an expression of common union and fellowship; matrimony as permissible only among those "spiritually kindred"; obedience to and respect for civil government except in the use of armed force; exclusion from the church of those who sin willfully and their social ostracism for the protection of the faith of others in the church; and future rewards and punishments for the faithful and the wicked.

The Lord's Supper is served twice a year in almost all Mennonite congrega-

tions, and in most of them baptism is by pouring. Most of them observe the foot-washing ordinance in connection with the Supper, after which they salute each other with the "kiss of peace." The sexes are separated in the last 2 ceremonies. All Mennonites baptize only on confession of faith, refuse to take oaths before magistrates, oppose secret societies, and follow strictly the teachings of the New Testament. They have a strong intrachurch program of mutual aid and a world-wide relief and eleemosynary service through an all-Mennonite relief organization called the Mennonite Central Committee.

The local congregation is more or less autonomous and authoritative, although in some instances appeals are taken to district or state conferences. The officers of the church are bishops (often called elders), ministers, and deacons (almoners). Many ministers are self-supporting, working in secular employments when not occupied with the work of the church. There are other appointed officers for Sunday school, young people's work, and so forth.

The Amish movement within the ranks of the Mennonites takes its name from Jacob Amman, a Swiss (Bernese) Mennonite bishop of the late seventeenth century who insisted upon strict conformation to the confession of faith, especially in the matter of the ban, or expulsion of members. This literalism brought about a separation in Switzerland in 1693; about 200 years later the divided bodies, with the exception of 3 Amish groups, were reunited.

Amish immigrants to the United States concentrated early in Pennsylvania and moved from there into Ohio, Indiana, Illinois, Nebraska, and other western states; some went into Canada. They have today a common literature. Many of the Amish, distinguished by their severely plain clothing, are found in the Conservative Amish Mennonite Church and the larger Old Order Amish Mennonite Church. They are still the "literalists" of the movement, clinging tenaciously to the "Pennsylvania Dutch" language and to the seventeenth-century culture of their Swiss-German forebears. They oppose automobiles, telephones, higher education, and so forth, but are recognized as very efficient farmers.

Beachy Amish Mennonite Churches

These churches are made up of Amish Mennonites who separated from the more conservative Old Order Mennonites over a period of years, beginning in Somerset County, Pennsylvania, in 1927. They were led by Bishop Moses M. Beachy, who died in 1946. There are today about 12 congregations and over 2,000 members.

They resemble the Old Order Amish in garb and general attitudes, but their discipline is more mild and relaxed, especially in the matter of shunning; they do not "shun" (refuse to recognize) those members of their group who leave to join other churches.

Church of God in Christ (Mennonite)

This church grew out of the preaching and labors of John Holdeman, a member of the Mennonite Church who became dissatisfied with what he thought was a lack of allegiance in that church to the principles laid down by Menno Simons, especially in its failure to enforce the ban. Holdeman completed his organization in Ohio in 1859. Since his death his followers have considerably relaxed the discipline based on his views. The Church of God in Christ is unique in refusing to take interest on money loaned; this is prohibited in its membership. There are 6,200 members in 33 churches.

Conference of the Evangelical Mennonite Church

Formerly the Defenseless Mennonite Church of North America, this is a branch of the Amish Mennonite Church which left that body in 1860 under the leadership of Henry Egli, seeking a more positive emphasis upon conversion. Members work closely with the Evangelical Mennonite Brethren, supporting missionary work in Tennessee, an orphanage at Flanagan, Illinois, and the foreign missionary stations of the Belgian Congo mission. There are 2,301 members in 21 churches.

Conservative Mennonite Conference

With 5,484 members in 40 churches this is a small body subscribing to the Dordrecht Confession of Faith. Its first general conference was held at Pigeon, Michigan, in 1910. It separated gradually from the Old Order Amish, installing such innovations as meetinghouses, Sunday schools, evening and "continued" meetings, and the use of English rather than German in worship.

Evangelical Mennonite Brethren

Formerly called the Conference of Defenseless Mennonites of North America, this group lists 2,580 members in 14 churches. It was established by Russian Mennonite immigrants 1873-74 and supports missionaries in China and Africa in co-operation with the Evangelical Mennonite Church and has identical polity and doctrine.

Evangelical Mennonite Church

Formerly known as (*Mennonite*) *Kleine Gemeinde* (Little Congregation), this body was organized as the result of a split among the Mennonites in Russia in 1812; the "little congregations" stood for a strict enforcement of discipline. They established several churches in the United States in the 1870's, where their membership has now declined to 25. Most of them are resident in Canada, where they report 2,000 members.

The General Conference Mennonite Church

This conference was organized at the instigation of several Iowa congregations who sought the uniting of all Mennonite bodies into one; the actual outcome was the formation of an additional body. They created the General Conference in 1860, drawing into it many Russian and German congregations and the Central Mennonite Conference, a former Amish body.

This conference accepts most established Mennonite doctrine and practice, but it does not require its women to cover their heads during prayer or worship, nor does it uniformly consider foot washing as a "command of Christ." Musical instruments are employed in many of the churches. Governmental organization parallels that of the Mennonite Church, with local and district conferences, and a general conference meeting every 3 years. The general conference elects a board of 9 trustees and appoints boards for home missions, foreign missions, and publications. This body of Mennonites stresses the autonomy of the local congregation even more than the Mennonite Church.

Home missionary effort consists chiefly of evangelistic work and supplying needy congregations with ministers. Foreign mission stations are located among the American Indians and in India and Japan. There are 2 colleges and 1 junior college, 5 homes for the aged, 7 hospitals, 3 girls' homes, and a nurses' training school. It is the second largest American Mennonite group, with 51,378 members and 250 churches.

Hutterian Brethren

These are the modern disciples of Jacob Hutter, a sixteenth-century Tyrolean Anabaptist who advocated communal ownership of property. He was burned as a heretic in Austria in 1536. Many of the Hutterites came from Russia to Canada and the United States about 1874; they have moved back and forth across the border ever since. Most of them today are of German ancestry and use the German tongue in their homes and churches. Aside from the "common-property" idea, they are quite similar to the Old Order Amish: they have a Bible-centered faith which they seek to express in brotherly love; they aim at the recovery of the New Testament spirit and fellowship; they feel that this requires nonconformity to the world, and accordingly they practice nonresistance; refuse to participate in local politics, dress differently, make no contributions to community projects, and have their own schools, in which the Bible is paramount. Their exclusiveness has made them unwelcome in certain sections of the country, and their status is uncertain at the moment. There are 31 colonies of Hutterites in South Dakota, Minnesota, and Montana, with a population of 3,204.

Krimmer Mennonite Brethren Conference

Made up largely of descendants of Russian immigrants, this group was founded in the Crimea by Jacob A. Wiebe in 1869. It has an unusual method of baptism, immersing candidates for membership backward, like the Baptists, instead of forward, as in other immersionist Mennonite churches. Continued efforts have been made to unite this branch with the Mennonite Brethren Church. The conference has a home missionary work among the Negroes of North Carolina and foreign missions in Mongolia and China. There were 2 colleges, 1 academy, 1 hospital, 1 home for the aged, and there were 1,792 members in 11 churches in 1958.

Mennonite Brethren Church of North America

Russian in background, this church stems from a Mennonite Brethren church organized on the Molotschna River in Russia by a Mennonite group seeking a rigid enforcement of the ban and closer attention to prayer and Bible study. Small bodies of these Russians reached America in 1874, spreading through the Midwest to the Pacific coast and into Canada.

A general conference meets triennially as the chief administrative body, gathering delegates from 5 district conferences. District conferences supervise a large work in evangelism; home missions are found among the Indians and Mexicans of Oklahoma; and foreign missions are maintained in India, Central and South America, Europe, Japan, and Africa. There are 24,711 members and 146 churches—which represents a phenomenal growth from 11,930 members in 65 churches in 1954.

Mennonite Church

This is the largest single group of Mennonites in this country, with 83,204 members and 612 churches; it is the church founded by the Germantown immigrants in 1683. It holds firmly to the Dordrecht Confession of Faith—though with a mild interpretation of "shunning" expelled members—and is progressive in practice. A general conference meets every 2 years as an advisory body; deacons and ministers who are not elected delegates from the district or state conference may debate but not vote; the bishops and other delegates from the district conferences render decisions by a majority vote. The district conferences set the disciplinary standards for their respective congregations. Bishops, ministers, and deacons serve as delegates; some districts also have lay delegates. Three conferences of the former Amish Mennonite Church have been merged with the district and state conferences of this church.

Church-wide autonomous boards and committees are in charge of missionary, educational, publishing, and philan-thropic work; they are not under the supervision of the general conference. Home missions stress evangelism; and foreign missions are found in Africa, India, Japan, Puerto Rico, and South America. There are 2 colleges, several academies, 1 hospital, 2 nurses' training schools, 3 orphans' homes, and 4 homes for the aged.

Old Order Amish Mennonite Church

Organized about 1865, this church adheres strictly to the older forms of worship and attire, using hooks and eyes instead of buttons on coats and vests, worshiping as a group in private homes and having no conferences. Members do not believe in conferences, missions, or benevolent institutions, and have aroused attention by their adamant opposition to centralized schools. Some of them, however, contribute to the missions and charities of the Mennonite Church. There are 17,785 members and 250 churches.

Old Order (Wisler) Mennonite Church

This church was named for the first Mennonite bishop in Indiana, Jacob Wisler, who led a separation from the Mennonite Church in 1870. Those who separated did so in protest against the use of English in the services and the introduction of Sunday schools. Joined in 1886, 1893, and 1901 by groups with similar ideas from Canada, Pennsylvania, and Virginia, they still maintain their church on the basis of these protests. Each section of the church has its own district conference; there are no benevolent or missionary enterprises, but some members contribute to the work of the Mennonite Church in those fields. There are 6,116 members and 44 churches.

Reformed Mennonite Church

This church represents a protest against the established Mennonite churches as "corrupt and dead bodies," and the stricter enforcement of Mennonite discipline, led by Francis Herr and his son John Herr in Lancaster County, Pennsylvania, in 1812. The Reformed Church has no written discipline but is rigid in enforcing the ban on members who violate or neglect what might be called their unwritten discipline. It adheres vigorously to the principle of nonresistance, has no missionary or educational work, and reports 616 members in 19 churches. This is the group described in the novel *Tillie, a Mennonite Maid* by H. R. Martin.

Stauffer Mennonite Church

This body has only 2 churches and 375 members; it was organized in 1845 by Jacob Stauffer at Lancaster, Pennsylvania, following a disciplinary dispute in the Groffdale, Pennsylvania, congregation. It is an extremely conservative

church, using the German language and having no educational, missionary, or benevolent work. A group known as the Weaver Mennonites left the church soon after its organization and now has 60 members.

Unaffiliated Mennonites

There are a number of what might be called "splinter" Mennonite churches which hold unaffiliated status with all the other groups. One of the largest of these bodies is known as the Unaffiliated Conservative Amish Mennonite Churches; it claims 2,034 members enrolled in 20 churches. According to the Mennonite Yearbook and Directory there are 4 other Mennonite congregations, with 950 members, who are included in the statistics reported for the Mennonite Church but who have no other relationship with that church.

METHODISTS

England's famed old Oxford University has been called the "cradle of lost causes," but at least one cause was born there which was not lost. This was Methodism. Known and ridiculed at Oxford in 1729, it claims today 13,611,336 adherents in the United States, 14,548,000 in North America, and 19,100,000 around the world. The influence of Methodism is even more impressive than its numbers.

In 1729 the Oxford Methodists (also dubbed "Bible Bigots," "Bible Moths," and the "Holy Club") were a tiny group of students who gave stated time to prayer and Bible reading; prominent among them were John and Charles Wesley and George Whitefield. They were methodically religious, talking of the necessity of being justified before they could be sanctified and of the need of holiness in human living, reading and

discussing William Law's *A Serious Call to a Devout and Holy Life* and *A Treatise on Christian Perfection*. The two Wesleys were sons of a clergyman of the Church of England; with the other members of the Holy Club they stood their ground against jeering students and went out to preach and pray with the poor and desperate commoners of England—prisoners in jail, paupers in hovels, bitter and nearly hopeless "underdogs of a British society that was perilously close to moral and spiritual collapse." Methodism started on a campus and reached for the masses.

The Wesleys came to Georgia in 1736. Charles came as secretary to General Oglethorpe, and John was sent by the Society for the Propagation of the Gospel as a missionary to the Indians. It was an unsuccessful and unhappy 2 years for John Wesley with but one bright spot; on shipboard en route to the colonies he met a group of Moravians and became deeply impressed by their piety and humble Christian living. Later when he returned to London, he went one night to meet with a religious society in Aldersgate Street, heard the preacher read Luther's preface to the Epistle to the Romans and felt his heart "strangely warmed" as the meaning of the reformer's doctrine of "justification by faith" sank into his soul. It was the evangelistic spark that energized his life and started the flame of the Wesleyan revival in England. From the pious Moravians via Wesley came the warm-hearted emphases upon conversion and holiness which are still the central themes of Methodism.

Whitefield and the Wesleys were too much afire to remain within the staid Church of England. When its doors were closed to them, they took to the open air, John preaching and Charles writing the hymns of the revival in streets, barns, and private homes and in the mining pits of Cornwall, preaching repentance, regeneration, turning from sin and the wrath to come, justification, holiness, and sanctification. The upper classes laughed, and the lower classes listened to the first words of hope they had heard in many a year. Converts came thick and fast; it became necessary to organize them into societies. The first Methodist society was attached to a Moravian congregation in Fetter Lane, London, in 1739 and later moved to its own quarters in an old, abandoned government building known as the Foundry, where the first self-sustaining Methodist society in London was organized in 1740.

Between 1739 and 1744 the organizational elements of Methodism were instituted; we read of a "circuit system" and of an "itinerant ministry," of class meetings and class leaders, of lay preachers and annual conferences. There was a phenomenal growth in membership; more than 26,000 Methodists were wor-shiping in England, Ireland, Scotland, and Wales in 1767. Their impact upon British society was startling; the crudities and barbarisms of the times were alleviated and a "French revolution" averted. It was primarily a lay movement.

Wesley did his best to keep the movement within the Church of England; an Evangelical Party grew within the church, but the greater numbers recruited from among the unchurched made a separate organization imperative. In 1739 Wesley drew up a set of general rules which are still held by modern Methodists and an ideal delineation of Bible rules and conduct. A Deed of Declaration in 1784 gave legal status to the yearly Methodist conference. But John Wesley was dead in 1791 before Methodism in England had the name of a recognized church, the Wesleyan Methodist Connection.

Meanwhile the movement had invaded the American colonies. Wesley had begun to send out leaders; the first of them were Joseph Pilmoor and Richard Boardman. Philip Embury, an Irish lay leader, encouraged by his cousin Barbara Heck, preached in New York and inspired the organization about 1766 of the first Methodist society overseas. By 1769 the New York Methodists had built Wesley Chapel, now known as John Street Methodist Church. To the south Captain Thomas Webb, a veteran of Braddock's ill-fated army, established societies in Philadelphia, and Robert Strawbridge started a revival in Maryland and built a log-cabin church at Sam's Creek. Devereux Jarratt, a transplanted evangelical Anglican minister, led a revival in Virginia which won thousands. The true center of Methodism in those days did indeed lie in the South; out of 3,148 Methodists in the colonies in 1735 about 2,384 lived south of Mason and Dixon's Line. Wesley, aware of the rapid spread of the movement in America, sent emissaries to take charge, among them Francis Asbury and his successor, Thomas

Rankin, the latter as the first full-fledged "superintendent of the entire work of Methodism in America." Rankin presided over the first conference in America, called at Philadelphia in 1773 and attended by 10 ministers.

There were about 1,160 Methodists represented in the conference of 1773; when the Liberty Bell rang in 1776, there were less than 7,000 in all the colonies, and they seemed doomed to disappear as quickly as they had been gathered. The majority of their preachers had come from England and were incurable British; they were so roughly handled by the patriots that by 1779 nearly every one of them had fled either to Canada or home to England. Wesley's pro-British attitude also roused resentment, and Francis Asbury working almost singlehanded had a difficult time keeping some of the churches alive. But a miracle happened; of all the religious groups in the colonies the Methodists alone actually seemed to prosper during the revolution. When the surrender came at Yorktown, their membership had grown to 14,000 and there were nearly 80 preachers. They were, after Yorktown, an American church, free of both England and the Church of England. Wesley accepted the inevitable; he ordained ministers for the colonies and appointed Asbury and Thomas Coke as superintendents, or bishops.

Coke brought with him from England certain instructions from Wesley, a service book and hymnal, and authority to proceed with the organization. A Christmas Conference held at Baltimore in December of 1784 organized the Methodist Episcopal Church, elected Coke and Asbury as superintendents (later called bishops), and adopted the Sunday Service (an abridgment of the Book of Common Prayer), and Articles of Religion as written by John Wesley, adding another article that as good patriots Methodists should vow allegiance to the United States government. The first general conference of the new church was

held in 1792, made up solely of ministers. It was not until 1872 that laymen were admitted to what had become by that time a quadrennial general conference. Membership soared: from 37 circuits and 14,000 members at the close of the revolution there came a membership of 1,324,000 by the middle of the following century.

Methodism not only swept through the cities; it developed an amazing strength in small towns and rural areas. Everywhere there were circuit riders—ministers on horseback riding the expanding frontier and preaching in mountain cabins, prairie churches, schoolhouses, and camp meetings of free grace and individual responsibility and the need of conversion and regeneration. Their itinerant ministry was perfectly adapted to the democratic society of the frontier. The Methodist Book Concern was established in 1789, putting into the saddlebags of the circuit riders a religious literature which followed the march of American empire south and west. The camp meeting, born among the Presbyterians though not always carried on by them, was adopted by the Methodists and exploited to the limit. Its revivalistic flavor and method were made to order for the followers of Wesley and Whitefield. There are still camp meetings in Methodism.

All was not peaceful, however, among all the Methodists; divisions came. Objecting, like good democrats, to what they considered abuses of the episcopal system, several bodies broke away: the Republican Methodists, later called the Christian Church, withdrew in Virginia; Methodist Protestants seceded in 1830. Between 1813 and 1817 large Negro groups formed independent churches: the African Methodist Church; the Union Church of Africans, now the Union American Methodist Episcopal Church; and the African Methodist Episcopal Zion Church. In 1844 came the most devastating split of all, the bisecting of the Methodist Episcopal

153

Church into 2 churches, the Methodist Episcopal Church, the northern body; and the Methodist Episcopal Church, South.

The cause of this major split was, of course, slavery. Bishop Andrew, a Georgian, owned slaves through inheritance; and his wife was also a slaveholder. It was not possible for him or his wife to free their slaves under the laws of Georgia. The general conference of 1844, held in New York City, requested him to desist from the exercise of his office so long as he remained a slaveholder. Incensed, the southern delegates rebelled, a provisional plan of separation was formulated, and the Southerners went home to organize their own church in 1845. Basic to the separation was the constitutional question of the power of the General Conference, which, the Southerners maintained, assumed supreme power in virtually deposing a bishop against whom no charges had been brought, who had violated no law of the church, and who had been given no trial. It was a split that concerned neither doctrine nor polity; it was purely political and social, and it was a wound that waited until 1939 for healing. In that year the Methodist Episcopal Church, the Methodist Episcopal Church, South, and the Methodist Protestant Church were reunited at Kansas City, Missouri.

The uniting conference of 1939 adopted a new constitution in 3 sections: the Articles of Religion, drawn up by John Wesley and based on the 39 Articles of Religion of the Church of England; the General Rules, covering the conduct of church members and the duties of church officials; and the Articles of Organization and Government, outlining the organization and conduct of conferences and local churches. This constitution cannot be changed by any general conference unless and until every annual conference has acted on the changes proposed.

In matters of faith there has been very little occasion for confusion or differ-ence among Methodists; heresy trials and doctrinal quarrels have been noticeably absent. Historically they have never built theological fences or walls to keep anyone out; they have stressed the great foundation beliefs of Protestantism and offered common ground acceptable to those uninterested in theological trivialities. Some of the churches repeat the Apostles' Creed in their worship, but not all of them, though the discipline of the church provides for its use in formal worship. Their theology is Arminian, as interpreted by Wesley in his sermons, his notes on the New Testament, and his Articles of Religion.

They preach and teach doctrines of the Trinity, the natural sinfulness of mankind, man's fall and need of conversion and repentance, freedom of the will, justification by faith, sanctification and holiness, future rewards and punishments, the sufficiency of the Scriptures for salvation, perfection and the enabling grace of God. Two sacraments, baptism and the Lord's Supper, are observed; baptism is administered to both infants and adults, usually by sprinkling. Membership—full, preparatory, or "affiliate" (the latter arranged for people away from their home church who wish to affiliate where they live)—is based upon confession of faith or by letter of transfer from other evangelical churches; admission of children to membership is usually limited to those 13 years of age or over, though in the South the age may be 2 or 3 years younger. There is wide freedom in the interpretation and practice of all doctrine; liberals and conservatives work in close harmony.

The local churches in Methodism probably enjoy less freedom than most Protestant churches; they are called charges, to which pastors are appointed by the bishop at the annual conference. Official boards are made up of stewards and trustees and other church officers. Trustees manage the property interests of the church; stewards handle finances and generally guide the spiritual work.

154

Quarterly, annual, and general conferences prevail in most Methodist bodies; while Methodist government is popularly called episcopal, it is largely governmental by this series of conferences. The quarterly conference meets in the local charge or on the circuit with the district superintendent presiding. It fixes the salary of the pastor, sets the budget, elects the church officers, and sends delegates to the annual conference where it seems advisable, as it usually does in large or "station" charges. The quarterly conference may delegate to the official board of the local church responsibility for many of these duties. Some areas have district conferences between the quarterly and the annual conferences, but it is not a universal arrangement in the church. Annual conferences cover defined geographical areas, ordain and admit ministers to the ministry, vote on constitutional questions, supervise pensions and relief, through act of the bishop exchange pastors with other annual conferences, and every fourth year elect lay and ministerial delegates to the general conference. The general conference is the lawmaking body of the church, meeting quadrennially; the bishops preside, and the work of the conference is done largely in committees, whose reports when adopted by the general conference become Methodist law.

Worship and liturgy are based upon the English prayer book with widespread modifications. The language of the Prayer Book is much in evidence in the sacraments of the Methodist churches. In many forms of worship, however, each congregation is free to use or change the accepted pattern as it sees fit.

There are 26 separate Methodist bodies in the U.S. of which The Methodist Church is numerically the strongest.

The Methodist Church

This group includes the 3 branches united at Kansas City in the general conference of 1939: the Methodist Episcopal Church, the northern body; the Methodist Episcopal Church, South; and the Methodist Protestant Church. The history of the Methodist Episcopal Church has already been outlined. The Methodist Episcopal Church, South, was organized at Louisville, Kentucky, in 1845 and held its first general conference a year later in Petersburg, Virginia, under the presidency of Bishops James O. Andrew and Joshua Soule. The southern church brought to the 1939 merger 3 universities, 26 colleges, 22 junior colleges, 20 secondary schools, and a membership of more than 3,000,000. The Methodist Protestant Church was organized in revolt against the rule of the clergy in the Methodist Episcopal Church and the exclusion of laymen from its councils; it was formally organized in 1830 at Baltimore with about 5,000 members. There were over 50,000 members in the Methodist Protestant Church in 1939, 5 educational institutions, and foreign missions in China, India, and Japan.

The polity of The Methodist Church follows the general polity of all Methodism. There are 100 annual conferences in the United States with a total of 39,236 pastoral charges, 27,750 ministers, 9,910,741 members, and 1,536,419 preparatory members. With the union of 3 bodies at Kansas City in 1939 a system of 6 jurisdictional conferences was added; these meet every 4 years after the general conference has adjourned to elect the bishops of the denomination and the representatives of the larger boards and commissions. In lands outside the continental United States central conferences correspond somewhat to the jurisdictional conferences. They meet quadrennially, and when authorized to do so may elect their own bishops. The bishops of each jurisdictional or central conference collectively are called its College of Bishops.

The general conference is the lawmaking body of The Methodist Church; it

155

consists of 835 delegates, half laymen and half ministers, elected on a proportional basis by the annual conferences. A judicial council has been created to determine the constitutionality of any act of the general conference which may be appealed, and to hear and determine any appeal from a bishop's decision on a question of law in any district, annual, central, or jurisdictional conference. It is made up of 5 ministerial and 4 lay members, and has become so important that it is often called the "Supreme Court of The Methodist Church." Its decisions are final.

Bishops are elected for life, with retirement set at 72; there are 60 of them in the United States and abroad in charge of the areas of the church, such as the New York Area, the Denver Area, and so forth. Together they constitute the Council of Bishops, which meets at least once a year and usually twice a year "for the general oversight and promotion of the temporal and spiritual affairs of the entire Church."

The work of The Methodist Church is "big business." It holds property in the United States valued at $2,555,-838,779. This figure does not include educational plants, valued at $592,073,020, nor hospitals and homes for the aged. It has spread over 50 countries; 16 of its bishops administer work overseas. Over 200,000 students are enrolled in 135 educational institutions, from secondary schools to graduate schools and seminaries; these include 12 schools of theology, 1 school of medicine, 8 universities, 76 colleges, 21 junior colleges, 14 secondary schools and 3 others. There are 76 hospitals, 104 homes for the aged, 49 homes for children, and 7 homes for businesswomen, serving a total of 1,520,-913 persons (in 1959). There are 60 foreign conferences or missions. In these, in 1958, there were 4,600 native preachers, 2,320 "supplies," 886,552 full and 583,242 preparatory members.

The Methodist Publishing House is the oldest and largest religious publishing concern in the world. *Together,* the denomination's most widely circulated magazine, has nearly a million subscribers, and there are 37 other periodicals sponsored by the church, exclusive of its Sunday-school materials.

The World Methodist Council, organized in 1881 and designed to draw the numerous branches of the whole Wesleyan Movement closer together in fellowship and devotion to their mutual heritage, has become increasingly active in recent years. Nine Ecumenical Methodist Conferences have been held by this Council since 1881; the next one will be held in Oslo in 1961. Headquarters have been established at Lake Junaluska, North Carolina.

The bishops, boards, and committees of this church administer a fast-growing, global work, but its influence can hardly be measured by its size and spread. The May 10, 1949 issue of *Newsweek* said that

Methodist strength lies not so much in figures as in the vitality of the Church itself. . . . [Its members] emphasize brotherhood and friendliness in their religion. Unhampered by a strict theology, they lead with their hearts instead of their heads.

With an evangelistic passion for conversion and righteous living in the individual, on one hand, and a social passion matched by few other Protestant bodies, on the other, The Methodist Church has had an effect upon the individual and upon society which cannot be read in its statistics.

African Methodist Episcopal Church

With 1,166,301 members and 5,878 churches (as of 1951) this is the second largest Methodist group in the United States. Its genesis lies in the withdrawal in 1787 of a group of Negro Methodists from the Methodist Episcopal Church in Philadelphia; their objection was directed largely against practices of discrimination. They built a chapel and ordained a

Negro preacher through the assistance of Bishop William White of the Protestant Episcopal Church. In 1793 Bishop Francis Asbury dedicated Bethel Church in Philadelphia, a church whose members prohibited any white brother from "electing or being elected into any office among [them], save that of a preacher or public speaker." In 1799 Bishop Asbury also ordained Richard Allen to preach. Other similar Methodist Negro bodies were formed; the African Methodist Episcopal Church was formally organized in 1816. In the same year Richard Allen was consecrated as its first bishop, again by Bishop Asbury. It was a church confined in the years preceding the Civil War to the northern states; following the war its membership increased rapidly in the South, and today it is represented in nearly every state in the union.

Both doctrine and polity follow that of other Methodist bodies. General boards are constituted by nomination of the bishops, of which there are 17 appointed at the general conference. The general conference also examines all judicial power and prerogatives. Each department of church work is supervised by a board of 18 members, one for each episcopal district. The church has a widespread home missionary program, foreign missionary work in Africa and the West Indies, 17 educational institutions, and 5 periodicals.

African Methodist Episcopal Zion Church

This church dates from 1796, when its first organization was instituted by a group of Negro members protesting discrimination in the John Street Church in New York City. Their first church, built in 1800, was called Zion; the word was later made part of the denominational name. The first annual conference of the body was held in this church in 1821 with 6 Negro Methodist churches in New Haven, Philadelphia, and Newark, New Jersey, represented by 19 preachers and presided over by the Rev. William Phoebus of the white Methodist Episcopal Church. James Varrick, one of the John Street dissenters, was elected their first bishop at this conference. The name African Methodist Episcopal Zion Church was approved in 1848.

This church spread quickly over the northern states; by the time of the general conference of 1880 there were 15 annual conferences in the South. Livingstone College at Salisbury, North Carolina, the largest educational institution of the church, was established by that conference. Departments of missions, education, and publications were established in 1892; later came administrative boards to direct work in church extension, evangelism, finance, ministerial relief, and so on. Home missions are supported in Louisiana, Mississippi, and in several states beyond the Mississippi, principally in Oklahoma. Foreign missionaries are found in Liberia, the Gold Coast colony, West Africa, South America, and the West Indies. There are 6 educational institutions, several foreign mission stations, and there are 780,000 members in 3,090 churches.

African Union First Colored Methodist Protestant Church, Inc.

A Negro body organized in 1866, this is a union of 2 former churches known as the African Union Church and the First Colored Methodist Protestant Church. Doctrine is in accord with most of Methodism, but there are differences in polity; there are no bishops, and ministers and laymen have equal power in annual and general conferences. There is no foreign missionary program; home missions are maintained by a group of women known as the Grand Body. A general board, with a president, secretary, and treasurer, directs the denominational effort; the board meets annually and the general conference quadrennially. There are 5,000 members and 33 churches.

Apostolic Methodist Church

This is the smallest of the Methodist churches. Organized in Florida in 1932, it is ultrafundamentalist in doctrine, and lists less than 100 members in 3 churches.

Christian Methodist Episcopal Church

Known until 1954 as the Colored Methodist Episcopal Church, this church was established in 1870 in the South in an amicable agreement between white and Negro members of the Methodist Episcopal Church, South. There were at the time at least 225,000 Negro slave members in the Methodist Episcopal Church, South, but with the Emancipation Proclamation all but 80,000 of these joined the 2 independent bodies which had left the southern white church to join the northern church. When the general conference of the Methodist Episcopal Church, South, met at New Orleans in 1866, a commission from the Negro membership asked for a separation into a church of their own. The request was granted, and in 1870 the organization of the Colored Methodist Episcopal Church was realized. They held this name until the meeting of their general conference at Memphis in May of 1954, when it was decided to change it to the Christian Methodist Episcopal Church.

Their doctrine is the doctrine of the parent church; this denomination adds a local church conference to the quarterly, district, annual, and general conferences usual in Methodism. Seven boards supervise the national work, each presided over by a bishop assigned as chairman by the College of Bishops. The general secretaries of the various departments are elected every 4 years by the general conference. There were 392,167 members and 2,469 churches in 1951.

There are 2 periodicals, and 5 colleges are maintained.

Colored Methodist Protestant Church

Organized in Maryland in 1840, this is a remnant group of Methodist Protestant background; there is but one congregation today, with about 200 members.

Congregational Methodist Church

This church was constituted in Georgia in 1852 by a group withdrawing from the Methodist Episcopal Church, South, in objection to certain features of the episcopacy and the itinerancy. Two thirds of its membership in turn withdrew to join the Congregational Church in 1887-88.

Local pastors are called by the local churches; district conferences grant licenses, ordain ministers, and review local reports. District, annual, and general conferences are all recognized as church courts, ruling on violations of church law, citing offending laymen or ministers, and holding the power of expulsion over unworthy members. There is a restricted home and foreign missionary program. A junior college, known as Westminster College and Bible Institute, is maintained at Tehuacana, Texas. As of 1960, approximately 15,000 members were reported in 253 churches.

Congregational Methodist Church of the U.S.A.

Organized at Forsythe, Georgia, in 1852, this group claims to be the parent body from which the Congregational Methodist Church dissented to form its own organization. Originally under the jurisdiction of the Methodist Episcopal Church, South, they withdrew from that church in disagreement over the episcopal and itinerant systems, claiming that this system lacked biblical authority and democratic principles, to set up a

158

church that would be congregational in government. There are local and district conferences, and about 7,000 members in 65 churches. The church was incorporated at Anniston, Alabama, in 1937.

Cumberland Methodist Church

This is one of the smaller Methodist bodies, listing currently 4 churches and an inclusive membership of 65. Its leaders withdrew from the Congregational Methodist Church in protest against certain elements of polity and doctrine. It was organized at Laager, Grundy County, Tennessee, on May 5, 1950. A general board is the chief administrative body, and a president is elected instead of the usual bishop. The membership is limited to the state of Tennessee.

Evangelical Methodist Church

Organized at Memphis, Tennessee, in 1946, this church is "fundamental in doctrine, evangelistic in program, and congregational in government." It represents a double protest against what were considered autocratic and undemocratic government on the one hand and a tendency toward modernism on the other in The Methodist Church, from which the body withdrew. There is great emphasis placed upon the protest against modernism.

The church is Arminian in theology and Wesleyan in doctrine. Members seek a return to the original revivalistic thought and program of Wesleyanism; they adhere more rigidly than most Methodists to the original standards of Wesley; extremely fundamentalist, they oppose the "substituting of social, educational, or any other variety of cultural salvation."

Local churches control and own their own property and select their own pastors. There are 5 districts, 5 district superintendents, and 1 general superintendent within the Western Conference;

6 districts, 6 district superintendents, and 1 general superintendent within the Eastern Conference. In addition, the territory of Mexico constitutes the only mission conference, called the Mexican Evangelistic Conference, with 1 general superintendent. The General Conference meets quadrennially. International headquarters are located at 301 Palm, Abilene, Texas. There are 102 churches, 221 ministers, and a total membership of 8,000.

Free Methodist Church of North America

This is one of the more conservative among the larger bodies of American Methodism, both in doctrine and in standards of Christian practice. Its founder was the Rev. B. T. Roberts, who with his associates objected to what was called "new school" Methodism, which they considered destructive to the Wesleyan standards of the church. They were "read out" of their churches and organized the Free Methodist Church at Pekin, New York, in 1860. The Genesee Conference, of which Roberts had been a member, restored his credentials to his son in 1910, but no reunion of the group with The Methodist Church has yet been effected. A merger with the Holiness Movement Church in Canada was approved in 1960.

Doctrinally, the Free Methodists call for a return to primitive Wesleyan teaching; they stress the virgin birth and deity of Jesus and his vicarious atonement and resurrection. No one may be received into membership without an experience of confession and forgiveness of sin, and the experience of entire sanctification is sought in all members. Strict adherence to the general rules of Methodism is demanded, and membership in secret societies is forbidden. There are 55,000 members in the U. S., and a world membership of 97,000—or 2 members abroad for every 3 in the

U. S. and Canada. Foreign missions are maintained in Africa, India, Japan, the Dominican Republic, Formosa, Hong Kong, the Philippines, Egypt, Brazil, Paraguay, and Mexico. There are 3 senior colleges, 5 junior colleges, and a seminary foundation in co-operation with Asbury Theological Seminary. The church has a general conference and 4 bishops.

Fundamental Methodist Church, Inc.

Known until August, 1956, as the Independent Fundamental Methodist Church, this church was instituted on August 27, 1942, at Ash Grove, Missouri, organized under its original title in 1944, and chartered under its present title in 1948. Its origin is traced back to the Methodist Protestant Church, of which it was a part until the merging of the 3 major Methodist churches in 1939. Dissatisfaction with the merger and the conviction that the primitive Wesleyan principles and theology would suffer thereby led to the withdrawal and the establishment of the new church. As the name suggests, there is an insistence here upon fundamental teaching.

There are no bishops in this church; nationally, they have a chairman, and a secretary. Government is more congregational than in most Methodist groups; there is a district superintendent in charge of each district of the church, and an annual conference for each district. There are 13 ministers, 14 churches, 639 members.

Holiness Methodist Church
(North Carolina and North Dakota)

Two Methodist bodies bear this name. The first was organized in 1900 in North Carolina and was formerly known as the Lumber River Mission Conference of the Holiness Methodist Church and later as the Lumber River Annual Conference of the Holiness Methodist Church.

(A small group of 7 churches and 570 members is still active in North Carolina under the name Lumber River Annual Conference of the Holiness Methodist Church, but information concerning its faith and work is unavailable.) Established to bring new emphasis to home missions and scriptural holiness, it stresses the doctrines of the Atonement, the witness of the Spirit, and "holiness in heart and life." Attendance at class meetings is required. There is no itinerant ministry as in most Methodist bodies, and pastorates are not limited. The whole church meets each year in an annual conference presided over by a bishop. There are about 1,000 members in 6 churches.

The second Holiness Methodist Church is a western group, and an outgrowth of the Northwestern Holiness Association, which was an auxiliary of the National Holiness Association. The original organization was made up of a group of evangelists and evangelistic bands working between Minneapolis and the Pacific coast; the organization was effected in 1911, and the name, Holiness Methodist Church, was adopted in 1920. While similar in polity and teaching to the Methodist Holiness Church in North Carolina, it has no connection with that body. The Holiness Methodist School of Theology is located in Minneapolis, and the official periodical, *Holiness Methodist Advocate*, is published from headquarters, also in Minneapolis. A general superintendent supervises the work of 27 clergymen. The work is largely evangelistic, at home and in one missionary station in Bolivia. Three camp meeting grounds are maintained in Minnesota, North Dakota, and Washington. There are 900 members in 27 churches.

Independent African Methodist Episcopal Church

This group was formed in 1907 at Jacksonville, Florida, by 12 ministers who left the African Methodist Episcopal Church following disputes with the district superintendents of that church. A new book of discipline, doctrines, and laws was written; the *Book of Discipline* is revised from time to time by the quadrennial general conference, but the 25 articles of religion it contains remain unchanged.

There are quarterly, annual, and general conferences. The annual conference ordains ministers as deacons, and the general conference ordains elders and bishops. In 1940 there were 1,000 members and 12 churches.

New Congregational Methodist Church

This church originated in an administrative quarrel in the Georgia conference of the Methodist Episcopal Church, South, over the consolidation of certain rural properties in the southern section of the state. Protesting, the New Congregational Methodist Church was organized in 1881 on the general plan of the Congregational Methodist Church. (There has recently been a division in this church, with a number of congregations uniting with the Congregational Methodist Church.) There are at present about 700 members in 11 churches—7 of which are in north Florida and 4 in south Georgia. There are two smaller groups in central Georgia and Indiana.

Government is a combination of Methodist and Congregational systems; the episcopacy is rejected, and congregations call and elect their own pastors; there are the usual (Methodist) local, district, and general conferences. An unusual feature of this church lies in their practice of foot washing.

People's Methodist Church

Conservative and "holiness," the founders of this church left The Methodist Church in North Carolina at the time of the merger of the 3 major Methodist churches. There are approximately 25 congregations and 1,000 members, and

a Bible school in Greensboro, North Carolina. No information on doctrine or polity is available.

Primitive Methodist Church, U.S.A.

This church had its initial organization in England. Lorenzo Dow, an American camp-meeting revivalist, went to England early in the nineteenth century to hold a series of camp meetings which resulted in the formation of a number of societies among his converts. Refused admission to the Wesleyan Connection, they formed the Primitive Methodist Church in 1812. The early Primitive bodies in this country were grouped in 1925-29 into eastern and western conferences. The early Wesleyan doctrines of redemption, repentance, justification, sanctification, and so forth, are held in this church. There are no bishops or district superintendents; denominational officers are the president, vice-president, secretary, and treasurer. There are annual conferences and a quadrennial general conference. Ministers, who have no time limit set upon their pastorates, are invited by the local churches, who designate their first, second, and third choices and extend their invitations in that order. All invited pastors are assigned to charges by the annual conference, and no ministerial candidates are received unless there are churches open for them. Work in education and missions is directed by the general conference; foreign missionaries are stationed in Guatemala, Kenya, and Brazil. There are 12,729 members and 92 churches. An official organ, *The Primitive Methodist Journal*, is published monthly.

Reformed Methodist Church

This is a church of New England origin, founded in Vermont in 1814 as the result of a bitter controversy over the episcopal system and Methodist Episcopal Church theology and practice. The Reformed Methodist Church

161

rid itself of bishops and became thoroughly identified with the holiness movement. There are about 500 members in a dozen churches, and their membership and influence seem to be dwindling from year to year.

Reformed Methodist Union Episcopal Church

This church was started in 1885 at Charleston, South Carolina, in a withdrawal from the African Methodist Episcopal Church, the immediate cause of the division being a dispute over the election of ministerial delegates to the general conference. Intended at first as a nonepiscopal church, the body adopted the complete polity of the Methodist Episcopal Church in general conferences of 1896 and 1916. Its first bishop was consecrated in 1899 by a bishop of the Reformed Episcopal Church. Class meetings and love feasts are featured in the local congregation; there are 11,000 members and 30 churches.

Reformed New Congregational Methodist Church

This church was organized in 1916 by J. A. Sander of the Independence Mission and Earl Wilcoxen of the Congregational Methodist Church, with an independent polity. It opposes divorce, secret societies, and personal adornment. It reported 329 members in 8 churches in 1936.

Reformed Zion Union Apostolic Church

This church was organized at Boydton, Virginia, in 1869 by Elder James R. Howell, a minister of the African Methodist Episcopal Zion Church in New York, in protest against white discrimination and against the ecclesiasticism of other Negro Methodist churches. This was originally known as the Zion Union Apostolic Church; internal friction com-

pletely disrupted the body by 1874, and in 1881-82 it was reorganized under the present name. There are no basic departures from standard Methodist doctrine or polity except that only one ordination, that of elder, is required of its ministers. There are 12,000 members, 52 churches.

Southern Methodist Church

Doctrinally and spiritually, the Southern Methodist Church remains the same as the body from which it came—the Methodist Episcopal Church, South. They opposed the merger of that church with the northern Methodist Episcopal Church, in 1939, on the grounds of "alarming infidelity and apostasy found therein." They regard the Southern Methodist Church not as a separatist group, but as a church "brought into existence to perpetuate the faith of John Wesley."

There are no bishops here, but there are the orthodox annual and general Methodist conferences; a president, usually a clergyman, is elected every 4 years. The church is a constituent member of the conservative American and International Councils of Churches. Somewhat unique among Methodist churches, this one has a strong statement on racial segregation, teaching that "holy writ teaches the separation of peoples at least to the extent of three basic races, namely, Caucasian, Mongoloid, and Negroid."

Union American Methodist Episcopal Church

This was one of the first Negro bodies to establish an independent Methodist church. Members left the Asbury Methodist Church in Wilmington, Delaware, in 1805. They worshiped out of doors and in private homes until 1813, when they built their first church and incorporated under the title Union Church of Africans; the change to the present name was made in 1852. Deflections of

162

membership in 1850 were responsible for the formation of still another body, the African Union Church, which forced the change to the present name of the Union American Methodist Episcopal Church.

General, annual, district, and quarterly conferences are held; general conferences are called only to consider proposed changes in name, law, or polity. There are 2 educational institutions, and the church claims 27,000 members in 250 churches.

Wesleyan Methodist Church of America

This church represented at the time of its founding in 1843 a protest against slavery and the episcopacy which predated by one year the historic division of the Methodist Episcopal Church and the Methodist Episcopal Church, South. With the slavery issue settled by the Civil War other differences of a spiritual or reform character—entire sanctification and opposition to the liquor traffic —seemed important enough to continue

the separate existence of the Wesleyan Methodist Church.

The original Wesleyan doctrines, especially those dealing with sanctification, are all-important in this church; otherwise it is in accord with accepted Methodist belief and procedure. Candidates for membership are required to disavow the use, sale, or manufacture of tobacco and alcoholic beverages, and to refrain from membership in secret societies.

An enlarging evangelistic and missionary activity is directed from world headquarters in Marion, Indiana. In 1959, 30 conferences were listed, and missionaries were at work in Australia, South and Central America, the West Indies, Japan, West Africa, India, and Taiwan. There are 5 colleges, and a total of 50,449 members in 1,220 churches at home and abroad.

In 1955 the Wesleyan Methodist Church rejected union with the Free Methodist Church, and in 1959 union with the Pilgrim Holiness Church was narrowly defeated. Wide-ranging reorganization of the church was approved in the General Conference of 1959.

MORAVIANS

In a sense the Moravian Church had its first apostles in Cyril and Methodius, who were missionaries among the Slavs in the ninth century. As early as this Moravians and Bohemians in old Czechoslovakia were struggling for political and religious freedom. Later they followed John Huss, martyred in 1415, and Jerome of Prague, martyred in 1416. Their first association was formed in Bohemia in 1457. At the beginning of the Reformation there were more than 500 Brethren, or Moravian, churches with about 175,000 members.

As a church they opposed the corruption of the Roman Catholic Church and stressed purity of morals, apostolic discipline, and true scriptural teaching.

For a time they inclined toward a very literal interpretation of the Sermon on the Mount and denounced war, the taking of oaths, and all unions of church and state. They called themselves *Jednota Bratraska*, the Church (or Communion) of Brethren; this is the correct translation of their later term *Unitas Fratrum*. They accepted the Apostles' Creed, rejected the purgatory and worship of the saints of the Roman Catholic Church as well as its authority, practiced infant baptism and confirmation, and put conduct above doctrine.

The Thirty Years' War all but annihilated their first societies; persecution drove them into Hungary, Holland, Poland, and Saxony. A small band found refuge on the estate of Nicholas Louis, Count of Zinzendorf, in Saxony, where they built the town of Herrnhut (1722-27). Zinzendorf was a Lutheran who had close contact with the Pietist movement, and he became so influential among the Moravians that they used for a time the Augsburg Confession of Faith of Lutheran Saxony. They adopted the name *Unitas Fratrum* from their ancient church and in 1735 again established the episcopacy which had been preserved through John Amos Comenius and his son-in-law Jablonsky. The *Unitas Fratrum* came to be popularly known as the Moravian Church because the leaders of the renewal had come from Moravia.

Moravian Church (*Unitas Fratrum*)

The Moravian Church arrived in America in 1734 when a group of the Brethren from Germany came to Georgia to carry on missionary work among the Indians. John Wesley was a passenger on the same ship with them, and this was the beginning of his important relations with the Moravians. Political disturbances in Georgia soon disrupted their colony; and a group accompanied George Whitefield to Pennsylvania, where they settled in 1740. Three uniquely and exclusively Moravian towns grew swiftly in Pennsylvania at Bethlehem, Nazareth, and Lititz, based on the communities in Germany, Holland, and England. They remained exclusively Moravian until the middle years of the nineteenth century.

Zinzendorf came to America in 1741, attempted to merge all the colonial Germans into one body, and failed. He stayed on, however, to help with the establishment of Bethlehem and Nazareth and to lay the foundations of the Moravian missionary work among the Indians. By 1775 there were 2,500 Moravians in Pennsylvania alone.

The Moravians have no doctrine peculiar to them; they are broadly evangelical, insisting upon a principle of "in essentials unity, in nonessentials liberty, and in all things charity." Their scriptural interpretations agree substantially with the Apostles' Creed, the Westminster and Augsburg confessions, and the Articles of Religion of the Church of England. They hold the Scriptures to be the inspired word of God and an adequate rule of faith and practice; and they have doctrines dealing with the total depravity of man, the real Godhead and the real humanity of Christ, justification and redemption through the sacrifice of Christ, the work of the Holy Spirit, good works as the fruits of the Spirit, the fellowship of all believers, the second coming of Christ, and the resurrection of the dead to life and judgment. Their main doctrinal emphasis may be said to be upon the love of God manifested in the redemptive life and death of Jesus, the inner testimony of the Spirit, and Christian conduct in everyday affairs.

The sacrament of infant baptism by sprinkling is practiced, through which children become noncommunicant members until confirmation. There are 60,000 members in 160 churches. Members are admitted by vote of the congregational board of elders. The Lord's Supper is celebrated at least 6 times a year, and the old custom of the love feast is preserved. A variety of liturgies is used in worship: the church is notable for one especially beautiful outdoor service held at Easter.

The Moravian Church is divided in the United States into 2 provinces, northern and southern, and works under a modified episcopacy. Congregations are grouped into provincial and district synods; internationally they are joined in a "unity" with a general synod meeting as a world body every 10 years. The highest administrative body in each American province is the provincial synod, composed of ministers and laymen and meeting every 5 years; it directs missionary, educational, and publishing work, and elects a provincial elders' conference, or executive board, which functions between synod meetings. Bishops are elected by provincial and general synods. They are spiritual, but not administrative, leaders in the church.

Missionary work has always been a first concern of the Moravians; with a comparatively small membership they conducted the most efficient missionary work among the Indians of any of the early colonial churches. The world-wide Moravian Church now supports work in 13 foreign missionary fields, including North, Central, and South America, Africa, Tibet, and Palestine. A home missions work among the Eskimos of Alaska has been carried on since 1885. The church maintains 2 colleges, a theological seminary, and 2 girls' boarding schools. Both of the latter trace their origins back to the pre-Revolutionary period.

Bohemian and Moravian Brethren

Consisting of 2 churches and 230 members, this group was founded in Iowa between 1858 and 1895. It has no connection with other Moravian churches but maintains "friendly relations" with the Presbyterian and Reformed Bohemian churches of the East and Northwest in educational and missionary work. Members accept the Helvetic and Westminster confessions and use the Heidelberg and Westminster catechisms. Polity is Presbyterian with local church government in the hands of boards of elders and trustees.

Evangelical Unity of the Czech-Moravian Brethren in North America

This group originated among Czech and Moravian immigrants arriving in Texas about 1850. In 1864 they organized as the Bohemian and Moravian Brethren and in 1903 as the Evangelical Union of Bohemian Brethren. A number of Iowa churches united with the Evangelical Union in 1919, and the present name was adopted. There are few departures from the doctrine and polity of the Moravian Church in America (*Unitas Fratrum*) except that the synod meets every 2 years. The church has no colleges or seminaries. In 1959 it reported 6,028 members and 32 churches confined to Texas.

NATIONAL DAVID SPIRITUAL TEMPLE OF CHRIST CHURCH UNION (INC.), U.S.A. (THE UNIVERSAL CHRISTIAN SPIRITUAL FAITH AND CHURCHES FOR ALL NATIONS)

This is a body founded in 1932 by the Rev. Dr. David William Short, a former minister of the Missionary Baptist Church. Dr. Short wished to "proclaim the Orthodox Christian spiritual faith"; he was convinced that no man had the right or spiritual power "to make laws, rules, or doctrines for the real church founded by Jesus Christ," and that the denominational churches had been founded in error and in disregard of the apostolic example. He held wisdom, knowledge, faith, healing, miracles, prophecy, discerning of spirits, and divers kinds of tongues to be spiritual gifts of the Holy Ghost and as parts of the church of Christ. He believed that all races should and must be accepted in the true church.

The members of this church consider

themselves to be the true and universal church of Christ and not just another denomination. They rely entirely upon the Holy Ghost for inspiration and direction; their church constitution they claim to be found in I Cor. 12:1-31 and Eph. 4:11. Their organization is made up of pastors, prophets, prophetesses, bishops, archbishops, elders, overseers, divine healers, deacons, mothers, choir members, missionaries, altar boys, and altar girls. Archbishop Short is the chief governing officer; there is a national executive board, which holds a national annual assembly.

A restricted home missionary work is conducted in hospitals, and a nursing home is maintained. A monthly newspaper, *The Christian Spiritual Voice*, is published at Kansas City, Missouri. Archbishop Short is also founder, president, and mentor of the St. David Orthodox Christian Spiritual Seminary, which was dedicated in 1949 at Des Moines, Iowa. The membership is reported at 43,850 in 65 churches.

NEW APOSTOLIC CHURCH OF NORTH AMERICA

THE NEW APOSTOLIC Church of North America is a variant or schism of the Catholic Apostolic Church movement in England. It claims common origin with the Catholic Apostolic Church in the appointment of an apostle in the parent body in 1832. Debate arose in 1860 over the appointment of new apostles to fill vacancies left by death. Insisting that there must always be 12 apostles at the head of the true church, Bishop Schwarz of Hamburg was excommunicated from the Catholic Apostolic Church in 1862 for proposing the election of new apostles. A priest named Preuss was elected to the office of apostle "through the spirit of prophecy" to lead the dissenting body, and Bishop Schwarz served under him until his own elevation to the apostolic office.

Under Preuss and Schwarz the New Apostolic Church spread from Europe to America, where today it is organized into apostles' districts, bishops' districts, and elders' districts. Each church has a rector and one or more assistants (priests, deacons, and so forth), who serve usually without remuneration. All ministers and other "office-bearers" are selected by the apostleship. The American church is a constituent part of the international organization supervised by Chief Apostle J. G. Bischoff in Frankfurt, Germany.

Just as the true church must be governed on the scriptural pattern by 12 apostles, members of this church believe that only the apostles have received from Christ the commission and power to forgive sin. The New Apostolic Church accepts the Apostles' Creed and stresses the authority and inspiration of the Bible, the apostolic ordinance of the laying on of hands, the necessity of gifts of the Holy Spirit (which include prophecy, visions, dreams, divers tongues, songs of praise, wisdom, discrimination of spirits, the power of healing and performing wonders), tithing, and the speedy, personal, premillennial return of Christ. Three "means of grace" are found in 3 sacraments: baptism (including children), Holy Communion, and Holy Sealing (the dispensing and reception of the Holy Spirit). Work "along broader interior and missionary lines" is conducted in the United States and Canada. There are 16,500 members in 210 churches and 39 missions in the United States, and about 600,000 in 4,000 branches in the international organization in Canada, England, Germany, Switzerland, Holland, France, Australia, South Africa, and South America.

OLD CATHOLIC CHURCHES

Old Catholic churches in the United States are outgrowths but unconnected branches of the Old Catholic movement and churches of Europe. The European bodies originated in a protest against the doctrine of papal infallibility adopted by the Roman Catholic Vatican Council of 1870; Roman priests in Germany who refused to accept the doctrine were excommunicated and organized the Old Catholic Church under the leadership of Bishop Doellinger in 1871. A similar break occurred in Holland and Switzerland, where other Old Catholic churches were established.

This revolt did not break completely with Roman Catholicism. It rejected papal infallibility, the doctrine of the Immaculate Conception, compulsory celibacy of the priesthood, and in some instances the filioque clause of the Nicene Creed, but kept much of the other doctrine, creeds, customs, and liturgy of the Roman Catholic Church. It was also most anxious to preserve the orders and the apostolic succession of its priests and bishops inasmuch as they considered apostolic succession as vital in a valid Christian ministry. Much confusion has resulted in conflicting claims of succession and validity of orders, especially in American Old Catholic churches. All Old Catholic bodies in this country were at one time or another connected with European bodies, but that is not true today. With the exception of the Polish National Catholic Church, none of the American Old Catholic churches are recognized by European churches or authorities, and most American groups have severed their connections with churches abroad. Someone has said that most of the Old Catholics in America are either dissatisfied Anglicans or former Roman Catholics; and there is some truth in that, if not all the truth. Several attempts have been made, however, to merge Old Catholic churches with those of the Church of England or the Greek Church, and gestures have been made toward membership in the World Council of Churches.

Old Catholic missionaries were in America soon after 1870, establishing scattered congregations. Father Joseph Réné Vilatte, a French priest ordained by the Old Catholics in Switzerland, attempted to organize these congregations and at once became the storm center of the rising confusion. Vilatte himself vacillated between rival bodies; he studied in a Presbyterian college at Montreal and twice returned to submit to the Roman Catholic Church, dying at last in a French monastery. Vigorously opposed within his own church and by American Protestant Episcopalians, whose ranks he refused to join, he went to Switzerland in 1885 for ordination as an Old Catholic bishop and was finally consecrated as an archbishop by Archbishop Alvarez of Ceylon, who claimed orders through the Syro-Jacobite Church of Malabar. He returned to America to found the American Catholic Church.

Separated and competing as they are, the Old Catholics in the United States have a firm common doctrinal basis. This doctrine is similar to that held by the Greek and Latin churches before those 2 bodies separated; among the Old Catholics it is now more Eastern Catholic than Western. They accept the 7 ecumenical councils of the church held before the division into Eastern and Western bodies in 1505; they generally reject the filioque clause of the Nicene Creed, all dogmas of papal infallibility and celibacy, and all advocacy of the union of church and state. Bible reading is encouraged, and national tongues rather than Latin are used in all worship. There is a strange blend here of orthodoxy and rationalism both in doctrine and in ritual.

There are 4 main divisions of Old Catholic churches in the United States, with an approximate total of 100,000 members in 129 churches—the American Catholic Church; the American Catholic

Church, Archdiocese of New York; the North American Old Roman Catholic Church; and the Old Catholic Church in America. The African Orthodox Church, a Negro group, is listed often as an Old Catholic body; but actually it is Protestant Episcopalian in origin and connection. Three other groups—the Polish National Catholic Church of America, the Lithuanian National Catholic Church, and the Uniat Churches—may be said to have certain common origins and doctrines with the Old Catholic churches but have been listed separately in this book in consideration of their distinctively nationalistic character.

American Catholic Church

This church was established by Father Vilatte, as already described in Chicago. Before returning to the Roman Catholic Church, Vilatte consecrated Bishop F. E. J. Floyd, a former Protestant Episcopal priest, who assumed the primacy and title of archbishop in the reorganized church. There are actually 2 small bodies within the American Catholic Church, both seriously affected by withdrawals from its membership and now reporting about 5,000 members in 29 churches. Faith and polity are generally that of other Old Catholic groups. There is an archbishop, 2 auxiliary bishops, and a titular bishop. In 1951 the Apostolic Episcopal Church was merged with the American Catholic Church.

The American Catholic Church, Archdiocese of New York

This church was organized by its present archbishop, the Most Rev. James Francis Augustine Lashley, in 1927 and incorporated in 1932. Its orders are derived from the Syrian Church of Antioch through Father Vilatte, and it had a membership of 8,435 in 20 churches in 1947, all of which are located in New York City and Brooklyn. Roman Catholic forms of ordination and consecra-

tion are followed in the investing of holy orders.

North American Catholic Church

The largest Old Catholic body in the United States, this church has 78,278 members and 60 churches. Various independent congregations have united with this group from time to time, giving it its present impressive strength. Church officers, including archbishops, bishops, general vicars, priests, and delegates, are elected by the local congregations and confirmed by the primate; each foreign group of churches has a bishop of its own nationality. There is a theological seminary in Chicago; and there are several home for religious orders, aged priests, and needy laymen. The church is identical with the Roman Catholic Church in worship and doctrine, acknowledging "the supremacy of the successor to St. Peter" but with Masses held in the vernacular of the people. The clergy are allowed to marry. It was received into union with the Eastern Orthodox Church by the Archbishop of Beirut on August 5, 1911, and by the Orthodox Patriarch of Alexandria on February 26, 1912.

The Old Catholic Church in America

Deriving its episcopate from the Old Roman Catholic Church of Holland and from the Eastern Orthodox Church, this body represents the Old Catholic churches of Poland, Lithuania, France, Morocco, Central America, and Yugoslavia. It accepts the decrees of the 7 ecumenical councils, holds Mass in English, permits its priests to marry before ordination, and employs the rituals, slightly modified, of both Roman Catholic and Eastern Orthodox churches. An unusually effective intercommunion has been established among the Protestant Episcopal, Anglican, Polish National Catholic, and Old Catholic churches,

168

which may be the first step toward a merger of these bodies.

There are 6,000 members in 22 churches.

The Reformed Catholic Church (Utrecht Confession) Province of North America

This is the American branch of an international group of Reformed Catholic Churches (others are found in Great Britain, France, and Germany). They hold highly valid orders derived from Roman Catholic and Eastern Catholic sources, from the initial period of the church in the seventeenth century.

Doctrine, generally, is based on the Nicene Creed and the pronouncements of the ecumenical councils prior to the Great Schism. A primate and a chancellor stand as the top officers of the church, and a provincial convocation meets every three years.

There are 2,217 members in 20 churches, as of 1957.

OPEN BIBLE STANDARD CHURCHES, INC.

Open Bible Standard Churches, Inc. was originally composed of two revival movements: namely, Bible Standard, Inc., founded in Eugene, Oregon, in 1919; and Open Bible Evangelistic Association, founded in Des Moines, Iowa, in 1932. Similar in doctrine and government, the 2 groups amalgamated on July 26, 1935, taking the combined name, "Open Bible Standard Churches, Inc." with headquarters in Des Moines, Iowa.

The Pacific coast group, with activities centered in Oregon, spread through Washington, California, and into the Rocky Mountain areas of the West; the Iowa group expanded into Illinois, Missouri, Ohio, Florida, and Pennsylvania. There are now churches in 24 states, with the main concentration in the central and far-western states.

The teachings are "fundamental in doctrine, evangelical in spirit, missionary in vision, and pentecostal in testimony"; they include emphasis on the blood atonement of Christ, divine healing, baptism of the Holy Spirit, personal holiness, the premillennial return of the Lord, and baptism by immersion.

Churches are grouped into 5 geographical divisions, subdivided into 17 districts. Seventeen district superintendents who are also pastors guide the work under the supervision of divisional superintendents. Individual churches are congregationally governed, locally owned, and are affiliated by a charter with the national organization. The 10 departments function under the leadership of departmental heads with the advice of a committee and are represented on the general board of directors. The highest governing body is the General Conference, which meets annually and is composed of all licensed and ordained ministers and 1 lay delegate from each church.

There are 48 missionaries at work in 8 foreign countries, and 5 Bible training colleges for the training of national workers. In the United States there are 5 Bible institutes and Bible colleges, with a total enrollment of about 400 students, located at Des Moines, Iowa; Eugene, Oregon; Dayton, Ohio; St. Petersburg, Florida; and Pasadena, California.

A board of publications is responsible for the preparation of conference publications; a nationally owned book store and press, known as "Inspiration Press and Book Store," is located at Des Moines and circulates a monthly periodical, *The Message of the Open Bible*, and lesson materials for their Sunday schools.

The denomination is a constituent member of the Pentecostal Fellowship of North America and of the National Association of Evangelicals. As of 1960, there were approximately 26,000 constituents in 263 churches.

PENTECOSTAL BODIES

Pentecostalism is a most inclusive term applied to a large number of revivalistic American sects, assemblies, and churches. Many of them have come out of either Methodist or Baptist backgrounds, and they are primarily concerned with perfection, holiness, and the Pentecostal experience.

They offer statements of faith which are often long and involved and highly repetitious, but through which may be traced certain common strains and elements. Most of them believe in the Trinity, original sin, man's salvation through the atoning blood of Christ, the virgin birth and deity of Jesus, the divine inspiration and literal infallibility of the the Scriptures, manifestations and "blessings" of the working of the Holy Spirit often running into excessive emotionalism—shouting, trances, jerking, hand clapping, "tongue talking," and so forth—the fiery Pentecostal baptism of the Spirit, premillennialism, and future rewards and punishments. Two sacraments are found in most of their sects—baptism, usually by immersion, and the Lord's Supper. Foot washing is frequently observed in connection with the Supper. Many practice divine healing, and speaking in tongues is widespread.

Ultrafundamentalistic, varying in size from small group meetings to huge mass meetings, and working independently of any recognized denominational organization, Pentecostalists are found in every state in the Union with their greatest strength in the South, West, and Middle West. They use a great variety of names; only those including the word "Pentecostal" are included here, and they are comparatively small sects. The majority of American Pentecostalists may be found in the Tomlinson groups of the Church of God and their offshoots. No accurate count of their total membership is possible inasmuch as many groups never offer statistics of any kind.

Calvary Pentecostal Church, Inc.

This church was founded at Olympia, Washington, in 1931 by a group of ministers who sought a ministerial fellowship rather than a separate denomination, and freedom from the sectarian spirit. The body was incorporated in 1932, and a home and foreign missionary society was incorporated in the same year. Home missions work today consists mainly of evangelistic work, relief to weak churches, and the establishment of new churches. A general superintendent and executive presbytery board administer the work of the church; the general body meets in convention annually or semiannually. Seminary, college, or even Bible-school education is considered beneficial but is no requisite for the ministers of this church. Ministers include both men and women; those who give evidence of having heard the call of God to preach are qualified by ordination. There are 35 churches and 20,000 members.

Emmanuel Holiness Church

This is a group organized on March 19, 1953, at the Columbus County Camp Ground in Whiteville, North Carolina. The founders had come to a general conference of the Pentecostal Fire-Baptized Holiness Church but withdrew from that church in protest against certain positions taken by the conference on polity

170

and doctrine. They now have a membership of 1,200 in 56 churches. Their chief administrative body is a general assembly, and a general overseer is their church officer. A periodical, *Emmanuel Messenger*, is published at Anderson, South Carolina.

Pentecostal Holiness Church

This church was organized in 1898 at Anderson, South Carolina, by a number of Pentecostal associations which at the time used the name Fire-Baptized Holiness Church. A year later another group organized as the Pentacostal Holiness Church; the two bodies united in 1911 at Falcon, North Carolina, under the latter name. A third body, the Tabernacle Pentecostal Church, joined them in 1915. There are 51,688 members in the United States, in 1,214 churches, and 19,597 in 419 churches in foreign mission fields.

The theological standards of Methodism prevail here, with certain modifications. It accepts the premillennial teaching of the Second Coming and believes that provision was made in the Atonement for the healing of the body. Divine healing is practiced, but not to the exclusion of medicine. Three distinctive experiences are taught: two works of grace—justification by faith and sanctification, as a second work of grace—and the Spirit Baptism, attested by speaking in other tongues. Services are often characterized by "joyous demonstrations."

Polity also is Methodistic; there are annual conferences and a quadrennial general conference which elects one general superintendent (bishop) to hold office for 4 years only. The general conference also elects 4 assistant general superintendents, a general secretary, and a general treasurer of the church, these constituting the general executive board. There is a general board of administration composed of the executive board and the superintendents of all annual conferences in the United States except the home missions conferences. There are 28 annual conferences in the United States, 3 in Canada, 1 in England, and 1 white or European conference in South Africa. Foreign missions are found in Hong Kong, India, South Africa, Central Africa, West Africa, South America, Central America, the Hawaiian Islands, Alaska, Mexico, and Cuba. There is a junior college (Emmanuel College) at Franklin Springs, Georgia; a junior college (Southwestern Bible College) at Oklahoma City, Oklahoma; a theological seminary (Holmes Theological Seminary) at Greenville, South Carolina; a children's home (Falcon Children's Home) at Falcon, North Carolina; a home for the aged (Carmen Home) at Carmen, Oklahoma.

There is a publishing house which also houses general offices for the church (Advocate Press) at Franklin Springs, Georgia, the international headquarters of the denomination.

Pentecostal Fire-Baptized Holiness Church

This church was organized in 1911 by a small group who declined to continue in the union of the Fire-Baptized Holiness Church and the Pentecostal Holiness Church; their objection had to do mainly with matters of discipline in the wearing of ornaments and elaborate dress. They withdrew from the union in 1918 and were joined in 1920 by the Pentecostal Free Will Baptist Church.

Members of this church are forbidden to buy or sell, or to engage in any labor or business for which they may receive "pecuniary remuneration." They are also forbidden "filthiness of speech, foolish talking or jesting, slang, attendance at fairs, swimming pools or shows of any kind, the use of jewelry, gold, feathers, flowers, costly apparel, neckties."

The sect is strongly premillennialist and perfectionist; "joyous demonstrations" are prominent, finding expression

171

in hand clapping, crying, and shouting. State conventions support convention evangelists, and there is a general convention which elects a 7-member board of missions. Foreign missions are supported in Mexico. There are 576 members and 40 churches.

Church of God in Christ (Pentecostal)

This is a small body with 210 members and 9 churches in 1936. It was founded in the early 1930's and is under the supervision of a bishop, who has headquarters at Bluefield, West Virginia. Local churches are reported to have been established in Michigan, West Virginia, Illinois, Ohio, Tennessee, Texas, and Alabama.

International Pentecostal Assemblies

This body is the successor to the Association of Pentecostal Assemblies founded in 1921 and the National and International Pentecostal Missionary Union founded in 1914. Doctrine follows the usual Pentecostal standards; the sick are anointed with oil and healed by prayer, foot washing is optional, and there is strong opposition to participation in war. The last membership report, in 1952, listed 5,000 members in 50 churches under the general supervision of an official board which directed the activities of the church in 23 states at home and on several foreign mission fields. The entire work is supported by tithing of the membership.

Pentecostal Assemblies of the World, Inc.

This was an interracial body at the time of its organization in 1914; the white members withdrew in 1924 to form the Pentecostal Church, Inc., which in turn became a constituent body of the United Pentecostal Church, Inc., in 1945. Origin is traced "directly back to Pentecost, A.D. 33." Doctrine reveals no

important departure from that of Pentecostalism in general. Secret societies are opposed, as are church festivals and collecting money on the streets; the wearing of jewelry, attractive hosiery, bobbed hair, bright ties, low-necked dresses is forbidden. Divorce is not permitted when both man and wife have had the "baptism of the Holy Ghost"; but when the unbeliever in a marriage contract procures a divorce, the believer may remarry.

Organization is similar to that of The Methodist Church: a general assembly meets annually under a presiding bishop; there are a secretary-treasurer for foreign missions, a committee of 3 on evangelism, and a board of 24 district elders. An executive board composed of bishops is elected each year by the ministerial members of the assembly. Local assemblies are presided over by district elders. There is evangelistic work conducted in the United States and in several missions abroad. In 1951 there were 50,000 members in 600 churches.

Pentecostal Church of God of America, Inc.

This church was organized at Chicago in 1919, incorporated in Missouri in 1936, and held its first national convention in 1940. The words "of America" were added to its name to distinguish it from a Kansas City body bearing a similar name. It is typically Pentecostal in faith, with immersion, Spirit baptism, speaking in tongues, foot washing and divine healing.

In the United States 100,000 members are reported in 994 churches. Officers include a general superintendent, secretary-treasurer, director of world missions, executive secretary-treasurer of world missions, director of Indian missions, district superintendents, and district presbyters.

A general convention meets biennially; district conventions, annually. More than

300 mission churches are supported in 13 countries abroad.

Pentecostal Church of Christ

Founded by John Stroup at Flatwoods, Kentucky, in 1917 and incorporated at Portsmouth, Ohio, in 1927, this church subscribes to the usual Pentecostalist doctrines of the Trinity, the personal spiritual experiences of regeneration, sanctification and baptism by the Spirit, and it puts strong emphasis upon divine healing. They have 41 churches, 1,190 members. A monthly periodical, *Pentecostal Witness*, is published in London, Ohio.

United Pentecostal Church, Inc.

This church is made up of a union of 2 Pentecostal bodies merged in 1945: the Pentecostal Assemblies of Jesus Christ and the Pentecostal Church, Inc. The first body was the result of a merger of several groups which refused to enter the General Council of the Assemblies of God, and the latter consisted of the white members who withdrew from the Pentecostal Assemblies of the World when it ceased to be an interracial body in 1924. One of the few white Pentecostal organizations believing in the necessity of water baptism in the name of Christ (Acts 2:38), the United Pentecostal Church, Inc., has 1,680 churches, 3,536 ministers, approximately 150,000 members organized into 26 districts in the United States, the superintendents of which make up their (annual) general board, or top administrative body. They support 70 missionaries and over 200 native workers abroad, maintain 15 summer campgrounds in this country, and have established headquarters, a modern printing plant, and publishing house at St. Louis, Missouri.

PILGRIM HOLINESS CHURCH

The Rev. Martin Wells Knapp, a Methodist minister, organized the International Apostolic Holiness Union in 1897 in his home at Cincinnati, Ohio, to encourage the preaching of the original Wesleyan doctrines of holiness, premillennialism, divine healing, and a return to "apostolic practices, methods, power, and success." His intention was to form a union of Holiness and Pentecostal groups in agreement with his ideas; but eventually, through a rather bewildering series of mergers, the proposed union became a full-fledged denomination. The bodies joining his union were the Holiness Christian Church, the Pentecostal Rescue Mission of Binghamton, New York, the Pilgrim Church of California, the Pentecostal Brethren in Christ in Ohio, the People's Mission Church of Colorado, and numerous other small bodies. These, united in the Pilgrim Holiness Church, now have a strength of 47,703 members in 1,790 churches. About 1,010 of these churches with 32,310 members are in the United States and Canada, and 780 churches with 15,393 members are in foreign lands. There are churches in 37 states and in the province of Ontario in Canada.

The Pilgrim Holiness Church is close to the Church of the Nazarene in both doctrine and polity, although doctrine is described as Arminian and Methodist and government as a "combination of Episcopal and Congregational forms." Theologically it is conservative, stressing the Trinity, the new birth, entire sanctification, divine healing, premillennialism, and the inspiration and infallibility of the Scriptures. Baptism, the mode of which is optional, and the Lord's Supper are practiced as sacraments. Members are admitted on confession of faith

173

following appearances before an advisory board and the church congregation. Both men and women are accepted as ministers.

Local churches are governed by a church board composed of the pastor, elders, deacons, and other church officers; women may be elected deaconesses. District organizations meet annually, made up of ministers and laymen; they elect district councils which hold authority over the ministers and churches of their various districts. A general conference meets every 4 years and elects 3 general superintendents, secretary, treasurer, secretaries for foreign missions, church extension, Sunday schools, youth work, and a publishing agent. Home missionaries work largely in the South; foreign missions are located in Africa, Mexico, South America, the Philippines, and the West Indies. There are 5 Bible colleges and 1 liberal arts college.

POLISH NATIONAL CATHOLIC CHURCH OF AMERICA

Organized at Scranton, Pennsylvania, on March 14, 1897, the Polish National Catholic Church was born in resentment against certain resolutions passed by the Roman Catholic Council of Baltimore in 1884. These resolutions seemed to the dissenting Polish congregations to give the Roman hierarchy and priesthood an unwarranted religious, political, financial, and social power over their parishioners, and to permit an "unlawful encroachment upon the ownership of church property and to pave the way for the political exploitation of the Polish people." (Some feel that the cause of the dissention roots even farther back, in the demand in Poland in the Reformation era for a Polish National Church.) Resentment smoldered gradually into open revolt and resulted in the founding of an independent Polish body with approximately 20,000 members mainly in the eastern states. This is the only break of any considerable size from the Roman Catholic Church in the United States; but there are other groups among Slovaks, Lithuanians, Ruthenians, and Hungarians which have also broken away. Several of the Slovak and Lithuanian parishes have merged with the Polish National Catholic Church.

A constitution for the new church was adopted by the Scranton parish in 1897, claiming the right for the Polish people to control all churches built and maintained by them, to administer such church property through a committee chosen by the parish, and to choose their own pastors. The first synod was held at Scranton in 1904, with 147 clerical and lay delegates representing parishes in Pennsylvania, Maryland, Massachusetts, Connecticut, and New Jersey. The Rev. Francis Hodur, the organizer and dominant figure in the group, was chosen bishop-elect; he was consecrated bishop in 1907 at Utrecht, Holland, by 3 bishops of the Old Catholic Church. This synod also ordered all Latin service books translated into Polish and established a seminary at Scranton.

The doctrine of the church is founded upon the Scriptures, the holy traditions, and the 4 ecumenical synods of the undivided church; the Apostles' and the Nicene creeds are accepted. Doctrine is expanded in a confession of faith which includes statements of belief in the Trinity; the Holy Spirit as man's source of grace, power, and peace; the necessity of the spiritual unity of all believers; the church as teacher and confessor; the equality of all people as the common children of God; immortality and the future justice and judgment of God. The doctrine of eternal damnation or punishment is rejected.

Even sinful man, after undergoing an intrinsic regeneration through contrition, penance, and noble deeds, may have a chance to regain the grace of God. . . . Man, by following the Supreme Being, is in this life capable of attaining a certain degree of the happiness and of the perfection which is possessed of God in an infinite degree. . . . Faith is helpful to man toward his salvation, though not without good works.

Sin is

a lack of perfection, a consequence resulting from a lack of spiritual, godly life within the being, in whom predominates a mean, animal life, and as mankind progresses in this knowledge of the causes of life and nature of God, and comes nearer and nearer to Him, sin will gradually grow less and less until it vanishes entirely. Then man will become the true image and child of God, and the kingdom of God will prevail upon earth.

Seven sacraments are observed, with baptism and confirmation being recognized as one sacrament; actually confirmation is a complement of baptism. The word of God "heard and preached" is proclaimed as a sacrament. Two forms of confession are in general use—a private or "ear" confession and a general public confession for adults only.

A general synod is the highest authority in the government of the church. It meets every 4 years, except for such special sessions as may be considered necessary, and is composed of bishops (of whom there are now 7), clergy, and lay delegates from every parish. Administrative power rests with Prime Bishop the Most Rev. Leon Grochowski, successor to the late Bishop Hodur. A

church council meets twice annually, or on call, and is composed of all the bishops, 4 clerical, and 4 lay delegates elected by the general synod. In like manner the authority of the diocese is vested in a diocesan synod which meets every 4 years. Each parish is governed by an elected board of trustees. There are 274,658 members in 157 churches in the United States and 5,412 members in Canada. The Polish language is used in the worship and in the educational program in parish schools, taught largely by pastors; but English may be used if necessary for sacraments, sermons, gospel, and other church rituals, with permission of the bishop. The clergy may marry, but only with the knowledge and permission of the bishop and the lay members of the congregations.

The Polish National Union, a fraternal and insurance organization, was established by the church at Scranton in 1908, set up on parish lines and as an adjunct to parish life. It consists of 12 districts divided into 257 branches and has 35,000 members, all of whom are not required to be members of the church. A missionary work was begun in Poland in 1919, and by 1951 had 119 parishes and a theological seminary in Krakow. Missionary Bishop Padewski was imprisoned by the Communists at Warsaw and died in prison in 1951; since then these churches in Poland have come under the control of the Red government. A home for the aged and disabled was established by the church and the Polish National Union at Spojnia Farm, Waymart, Pennsylvania, in 1929.

An unusually effective intercommunion has been established between the Protestant Episcopal, Anglican, Old Catholic, and Polish National Catholic Churches.

PRESBYTERIANS

Presbyterianism has two firm and deep roots: one goes back to the Greek word

presbuteros (elder) and has to do with the system of church government of ancient and apostolic times; the other goes back to John Calvin and the Protestant Reformation and has to do with the form of government used by all people calling themselves Presbyterian and holding the faith of the Reformed churches.

Calvin (1509-64) was a Frenchman trained for the law. Turning to theology, his keen, legalistic mind and his lust for freedom from the rigid, confining forms of Roman Catholicism drove him as a fugitive from Roman reprisal to the city of Geneva, where he quickly grasped the reins of leadership in the Reformed sector of the Reformation. Resolute and often harsh to the point of cruelty with those who opposed him, he established himself and his theological system at the heart of a "city of God" in the Swiss capital, making it, according to Macaulay, the "cleanest and most wholesome city in Europe."

Calvin's whole thought revolved about the concept of sovereignty:

the sovereignty of God in His universe, the sovereignty of Christ in salvation, the sovereignty of the Scriptures in faith and conduct, the sovereignty of the individual conscience in the interpretation of the Will and Word of God.

His system has been summarized in 5 main points: human impotence, unconditional predestination, limited atonement, irresistible grace, and final perseverance. God, according to Calvinism, rules the world; man is completely dominated by and dependent upon him; man is also totally depraved and unable to save himself (the doctrine of total depravity); God chooses or elects to save some and predestines others to be lost (the doctrine of predestination); even babes may be damned and without hope (infant damnation). But both elect and damned have definite rights and duties: man has a covenant with God, which must be honored; whatever his state he must keep faith in God's grace and ultimate goodness.

Out of this Calvinism came miracles of reform; few reformers have made as many contributions as John Calvin in so many fields at once—in education, in the building of an intelligent ministry, in the liberation of the oppressed and persecuted, and in the establishment of democratic forms of government in both church and state. In his thought lay the germ which in time destroyed the divine right of kings. He gave a new dignity to man, and representative government to man's parliaments and church councils. He struck the final blow at feudalism and offered a spiritual and moral tone for dawning capitalism.

Strictly speaking, John Calvin did not found Presbyterianism; he laid the foundations upon which it was reconstructed in Switzerland, Holland, France, England, Scotland, and Ireland. He inspired fellow Frenchmen out of whose ranks came the Huguenots; by 1560 there were 2,000 churches of Presbyterian complexion in France. He influenced the Dutchmen who established the Dutch Reformed Church in Holland. He gave courage to British Presbyterians in their bitter struggle against Catholic Bloody Mary. To him came Scots who became Covenanters; to him came John Knox, who went home to cry "Great God, give me Scotland, or I die." Knox and the Covenanters set Scotland afire and made it Protestant and Presbyterian.

A delegation of Scots sat in the Westminster Assembly of Divines along with 121 English ministers, 10 peers, and 20 members of the House of Commons, resolved to have "no bishop, and no king." This Westminster Assembly is a milestone in Presbyterian history. Meeting at the call of Parliament to resolve the struggle over the compulsory use of the Anglican Book of Common Prayer, it sat for nearly 5 years (1643-48) in 1,163 sessions, produced a Larger and a Shorter catechism, a directory for the public worship of God, a form of government, and the Westminster Confession of Faith, which, built upon the Old and New Testaments, became the doctrinal standard of Scotish, British, and American Presbyterianism.

Dominant in the Westminster Assembly, the Presbyterians soon dominated the British government. Cromwell completed the ousting of a monarch and established a commonwealth; the commonwealth crashed, the monarchy returned, and the fires of persecution flamed again. British Presbyterians fled to America with the Puritans; an attempt to establish episcopacy in Scotland after 1662 sent many Presbyterians out of Scotland into Ireland, where economic difficulties and religious inequalities drove them on to America. The Presbyterian British, and even more the Presbyterian Scotch-Irish, became the founders of Presbyterianism in America. Beginning in 1710 and running into mid-century, from 3,000 to 6,000 Scotch-Irish came annually into the American colonies, settling at first in New England and the middle colonies, then spreading out more widely than any other racial group ever to reach our shores.

There were Presbyterian congregations in the colonies long before the Scotch-Irish migration of 1710-50. One was worshiping in Virginia in 1611; others were worshiping in Massachusetts and Connecticut in 1630. Long Island and New York had congregations by 1640 and 1643. What is probably the oldest continuing Presbyterian church in the United States was founded by the Rev. Francis Makemie at Rehoboth, Maryland, in 1683. Makemie ranged the coast from Boston to the Carolinas, planting churches and giving them unity with one another; 6 groups were united into the first presbytery in Philadelphia in 1706; in 1716 this first presbytery had become a synod made up of 4 presbyteries and held its first meeting in 1717.

The United Presbyterian Church in the U.S.A.

Overwhelmingly the largest single body of Presbyterians in America, this church is the result of a merger (1958) of two groups in the United States: The Presbyterian Church in the U.S.A., and the United Presbyterian Church of North America. We shall consider them first, separately, under their original names, and then as a united church.

PRESBYTERIAN CHURCH
IN THE U.S.A.

The Presbyterian Church in the U.S.A. dates back to the organizing of the General Presbytery in 1706. The first general synod of its spiritual forefathers, meeting in 1729, adopted the Westminster Confession of Faith with the Larger and Shorter catechisms "as being, in all essential and necessary articles, good forms of sound words, and systems of Christian doctrine." The same synod denied to the civil magistrates any power whatever over the church or any right to persecute anyone for his religious faith.

Free in the new land with their Scotch-Irish fire and Covenanter background, the Presbyterians quickly set about procuring trained ministers; creeds and colleges have been their stock in trade from the earliest days. William Tennent, Sr. organized a "log college" in a cabin at Neshaminy, Pennsylvania. He started with 3 of his 4 sons as his first pupils, and this family school grew into the most important Presbyterian institution of higher learning in America. Out of it came the College of New Jersey (now Princeton University), and a stream of revivalistic Presbyterian preachers who played leading roles in the Great Awakening of the early eighteenth century. Prominent among them were William Tennent, Jr. and his brother Gilbert, who met and liked the British revivalist George Whitefield and followed him in preaching an emotional "new birth" revivalism which came into conflict with the old creedal Calvinism. The camp-meeting revival grew out of the Great Awakening enthusiasm; it was born as a Presbyterian institution and was continued by the Methodists when the Presbyterians dropped it.

Presbyterian objection to emotional revivalism went deep; it split their church. Preachers took sides; those of the "old side" opposed revivalism, while those of the "new side" endorsed it, claiming that less attention should be paid to college training for the ministry and more to the recruiting of regenerated common men into the pulpit. The two sides quarreled until 1757, when they reunited; in 1758, the first year of the united synod, there were 98 ministers in the Presbyterian Church in the colonies, 200 congregations, and 10,000 members. One of the ablest of the new-side preachers was John Witherspoon, president of Princeton (founded in 1746), member of the Continental Congress, and the only ministerial signer of the Declaration of Independence.

Witherspoon may have been instrumental in the call of the general synod upon the Presbyterian churches to "uphold and promote" the resolutions of the Continental Congress. The Scotch-Irish accepted the revolution with relish; the persecution they had experienced in England and Ulster left them as natural dissenters and solidly anti-British. Their old cry, "No bishop, and no king," was heard as far off as England; Horace Walpole remarked that "Cousin America" had run off with a Presbyterian parson.

The Presbyterians moved swiftly to strengthen their church after Yorktown, meeting as a synod at Philadelphia in 1788 at the same time that the national constitutional convention was in session in the same city. The national administrative bodies of American Presbyterianism were known as the General Presbytery from 1706-16; as the General Synod from 1717-88, and as the General Assembly from 1789 to the present time. John Witherspoon was a delegate at the Presbyterian gathering and with James

Wilson helped put into the governmental statutes of the nation and the Presbyterian Church those principles of democratic representation which make them so amazingly alike even though he was not a member of the Constitutional Convention.

From 1790 to 1837 membership in the Presbyterian Church in the U.S.A. increased from 18,000 to 220,557. This growth was due to the revival which swept the country during those years and to the Plan of Union with the Congregationalists. Under this plan Presbyterian and Congregational preachers and laymen moving into the new western territory worked and built together; preachers of the 2 denominations preached in each other's pulpits, and members held the right of representation in both Congregational association and Presbyterian presbytery. The plan worked well on the whole, absorbing the fruits of the national revivals and giving real impetus to missionary work both at home and abroad. Then came disagreements between old-school and new-school factions within the church over matters of discipline and the expenditure of missionary money. The general assembly of 1837 expelled 4 new-school presbyteries, which promptly met in their own convention at Auburn, New York. The Presbyterian Church in the U.S.A. was split in two between new-school men who wanted to keep the plan of union and old-school men who were suspicious of the "novelties of New England (Congregational) theology."

These years promised to be an era of expansion for the Presbyterians. Marcus Whitman drove the first team and wagon over the south pass of the Rockies into the great Northwest. After him came hosts of Presbyterian preachers and laymen building churches, schools, colleges, seminaries. From 1812 to 1836 the Presbyterians in the United States built their first great theological seminaries: Princeton, Auburn, Allegheny, Columbia, Lane,

McCormack, Union in Virginia, and Union in New York City. They also set up their own missionary and educational societies. But the era of unity suddenly became an era of schism. Even earlier than the old-school–new-school division the Cumberland presbytery had broken away in 1810, following a dispute over the educational qualifications of the ministry, to form the Cumberland Presbyterian Church. Antislavery sentiment was increasing. A strong protest was made in 1818, but it was later modified. In 1846 the old-school assembly regarded slavery in the southern states as no bar to Christian communion; but the new-school assembly took action in the same year, condemning it without reservation. By 1857 several southern synods had withdrawn to organize the United Synod of the Presbyterian Church, and the greater and final break came in 1861 when 47 southern presbyteries formed their General Assembly of the Presbyterian Church in the Confederate States of America. In 1865 the United Synod and the Confederate churches merged into what is now known as the Presbyterian Church in the United States. The Synod of Kentucky united with it in 1869 and the Synod of Missouri in 1874.

The old-school and new-school bodies, holding separate assemblies since 1837, were reunited in 1870 on the basis of the Westminster Confession; they were joined in 1906 by a large majority of the Cumberland churches and in 1920 by the Welsh Calvinistic Methodists.

From the 1920's through the 1950's, two strong emphases were noticeable in this church: one was the emphasis upon theology, seen in the struggle between liberals and conservatives; and the other was the emphasis upon Presbyterian unity. The latter was evident in the proposed merger with the Protestant Episcopal Church, which was not realized, and in the 1958 merger of the Presbyterian Church in the U.S.A. with the United Presbyterian Church of North America.

UNITED PRESBYTERIAN CHURCH OF NORTH AMERICA

The United Presbyterian Church of North America was formed by the merging of the Associate Presbyterian Church and the Associate Reformed Presbyterian Church at Pittsburgh in 1858. The doctrines, traditions, and institutions of the two combining bodies were preserved; government in the United church followed the Presbyterian form with session, presbytery, synod, and a general assembly which met annually.

In matters of faith this church rested upon the broad foundation of the Westminster Confession with certain modifications, one of which amended the chapter in the confession on the power of civil magistrates. A confessional statement of 44 articles was drawn up by the United Presbyterian Church in 1925; it contained the substance of the Westminster standards and symbols but restricted divorce cases to marital unfaithfulness, denied infant damnation, extended sacramental privileges to all who professed faith in Christ and led Christian lives, withdrew the protest against secret or oath-bound societies, abandoned the exclusive use of the Psalms, maintained insistence upon the verbal inspiration of the Scriptures, affirmed the sufficiency and fullness of the provisions of God for the needs of a fallen race through the atonement of Christ, emphasized the renewing and sanctifying power of the Holy Spirit, and held salvation to be free to all sinners.

The usual boards, conducting work in missions, education, publications, pensions, and relief were combined with the boards and commissions of the Presbyterian Church in the U.S.A., with the merger. To this merger, the United Presbyterians brought 251,344 members, 833 churches, 6 colleges, 1 theological seminary, several homes for the aged, 1 hospital and 1 orphan's home, and missionary establishments in Egypt, Ethiopia, Pakistan, and the Sudan.

All Presbyterian bodies in this country subscribe to the principles and theology of the Westminster Confession. Some modifications or enlargements have come as the church has developed, but the Confession is its cornerstone. While no new "statement of faith" has yet appeared, the United Presbyterian Church in the U.S.A., proceeding from the Confession, puts its main emphasis upon the sovereignty of God in Christ in the salvation of the individual; and the salvation of every individual believer is recognized as a part of the divine plan. Salvation is not a reward for either faith or good works; it is the free gift of God. Regeneration, too, is an act of God; man is powerless to save himself, but once saved he remains saved.

Each congregation has its local session which acts in receiving and disciplining members and in the general spiritual welfare of the church. Congregations in limited districts are grouped in presbyteries, which examine, ordain, and install ministers; review reports from the sessions; and hear cases or complaints brought before them. The synod supervises the presbyteries of a larger district, reviews the records of its constituent presbyteries, hears complaints and appeals from the presbyteries, organizes new presbyteries, and functions in an administrative capacity in all denominational matters lying within its jurisdiction. The highest judiciary of the church is the annual general assembly, made up of clerical and lay delegates elected by the presbyteries on a proportional basis. The general assembly settles all matters of discipline and doctrine referred to it by the lower bodies, establishes new synods, appoints boards and commissions, and reviews all appeals. Its decisions are final except that it cannot itself amend the constitution of the church. The officers of the general assembly are the stated clerk as the chief executive officer of the denomination, elected for 5 years with the privilege of re-election, and the moderator, chosen each year to preside over the sessions of the general assembly.

The general assembly has provided for a general council and a permanent judicial commission. The general council is appointed to function between meetings of the assembly; it is composed of the moderator and 2 living ex-moderators; 2 members each, representing the 4 boards of the church; 1 representative of the council on theological education; and 18 "members at large." The stated clerk, the secretary of the general council, the secretary of finance, the secretary of stewardship and promotion, and the general secretary of each of the 4 boards are corresponding members with the right of the floor but without vote. This council is an important body; it has wide powers assigned by the assembly, and it formulates much of the policy under which the boards carry on their work. The council idea is carried down through the synods and presbyteries, which elect similar bodies with comparative powers. The permanent judicial commission is composed of 8 ministers and 7 ruling elders, no two of whom belong to the same synod. It was created in 1907 to act as a supreme judicial court. Judicial cases not affecting the doctrine or constitution of the church terminate with the synod as the final court of appeal; all others terminate with the general assembly.

Administrative direction of the work of the church is in the hands of the boards, reduced to 4 in 1923; the Board of National Missions, the Commission on Ecumenical Mission and Relations, the Board of Christian Education, and the Board of Pensions. The work now conducted by the Board of National Missions was begun by the general presbytery in 1707; the general synod of 1717 set up a "fund for pious uses," which eventually became the Presbyterian Ministers' Fund—the oldest life insurance concern in the United States. Home missions work was conducted for some time through the American Board of Commissioners for Foreign Missions, organized in 1810; a series of adjustments and consolidations resulted in the formation of the present Board of National Missions in 1923. The work of the board is carried on in all the 50 states and in the West Indies; it includes aid to churches, city and rural (about 90 per cent of the churches in the United States are said to have begun with the help of national mission funds), Sunday schools in pioneer areas, schools from primary to college level, hospitals and clinics, agricultural and community projects. The program employs more than 3,000 missionaries, ordained ministers, teachers, doctors, nurses, and community workers.

The Commission on Ecumenical Mission and Relations, elected by the general assembly, has 66 members (lay and clerical, men and women). It supports 1,369 missionaries and interchurch service representatives in 39 countries and maintains or co-operates in the work of 56 universities, colleges, and training schools; 118 secondary schools; 1,252 schools of lower grades; 77 hospitals; and 275 dispensaries and clinics. The Board of Christian Education, with 48 members, provides Presbyterian youth, children, and parents with study materials and supervises the work of Westminster Foundations on 114 college campuses. Its work reaches into 45 church-related colleges, 3 Christian education training schools, and 9 theological seminaries. Its publications are issued by the Westminster Press, one of the most efficient church publishing houses in American Protestantism. The Presbyterian periodicals *Today* and *Presbyterian Life* are published independently. The Board of Pensions administers a fund of $110,000,-000, together with relief grants administered in co-operation with the Minister's Emergency Relief Fund.

So, with few minor modifications, doctrine and polity remained the same with the merging of the Presbyterians in the U.S.A. and the United Presbyterians; together, they have in 43 countries some 45 seminaries, 53 hospitals, 79 clinics, 86 colleges in the United States, 150 neighborhood houses, 200 student centers, and 435 schools. Other reunions with other Presbyterian bodies, now under consideration, will greatly swell this total. Total membership of the United Presbyterian Church in the U.S.A. is 3,209,682 in 9,389 churches.

In 1960 there were 10 different Presbyterian denominations in the United States with a total membership of 4,126,583; of these, 3,964,085 are found in the two major divisions: the United Presbyterian Church in the United States of America and the Presbyterian Church in the United States. Of these 10 churches 7 are working together, in the western area of the Alliance of Reformed Churches Throughout the World Holding the Presbyterian Order, organized in 1875.

Presbyterian Church in the U.S.

This church in 1960 was composed of 6 synods with a total of 869,452 members and 3,984 churches. Often called "The Southern Presbyterian Church" (an objectionable term, to many, for its inference of regionalism) it has work and churches in 18 states and the District of Columbia. The organization of this church has already been described (see p. 179). Relations between the Presbyterian Church in the U.S.A. and the Presbyterian Church in the United States, disrupted by the Civil War, became cordial again once that war was over. Fraternal relations were re-established in 1882, and in 1888 the two groups held a joint meeting in Philadelphia to celebrate the centenary of the adoption of the Presbyterian Constitution of 1788. In 1897 they also united to observe the 250th anniversary of the Westminster Assembly.

The original differences between these two bodies have been resolved, but others remain to keep them apart; prominent among these are the question of conservative versus liberal theology and the problem involved in the assimilation or segregation of Negro members and churches. Neither of these current problems, however, seem impossible of solution. Conservatism and liberalism in theology are fairly prevalent in both groups, and it becomes increasingly difficult to draw any firm line in this area. While racial problems were prominent in the declination of the Presbyterian Church in the United States to join the proposed three-way merger with the Presbyterian Church in the U.S.A. and the United Presbyterian Church in 1954-55, continuing efforts are being made to work out an acceptable Christian solution in this situation.

Doctrinally this church is conservatively Calvinistic. As in most Reformed churches, ministers, elders, and deacons are required to give adherence to a confessional statement. Women are excluded from the ministry and eldership, but are encouraged to enlist in other fields of Christian work. Polity, like doctrine, follows the general Presbyterian pattern.

Five boards and 9 other agencies execute the work of the church. The boards are World Missions, Christian Education, Church Extension, Annuities and Relief, and Women's Work. A general council concentrates on stewardship, public relations, research, and church finance. Various other permanent and standing committees are also appointed by the assembly.

In the Presbyterian Church in the United States there are 16 Synods, 83 presbyteries, 3,068 ministers, 3,984 churches, and 869,452 communicants in 18 states. The church supports 4 theological seminaries—Austin, Columbia, Louisville, and Richmond—27 institutions of collegiate or higher rank, 4 secondary schools, 2 mission schools, and 15 orphans' homes and schools. Students' work is maintained in 30 colleges with full-time student work and in 19 other colleges with part-time workers. Approximately 61 presbyteries are receiving aid for work among the Indians in Texas and Oklahoma, mountain work in the Ozarks and the Appalachians, Latin-American work in Texas, and work among southern Negroes; 483 missionaries are serving abroad in Formosa, Africa, Brazil, Japan, Korea, Mexico, Ecuador, Iraq, and Portugal. There are about 140,000 foreign communicants, over 1,200 organized congregations, 4,000 outstations, approximately 4,000 trained native workers, 2,400 mission schools attended by 60,000 students, and 13 hospitals in which 126,000 patients were treated in 1958. There are 29 periodicals published by the Board of Education, which also operates John Knox Press.

Associate Presbyterian Church of North America

This church maintains the traditions of the secession movement of 1733 in the Church of Scotland. Missionaries from Scotland organized the Associate Presbytery in America in 1754. This presbytery merged with the Reformed Presbytery in 1782; 2 ministers and 3 ruling elders refused to accept the union and continued the organization of the Associate Presbytery of Pennsylvania. Other presbyteries joined the Pennsylvania group, which in 1801 was named the Associate Synod of North America. In 1858 this associate synod and the Associate Reformed Presbyterian Church of North America consummated a union under the name United Presbyterian Church of North America. Eleven ministers refusing to enter this union continued the Associate Presbyterian Church.

This church believes in restricted Communion, expels members who join secret orders, and uses the Psalms exclusively in worship services. It follows the Westminster Confession and has an associate testimony of its own explaining its doctrinal position. Polity differs in no essential elements from that of other Presbyterian churches. Home missions are conducted by itinerant pastors, and foreign missionary work is supported in India. There are no colleges or other schools; there are 500 members and 7 churches.

Associate Reformed Presbyterian Church (General Synod)

This is a synod of the former Associate Reformed Presbyterian Church; it is a body of Covenanter origins and traditions. ("Covenanter" here refers to the Reformed branch of the church. The Associate Prebyterian Church of North America, in distinction, is of Seceder origin; the Associate Reformed Church is a result of the union of the Associate and Reformed groups.) Feeling that the distances which separated them from their fellow members in the North were too great, the synod of the Carolinas withdrew in 1822 from the Associate Reformed Church to form the Associate Reformed Synod of the South. Following the creation of the United Presbyterian Church in 1858 (which this group never joined), they dropped the phrase "of the South," thereby becoming the Associate Reformed Presbyterian Church. They became a General Synod in 1935.

The standards of the Westminster Confession are followed. For some years the only music in this church was in the singing of the Psalms; this position was modified in 1946, permitting the use of other selected hymns. Foreign mission stations are located in Pakistan and Mexico; Erskine College and Erskine Theological Seminary are maintained at Due West, South Carolina; summer assembly grounds are at "Bonclarken," Flat Rock, North Carolina. Total membership is placed at 27,629 in 149 churches.

Bible Presbyterian Church

Within a year after the founding of the Orthodox Presbyterian Church (see p. 184) in 1936, a group under the leadership of the Rev. Carl McIntire withdrew to organize the Bible Presbyterian Church. They continued the protest against tendencies which they considered to be "modernistic, pacifistic and communistic" not only within Presbyterianism but within American Protestantism generally.

This protest has been continued and widened in the organization, under the inspiration of McIntire, of the American and International Councils of Churches, in both of which the Bible Presbyterian Church holds a prominent place; these two organizations oppose the teaching and work of the National Council of the Churches of Christ in the U.S.A. and the World Council of Churches. On the positive side the Bible Presbyterian Church advocates a conservative theology, built around the doctrines of the verbal inspiration and infallibility of the Bible, the premillennial return of Christ, and "separation from worldly practices and belief."

Its churches, at first limited to the eastern coast, have spread across the nation; in 1958 they are reported to have 8,870 members, 212 ministers, 103 churches, and 14 additional churches "in affiliation" with 500 members. A theological school, Faith Theological Seminary, is located in Philadelphia; there are independent home and foreign missions boards. A general synod meets annually.

Colored Cumberland Presbyterian Church

This church was built on the 20,000 Negro membership of the pre-Civil War Cumberland Presbyterian Church with the full approval of the general assembly of that church, held in 1869. The first 3 presbyteries were organized in Tennessee, where the first synod, the Tennessee Synod, was organized in 1871. In doctrine this church follows the Westminster Confession with 4 reservations: (1) there are no eternal reprobates; (2) Christ died for all mankind, not for the elect alone; (3) there is no infant damnation; and (4) the Spirit of God operates in the world coextensively with Christ's atonement in such manner "as to leave all men inexcusable." Polity is genuinely Presbyterian except that bishops are included as pastors among its officers. There were 19 presbyteries, 4 synods—Alabama, Tennessee, Kentucky, and Texas—121 churches, and 30,000 members found in all sections of the country in 1949. In May of 1940 the general assembly accepted an overture from a presbytery of 17 churches and 1 school in Liberia, Africa, and voted to make it a part of the Colored Cumberland Presbyterian Church.

Cumberland Presbyterian Church

An outgrowth of the Great Revival of 1800, the Cumberland Presbytery was organized on February 4, 1810, in Dickson County, Tennessee, by 3 Presbyterian ministers, the Revs. Finis Ewing, Samuel King, and Samuel McAdow. Contributing factors to the organization were a rejection by the founders of the doctrine of fatality of the Westminster Confession of Faith, and an insistence that the rigid standards of the Presbyterian Church for the education of the clergy be relaxed in the light of extraordinary circumstances existing on the American frontier. The presbytery for a time sought admission into the Presbyterian Church, but, failing in this effort, developed eventually into a denomination. A union with the Presbyterian Church, U.S.A., in 1906 was only partially successful. A considerable segment, to whom the terms of union were unsatisfactory, perpetuated the Cumberland Presbyterian Church as a separate denomination.

This church reports 88,000 members in 990 congregations located for the most part in 11 southern states, with some congregations in the states of Indiana, Illinois, Ohio, Michigan, Iowa, Kansas, New Mexico, and California.

The church sponsors missionaries in Colombia, South America, Japan, China, and the Hong Kong area. The Cumberland Presbyterian Theological Seminary is located at McKenzie, Tennessee. Bethel College is sponsored by the church at the same location. The Cumberland Presbyterian Children's Home is located at Denton, Texas. The Cumberland Presbyterian Center—publishing plant, bookstore, and denominational board offices—is located at Memphis, Tennessee.

The Orthodox Presbyterian Church

This church was organized June 11, 1936, in protest against what were believed to be modernistic tendencies in the Presbyterian Church in the U.S.A. (now the United Presbyterian Church in the U.S.A.). Led by the late Rev. J. Gresham Machen, the dissenters had formed a foreign missionary society which they were ordered to disband; refusing, they were tried, convicted, and suspended from the Presbyterian Church in the U.S.A. They organized the Presbyterian Church of America; an injunction brought against the use of that name by the parent body resulted in the change in 1939 to the name Orthodox Presbyterian Church.

The Westminster Confession and the Westminster Larger and Shorter catechisms are accepted as subordinate doctrinal standards or creedal statements. Stronger emphasis is laid upon the infallibility and inerrancy of the Bible (the books of the Bible were written by men "so guided by Him that their original manuscripts were without error in fact or doctrine"); original sin; the virgin birth, deity, and substitutionary atonement of Christ; his resurrection

184

and ascension; his role as judge at the end of the world and the consummation of the Kingdom; the sovereignty of God; and salvation through the sacrifice and power of Christ for those "whom the Father purposes to save." Salvation is "not because of good works, [but] it is in order to good works."

The Presbyterian system of government is followed; a general assembly meets annually. The church constitution contains the creedal statement of the group, a form of government, book of discipline, and directory for the worship of God. Committees appointed by the general assembly conduct work in home missions and church extension, foreign missions, and Christian education. There are 10,233 members in 92 churches.

Reformed Presbyterian Church in North America, General Synod

This is the original New Light group which was organized following the division of the Reformed Presbyterian Synod in 1883. It is similar to the preceeding body except that it allows its members to vote and hold public office. It accepts the Westminster standards and Reformed Principles Exhibited as their subordinate standards; uses hymns as well as Psalms in worship, and organs and pianos in their singing; preaches the headship of Christ over all nations; and advocates public social covenanting (although this is not practiced as much today as formerly). Polity is distinctively Presbyterian. There are 3 presbyteries with 19 congregations and 2,060 communicant members (including ministers) in the United States, one presbytery with 5 congregations, and 2 mission stations and 171 communicant members in India.

Reformed Presbyterian Church of North America (Old School)

A body of direct Covenanter lineage, its first minister came to this country from the Reformed Presbytery of Scotland in 1752. Most of the early membership joined the union with the Associate Presbytery in 1782, but a small group remained outside the union and reorganized in Philadelphia under the name Reformed Presbytery in 1798. A synod was first constituted at Philadelphia in 1809, only to split in 1833 into Old Light and New Light groups in a dispute over citizenship. The synod of the Reformed Presbyterian Church (Old Light) refused to allow its members to vote or participate generally in public affairs; the general synod of the Reformed Presbyterian Church (New Light) imposed no such restrictions.

The government of this church is thoroughly Presbyterian except that there is no general assembly. The Westminster Confession is the doctrinal standard. The members pledge themselves to "pray and labor for the peace and welfare of our country, and for its reformation by a constitutional recognition of God as the source of all power, of Jesus Christ as the Ruler of Nations, of the Holy Scriptures as the supreme rule, and of the true Christian religion." Until that reformation is accomplished, they refuse to vote or hold public office. They observe close Communion and use only the Psalms in worship. No instrumental music is permitted in their services, and members cannot join any secret society.

Home missionaries work among the Indians, Negroes, and Jews in America; foreign missionaries are at work in Cyprus and Japan. There are a church at Beaver Falls, Pennsylvania, a theological seminary at Pittsburgh, and a home for the aged; 6,214 members were reported in 72 churches in 1954.

PROTESTANT EPISCOPAL CHURCH

It is stated in the preface of the Book of Common Prayer of the Protestant Episcopal Church that "this Church is far from intending to depart from the Church of England in any essential point of doctrine, discipline, or worship." Therein lies the hint of its origin: the Protestant Episcopal Church constitutes the "self-governing American branch of the Anglican Communion." For a century and a half in this country it bore the name of the Church of England.

Its history runs back to the first missionaries who went to the British Isles from Gaul prior to the Council of Arles in A.D. 314. It is traced down through the days when Henry VIII threw off the supremacy of the pope (Henry, according to Anglican scholars, did not found the Church of England; it was a church that had always been more British than Roman); through the reign of Edward VI, when the Book of Common Prayer and 42 Articles of Religion were written; through the period of Catholic restoration under Bloody Mary and through her successor Protestant Elizabeth, who put the united church and state under the Protestant banner and sent Sir Francis Drake sailing to build an empire.

Drake came ashore in what is now California in 1578. His Church of England chaplain, Francis Fletcher, planted a cross and read a prayer while Drake claimed the new land for the Virgin Queen. Martin Frobisher had reached Labrador in 1576, also with a chaplain. After them came colonists to Virginia under Sir Humphrey Gilbert and Sir Walter Raleigh; Raleigh's chaplain baptized an Indian named Manteo and a white baby named Virginia Dare before the settlement vanished. With Captain John Smith came Chaplain Robert Hunt, who stretched a sail between two trees for a shelter and read the service from the Book of Common Prayer.

In the South the transplanted Church of England quickly became the Estab-

lished Church. It was at heart a tolerant and catholic church, but the control of the crown brought an almost ruthless authority which made the church suspect in the eyes of those colonists who had come here seeking freedom from all such authority. The Virginia House of Burgesses set the salary of the Virginia clergyman at "1,500 pounds of tobacco and 16 barrels of corn." It was a British clergy supported by public tax and assessment and by contributions from the Church in England through the Society for the Propagation of the Gospel. And it was technically under the jurisdiction of the Bishop of London. In that fact lay one of its almost fatal weaknesses: colonial ministers had to journey to England for ordination, and few could afford it. This, coupled with the rising tide of the American Revolution, placed the colonial Church of England in an unenviable position.

Yet the church did well. Membership grew rapidly. William and Mary College was established in 1693, and the Church of England became the predominant church in the South. King's Chapel in Boston, the first Episcopal church in New England, was opened in 1689; in 1698 a church was established at Newport, Rhode Island, and another, called Trinity Church, in New York City. In 1702 a delegation from the Society for the Propagation of the Gospel came from England to survey the colonial church and found about 50 clergymen at work from the Carolinas to Maine. The visitors sensed the need for American bishops to ordain American clergymen; they also sensed the increasing opposition of the American patriot to a British-governed church.

The Revolution almost destroyed the colonial Church of England. Under special oath of allegiance to the king the clergy either fled to England or Canada, or remained as Loyalists in the colonies in the face of overwhelming persecution. That many of them were loyal to the

American cause meant little; the Rev. William White was chaplain of the Continental Congress, the Rev. Charles Thurston was a Continental colonel, and in the pews of the Episcopal Church sat Washington, Jefferson, Patrick Henry, John Jay, Robert Morris, John Marshall, Charles and "Light-Horse Harry" Lee, and John Randolph. But their presence could not stem the tide. The Anglican house was divided, and it fell. At the war's end there was no episcopacy, no association of the churches, not even the semblance of an establishment. Few thought of any future for this church, which suffered between Lexington and Yorktown more than any other in the colonies.

There was, however, a future—and a great one. In 1782 there appeared a pamphlet entitled *The Case of the Episcopal Churches in the United States Considered,* written by William White. It was a plea for unity and reorganization, and it proposed that the ministry be continued temporarily without the episcopal succession since the latter "cannot at present be obtained." In 1783 a conference of the Episcopal churches met at Annapolis, Maryland, and formally adopted the name Protestant Episcopal Church—"Protestant" to distinguish it from the Church of Rome, "Episcopal" to distinguish it from the Presbyterians and the Congregationalists. In the same year the clergy in Connecticut elected Samuel Seabury as their prospective bishop; he went to England and waited a year for consecration at the hands of English bishops. This was denied, and he then went to Scotland to be consecrated bishop in 1784. Ultimately Parliament and the Church of England cleared the way, and two other bishops-elect from New York and Pennsylvania were consecrated by the Archbishop of Canterbury in 1787. In 1789 the constitution of the Protestant Episcopal Church was adopted in Philadelphia, the Book of Common Prayer was revised for American use, and the Prot-

estant Episcopal Church became an independent, self-governing body.

There were complete harmony and expansion for the next half century. There were established new churches and church institutions: Sunday schools, Bible, prayer book, and tract societies, theological seminaries, colleges, boarding schools, guilds for men and women, and the Domestic and Foreign Missionary Society. Diocesan organizations replaced state organizations; new bishops moved into the new West. Bishops J. H. Hobart in New York, A. V. Griswold in New England, Benjamin Moore in Virginia, and Philander Chase in Ohio worked miracles in overcoming the revolutionary prejudices against the church. W. A. Muhlenberg, one of the great Episcopalian builders,

organized the first free church of any importance in New York, introduced the male choir, sisterhoods and the fresh air movement, while his church infirmary suggested to his mind the organization of St. Luke's Hospital [in New York], the first church hospital of any Christian communion in the country.

Muhlenberg was a man of wide vision; he inspired a "memorial" calling for a wider catholicity in the Protestant Episcopal Church, which resulted in the famous Lambeth Quadrilateral on Church Unity in 1888 and the movement which produced the further revision of the American Book of Common Prayer in 1892.

With the outbreak of the Civil War disruption again threatened the Protestant Episcopal Church, but it did not come. Among the major Protestant churches this one alone suffered no division. New England churchmen may have been abolitionists, and a Louisiana bishop, Leonidas Polk, may have been a general under Lee, but Polk prayed for Bishop Charles Pettit McIlvaine of Ohio in public, and the Ohioan prayed for Polk, and they were still in one church. A temporary Protestant

Episcopal Church in the Confederate States was organized to carry on the work in the South, but the names of the southern bishops were called in the general convention in New York in 1862; and once the war was over, the Episcopalian house was in 1865 quickly reunited.

The years following Appomattox were years of new growth. A dispute over churchmanship, rising out of the Oxford Movement in England, resulted in the separation of a group into the Reformed Episcopal Church in 1873, but otherwise Episcopalian unity held fast. New theological seminaries were established, and old ones were reorganized and strengthened. This period saw the organization of Church Congress, the Brotherhood of St. Andrew, and numerous other church agencies. The expansion continued into the next century; two world wars failed to halt it. In 1830 the Protestant Episcopal Church had 12 bishops, 20 dioceses, 600 clergymen, and 30,000 communicants; in 1930 it had 152 bishops, 105 dioceses, 6,000 clergymen, and 1,250,000 communicants.

The Episcopalian form of government closely parallels that of the federal government. The basic unit is the parish, governed by a priest, who is called a rector; wardens, who have charge of church records and the collection of alms; and vestrymen, who have charge of all church property. There are also lay readers and deaconesses in the local congregation. Parishes are grouped geographically into 77 dioceses, each of which includes not less than 6 parishes; the dioceses, which elect the bishops, were at first identical with the states, but with the growth of the church larger dioceses became necessary. Government in the diocese is vested in the bishop and the diocesan convention, made up of clerical and lay representatives and meeting annually. It is self-governing but appoints a standing committee as the ecclessiastical authority for all purposes declared by the general convention. Sec-

tions of states and territories not organized into dioceses are established by the house of bishops and the general convention as missionary districts, which may be elevated into dioceses or consolidated with other parts of dioceses as new dioceses. In addition to the 10 domestic missionary districts there are 10 overseas missionary districts and 5 extracontinental missionary districts.

Dioceses and missionary districts are grouped into 8 provinces, each governed by a synod consisting of the bishop, 4 presbyters, and 4 laymen elected by each constituent diocese and missionary district. Once in 3 years there is a general convention composed of a house of bishops and a house of deputies with lay and clerical delegates having equal representation. The 2 houses sit and deliberate separately; both must approve of a measure before it can become law. The ecclesiastical head of the church is the presiding bishop elected by the general convention; he serves until the age of retirement, set at 68.

In 1919 the general convention provided for a national council to act between sessions of the convention. It is one of the most important administrative agencies of the church, made up of 32 members consisting of bishops, priests, laymen, and laywomen; the presiding bishop is president, and the council facilitates the work of the church in 6 departments: foreign missions, domestic missions, religious education, Christian social service, finance, and promotion. The general divisions of laymen's work, women's work, and research work in co-operation with all 6 of the departments.

The Episcopalian accepts 2 creeds—the Apostles' and the Nicene. The articles of the Church of England, with the exception of the twenty-first and with modifications of the eighth, thirty-fifth, and thirty-sixth, are accepted as a general statement of doctrine; but adherence to them as a creed is not re-

188

quired. The clergy make the following declaration:

I do believe the Holy Scriptures of the Old and New Testaments to be the Word of God, and to contain all things necessary to salvation, and I do solemnly engage to conform to the doctrine, discipline, and worship of the Protestant Episcopal Church in the United States of America.

The church expects of all its members "loyalty to the doctrine, discipline, and worship of the one holy Catholic Apostolic Church, in all the essentials, but allows great liberty in nonessentials." It allows for more variation, individuality, independent thinking, and religious liberty than most of our larger Protestant churches. Liberals and conservatives, modernists and fundamentalists, find cordial and common ground for worship in the Prayer Book, which next to the Bible has probably influenced more people than any other book in the English language.

There are 2 sacraments, baptism and the Lord's Supper, recognized as "certain sure witnesses and effectual agencies of God's love and grace." Baptism by pouring or immersion is necessary for regeneration for either children or adults; baptism by any church in the name of the Trinity is recognized as valid baptism, baptized children are confirmed as members by the bishop, and those not baptized in infancy or childhood must accept the rite before confirmation. Without stating or defining a holy mystery the Episcopal Church believes in the real presence of Christ in the elements of the Supper. The church also recognizes the sacramental character of confirmation, penance, orders, matrimony, and unction.

Some Episcopalians are high churchmen with elaborate ritual and ceremony; others are low churchmen with a ritual less involved and with more of an evangelistic emphasis. There are Anglo-Catholics, stressing the catholicity of the church; they constitute about one third of the members. All, however, have a loyalty to their church which is deep and lasting; in more than 300 years this church has known only one minor division; today it stands sixth among all denominations: it had 3,359,048 members in 7,485 churches in the United States in 1958.

Stanley I. Stuber has called this the "Church of Beauty," and it is an apt description. Its prayer book is matchless in the literature of religious worship, containing the heart of the New Testament and the best of Old Testament devotions. Members have built stately cathedrals in this country, among them the Cathedral of St. John the Divine in New York City, which is the third largest cathedral in the world, and the National Cathedral at Washington, sometimes called the American Westminster Abbey. Stained-glass windows, gleaming altars, vested choirs, and a glorious ritual give the worshiper not only beauty but a deep sense of the continuity of the Christian spirit and tradition. Next to their stress on episcopacy their liturgical worship is a distinguishing feature; varying in degree according to high or low church inclinations, it has its roots in the liturgy of the Church of England and includes the reading, recitation, or intonation by priest, people, and choir of the historic general confession, general thanksgiving, collects, Psalter, and prayers, all of which are written in a beauty and cadence second only to that of the King James Version of the Bible.

Home missions, supported or aided by national missionary funds, are found in 32 dioceses and missionary districts in the United States. Special emphasis is placed upon work in town and country areas, in college communities, and in Negro, Indian, and Spanish-speaking fields. Overseas missions are located in all American territories—the Panama Canal Zone, Guam, the Virgin Islands, and Puerto Rico—and in Brazil, Cuba, the Dominican Republic, Haiti, India, Japan, the Near East, Liberia, Mexico, Oki-

189

nawa, Taiwan, Central America, and the Philippines. The church sponsors or maintains 12 theological seminaries, 6 colleges, 1 university, 3 training schools for deaconesses, 180 secondary schools for boys and girls in the United States, Alaska, Hawaii, and the Philippines, 76 homes for the aged, 78 institutions for child care, 79 hospitals and convalescent homes, and work for seamen in 8 dioceses in America. This church is unique in Protestantism for its orders of monks and nuns; there are 11 orders for men and 15 for women, employed in schools, hospitals, and various forms of missionary work.

The Protestant Episcopal Church has an undeserved reputation for exclusiveness and non-co-operation with other Protestant bodies; actually it has been most co-operative. The Lambeth Quadrilateral, already mentioned, was adopted by the house of bishops at the general convention of 1886 and accepted with modifications 2 years later. It had 4 points for world unity of the churches: the Scriptures as the word of God, the Apostles' and the Nicene creeds as the rule of faith, the 2 sacraments of baptism and the Lord's Supper, and the episcopate as the central principle of church government. In 1910 the general convention appointed a commission to arrange for a World Conference on Faith and Order; the first conference was held at Geneva in 1920, the second in 1927 at Lausanne, the third at Edinburgh in 1937. The church is active in the National Council of the Churches of Christ in America and in the World Council of Churches. An unusually effective intercommunion has been established among the Anglican, Old Catholic, Polish National Catholic, and Protestant Episcopal Churches, which may be the first step toward a merger of these bodies.

REFORMED BODIES

When the Belgic Confession was written in 1561 as the creedal cornerstone of the Reformed churches in Belgium and Holland, the "Churches in the Netherlands which sit under the Cross" gave thanks to their God in the preface of that document, where they said, "The blood of our brethren . . . crieth out." There was real cause for crying out, for the Reformation was spreading into the Netherlands from Switzerland in the midst of the long Dutch struggle against Catholic Spain. The Dutch Reformed Church was cradled in cruelty.

Those Reformation-founded churches called Reformed, as distinguished from those called Lutheran, originated in Switzerland under Zwingli, Calvin, and Melanchthon; they were Reformed in Switzerland, Holland, and Germany; they were Presbyterian in England and Scotland, and Huguenot in France; still others in Bohemia and Hungary used national names. As they moved overseas to the American colonies, they formed into 4 groups of churches: 2 from Holland became the Reformed Church in America and the Christian Reformed Church; 1 from the German Palatinate became the Reformed Church in the United States, now the Evangelical and Reformed Church; the fourth, coming from Hungary, became the Free Magyar Reformed Church in America. All of them were and still are Calvinistic and conservative, basing their doctrine generally upon the Heidelberg Catechism, the Belgic Confession, and the canons of the Synod of Dort, and using a modified Presbyterian form of government.

Reformed Church in America

This church had an unorganized membership along the upper reaches of the Hudson River in the neighborhood of

Fort Orange (Albany), New York, in 1614. Members had no regularly established congregations or churches; but they were numerous enough to require the services of Reformed ministers, two of whom came from Holland in 1623 as "comforters of the sick." By 1628 the Dutch in New Amsterdam had a pastor of their own in Dominie Jonas Michaelius and an organized Collegiate Church, which was to become the oldest church in the middle colonies and the oldest church in America with an uninterrupted ministry.

When the English took New Amsterdam in 1664, Dutch churches were thriving in Albany, Kingston, Brooklyn, Manhattan, and at Bergen in New Jersey. As the immigration from Holland ceased, there were perhaps 8,000 Dutch churchmen and churchwomen in the country, holding their services in Dutch and served by either native clergymen or pastors sent from Holland. It was difficult and expensive to send native-born ministerial candidates to Holland for education and ordination; the question rent the Reformed Church and was finally resolved in the building of a college and seminary at New Brunswick (Queen's College, later Rutgers). It was the first theological seminary to be built in this country, and it was fathered by the famous Dominie Theodore Frelinghuysen, who also took a leading part in the revival called the Great Awakening.

A sharp controversy disputing the authority of the classis of Amsterdam resulted in the complete independence of the Dutch churches in America; a general body and 5 particular bodies were created, a constitution was drawn up in 1792, and the general synod was organized in 1794. The names Dutch Reformed Church in North America and Reformed Dutch Church in the United States of America were both in use in 1792; in 1819 the church was incorporated as the Reformed Protestant Dutch Church, and in 1867 it became the Reformed Church in America.

The American Revolution had little effect upon the Reformed Church in America except to offer the Dutchmen a chance to even matters with the English. Once the war was over, Scotch, English, and Germans began joining the church, creating a problem in the use of the Dutch tongue which took years to resolve. A second Dutch immigration from the Netherlands started in the middle of the nineteenth century, bringing whole Dutch congregations with their pastors. One group, led by Dominie Albertus van Raalte, settled in western Michigan and established the community called Holland, known today for Hope College, Western Theological Seminary, and an annual tulip festival. Van Raalte and his group became part of the Reformed Church in America in 1850. Another colony, led by Dominie Scholte, settled in Pella, Iowa, in 1847-48 and in 1856 merged with the Reformed Church in America except for a small dissenting group.

Domestic missions began in 1786; actually, missionary work among the Indians had begun much earlier. Needy and destitute churches in New York, Pennsylvania, and Kentucky were assisted by the domestic missionaries of the classis of Albany for many years, and in 1806 the general synod took over administration of all missionary agencies. This church co-operated with the American Board of Commissioners for Foreign Missions. In 1832 the Board of Foreign Missions was created but continued to work through the American Board until 1857, from which time it has operated independently. Insisting from the start upon 7 years of college and seminary training for its ministers, the church established the Education Society of the Reformed Church in America in 1828 and changed it to the Board of Education of the General Synod in 1831.

The explicit statements and principles

of the Belgic Confession, the Heidelberg Catechism, and the Synod of Dort are still the doctrinal standard of the Reformed Church in America. The mild and gentle spirit of the confession with its emphasis upon salvation through Christ is a central theme; the primacy of God and his power in human life are at the heart of the preaching of the church as they are at the heart of the canons of Dort; and the Heidelberg Catechism, based as it is on the Apostles' Creed, is employed in all catechetical classes. The divine authority of the Scriptures is important here; "the final authority in the Reformed faith is the Holy Scripture, the living Word of God, spoken to every man through the Holy Spirit of God."

Worship is semiliturgical, but it is an optional liturgy; only the forms for baptism and the Lord's Supper, the 2 recognized sacraments of the church, are obligatory. It is a corporate or congregational way of worship, blending form and freedom and distinguishing this from other Protestant communions.

Government of the church stands midway between the episcopal and Presbyterian forms; it might be called "modified Presbyterian." The governing body in the local church is the consistory, made up of elders, deacons, and the pastor, who is always president. Elders are charged with the guidance of the spiritual life of the church, and deacons are in charge of benevolences; but they generally meet and act as one body. A number of churches in a limited area are grouped into a classis, which has immediate supervision of the churches and the ministry, and is composed of all the ministers of the area and an elder from each consistory. Classes are grouped into particular synods, of which there are 6, meeting annually and made up of an equal number of ministers and elders from each classis, and supervising the planning and programing of the churches within the area. The highest court of the church is the general synod,

representing the entire church, meeting once a year, and consisting of delegations of an equal number of ministers and elders from each classis. The size of the delegation, however, varies in accordance with the size of the classis. The general synod directs the missionary and educational work through its various boards. The president of the general synod, elected by the delegates, holds office for 1 year.

The Board of Foreign Missions directs 164 active missionaries abroad in the Philippine Islands, south India, Japan, Arabia, Iraq, Mesopotamia, and Africa; a total of $1,175,758 was received to finance foreign missions for the year ending December 31, 1958. The Board of Domestic Missions offers help to needy and mission churches, administers the church building fund and the Southern Normal School in Brewton, Alabama. It also directs work among Dutch immigrants in Canada and among Italians, Chinese, and Jews in the United States; operates missions in Kentucky; supports other missionary projects among Japanese-Americans, Italians, Indians, migrants, and sharecroppers; provides scholarships in the denominational colleges, and carries on evangelistic work in Mexico and among urban American Negroes. In 1958 the churches and various organizations contributed $1,158,171 for the work of the board. The Board of Education offers funds for student aid in 3 colleges and 2 theological seminaries, and plans the work for Sunday schools, catechetical classes, young peoples' activities, and adult groups. Living donors in 1958 contributed $708,437 to this board. The Board of Pensions administers annuities, pensions, and relief funds for widows, disabled ministers, and orphans. About 552 persons received a total of $282,257 from these funds in 1957-58.

The Reformed Church in America in 1959 listed 219,770 members in 867 churches.

Christian Reformed Church

This is the second largest Reformed body in the United States, with 184,346 members and 402 churches reported in 1959. It began with the dissent of a number of members and 2 Michigan ministers of the Reformed Church in America, who found themselves in disagreement with the parent church on certain matters of doctrine and discipline. A conference held at Holland, Michigan, in 1857 effected the separation of the Holland Reformed Church from the Reformed Church in America. Through a series of changes in name the Holland Reformed Church became the present Christian Reformed Church.

Dissension split its ranks soon after organization; by 1863 there were only 3 Christian Reformed pastors for the entire body. Immigration from Holland and anti-Masonic agitation in the Reformed Church in America, however, brought several groups into merger and gave the church a new lease on life. The Christian Reformed Church today is largely an English-speaking church with a few congregations still using Holland Dutch. Doctrine shows no important differences from Reformed standards; the 3 historic creeds are accepted. Organization bears the usual Reformed markings, including 30 classes which meet every 4 months (in some cases every 6 months) but with no intermediate or particular synods between the classes, and a general synod made up of 2 ministers and 2 elders from each classis, meeting annually.

Interest in missions, ministerial training, Christian primary and high schools, labor unions, and tuberculosis and psychopathic hospitals distinguishes this denomination. Thirty-three home missionaries work among the Navajo and Zuni Indians, among American Jews, Negroes, and Chinese in New York City and Chicago, and in unchurched communities in other American cities. Forty-six foreign missionaries work in Japan, South America, northern Nigeria, Cuba, and Formosa; there are churches and stations in Canada. Calvin College and Seminary are located at Grand Rapids, Michigan, and there are a number of Christian school societies made up of parents who support the denomination's Christian schools. There are 18 homes for the aged, 2 junior colleges (Durat College at Sioux Center, Iowa, and Trinity College at Chicago), and a publishing house at Grand Rapids.

Hungarian Reformed Church in America

With 38 churches and 10,000 members, the Hungarian Reformed Church in America was organized in 1904 under the supervision of the Reformed Church of Hungary. The Reformed Church of Hungary transferred most of these American congregations to the Reformed Church in the United States in 1922 under the Tiffin Agreement, made at Tiffin, Ohio. When the Reformed Church in the United States united with the Evangelical Synod of North America in 1934, 3 Hungarian congregations that had refused to accept the Tiffin Agreement, together with 4 other Hungarian congregations, merged to form the Free Magyar Reformed Church in America. The present name was adopted in 1958.

This church is divided into eastern and western classes, which together constitute a diocese. Both classes have a dean and a lay curator; the diocese is headed by an archdean and a chief lay curator. In polity it occupies middle ground between episcopacy and Presbyterianism. The doctrine and polity of the mother church in Hungary are followed; the church recognizes the Second Helvetic Confession and the Heidelberg Catechism as "symbolic books." The diocese meets annually; there is a constitutional meeting every 3 years. Local churches are found in New York, New Jersey, Pennsylvania, Ohio, and Michigan.

Netherlands Reformed Congregations

This is the smallest of all the Reformed groups in the United States; it has 14 churches and 2,223 members. Its short history (from 1907) began with a secession from the State Church in Holland; immigrants coming to the United States from Holland organized in that year, basing their belief on the Belgium Confession, the Heidelberg Catechism, and the Canons of Dort. There are 8 Sunday schools and 4 clergymen; a synod meets every 2 years.

Protestant Reformed Churches of America

Three consistories of the Classis Grand Rapids East and Grand Rapids West of the Christian Reformed Church, with their pastors, were separated from that church as the result of a disagreement over the doctrine of common grace (Arminianism). The debate began in 1925; the dissenters were formally organized as Protestant Reformed Churches of America in 1926. They stand for particular grace, for the elect alone, and hold to the three Reformed

Confessions—the Heidelberg Catechism, the Belgic or Netherlands Confession, and the Canons of Dortrecht—as the basis of their belief in the infallible word of God. In government they are Presbyterian, subscribing to the 87 Articles of the Church Order of Dortrecht. Their General Synod meets annually, in June.

A small theological seminary is maintained at Grand Rapids. An association of Protestant Reformed men in the same city publishes a bimonthly periodical known as *The Standard Bearer*, and another publication, a monthly called *Beacon Lights*, is issued by the denomination's Young Peoples Federation. There are 1,414 communicant members in 19 churches located in Michigan, Illinois, Iowa, Wisconsin, Minnesota, Colorado, California, and Washington.

The ranks of this church were split in 1953 by the deflection of a considerable number of churches and members under the leadership of Rev. H. de Wolf, a former leader of the earlier (Hoeksema) group; they have formed another denomination bearing the same name.

REFORMED EPISCOPAL CHURCH

The Reformed Episcopal Church was organized in New York City in 1873 by 8 clergymen and 20 laymen who formerly had been priests and members of the Protestant Episcopal Church. A long debate over the ritualism and ecclesiasticism of the Protestant Episcopal Church lay behind the separation; the immediate cause of the division lay in the participation of Bishop George David Cummins of Kentucky in a Communion service held in the Fifth Avenue Presbyterian Church in New York City. In the face of criticism and in the conviction that the catholic nature and mission of the Protestant Episcopal Church were being lost, Bishop Cum-

mins withdrew to found the new denomination.

Doctrine and organization are similar to that of the parent church with several important exceptions. The Reformed Episcopal Church rejects the doctrine that the Lord's table is an altar on which the body and blood of Christ are offered anew to the Father, that the presence of Christ in the Supper is a presence in the elements of bread and wine, and that regeneration is inseparably connected with baptism. It also denies that Christian ministers are priests in any other sense than that in which all other believers are a "royal priesthood." Clergymen ordained in other churches are not reordained on entering the ministry of the Reformed Episcopal Church, and members are admitted on letters of dismissal from other Protestant denominations.

Worship is liturgical but not repressively or exclusively so; at the morning services on Sunday the use of the prayer book, revised to remove certain objectionable sacerdotal elements, is required. At other services its use is optional, while at any service extempore prayer may be used by the minister.

Parish and synodical units prevail in the administration of the church; the triennial general council of the Re-

formed Episcopal Church is not like the general convention of the Protestant Episcopal Church, however, as its bishops do not constitute a separate house.

A home missionary work is conducted among the Negroes of the South; and foreign missions are maintained in India, Equatoria, Sudan, and northern Rhodesia, Africa, and Germany. In India and Africa there are 20 primary schools, 2 hospitals, and 1 orphanage. There are 2 seminaries in the United States located at Philadelphia and Summerville, South Carolina. In 1957 the church listed 8,900 members in 68 local churches.

THE ROMAN CATHOLIC CHURCH

Across the first 1,000 years of Christendom the principal church was the Roman Catholic Church; for the first 1,500 years, up to the time of the Protestant Reformation, the Western world was almost solidly Roman Catholic. The eleventh-century separation left the faith divided between Roman Catholic and Eastern Orthodox sectors; and the Reformation left continental Europe and the British Isles divided between Roman Catholic, Lutheran, and Reformed Churches, with the prospect of still further division as denominationalism increased.

The Roman Catholic Church dates its beginning from the moment of Christ's selection of the apostle Peter as guardian of the keys of heaven and earth and as chief of the apostles, and it claims this fisherman as its first pope. It gained real authority and power when it arose as the only body strong enough to rule after the fall of the city of Rome in A.D. 410. A house of terror ravaged first by Goths, Vandals, and Franks and then by Saxons, Danes, Alemanni, Lombards, and Burgundians, Europe found its only steadying hand in the Roman Catholic Church. Without the church anarchy

would have been king from Britain to the Bosphorus. The first mention of the term Catholic (meaning "universal") Church was made by Ignatius about A.D. 110-15, but the first real demonstrations of its Roman authority came as it won the barbarians to its banners while it kept the flame of faith burning in its churches and the candle of wisdom alive in its monastic schools. The "City of God" of which Augustine wrote so brilliantly was in fact the Church of Rome. Augustine deeply influenced its theological and philosophical structure, and he gave the papacy its finest justification and defense. He left it strong enough to give crowns or deny them to Europe's kings.

The church beat back the threats of its enemies at home and from afar; it converted the barbarian, won against the Saracen, and employed the Inquisition against the heretic boring from within. It brought the hopeful interval known as the Peace of God; it also supported chivalry and feudalism, fought the Crusades, created a noble art and literature, and sent friars in gray called Franciscans as the missionaries of peace to the world and friars in black called

Dominicans to instruct in the dogma of the church. It built schools and cathedrals, dominated Europe, and reached for the world with Loyola and his Jesuits. Africa, India, China, and Japan were visited by Roman Catholic missionaries.

Inevitably there came the temptations of power and prosperity within the church and opposition to its growing power and prosperity from without. Then came the Reformation. Roman Catholic scholars readily admit that there were corrupt individuals within the church, that many of its members had sinned and that some of its hierarchy had done wrong, and that reform was necessary. Indeed, reform was under way before the Reformation broke; Martin Luther himself was a Catholic reformer within the church before he became a Protestant. Erasmus and Savonarola wrote and preached against the corruption and worldliness of certain Roman Catholic leaders and laymen, but they stayed within the church. That all these reformers had a case against the members of the Roman Church is not denied by the Roman Catholics; they do, however, maintain that while priests and bishops and even popes may err, the one true church cannot err, and that Luther was wrong in rebelling against the church. But rebel he did, and the Roman Church suffered its most fateful division.

There were, too, other reasons for the revolt. There was the growth of nationalism and secularism, the ambitions of political princes and rulers with great personal ambitions who wanted no interference from the church. And there was the Renaissance, with its revival of Greek and Roman pagan influences and emphases. All these forces worked together to produce the Reformation; even the Counter Reformation already at work within the structure of the Roman Church, which came to a head in the Council of Trent, could not stop it, for the Protestant insistence upon Christ as the head of the Christian church, the Bible as its authority, the Holy Spirit as its inspiration, the fellowship of its membership as its strength, personal experience in Christ as the way to salvation, and the right of individual interpretation of the Scriptures denied too much of the authority and dogma of the Roman Catholic church for any compromise to be effective.

But long before Luther, Roman Catholics had reached America. The first Roman Catholic diocese on this side of the Atlantic was established in Greenland in 1125; there were bishops in residence there until 1377. A bishop of Catholic Spain came with Columbus in 1492; missionaries came with Coronado and with the other early Spanish explorers. Most of them perished; one of them started the first permanent parish in America at St. Augustine, Florida, in 1565.

French Catholic explorers, *voyageurs*, and colonizers—Cartier, Joliet, Marquette, and others—were generally Roman Catholics supported by missionary groups. Among them were the Recollets, Jesuits, Sulpicians, Capuchins, and the secular clergy. New France became a vicariate apostolic in 1658 with Bishop Laval at its head. The See of Quebec (1674) had spiritual jurisdiction over all the vast province of France in North America, reaching down the valley of the Mississippi to Louisiana.

In 1634 the Roman Catholics founded Maryland; later they were restricted by law in Maryland and in other colonies, and the restrictions were not removed until after the Revolution. In the face of these restrictions and in view of the fact that most of the colonial immigrants were Protestants and not Catholics, the Roman Catholic Church grew slowly. In 1696 there were only 7 Catholic families in New York, and 80 years later they were still traveling to Philadelphia to receive the sacraments. In 1763 there were less than 25,000 Catholics in all the colonies; they were under the jurisdiction of the vicar apostolic of London.

Catholics in large numbers were in the Continental Army during the Revolution. Among the signatures on the Articles of Confederation, the Declaration of Independence, and the Constitution are found those of Thomas Fitzsimmons, Daniel Carroll, and Charles Carroll of Carrollton, all of whom were Catholics. The Revolution brought them a complete and genuine freedom, religious as well as political; religious equality became the law with the adoption of the Constitution in 1787.

There was no immediate hierarchal superior in the United States when the war ended, and the vicar apostolic in London refused to exercise jurisdiction over the "rebels." After long investigation and delay and an appeal to Rome the Rev. John Carroll was named superior, or prefect apostolic, of the church in the 13 original states; and the Roman Catholic Church in this country became completely independent of the Roman Catholic Church in England. At that time there were 15,800 Catholics in Maryland, 700 in Pennsylvania, 200 in Virginia, and 1,500 in New York, with many others along the Mississippi, unorganized and with no priests. At the turn of the century there were 80 churches and about 150,000 Roman Catholics; by 1890 there were 6,231,417 —an amazing growth due primarily to the flood tide of immigration from the Roman Catholic countries of Europe.

Baltimore became the first American diocese in 1789 and an archdiocese in 1808. Other dioceses and archdioceses were formed as the church expanded, covering the country from coast to coast. Three plenary or national councils were held at Baltimore in 1852, 1866, and 1884. Archbishop John McCloskey became the first American cardinal in 1875, and Archbishop James Gibbons of Baltimore was elevated to the same rank in 1877. The Catholic University of America was founded at Washington, D.C., by the third plenary council in 1884. The first apostolic delegation met there in 1893.

The Civil War and two world wars failed to disturb the work of the church or to interrupt its growth. Indeed the First World War produced one of the ablest hierarchal Roman Catholic agencies in the country, the National War Council, now known as the National Catholic Welfare Conference. The national and international strength of Catholicism was dramatized in the twenty-eighth International Eucharistic Congress held at Chicago in 1926 with more than 1,000,000 Catholics from all parts of the world participating. There were 18,605,003 Catholics in the United States in 1926; in 1960 the Roman Catholic Church was the largest church in the United States, with 40,871,302 members in 23,346 churches.

The faith and doctrine of Catholicism are founded upon "that deposit of faith given to it by Christ and through His apostles, sustained by the Bible and by tradition." Thus they accept 3 creeds (the Apostles', the Nicene, and the Athanasian), the Bible, and tradition (the official teaching of the church) as the sources of their faith. (They also accept the creed of Pope Pius IV, which affirms all the articles of the Nicene Creed, the traditions of the apostles, the sacraments, the sacrifice of the Mass, purgatory, indulgences, the invocation of the saints, and the Holy See.) Specifically, the National Catholic Almanac for 1960 offers the following main points of Catholic faith in a "Summary of Catholic Belief":

God: There is one God, a pure spirit, Creator of heaven and earth, without beginning or end, all holy, all good, omnipresent, knowing and seeing all, omnipotent, infinite in perfection.

The Holy Trinity: There are three Persons in God, equal, and of the same substance: the Father; the Son, begotten of the Father; the Holy Spirit, proceeding eternally from the Father and the Son. All three are

197

eternal and infinitely perfect; all three are the same Lord and the same God.

Creation and the Fall: God created the angels to be with Him forever; some of them fell from grace, were consigned to hell and became devils. God created Adam and Eve, the first parents of the human race, and he placed them in Paradise, whence they were justly banished in consequence of Adam's sin. Because of the fall of Adam, all were born in the state of original sin and would be lost if God had not sent a Saviour.

Jesus Christ, Redeemer: The Saviour is Jesus Christ, the Son of God—equal to the Father and the Holy Spirit in all things—and perfect Man—with a human soul and body. The divine Person of Christ unites His divine and human natures. Christ was conceived in the womb of the Virgin Mary by the power of the Holy Spirit, without any man for His father; Mary, His Mother, remained a pure virgin. During His life Christ founded the Catholic Church. He offered Himself as a sacrifice for the sins of the world by dying on the cross to gain mercy, grace and salvation for mankind. After His death and burial Christ arose on the third day and manifested Himself to His disciples for 40 days before ascending into heaven, where he continually intercedes for us. He sent down His Holy Spirit upon His apostles, to guide them and their successors in truth.

The Church: Christ is the invisible head of the Catholic or universal Church; the Holy Spirit is its guiding Spirit of Truth (Soul of the Church). Christ founded the Church on a rock of infallibility and invincibility. The Church has these marks: one, because its members profess one faith and one communion under one pastor (the pope), the successor of St. Peter, to whom Christ committed His whole flock; holy, because the Holy Spirit abides in the Church, which teaches holiness in doctrine and morals, has the supernatural means to holiness, and in every age produces living examples of holiness; catholic, because it has existed in all ages, has taught all nations the truth, and teaches the whole body of divine revelation; apostolic, because it derives its doctrines, mission and succession from the apostles.

Rule of Faith: The Scriptures, Old and New Testaments, were deposited by the apostles with the Church, which is their guardian and protector, and the interpreter and judge of all controversies concerning them. The Scriptures and Tradition, as authentically interpreted and taught by the Church, comprise the proximate rule of faith.

Sacraments: Christ instituted seven sacraments: baptism, confirmation, Holy Eucharist, penance, extreme unction, holy orders, matrimony.

Mass: Christ instituted the Sacrifice of His Body and Blood as a remembrance and unbloody renewal of His Passion and death, which is perpetuated in the Mass. Christ is immolated upon the altar at Mass, being Himself both priest and victim. Through the Mass, men participate in the sacrifice and merits of Christ, adore God, thank Him, make reparation for sin and petition for blessings.

Communion of Saints: In the Church there is a communion of saints—i.e., a union of grace and good works embracing the faithful on earth (Church Militant), in purgatory (Church Suffering) and in heaven (Church Triumphant). Members of the Church Militant are in communication with each other through prayer and good works. They communicate with the Church Suffering by prayer for the souls in purgatory. The faithful on earth communicate with the blessed in heaven by imitating them, honoring them by prayer and by seeking their intercession with God. The blessed in heaven communicate with the Church Militant and the Church Suffering by praying for the souls on earth and in purgatory.

Necessity of Grace: Without divine grace man cannot make even one step toward heaven; all merits result solely from cooperation with the grace of God. Christ died for all men. God is not the author of sin. His grace and His knowledge does not take away the free will of man. Prayer and good works are necessary for salvation.

Death, Judgment, Heaven, Hell: Christ will judge all men in a particular manner at the time of death; according to their spiritual condition, they will be consigned to heaven, purgatory or hell. At the end of the world, the dead, good and bad, shall rise from their graves to be judged in a general judgment, according to their works: the good shall go to heaven, body and soul, to be happy for all eternity; the wicked shall be condemned, body and soul, to the everlasting torments of hell.

Baptism, necessary for membership in the church, is administered to both infants and adults by pouring; all baptized persons are listed as members of the church. Confirmation by the laying on of hands by a bishop and anointing with the holy chrism in the form of a cross follows baptism. The Eucharist (Lord's Supper) is served to laymen, laywomen, and children usually following a fast; the laity receive it in the form of bread alone, and the body and blood of Christ are considered as actually present in the eucharistic elements. The sacrament of penance is one through which post-baptismal sins are forgiven. Extreme unction is administered to the sick who stand in danger of death. The sacrament of orders, or holy orders, is one of ordination for the bishops and priests of the church. Marriage is a sacrament which "cannot be dissolved by any human power"; this rules out divorce. Members are required to attend Mass on Sundays and obligatory holy days, to fast and abstain on certain appointed days, to confess at least once a year, to receive the Holy Eucharist during the Easter season, to contribute to the support of the pastors, and to observe strictly the marriage regulations of the church.

The government of the Roman Catholic Church is hierarchal and completely authoritarian; no layman may have any voice in the government; parishes cannot call their own priests, but the parish laymen are often consulted on certain phases of parish work. At the head of the government stands the pope, who is also bishop of Rome, the "Vicar of Christ on earth, and the Visible Head of the Church." His authority is supreme in all matters of faith and discipline. Next to him is the College of Cardinals, never more than 70 in number and of 3 orders—cardinal deacons, cardinal priests, and cardinal bishops, indicating not their jurisdictional standing but their position in the cardinalate. Generally cardinal priests are bishops or archbishops, and the cardinal deacons are priests; many of the cardinals live in Rome, acting as advisers to the pope and as heads of members of the various congregations or commissions supervising the administration of the church. When a pope dies, the cardinals elect his successor; they hold authority in the interim.

The Roman Curia is the official body of papal administrative offices through which the pope governs the church; it is composed of congregations, tribunals, and curial offices. The congregations include the Congregation of the Holy Office, Consistorial Congregation, Congregation of the Sacraments, Congregation of the Council, Congregation of the Affairs of Religious, Congregation of Sacred Rites, Congregation of Ceremonies, Congregation of Seminaries and Universities, Congregation for the Propagation of the Faith, Congregation for Extraordinary Ecclesiastical Affairs, and Congregation for the Oriental Church. Curia tribunals include the Sacred Penitentiary, the Sacred Roman Rota, and the Apostolic Segnatura. The offices of the Curia include the Cancellaria, Dataria, Secretariate of State, and others.

In the United States the government of the church has its top representative in the apostolic delegate at Washington; and there are 5 cardinals, 32 archbishops, 190 bishops, and 53,796 priests. The archbishop is in charge of the archdiocese and has precedence in his province. There are 26 archdioceses, 113 dioceses grouped into 26 provinces. Bishops are the ruling authority in the dioceses, but appeals from their decisions may be taken to the apostolic delegate and even to Rome. The diocese also has a vicar-general who acts under certain conditions as representative of the bishop; there is also a diocesan chancellor or secretary, a council of consultors, and a number of boards of examination and superintendence. The parish pastor is responsible to the bishop; he is appointed by the bishop or archbishop and holds authority to celebrate the Mass and administer the sacraments with the help of such other priests as the parish may need.

Bishops are appointed from Rome, usually upon suggestions from the hierarchy in the United States; they in turn send to the Holy See at Rome every 2 years the names of priests fitted to become bishops and often make suggestions as to the best of the priests available. The clergy in the Roman Catholic Church may be members in minor orders, subdeacons, deacons, or priests. Candidates for orders studying in divinity schools are called seminarians; following their vows of chastity they are ordained by the bishop as subdeacons, deacons, or priests. There are 96 diocesan seminaries, 429 religious and scholasticate seminaries, and a total of 39,896 seminarians in the United States.

Religious orders are of 2 kinds: Monastic and religious congregations of priests, and the various brotherhoods and sisterhoods. This would not include the Franciscans or Dominicans, who are neither monastic nor religious congregations. The Official Catholic Directory for 1960 lists a total of 162 separate religious orders of priests, 24 religious orders of brothers, and 687 religious orders of women. Most of the members of orders take perpetual, but solemn, vows. A president or superior heads each order; he is often represented in different countries by subordinates or councils, although some orders form completely independent communities. Ordained clerical members of the orders are known as regular clergy to distinguish them from the parish priests, who are called diocesan clergy; both classes of clergy go through the same forms of ordination and induction. There are also lay members in the orders, who take vows but are not inducted or ordained into the priesthood. Lay brothers, of whom there are 10,473 in the United States, assist the ordained leaders in the work of the order. All orders are divided into provinces or communities, and their members are under the jurisdiction of the head of the province or community. Those in the sisterhoods (there are 168,527 sisters in the United States) and brotherhoods are required to take vows but are not ordained; they are engaged primarily in educational, philanthropic, and charitable work.

Three ecclesiastical councils form an important part of the Catholic system; they are known as general or ecumenical, plenary or national, and provincial councils. A general council is called by the pope or with his consent; it is composed of all the Roman Catholic bishops of the world, and its actions on matters of doctrine and discipline must be approved by the pope. Plenary councils are made up of the bishops resident in the country; their acts, too, must be submitted to the Holy See for confirmation and correction before promulgation; they do not define but repeat the doctrine defined by the general councils, and they apply a universal discipline determined by these councils and the Holy See through explicit statutes in each country and province; they may initiate such discipline as national circumstances demand. These councils function as legislative bodies and are known in every country in the world in which the church is represented. Below them are smaller diocesan and provincial councils which make further promulgation and application of the decrees passed by the other councils and approved by the pope.

Nationally the Roman Catholic Church in the United States is thus governed by its hierarchy, made up of 182 members, and by its priesthood. Church property is controlled by a board of trustees appointed in each diocese by the bishop. The board includes a majority of priestly members and a minority of laymen; property is held under the title of the bishop or archbishop. The total work from the local parish to the highest offices and divisions is financed by pew rents, plate collections, baptismal and wedding offerings, Masses, and so on. The priest controls all moneys, retaining enough for his salary—which is determined by the diocese and is uniform throughout the diocese—and the running expenses of the parish, and putting the balance to the credit of the church.

Masses are held on Sundays from 5 A.M. to noon. High Mass, with the liturgy sung in part by priest and choir and with a sermon, is held between 10 A.M. and noon; all others, called low Masses—in which the Mass is read and a short instruction but no sermon is given—are celebrated at various hours between 5 and 12. Vespers are sung in the afternoon and evening. Mass and liturgy, except in Eastern Rite churches and in a few Uniat churches, are always in Latin; but sermons, instruction, and the reading of the Bible are in the language of the congregation.

With the most centralized government in Christendom the Roman Catholic Church has accomplished a work almost unbelievable in scope. The Holy See at Rome has representatives in 58 countries of the world; 41 are of diplomatic status, and 17 are apostolic delegations, nuncios, internuncios, or other representatives. As of January 1, 1960, there were Roman Catholic churches established in 217 countries, with a world total of 527,643,000 members.

Missionary work in the United States is conducted under the direction of the American Board of Catholic Missions, under which the Commission for Catholic Missions for the Colored People and the Indians is at work. Some 595,155 American Negroes are Roman Catholics; in 1959 there were 493 Negro Catholic churches served by 719 priests, and 340 Negro Catholic schools with an enrollment of 90,756 pupils. There were also 120,110 Catholic Indians (about one third of the Indian population of the United States and Canada is Catholic),

served by 231 priests in 415 churches; there are 57 mission schools for Indians, with 8,367 students enrolled.

The Society for the Propagation of the Faith is the over-all representative foreign missionary body. In 98 foreign countries, more than 6,000 Catholic Americans are engaged in missionary work. There are 57 religious institutes or groups sending priests, brothers, and scholastics abroad, and 82 communities of sisters.

Education has been a primary interest of American Catholics ever since the establishment of a classical school in St. Augustine, Florida, in 1606; the first Catholic college was established at Mewton, Maryland, in 1677. Jesuits in Philadelphia founded "the mother of all parochial schools in the English-speaking colonies" in 1782, and parochial schools since that time have been the basic educational unit of the Roman Catholic Church. As of 1960, there are 9,897 elementary parochial schools with 4,195,781 students, 475 private elementary schools with 90,115 students, 1,567 diocesan and parochial high schools with 520,128 students, 866 private high schools with 324,171 students, 265 colleges and universities with 302,908 students, 20 diocesan teachers' colleges and normal schools, and 33 junior colleges. Elementary education is almost exclusively in the hands of religious orders of women, while secondary schools and colleges have teaching staffs of religious orders of both men and women, and lay teachers as well. There are 160,632 full-time teachers in Catholic schools, of whom 10,890 are teaching priests, 4,778 are teaching brothers, 98,471 are teaching sisters, and 45,506 are lay teachers; they instruct a total of nearly nine million students.

Roman Catholic charity and welfare work is conducted by many different organizations, religious and otherwise. The National Conference of Catholic Charities acts as a general information and co-operating body, but the bulk of the work is conducted by several religious orders of men and women devoted (full time) to the relief of the poor in homes or in institutions. There are also bureaus of charities in many of the dioceses. The Society of St. Vincent de Paul is perhaps the largest and most effective charity organization; across the last 37 years this society has administered a fund of $95,861,663 for the relief of the poor. Numerous other groups—the Little Sisters of the Poor, the Sisters of Charity, the Daughters of Charity of the Society of St. Vincent de Paul, the Sisters of Mercy, and the Third Order of Franciscans—are active among the poor in Catholic hospitals, orphanages, and homes for the aged. There are 808 general hospitals treating 12,819,798 patients annually and 137 special hospitals treating 209,686 each year; 326 homes for the aged, with 31,098 guests; 279 orphanages and infant asylums caring for 25,589 children, plus 20,667 children in foster homes. Nearly 50,000 American children are dependent on the Roman Catholic Church.

The members of the hierarchy in the United States are also members of the National Catholic Welfare Conference, a clearinghouse of information on the activities of Catholics which works to make the teachings of the church more effective. This is not a council or a legislative body, so the resolutions of its meetings do not have the force of law. It merely facilitates discussion of all policies affecting the interests and activities of the church, and unifies, co-ordinates, and organizes the work in social welfare, education, immigrant aid, civic education, and other activities. Every bishop in the United States and its territories and possessions has a voice in the conference; it is governed by an administrative board of 10 bishops and archbishops elected by the hierarchy. Under its direction 8 departments function: executive, education, press, immigration, social action, legal, youth, and lay organizations. In addition there are special episcopal committees on Catholic missions, Christian doctrine, motion pictures, the propagation of the faith (foreign service), obscene literature, the North American College, seminaries, relief, war emergencies, the pope's peace points, and refugees. This board is one of the most important and effective in the American church.

THE SALVATION ARMY

William Booth, an ordained minister in the Methodist New Connexion body in England, regretfully left the pulpit of that church in 1861, to become a free-lance evangelistic preacher. This step led him, in 1865, to the slum areas in London's East End and to a dedication of his life to the poverty-stricken, unchurched masses in that area. His first plan was to make his work supplementary to that of the churches, but this proved impractical because many converts did not want to go where they were sent, often they were not accepted when they did go, and Booth soon found that he needed his converts to help handle the great crowds that came to his meetings. He began his work in Mile End Waste under the name of The Christian Mission; in 1878, the name was changed to The Salvation Army.

Being a Methodist, Booth first organized his movement along lines of Methodist polity, with annual conferences at which reports were made and programs planned. With the changing of the name to The Salvation Army, the whole organization became dominated by the new title. "Articles of War" (declaration of faith) were drawn up, and soon the mission stations became corps, members became soldiers, evangelists became officers, and converts were listed as prisoners. Booth was designated as "General," and gradually he set up his organization on a military pattern which provided a direct line of authority and a practical system of training personnel for effective action. The leader reasoned that it was "just as valid to build an army of crusaders to save souls as it has been to send armies to recover a sepulchre."

The work spread quickly over England, Scotland, and Wales, and in 1880 it was established in the United States by a pioneer group under the direction of Commissioner George Scott Railton. Once committed to a policy of expansion, Booth lost no time in sending pioneering parties in different directions, reaching Australia and France in 1881; Switzerland, Sweden, India, and Canada in 1882; Iceland and South Africa in 1883; and Germany in 1886. Today, The Salvation Army is working in 86 countries and colonies with 25,000 officers, preaching the gospel in some 120 languages in 17,000 evangelical centers, and operating more than 3,000 social welfare institutions, hospitals, schools, and agencies.

Administratively, the Army is under the command of "The General of The Salvation Army," with top leaders in charge of 50 territorial and departmental commands of which 23 encompass the work in "missionary" lands or subsidized areas. The present national commander in the United States is Commissioner Norman S. Marshall. In this country the Army conducts its religious and social welfare program in all 50 states, implementing its purpose of preaching the gospel and effecting the spiritual, moral, and physical reclamation of persons coming under its influence through 8,547 centers of operation and including 6,337 service extension units. These are administered by more

than 5,000 officers, assisted by about 12,000 employees.

The unit of the Army is the corps, of which there may be several in one city. Each corps is commanded by an officer—ranging in rank from lieutenant to brigadier—who is responsible to a divisional headquarters. The 45 divisions in the United States each consist of a number of corps, and the work of each division is under the direct supervision of a divisional commander. The divisions are grouped into four territories—Eastern, Central, Southern, and Western—with headquarters in New York City, Chicago, Atlanta, and San Francisco. Territorial Commanders are in charge of the work in each territory, and the four territorial headquarters are composed of departments to facilitate the supervision and direction of all phases of Army work. National headquarters is the co-ordinating office for the entire country, and the national commander is the chief administrative officer, official spokesman, and president of The Salvation Army Corporation established under the laws of New York, and of local corporations in 14 other states. Property and revenues are in the custody of a board of trustees or directors, and citizens' advisory boards assist in interpreting the work of the Army to the general public.

Within the structure of the Army, converts who desire to become soldiers (members) are required to sign the Articles of War after which, as members, they give volunteer service. The function of officers is similar to that of ministers of other churches, and officers are commissioned to full-time Salvation Army service.

Basic training for each officer, regardless of his field of service—evangelical or social—is a two-year-in-residence course at one of the Army's four schools for officers' training located in New York, Chicago, Atlanta, and San Francisco. The chief source of officer-candidates is The Salvation Army corps.

After a soldier has served actively for at least six months, he may make application for officership and, if accepted, may enter the School for Officers' Training where his curriculum, in addition to formal study, includes practical field experience in corps and social service institutions as well as orientation in all possible areas of Salvation Army service. He is graduated from the school as a probationary lieutenant and, following additional studies, is eligible thereafter to attain the ranks of captain, major, brigadier, lieutenant colonel, colonel, lieutenant commissioner, and commissioner.

The motivating force of The Salvation Army in all of its work is the religious faith of its officers and soldiers; and the fundamental doctrines of the organization are stated in its Foundation Deed of 1878 in 11 cardinal affirmations. These statements document the Army's recognition of the Bible as the only rule of Christian faith and practice; of God, who is the creator and Father of all mankind; the Trinity of Father, Son, and Holy Ghost; Jesus Christ as Son of God and Son of man; sin as the great destroyer of man's soul and society; salvation as God's remedy for man' sins and man's ultimate and eternal hope made available through Christ; sanctification as the individual's present and maturing experience of a life set apart for the holy purposes of the kingdom of God, and an eternal destiny that may triumph over sin and death. While the Army has a dual function of church and social agency, its first purpose is the salvation of men "by the power of the Holy Spirit combined with the influence of human ingenuity and love." To the Salvation Army, its social services are merely a means of putting the socially disinherited—the needy in both the physical and spiritual realm—into a condition to be physically and spiritually uplifted. In meeting the needs of the "whole man," the Army has established a widespread social welfare program.

The work of the Army in the United States today includes 118 treatment centers aiding 56,000 men annually; 37 maternity homes and hospitals, of which two are general hospitals, with a total bed complement of 954 hospital beds, 566 bassinets and 1,149 maternity home beds, providing service for 18,000 hospital patients and 10,160 unmarried mothers of whom 7,257 unmarried mothers were in residence in maternity homes; 54 camps, providing camping experience for 16,521 children; 394 boys' and girls' clubs and community recreation centers, with a membership of 43,518; 30 Salvation Army-USO and Red Shield Clubs for servicemen, registering a total attendance of 2,924,979; 186 mobile canteens serving 437,372 persons in emergencies and 73,528 military personnel; Family Service Bureaus aiding 444,765 families; and hotels and lodges for men and women; nurseries; settlements; Missing Persons Bureau; care for alcoholics; Correctional Service Bureaus which work with prisoners and their families; community centers for all ages; and other allied services. The services are given without respect to race, color, creed, or condition; its work is financed through voluntary subscriptions, participation in Federated Funds, and its own annual maintenance appeals.

THE SCHWENKFELDER CHURCH

Kaspar Schwenkfeld von Ossig (1489-1561), a Silesian nobleman, was baptized and reared in the Roman Catholic Church and experienced a spiritual awakening in 1519. Disappointed in his hope to help reform the Roman Catholic Church from within, he played a leading role in the Reformation, advocating wider reading of the Bible by laymen, urging the need of the power, guidance, and leading of the Holy Spirit, and preaching that the elements of bread and wine in the Holy Communion were symbols that did not represent the body or change into the body and blood of Christ. This interpretation of the Lord's Supper, together with his insistence upon complete separation of church and state, led him into disagreement with Luther and Lutheranism. He founded a number of spiritual brotherhoods, whose members in time came to be known as Schwenkfelders.

The body has disappeared in Europe but persists in the United States in a church of about 2,500 members in 5 local congregations. A large body of them arrived in this country in 1734; their first formal society of Schwenkfelders was organized in 1782. Their 5 churches today are all located within a radius of 50 miles of Philadelphia.

All theology, they hold, should be constructed from the Bible alone; but the Scriptures are considered as dead without the indwelling Word. Christ's divinity was progressive, his human nature becoming more and more divine without "losing its identity"; faith, regeneration, and subsequent spiritual growth work a change in human nature; but justification by faith is not to be permitted to obscure the positive regeneration imparted by Christ.

Their theology is thus Christocentric. In polity they are congregational, each church being incorporated, self-sustaining, and conducting its affairs through its district or local conference. A general conference composed of all the local churches meets twice a year to develop the larger program of education and missions. Church worship is free and nonliturgical.

The general conference sponsored the founding of the Perkiomen School for boys at Pennsburg, Pennsylvania, in 1892; and a majority of the board of trustees of that school are still members of Schwenkfelder churches. Since 1884 members have been engaged in preparing a critical edition of the works of their founder.

SERVANTS OF YAH

The Servants of Yah seem to be dedicated to much the same crusade as the Life Messengers (p. 132), with the exception that the Servants have a definite body of positive teaching in their efforts to counteract the teachings and influence of Jehovah's Witnesses. They are people formerly associated with The Watch Tower Bible and Tract Society but who left that Society "for one reason only, viz., the call of Prophecy."

According to the Servants of Yah, the Bible is "entirely Prophecy," and prophecy being fulfilled *only* in our own times. No part of it refers to a past history of ancient peoples; rightly translated, all its superstitious doctrines disappear to reveal the true character of God (Yah), and the Servants of Yah have it rightly translated. The genuine word of God had never been known before the Yah translation; it had been "covered over by the handiwork of man." In the Old Testament, "the original text consisted of consonants only, but became buried beneath the Jewish vowel points, which made the text read quite differently. By the use of these vowel points the ancient Jews were able to manufacture and weave into the text their many 'fables and genealogies,' while the true message was lost. In the New Testament, the Living Yah has hidden His message in a Hebrew text within the Greek."

Doctrines denied include that of (the

Jehovah's Witness) Armageddon, the flood of Genesis, the teaching of Satan and demons, hell, and literal (water) baptism. American headquarters are located at GPO Box 542, Brooklyn 1, New York, and a European office is maintained in Vienna.

SOCIAL BRETHREN

This is a body organized in Illinois in 1867 by a small group of persons from various denominations, holding quite orthodox doctrines but disagreeing in certain matters of interpretation of Scripture, discipline, and decorum. In 1958 they reported 2 associations, each meeting annually, 1 general assembly meeting biannually, 29 churches located in Illinois, Michigan, and Indiana, and 1,520 members.

Their confession of faith emphasizes the following points:

The infinite power, wisdom and goodness of God, in whom are united three persons of one substance, power and eternity, the Father, Son and Holy Ghost.

The authority and consistency of the Scriptures, comprising the Old and New Testaments, as containing all things necessary to salvation, "so that whatsoever is not read therein nor may be proved thereby is not required of any man that it should be believed as an article of faith or thought to be requisite or necessary to salvation."

Regeneration and sanctification through Christ.

Eternal salvation of the redeemed and eternal punishment for apostasy.

The ordinances of baptism and the Lord's Supper for true believers only. Baptism may be by sprinkling, pouring or immersion.

Lay members of the church should have the right of suffrage and free speech, but ministers are called to preach the Gospel and not for political speeches.

Polity is a fusion of Baptist and Methodist structures and customs; and the work of the Social Brethren, aside from efforts in mutual aid and assistance, is largely evangelical.

SPIRITUALISTS

Spiritualism is as old as man's longing to communicate with his dead; as an organized religion it began at Hydesville, New York, in 1848 with the Fox sisters. The sisters heard repeated knockings or rappings in their cottage at Hydesville and later in Rochester, and believing them to be signals from the spirit world worked out a code of communication. Their séances became famous, and interest in Spiritualism spread rapidly. However, in 1847 Andrew Jackson Davis had published a book entitled *Nature's Divine Revelations*, which stated the fundamentals and philosophy of Spiritualism; the séances of the Fox sisters only substantiated the writings of Davis.

The first Spiritualist organizations were small, scattered, and without legal sanction. Little groups gathered about the mediums, and in cities the congregations soon became large. The first attempt at national organization did not come until 1863 and lasted for only 9 years. In 1893 the National Spiritualist Association was organized at Chicago; it is today the outstanding Spiritualist body in the United States. Small, independent congregations are still scattered across the country, independent in polity and worship and unwilling to grant any real authority to a centralized government; but many state and sectional Spiritualist groups function under the general direction of the president and board of the N.S.A.

The movement is known popularly for its mediums, séances, clairvoyance, and so on. Ouija boards, table tipping, and spirit rappings and conversations have attracted thousands anxious to communicate with their departed ones. But Spiritualism has genuine religious bases and connotations as well as psychic experiments. The movement has become a church, comforting and strengthening and healing thousands within and without its membership. The N.S.A. offers a Declaration of Principles, which reads as follows:

1. We believe in Infinite Intelligence.
2. We believe that the phenomena of Nature, both physical and spiritual, are the expression of Infinite Intelligence.
3. We affirm that a correct understanding of such expression and living in accordance therewith constitute true religion.
4. We affirm that the existence and personal identity of the individual continue after the change called death.
5. We affirm that communication with the so-called dead is a fact scientifically proven by the phenomena of Spiritualism.
6. We believe that the highest morality is contained in the Golden Rule. . . .
7. We affirm the moral responsibility of the individual, and that he makes his own happiness or unhappiness as he obeys or disobeys Nature's physical and spiritual laws.
8. We affirm that the doorway to reformation is never closed against any human soul, here or hereafter.
9. We affirm that the practice of Prophecy, as authorized by the Holy Bible, is a divine and God-given gift, re-established and proven through mediumship by the phenomena of Spiritualism.

The teaching of God as love is central in Spiritualism; the Lord's Prayer is used in both public worship and private séance. Christ is recognized as a medium; the Annunciation was a message from the spirit world, the Transfiguration was an opportunity for the materialization of the spirits of Moses and Elias, and the Resurrection was evidence that all men live on in the spirit world. Man's soul is often called the "astral body"; at death the material body dissolves, and the soul as the body of the spirit progresses through a series of spheres to a higher and higher existence. There are 2 lower spheres in which those of lower character or sinful record are purified and made ready for the higher existences. Most of the departed are to be found in the third sphere, called the Summer Land; above this are the Philosopher's Sphere, the Advanced Contemplative and Intellectual Sphere, the Love Sphere, and the Christ Sphere. All reach the higher spheres eventually; Spiritualists do not believe in heaven or hell, or that any are ever lost.

Services and séances are held in private homes, rented halls, or churches. Most Spiritualist churches have regular services with prayer, singing, music, selections read from the *Spiritualist Manual*, a sermon or lecture, and spirit messages from the departed. The churches and ministers are supported by freewill offerings; mediums and ministers also gain support from classes and séances in which fees are charged. The attendance at church services is invariably small; one authority estimates the average congregation at 20 to 25. But membership cannot be estimated on the basis of church attendance; for every enrolled member there are at least 15 who are not enrolled but are interested in the movement and in attending its services. Nearly 180,000 Spiritualists were reported as members of their churches in 1954, but this is not comprehensive or inclusive of all using the services of the church.

Administration and government differ slightly in the various groups, but most of them have district or state associations and an annual general convention. All have mediums, and most have ministers in charge of the congregations. Requirements for licensing and ordination also differ, but a determined effort is being made to raise the standards in education and character in the larger groups.

International General Assembly of Spiritualists

Organized at Buffalo, New York, in 1936, this is a co-operative body endeavoring to establish cohesion and unity in the Spiritualist movement. It had an inclusive membership of 164,072 and 209 churches in 1956 and was organized originally as an auxiliary of the General Assembly of Spiritualists in New York to care for churches outside that state. Its present purpose is to charter new Spiritualist churches; headquarters are located at Norfolk, Virginia.

The National Spiritual Alliance of the U.S.A.

This body was founded in 1913 by the Rev. G. Tabor Thompson and has its headquarters at Lake Pleasant, Massachusetts, where it was incorporated. Holding general Spiritualist doctrines, the alliance stresses subnormal and impersonal manifestations and intercommunication with the spirit world. Salvation is held to be through the development of personal character; "one reaps as he sows, yet . . . all things are working together for good and evolution obtains perpetually in all persons."

The local churches of the alliance elect their own officers and choose their own ministers; a 3-day convention is held annually with delegates from all the churches electing their national officers —president, secretary, and treasurer. An official board of directors directs the missionary work of ministers and certified mediums; college training is not required of a minister, but he must have passed a course of study arranged by the alliance. Mediums may baptize, but only ministers may officiate at the ceremonies of ordination and marriage. The work of the alliance is mainly in benevolent, literary, educational, music, and scientific activities. There are 3,085 members and 32 churches.

National Spiritualist Association of Churches

With 8,001 members in 214 churches, this association is influential far beyond its immediate membership, furnishing literature for the whole movement and advocating higher qualifications in mediums and ministers. It has a seminary, the Morris Pratt Institute, for the training of its ministers; a great deal of the work of the seminary is by correspondence. A national director of education directs a training course for members, licentiates, lecturers, mediums, and ordained ministers. The N.S.A. holds an annual legislative convention which elects officers triennially. This is the orthodox body of American Spiritualism.

Progressive Spiritual Church

This church was founded in Chicago in 1907 by the Rev. G. V. Cordingley and has its own confession of faith. It was organized "to lift spiritualism above mere psychic research, to establish it upon a sound, religious basis, and to secure its recognition among other Christian denominations." The confession of faith states the members' belief in the communion of spirits, in man's restoration to everlasting life, in God as an absolute divine Spirit, and in angels who as departed spirits communicate with the living by means of mediums. Jesus Christ is recognized as a medium controlled by the spirit of Elias and the spirit of Moses and the spirit of John the Baptist. "The fingers of the hand of a medium under control can write and deliver divine messages and visions. . . . A divine understanding of dreams can be had. . . . The stars divine the pathway of life of every character." The Bible is acknowledged as the inspired word of God, a guide to the spirit life as well as to the phases and phenomena of Spiritualism—prophecies, spiritual palmistry, spiritual automatic writing, spiritual materialization, spiritual triumpet speaking, spiritual healing by magnetized articles, and so forth. Heaven and hell are believed to be conditions, not locations.

Four sacraments—baptism, marriage, spiritual communion, and funerals—are observed. Ministers, who may be of either sex, must pass a course of instruc-tion in the church seminary. Church officers include a supreme pastor, secretary, treasurer, and board of trustees. Local churches elect their own officers but are subject to the constitution and bylaws of the mother church. The work of the church is largely benevolent, social, literary, scientific, and psychical. There are 11,347 members and 21 churches.

TRIUMPH THE CHURCH AND KINGDOM OF GOD IN CHRIST

Founded in Georgia in 1902 by Elder E. D. Smith, this church teaches the cleansing from sin in all "justified" believers through the shed blood of Christ; entire sanctification as an instantaneous, definite work of second grace obtained through the faith of the consecrated believer; the second coming of Christ; and baptism by fire as a scriptural experience also obtainable by faith. General overseers are the chief officers of the body; they meet quadrennially in what is called the International Religious Congress; otherwise the work of the church is carried on by state, county, and local officers. There are 70,079 members and 690 churches.

UNITARIAN UNIVERSALIST ASSOCIATION

Historically, in the United States, our two outstanding liberal Christian groups have been the Unitarians and the Universalists. A merger of the two bodies was approved in May of 1960, and the Unitarian Universalist Association will be formally launched in May of 1961. We consider them here first as separate bodies, then as a unit, under their new name.

It has always been claimed by the Unitarians that their thought reaches back into the early Christian centuries, before the concept of Trinitarianism was developed. Unitarianism as we know it today, however, began with the Protestant Reformation, among Arminians and Socinians. The movement spread from independent thinkers and Anabaptists in Switzerland, Hungary, Transylvania, Holland, Poland, and Italy to England, where it found champions in such leaders as Newton, Locke, and Milton. No attempt was made to organize the movement in England until late in the eighteenth century.

American Unitarianism, however, developed independently out of New England Congregationalism. Members of the liberal wing of the Congregational Church in eastern Massachusetts, asked only to join a covenant in that church and never to subscribe to a creed, were branded as Unitarian while still within the Congregational membership. The first organized church to turn to Unitarianism as a body, however, was not a Congregational church but the Episcopal King's Chapel in Boston in 1796.

In the second half of the eighteenth century many of the older and larger Congregational churches moving toward Unitarianism were known as Liberal Christian churches or groups; the name Unitarian was finally accepted in 1815.

The basis for the split with Congregationalism came in 1805 with the appointment of Henry Ware as professor of theology at Harvard; it was made certain when William Ellery Channing of Boston preached his famous Baltimore sermon in 1819 and in it outlined the Unitarian view. In that sermon the liberals had their platform. A missionary and publication society known as the American Unitarian Association was formed in 1825, and with it began an activity looking forward to the formation of a separate denomination. A national conference was established in 1865.

Channing defined the true church in these words:

By his Church our Saviour does not mean a party bearing the name of a human leader, distinguished by a form or an opinion, and on the ground of this distinction, denying the name and character of Christians to all but themselves. . . . These are the church—men made better, made holy, virtuous by his religion—men who, hoping in his promises, keep his commands.

The Unitarians proceeded from this to formulate their views. They have no creed; the constitution of the general conference stated that "these churches accept the religion of Jesus, holding in accordance with his teaching that practical religion is summed up in the love to God and love to man." Cardinal points in their doctrinal attitudes are those of the oneness of God (as opposed to Trinitarianism), the strict humanity of Jesus, the perfectibility of human character, the natural character of the Bible, and the ultimate salvation of all souls. They deny the doctrine of total depravity and believe in the divine nature of man; Trinitarianism is rejected as unscriptural, and they reject the deity of Christ but say they believe in his divinity as all men are divine as the sons of God. Salvation is by character; character is not an end but a means, and salvation lies in being saved from sin here, not from punishment hereafter. Hell and eternal punishment are held to be inconsistent with the concept of a loving and all-powerful God; to admit that God would permit eternal punishment would be to admit that he was powerless to save. Heaven is a state, not a place. Unitarians do not accept the doctrine of the infallibility of the Bible; they believe that the Bible is not a book but a library of books, all of which cannot be accepted as of equal value and importance. These ideas have been prominent in Unitarianism, but within this ideological framework the widest possible freedom is encouraged in personal interpretation and belief; even students and teachers in Unitarian theological schools are not required to subscribe to any dogmatic teaching or doctrinal tests. Emphasis upon individual freedom of belief, democratic principles, hospitality to the methods of science in seeking truth, and less concern with traditional doctrinal matters characterize the Unitarian movement.

In accordance with its charter, the American Unitarian Association considered itself to be devoted to certain moral, religious, educational, and charitable purposes which to the non-Unitarian may be as enlightening as an analysis of their religious or doctrinal statements; under these purposes, the Association felt obligated to

(1) Diffuse the knowledge and promote the interests of religion which Jesus taught as love to God and love to man;

(2) Strengthen the churches and fellowships which unite in the Association for more and better work for the kingdom of God;

(3) Organize new churches and fellowships for the extension of Unitarianism in our own countries and in other lands; and

(4) Encourage sympathy and cooperation among religious liberals at home and abroad.

Organization has always been liberally congregational; independent local churches were grouped in local, county, district, state and regional conferences, and were united in an international association for the purposes of fellowship, counsel and promotion of mutual interests.

At the moment of merger, there were 2 denominational seminaries and 2 preparatory schools, 386 churches and approximately 115,000 members. Foreign work was conducted through the International Association for Liberal Christianity and Religious Freedom with headquarters at Utrecht, Holland; the International Association has correspondents in 22 countries.

The Universalists draw their inspiration and find evidence of their thinking and philosophy in many cultural streams; much that is basic with Universalism is discovered throughout the world's several religions. Universalism is not exclusively a Christian denomination, having roots in both pre-Christian and contemporary world faiths, yet within the Christian frame of reference Universalists claim roots in the early Christian Gnostics, Clement of Alexandria, Theodore of Mopsuestia, in the Anabaptists of Reformation times and in seventeenth- and eighteenth-century German mystical universalists. American Universalism has its direct origin in the work of Dr. George DeBenneville, one of the German mystics; in John Murray, the British anti-Calvinist; and in Hosea Ballou, an original universalist thinker.

DeBenneville, the English-educated son of French Huguenot *émigrés*, studied medicine in Germany, came under the influence of the early Brethren and

Friends of God and the German pietists in Pennsylvania in 1741, and preached his gospel of universal salvation as he practiced medicine among the settlers and the Indians.

In 1759 James Relly of England wrote a book entitled *Union*, in which he opposed the Calvinistic doctrine of the election of the few. Relly's conviction of universal salvation deeply influenced John Murray, a Wesleyan evangelist who came to New Jersey in 1770; Murray found groups of universalist-minded people scattered along the Atlantic coast, and became minister to one such group in Gloucester, Massachusetts. The Independent Christian Church of Gloucester became the first organized Universalist Church in America in 1779. One of its charter members was Gloucester Dalton, a Negro. Murray served as a Revolutionary War chaplain in the armies of Washington and Greene.

The Universalists met at Philadelphia in 1790 to draft their first declaration of faith and plan of government. Government was established as strictly congregational; doctrinally, they proclaimed their belief in the Scriptures as containing a revelation of the perfections and the will of God and the rule of faith and practice, faith in God, faith in Christ as a mediator who had redeemed all men by his blood, in the Holy Ghost and in the obligation of the moral law as the rule of life. War was condemned; statements approving the settlement of disputes out of the courts, the abolition of slavery and the education of the Negro, testimony by affirmation rather than by oath, and free public education were approved. This Philadelphia Declaration was adopted by a group of New England Universalists in 1794; at about the same time Hosea Ballou, a schoolteacher and itinerant preacher in Vermont, was ordained to the Universalist ministry.

Ballou broke radically with Murray's thought; in 1805 he published a book, *Treatise on Atonement*, which gave Universalists their first consistent philosophy. Ballou rejected the theories of total depravity, endless punishment in hell, the Trinity and the miracles. Man, said Ballou, was potentially good and capable of perfectibility; God, being a God of infinite love, recognized man's heavenly nature and extraction and loved him as his own offspring. The meaning of the atonement he found, not in bloody sacrifice to appease divine wrath, but in the heroic sacrifice of Jesus, who was not God but a son of the eternal and universal God revealing the love of God and anxious to win all men to that love. It was an avowedly Unitarian-universalist statement of theology which deeply influenced American Universalism. Ballou made another lasting contribution with his insistence that the base of Christian fellowship lay not in creeds but in mutual good faith and good will; from this principle came two consistent aspects of modern Universalism—a broad, liberal latitudinarianism in theology and a universal concern for persons.

It must be kept clear that the Universalists have never had an *official* statement of faith or covenant. From time to time they have set down their basic principles, not as tests of membership nor to be used in any official way, but only to examine their emphases at a given moment in history. Accordingly, in four successive statements, they have grown progressively liberal and inclusive. The Philadelphia statement of 1790, for instance, had obvious trinitarian overtones and spoke in prevailing orthodox terms on the Scriptures, God, the Mediator, and the Holy Ghost; the Winchester Profession of 1805 humanized Jesus and thus directly opposed Trinitarianism, and re-emphasized salvation for the whole family of mankind; it also saw the Bible as one revelation of the character of God. A statement of five Universalist principles in Boston in 1899 liberalized their doctrine still further, and in 1935, in Washington,

D. C., they adopted their latest statement, which read as follows:

The bond of fellowship in this Convention shall be a common purpose to do the will of God as Jesus revealed it and to cooperate in establishing the kingdom for which He lived and died.

To that end we avow our faith in God as External and All-Conquering Love, in the spiritual leadership of Jesus, in the supreme worth of every human personality, in the authority of truth known or to be known, and in the power of men of good will and sacrificial spirit to overcome all evil and progressively establish the kingdom of God. Neither this nor any other statement shall be imposed as a creedal test, provided that the faith thus indicated be professed.

In 1942, the charter of the Universalist Church of America was changed to read: "To promote harmony among adherents of all religious faiths, whether Christian or otherwise." This was the final of a long series of steps calculated to meet the challenges of intellectual and social developments, and to safeguard the Universalist conviction that no doctrinal statements should be employed as creedal tests. Consequently Universalism has become a harmonious body of theists, naturalists, humanists, mystics, Christians, and non-Christians, who find great significance and meaning in a universal approach to life.

A keen sense of ethical responsibility has accompanied this sense of the importance of freedom among Universalists. They were very early active in movements of reform for prisons and working women; they opposed slavery from their earliest days, stood for separation of church and state, maintained a continuing interest in the fields of science, labor management, civil rights, and humane concern. They have placed medical workers in West Berlin and South German refugee centers in modern times; international student work camp teams are serving underprivileged children and refugee youth in Europe. American Universalists are feeding children in Japan; developing community centers in India; providing child care for Negro children in Virginia and a social center at an interracial public-housing development in Chicago; and doing work in various state mental hospitals. They have founded several colleges or universities—Tufts, St. Lawrence, Lombard (now part of the University of Chicago), Goddard, California Institute of Technology, Akron, Dean Junior College, and Westbrook Junior College. Through membership in the International Association for Religious Freedom, they contributed to the support of liberal religious groups in 22 countries abroad, and they maintain a close affiliation with Universalist groups in Holland, Japan, Korea, and the Philippines. At the time of the formation of the Unitarian Universalist Association, they had 68,949 members in 334 churches.

Joined now in their new association, neither Unitarians nor Universalists seem to have lost anything of their original ideology, theology, or purpose. Except for matters of organization and government, the churches involved will continue as they have been across the years; no minister, member, or congregation "shall be required to subscribe to any particular interpretation of religion, or to any particular religious belief or creed." The aims and purposes of the association are stated in their new constitution:

(1) To strengthen one another in a free and disciplined search for truth as the foundation of our religious fellowship;
(2) To cherish and spread the universal truths taught by the great prophets and teachers of humanity in every age and tradition, immemorially summarized in the Judeo-Christian heritage as love to God and love to man;
(3) To affirm, defend and promote the supreme worth of every human personality, the dignity of man, and the use of the democratic method in human relationships;
(4) To implement our vision of one world by striving for a world community founded on ideas of brotherhood, justice and peace;
(5) To serve the needs of member churches and fellowships, to organize new churches and fellowships, and to extend and strengthen liberal religion;
(6) To encourage cooperation with men of good will in every land.

Separate headquarters will be maintained by the 2 denominations until the new organizational structure is complete. Under the constitution recently approved, a general assembly is the over-all policy-making body for carrying out the purposes and objectives of the association. Both ministers and laymen are represented in this assembly. The General Assembly meets annually, in April or May, or in such special sessions as may be called by the Board of Trustees. The elected officers of the association (a moderator, president, 2 vice-presidents, secretary, and treasurer, all elected for 4-year terms), together with 20 other elected members, constitute the Board of Trustees, which appoints the executive and administrative officers of the association and generally carries out the policies and directives of the General Assembly. Members of this board have the usual powers of corporate directors as provided by law. The trustees meet 3 times a year, between regular meetings of the General Assembly. A series of committees is appointed to facilitate and co-ordinate the association's work. Under the General Assembly there is a nominating committee, program and business committees, and a commission on appraisal; under the Board of Trustees, an executive committee, a ministerial fellowship committee, finance committee, and investment committee.

All churches in the association are grouped into geographical regions; regional organization, based upon the principle of local church autonomy, will be developed by the General Assembly in consultation with the churches concerned.

UNITED BRETHREN

United Brethren in the United States are found in 3 churches—the Church of the United Brethren in Christ (Old Constitution), the United Christian Church, and the Evangelical United Brethren Church. Originally one group, they were the spiritual descendants of Philip William Otterbein and Martin Boehm (for their early historical background see Evangelical United Brethren Church, p. 101). At a general conference of the parent body held at York, Pennsylvania, in 1889 a dispute arose over proposed changes in the church constitution concerned mainly with permitting members to join lodges and secret societies. There was a division into 2 churches: the majority group under the name of the Church of the United Brethren in Christ and the minority in the Church of the United Brethren in Christ (Old Constitution). The larger body merged in 1946 with the Evangelical Church.

Church of the United Brethren in Christ (Old Constitution)

This is the dissenting group which opposed constitutional changes in 1889; their dissent is still one of discipline rather than of doctrine. In common with other United Brethren they believe in the Trinity; the deity, humanity, and atonement of Christ. Scriptural living is required of all members, who are forbidden the use of alcoholic drinks, membership in secret societies, and participation in aggressive but not defensive war. Baptism and the Lord's Supper are observed as ordinances of the church.

Quarterly, annual, and general conferences are held; the general conference meets quadrennially and is composed of only ministers, district superintendents (presiding elders), general church officials, and bishops. Both men and women are eligible to the ministry and are ordained only once as elders.

Missionary societies administer a work in evangelism and church aid in the United States and on foreign fields in Sierra Leone, West Africa, Jamaica, China, and the republic of Honduras in Central America. A college and seminary are located at Huntington, Indiana, with secondary schools in Jamaica and Sierra Leone. There are 20,896 members in 329 churches. Still insisting upon loyalty to the old constitution, they work in harmony with evangelical groups in other denominations.

United Christian Church

This church separated from the original body in 1862-70 "on account of conscientious convictions" dealing chiefly with questions of infant baptism, the bearing of arms in war, secret societies, and the wearing of fashionable clothes. The Rev. George W. Hoffman was one of its most influential leaders, and for years members were known as Hoffmanites.

Hesitant to create another denomination, this body had no formal organization until 1877. A confession of faith was approved that year, and the present name adopted a year later at Campbelltown, Pennsylvania. The confession of faith, constitution, and discipline now in use were approved in 1920.

Orthodox and evangelistic, doctrine in this church emphasizes the inspiration of the Scriptures, the Trinity, total depravity, justification, regeneration, entire sanctification, and strict Sabbath observance. Baptism (the mode of which is optional), the Lord's Supper, and foot washing are observed as ordinances. There are district, annual, and general conferences and an itinerant ministry; local preachers vote in the annual conference. Foreign missionaries are stationed in Africa and India; there are 595 members and 14 churches, as of 1955.

UNITED CHURCH OF CHRIST

Three churches of historic importance in America constitute the United Church of Christ: the Congregational Church, the Christian Church, and the Evangelical and Reformed Church. The first two were merged into the Congregational-Christian Churches in 1931, and were joined by the Evangelical and Reformed Church, in the new United Church of Christ, in 1957. Pending the approval of a constitution by the local churches represented in these denominations (hoped to be accomplished by mid-1961), the present denominational policies and administrations will continue. In the following account, the backgrounds, policies, and doctrines of the three bodies will be considered separately; to this is added an outline of polity and procedure for the United Church, as contained in the proposed constitution and bylaws.

Congregational Church

Congregationalism has been implicit in Christianity from the beginning; it began, as Gaius Glenn Atkins suggests, "without a name and with no sense of its destiny." Even before the Reformation broke over Europe, there were little dissenting groups of churchmen in England "seeking a better way" than that of the Established Church (Anglican Church or Church of England). As the Reformation developed in England, dissent took corporate form in the Puritan movement, of which Congregationalism was the most radical wing.

Until a few years ago it was generally believed that Congregationalism had its rise in separatism, a movement which began in the days of Queen Elizabeth and which held that the Church of England was unchristian; that to attempt to reform it from within was hopeless; and that the only course for a true Christian to take was to separate himself from it completely. Recent historians, however, have proved that though Robert Browne and other separatist leaders developed

sundry ideas which were identical with those of early Congregationalism, the 2 groups were wholly distinct, the former being perfectionists who refused co-operation with other branches of the church, the latter being as co-operative as possible without giving up their principles.

John Robinson, one of their most influential early leaders, first enters church history as a separatist; in 1609 he fled persecution in England and settled at Leiden in the Netherlands with the exiled congregation from Scrooby in Nottinghamshire. There he met William Ames, Congregationalism's first great theologian, and Henry Jacob, its first great pamphleteer and organizer. These men were also fugitives from the ecclesiastical courts of Britain. By them Robinson was converted from rigid separatism to the position of Congregationalism.

For 12 years Robinson and his congregation enjoyed peace and freedom under the Dutch; but haunted by the conviction that their sons would not grow up as Englishmen, a large part of the company sailed for America in 1620 aboard the historic "Mayflower." In a hostile new world, with the wilderness before them and the sea at their backs, they helped lay the foundations of the American commonwealth; the democratic ideals of their Plymouth colony, worked out slowly and painfully, were the cornerstone of the structure which gave us our free state, free schools, and free social and political life.

Other Congregational churches were established at Barnstable, Salem, and elsewhere along the Massachusetts coast. Between 1630 and 1640, 20,000 Puritans came to Massachusetts Bay. It was inevitable that the "Bay People" who came direct from England and the "Plymouth People" from the Netherlands should join forces, which they did, establishing thereby an all-powerful theocratic government over both settlements.

Church and commonwealth were this

theocracy's two instruments. It was a stern—and at times an intolerant—regime. Suffrage was limited to church members; Anne Hutchinson and Roger Williams were banished; Baptists were haled into court; and 4 Quakers were hanged on Boston Common. It was a dark but a comparatively short period, ending with the Act of Toleration in 1689.

In 1636 Thomas Hooker led a company of 100 to what is now Hartford, Connecticut; the freeman's constitution drawn up by Hooker and his associates became the model of the American Constitution. Dissenting from the rigidity of current church worship, Congregationalists such as Jonathan Edwards of Northampton played leading roles in the Great Awakening which broke in 1734; that revival was marked not only by the eloquence of George Whitefield but by the vigorous writings and preachings of Edwards, whose books are still regarded as American classics.

Emerging stronger than ever from the Revolution, in the preparation of which it played a great heroic part, Congregationalism was concerned for the next century with 5 significant developments: higher education, missions, the Unitarian separation, the formation of a national council, and the production of a uniform statement of belief. In the field of education this church had already made tremendous contributions: it had founded Harvard in 1636; Yale (1701) was a Congregational project for the education of its clergy; Dartmouth (1769) developed from Eleazer Wheelock's School for Indians. These, with Williams, Amherst, Bowdoin, and Middlebury, were among the first colleges in New England. By 1953 there were 48 colleges and 10 theological seminaries in the United States with Congregational Christian origin or connection.

Interest in missions among American Congregationalists began the day the Pilgrims landed at Plymouth. The Mayhews, David Brainerd, and John Eliot were soon at work among the Indians. Eliot spent 7 years mastering the Indian tongue, put the Bible in their language, and published an Indian catechism in 1653, the first book to be printed in their language. By 1674 there were 4,000 "praying Indians" in New England, with 24 native preachers. When the wagon trains went West after the Revolution, the families of Congregational ministers and missionaries were prominent. Manasseh Cutler, a preacher from Hamilton, Massachusetts, was instrumental in framing the famous Northwest Territory Ordinance of 1787; and other ministers led in the founding of Marietta, Ohio, the first permanent settlement in the Northwest Territory.

The American Board of Commissioners for Foreign Missions was organized in 1810 and was concerned at first with both home and foreign missionary work. On it served not only Congregationalists but representatives of Presbyterian, Dutch Reformed, and Associate Reformed churches. This was the first foreign missionary society in the country, and it was interdenominational. The first 5 men ordained were the 5 young men who had participated in the famous "haystack" meeting at Williams College. After them came missionaries to more than 30 foreign countries and in American territories, not the least of which was Hawaii, where Congregational missionaries within 25 years taught a whole nation of people to read and write, laid the foundations of a constitutional, democratic government, and made of their beautiful islands a sociological laboratory filled with many races living together in harmony and understanding. The Congregational achievement in Hawaii is one of the greatest in the whole history of Protestant missions.

The rise of denominationalism worked against the interdenominational complexion of the American Board, and by mid-century the non-Congregationalists had all withdrawn to go their separate ways. It is still known as the American

Board, but it is no longer interdenominational.

Moving westward, Congregationalists from New England came into contact with Presbyterians moving out from the middle and southern states. To avoid competition and duplication of effort, a plan of union was worked out under which ministers and members from both churches were exchanged and accepted on equal basis. Adopted in 1801, the plan eventually worked out to the advantage of the Presbyterians; it was discontinued in 1852, leaving the Presbyterians stronger in the West and the Congregationalists with a virtual church monopoly in New England. But the plan did much to inspire new Congregational missionary work. In 1826 the American Home Missionary Society was founded; it was active in the South before the Civil War and especially effective there toward the end of that conflict with its "contraband" schools for Negroes, one of which became Hampton Institute.

Meanwhile differences of opinion between theological liberals and conservatives were developing within the church. Strict Calvinists and Trinitarians were opposed by Unitarians, and a famous sermon by William Ellery Channing at Baltimore in 1819 made a division inevitable. The American Unitarian Association was established in 1825. Almost all the older Congregational churches in eastern Massachusetts went Unitarian; only one Congregational church was left in Boston. Debate and legal action over property and funds were not finished until about 1840.

In spite of the Unitarian deflection Congregationalism continued to grow. It assumed such proportions that a national supervisory body became necessary, and a series of national conventions or councils evidenced the growing denominational consciousness of the widely scattered independent local churches. A national council held at Boston in 1865 was so effective that a regular system of councils was established. Following conferences between the associations into which the churches had grouped themselves, the first of the national councils was called at Oberlin, Ohio, in 1871. Known today as the General Council of the Congregational Christian Churches, it meets biennially and acts as an overall advisory body for the entire fellowship.

The council of 1913 at Kansas City adopted a declaration on faith, polity, and wider fellowship which has been accepted by many churches as a statement of faith. While it did not in any way modify the independence of the local churches, it did give a new spiritual unity to the church. It reads as follows:

Faith.—We believe in God the Father, infinite in wisdom, goodness, and love; and in Jesus Christ, His Son, our Lord and Savior, who for us and our salvation lived and died and rose again and liveth evermore; and in the Holy Spirit, who taketh of the things of Christ and revealeth them to us, renewing, comforting, and inspiring the souls of men. We are united in striving to know the will of God, as taught in the Holy Scriptures, and in our purpose to walk in the ways of the Lord, made known or to be made known to us. We hold it to be the mission of the Church of Christ to proclaim the Gospel to all mankind, exalting the worship of the true God, and laboring for the progress of knowledge, the promotion of justice, the reign of peace, and the realization of human brotherhood. Depending, as did our fathers, upon the continued guidance of the Holy Spirit to lead us into all truth, we work and pray for the transformation of the world into the kingdom of God; and we look with faith for the triumph of righteousness and the life everlasting.

Polity.—We believe in the freedom and responsibility of the individual soul and the right of private judgment. We hold to the autonomy of the local church and its independence of all ecclesiastical control. We cherish the fellowship of the churches united in district, State, and national bodies, for counsel and cooperation in matters of common concern.

The Wider Fellowship.—While affirming the liberty of our churches, and the validity of our ministry, we hold to the unity and catholicity of the Church of Christ, and will unite with all its branches in hearty co-operation; and will earnestly seek, so far as in us lies, that the prayer of our Lord for His disciples may be answered, that they all may be one.

The "wider fellowship" is taken seriously; unity and co-operation across denominational lines have been outstanding characteristics of Congregationalism all through its history. Christian Endeavor, the largest young people's organization in all Protestantism, was founded by a Congregationalist, Francis E. Clark, in 1881; by 1885 it had become an interdenominational organization known all over the world as the United Society of Christian Endeavor. In 1924 the Evangelical Protestant Church of North America was received into the National Council of Congregational Churches as the Evangelical Protestant Conference of Congregational Churches; the two mergers with the Christian churches and the Evangelical and Reformed churches, coming comparatively close together, again witness to the widening fellowship and vision of the Congregationalists. Into the most recent merger they brought 47 church-related (not church-*controlled*) colleges, 11 theological seminaries, foreign mission stations in Africa, Mexico, Japan, the Philippines, India, Ceylon, Greece, Lebanon, Syria, Turkey, Korea, and Micronesia, and home missionaries in every state in the Union and Puerto Rico. Congregational-Christian membership in 1959 was 1,419,171, in 5,500 churches; they may not, however, take that many into the merger, due to the hesitancy of some local churches to adopt the proposed constitution.

Christian Church

The Christian churches, like the Congregational, were born in protest against ecclesiasticism and the denial of individual freedom in the church. There were actually 3 revolts which resulted in the establishment of Christian churches in New England and in the South.

The first came in 1792, when James O'Kelley, a Methodist minister in Virginia, withdrew from that church in protest against the development of the superintendency into an episcopacy, especially insofar as it gave the Methodist bishops absolute power in appointing ministers to their charges. O'Kelley and his followers organized under the name Republican Methodists; this was later changed to "Christian," with the new church insisting that the Bible be taken as the only rule and discipline, and that Christian character be made the only requirement of church membership.

Abner Jones, convinced that "sectarian names and human creeds should be abandoned," left the Vermont Baptists to organize at Lyndon, Vermont, in 1801 the First Christian Church in New England. This was done not so much in objection to Baptist organization or doctrine as from a desire to secure a wider freedom in religious thought and fellowship. Like O'Kelley, Jones insisted that piety and character were to be the sole test of Christian fellowship.

In the Great Awakening which swept Tennessee and Kentucky in 1801 there was a great deal of preaching which either ignored the old emphasis on the doctrines of the various denominations involved or was often in direct contradiction to them. Barton W. Stone, accused of anti-Presbyterian preaching, led a number of Presbyterians out of the Synod of Kentucky to organize a Springfield Presbytery. This presbytery was discontinued as its members gradually came to accept the ideology of James O'Kelley and Abner Jones, and adopted the name "Christians." Stone, an ardent revivalist, was deeply influenced by the preaching of Alexander Campbell and led many of his followers and churches into the fold of the Disciples of Christ. But the large majority of his Christian churches remained with the original Christian body.

The groups under O'Kelley, Jones, and Stone engaged in a long series of conferences which resulted in their union on 6 basic Christian principles:

1. Christ, the only head of the Church.
2. The Bible, sufficient rule of faith and practice.
3. Christian character, the measure of membership.
4. A right, individual interpretation of the Scripture, as a way of life.
5. "Christian," the name taken as worthy of the followers of Christ.
6. Unity, Christians working together to save the world.

No council or other body in the Christian Church has ever attempted to draw up any other creed or statement. Their creed is the Bible. Their interpretation of Bible teaching might be called evangelical, but no sincere follower of Christ is barred from their membership because of difference in theological belief. Open Communion is practiced; baptism is considered a duty, but it is not required; immersion is used generally, but any mode may be employed.

The union of the Congregational and Christian churches has been thoroughly democratic, leaving both free to continue their own forms of worship and each with its own polity and doctrine. Adhering strictly to the congregational idea, each local church is at liberty to call itself either Congregational or Christian, and the same choice is found in the self-governing district and state associations into which the churches are organized.

Evangelical and Reformed Church

The Evangelical and Reformed Church is the product of a union established at Cleveland, Ohio, on June 26, 1934, between 2 bodies of Swiss and German background with basic agreements in

doctrine, polity, and culture—the Evangelical Synod of North America and the Reformed Church in the United States.

The Evangelical Synod was the younger of the 2 bodies, originating with 6 ministers who met at Gravois Settlement near St. Louis in 1840 to form the Evangelical Union of the West. They were ministers of Lutheran and Reformed churches in the Evangelical United Church of Prussia. Two had been sent to America by the Rhenish Missionary Society and two by the Missionary Society of Basel; the other two were independent, one coming from Bremen and the other from Strassburg.

The Evangelical Union of the West was a co-operative ministerial association until 1849, when the first permanent organization was established. As the movement spread to the East and Northwest among German-speaking Lutheran and Reformed peoples, headquarters were established at St. Louis and a new name, the German Evangelical Synod of North America, adopted. A series of amalgamations with 4 other bodies of similar belief and polity—the German Evangelical Church Association of Ohio, the German United Evangelical Synod of the East, the Evangelical Synod of the Northwest, and the United Evangelical Synod of the East—resulted in the formation of the Evangelical Synod of North America, giving it a membership of 281,598 at the time of the merger with the Reformed Church in the United States.

The Reformed Church in the United States had its origin in Switzerland and Germany, and particularly in the flood tide of German immigration to Pennsylvania in the eighteenth century. More than half the Germans in Pennsylvania in 1730 were of the Reformed persuasion; their congregations were widely separated along the frontier; and lacking ministers, they often employed schoolteachers to lead their services. Three of their pastors, Johann Philip Boehm,

George Michael Weiss, and Johann Bartholomaeus Rieger, were deeply influenced by Michael Schlatter, who had been sent to America by the Synod (Dutch Reformed) of South and North Holland; with him they organized in 1747 a coetus (synod) in Philadelphia. It was a synod directly responsible to and in part financially supported by the synod in Holland, from which it declared its independence in 1793, taking the name of the German Reformed Church; and in that year it reported 178 congregations and 15,000 communicants. The word "German" was dropped in 1869; from that time on the denomination was called the Reformed Church in the United States.

Reformed Church missionaries went early across the Alleghenies into Ohio and south into North Carolina. An overall synod of the church divided the country into 8 districts or classes in 1819, and an independent Ohio classis was formed in 1824. Franklin College (now Franklin and Marshall) was founded at Lancaster, Pennsylvania, with the support of Benjamin Franklin; a theological seminary was opened at Carlisle and later moved to Lancaster; an academy which later became Marshall College was established in 1836. The Synod of Ohio established a theological school and Heidelberg University at Tiffin, Ohio, in 1850. The mother synod in the East and the Ohio Synod were united in the General Synod in 1836, which functioned until the merger with the Evangelical Synod of North America in 1934.

Difficulties arose in the early years of the last century over the languages used in the Reformed Church; the older Germans preferred the use of German, and the second-generation members demanded English. Inevitably in a church of such mixed membership there were conservatives and liberals in conflict. Some of the churches withdrew and formed a separate synod but returned in 1837 as wiser heads prevailed and compromises were made. New district synods of both German-speaking and English-speaking congregations were created, and 2 Hungarian classes were added in 1924 from the Old Hungarian Reformed Church.

By 1934 the boards of the church were directing a widespread home missions work and foreign missionary work in Japan, China, and Mesopotamia. There were 12 institutions of higher learning, 3 theological seminaries, and 3 orphanages. There were 348,189 members in the Reformed Church at the time of the 1934 merger, largely concentrated in Pennsylvania and Ohio.

Few difficulties were encountered in reconciling the doctrines of the 2 bodies when the union was finally accomplished. Both churches were German Calvinistic; the Reformed Church had been based historically on the Heidelberg Catechism and the Evangelical Synod on the Heidelberg Catechism, the Augsburg Confession, and Luther's Catechism. These 3 standards of faith were woven into one in the new constitution of the Evangelical and Reformed Church in these words:

The Holy Scriptures of the Old and New Testaments are recognized as the Word of God and the ultimate rule of Christian faith and practice.

The doctrinal standards of the Evangelical and Reformed Church are the Heidelberg Catechism, Luther's Catechism, and the Augsburg Confession. They are accepted as an authoritative interpretation of the essential truth taught in the Holy Scriptures.

Wherever these doctrinal standards differ, ministers, members, and congregations, in accordance with the liberty of conscience inherent in the Gospel, are allowed to adhere to the interpretation of one of these confessions. However, in each case the final norm is the Word of God.

Two sacraments—baptism, usually administered to infants, and the Lord's Supper—are accepted; confirmation, generally before the thirteenth or fourteenth years, ordination, consecration, marriage, and burial are considered as rites. Although hymns and forms of worship are provided for general use, a wide freedom of worship is encouraged.

Church polity, when this church joined the Congregational Christians in 1957, was modified Presbyterian; each local church was governed by a consistory or church council elected from its own membership. Local churches formed a synod, of which there were 34, each made up of a pastor and lay delegate from each charge; the synod met twice a year and had jurisdiction over all ministers and congregations, examined, licensed, and ordained all pastors and elected its own officers—a procedure quite different from that of the Congregationalist-Christian churches. It led many to wonder whether a union be-

tween two such different forms of government could possibly work; that wonder, or hesitancy, is a root cause for the dissension of the few churches that have thus far refused to co-operate in the merger.

The Evangelical and Reformed Church was a thriving church, in 1957-1960, when the details of union were being worked out. There were 810,000 members in 1959, in 2,740 churches, 8 colleges, 3 theological schools, 2 academies, foreign missionaries in India, Japan, Hong Kong, Iraq, Africa, and Honduras, and a widespread home missionary work in the United States among the people of the Ozarks, the American Indians, the Volga Germans, Hungarians, and Japanese.

On July 8, 1959, representatives of the Congregational-Christian churches and the Evangelical and Reformed Church adopted, at Oberlin, Ohio, a Statement of Faith for the United Church of Christ, into which they were merging. It reads as follows:

We believe in God, the Eternal Spirit, Father of our Lord Jesus Christ and our Father, and to his deeds we testify:
He calls the worlds into being, creates man in his own image and sets before him the ways of life and death.
He seeks in holy love to save all people from aimlessness and sin.
He judges men and nations by his righteous will declared through prophets and apostles.
In Jesus Christ, the man of Nazareth, our crucified and risen Lord, he has come to us and shared our common lot, conquering sin and death and reconciling the world to himself.
He bestows upon us his Holy Spirit, creating and renewing the Church of Jesus Christ, binding in covenant faithful people of all ages, tongues, and races.
He calls us into his Church to accept the cost and joy of discipleship, to be his servants in the service of men, to proclaim the gospel to all the world and resist the

powers of evil, to share in Christ's baptism and eat at his table, to join him in his passion and victory.
He promises to all who trust him forgiveness of sins and fullness of grace, courage in the struggle for justice and peace, his presence in trial and rejoicing, and eternal life in his kingdom which has no end.
Blessing and honor, glory and power be unto him. Amen.

This is "a testimony rather than a test of faith"; it is not intended to set forth doctrinal positions (the doctrines and theological positions of the three churches now within the United Church of Christ remain as they were before the union was accomplished), nor to stand as a substitute for the historic creeds, confessions, and covenants of the churches involved. It is not binding, in any creedal or theological sense, upon any local church in the denomination; no congregation is required to subscribe to the statement. But it does stand as a tribute to the faith, charity, and understanding of the merging groups.

Equally impressive is the understanding and co-operation evident in the governmental provisions of the constitution.

The United Church of Christ represents a union of Congregationalism and Presbyterianism—"it establishes congregationalism as the rule for the local congregation and presbyterianism as the basis for organization of the connectional life of the churches." (Harold E. Fey.) The constitution is explicit: "The autonomy of the local church is inherent and modifiable only by its own action. Nothing . . . shall destroy or limit the right of each local church to continue to operate *in the way customary to it.*" But beyond the local church, protected as it is, are associations, conferences, and the General Synod. Local churches in a geographical area are grouped into associations. The association is concerned with the welfare of the local churches within its area; assists needy churches; receives new churches into the United Church of Christ; licenses, ordains, and installs ministers; adopts its own constitution, bylaws, and rules of procedure; and is made up of the ordained ministers and elected lay delegates of the area. The association meets annually, and is related to the General Synod through its conference.

Associations are grouped into conferences, again by geographical areas. The voting members of the conference are ordained ministers of the associations in the conference, and lay delegates elected from the local churches. The conference acts on business, requests, counsel, and references from the local churches, associations, General Synod, and other bodies. It meets annually, and its main function is one of co-ordinating the work and witness of the local churches and associations, rendering counsel and advisory service, establishing conference offices, centers, institutions, and other agencies.

The General Synod is the top representative body of the church; it meets biennially and is composed of delegates chosen by the conferences, and of ex officio delegates (the elected officers of the church, members of the Executive Council, the moderator, and assistant moderators). The conference delegates are clergymen, laymen, and laywomen, in equal numbers; there are also associate delegates, with voice but without vote. General Synod has no power to "invade" local churches, associations, or conferences; it nominates and elects the officers of the church (a president, secretary, and treasurer) for 4-year terms, and a moderator who presides over the sessions of the General Synod and holds office for one year only (his duties are quite similar to those of a moderator among the Presbyterians).

The major boards, commissions, councils, offices, and "other instrumentalities" of the church are established by the General Synod; these include the Board for World Ministries (foreign missions), made up of 225 ministers, laymen, and laywomen; the Board for Homeland Ministries (home missions), also with 225 ministers, laymen, and laywomen; the Council for Higher Education composed of the executive heads of the academies, colleges, and theological schools of the church; the Council for Health and Welfare Services, administered by the heads of church institutions in these fields; the Council for Christian Social Action; Council for Church and Ministry; Council of Lay Life and Work; and the Stewardship Council. Public relations, TV, radio, and visual aids are in charge of an office of communication. Pension and relief activities are administered by a nonprofit corporation(s) responsible and reporting annually to the General Synod. Four committees (nominating, credentials, budget, and long-range planning) are also appointed by the General Synod, and it is authorized to appoint such other committees as they are necessary.

An executive council of 21 voting members (ministers, laymen, and laywomen) is elected by the General Synod to act for the synod in the interims between synod meetings. It determines the salaries of the officers of the church, appoints the editor of *United Church Herald* (the United Church periodical combining the old *Advance* and *Messenger* of the two church groups), prepares the agenda for all meetings of General Synod and appoints committees not otherwise provided; it also submits to General Synod "any recommendation it may deem useful" to the work of the church.

As of 1959, there were 1,419,171 members and 5,500 churches in the Congregational Christian churches; there were approximately 810,000 members in 2,740 churches in the Evangelical and Reformed Church. While some local churches in both groups may still decline to enter the merger, there would seem to be an approximate strength of over 2,000,000 members and 8,000 churches in the United Church of Christ.

UNITED HOLY CHURCH OF AMERICA, INC.

A Negro Pentecostal sect originating at Method, North Carolina, in a meeting held by the Rev. Isaac Cheshier in 1886, this body was successively called the Holy Church of North Carolina, the Holy Church of North Carolina and Virginia, and finally (1918) the United Holy Church of America. Its purpose is to establish and maintain holy convocations, assemblies, conventions, conferences, public worship, missionary and school work, orphanages, manual and trade training, . . . also religious resorts, with permanent and temporary dwellings.

Articles of faith contain statements of belief in the Trinity, the record of God's revelation of himself in the Bible, redemption through Christ, justification and instantaneous sanctification following justification, the baptism of the Holy Spirit, divine healing, Sabbath observance, and the ultimate reign of Christ over the earth. The chief officer is the president; a 9-member board of trustees supervises the general work of the church. There are 28,000 members in 432 churches.

UNITED MISSIONARY CHURCH

Up to 1947, this was "The Mennonite Brethren in Christ"; the present church, however, has no Mennonite connection and has grown away from all Mennonite influence. Members do a widespread work in evangelism, stressing holiness. Doctrinally, they believe in the Trinity, the virgin birth, the Atonement, second coming, and redemptive mission of Christ, the Bible as the inspired word of God. There are three diversions from the Dordrecht Confession of the Mennonites, in statements on entire sanctification, justification, and regeneration; divine healing; and the millennium. Baptism is by immersion.

There are three levels of governmental administration: local, district, and general conferences; there are district conferences in Michigan, Ohio, Pennsylvania, Indiana, Iowa, Nebraska, Kansas, South Dakota, Washington, Oregon, Idaho, and California, and two in Canada. A new constitution, drawn up in 1955 in connection with merger negotiations with the Missionary Church Association, gave a more centralized form to the government, with a general superintendent at the head of the church and the affairs of the denomination being administered generally between the superintendent and a general board. The general board, composed of representatives from the district conferences, meets at least semiannually; the general conference meets triennially, the district conferences annually, and local conferences at least annually.

Home missions are highly evangelistic; 111 foreign missionaries are at work in Africa, India, South America, Lebanon, Egypt, Formosa, Japan, Mexico, Columbia, the Dominican Republic, and Sierra Leone; co-operative work is done with the Missionary Church Association, the Christian and Missionary Alliance, and the Oriental Missionary Society. There are 2 Bible Colleges in Canada, and a liberal arts college—Bethel—at Mishawaka, Indiana. A nationwide radio broadcast, "Your Worship Hour," is sponsored by the Gospel Center Church in South Bend, Indiana; and two publications—*Gospel Banner* and *Missionary Banner*—have worldwide circulations. A total of 10,233 members are reported in 188 churches.

UNITY SCHOOL OF CHRISTIANITY

Charles Fillmore, bankrupt and a cripple, and his wife Myrtle, seriously ill with tuberculosis, discovered in 1887 "a mental treatment that is guaranteed to cure every ill that the flesh is heir to." The treatment, or system, is offered today in the Unity School of Christianity as a curative in many areas beyond physical healing. Unity is not a church or denomination, but a nonsectarian religious educational institution devoted to demonstrating that the teaching of Jesus Christ is a practical, seven-day-a-week way of life.

The Fillmores held that "whatever man wants he can have by voicing his desire in the right way into the Universal Mind," and this emphasis upon Mind they found originally in Christian Science. Both studied Christian Science, though neither was ever a part of the movement. They also studied New Thought, Quakerism, Theosophy, Rosicrucianism, Spiritism, and Hinduism; out of their studies came an ideology both old and original, built on ancient truths and concepts but moving in new directions.

Unity teaches that all thought goes back to God, who is "Principle, Law, Being, Mind, Spirit, All Good, omnipotent, omniscient, unchangeable, Creator, Father, Cause and Source of all that is." In the attribute of Mind is found the "meeting ground of man and God." Unity has a Trinity: "The Father is Principle, the Son is that Principle revealed in a creative plan. The Holy Spirit is the executive power of both Father and Son carrying out the creative plan." Jesus Christ is "Spiritual man . . . the direct offspring of Divine Mind, God's idea of perfect man." Man is a son of God filled with the Christ consciousness. It is through Christ, or the Christ consciousness, that man gains eternal life and salvation, both of which terms have meanings different from those in orthodox Christianity. Salvation here may be said to mean the attainment of that true spiritual body which replaces the physical body when man becomes like Christ. This transformation takes place not in any hereafter but "here in this earth" through a series of reincarnations and regenerations. Man suffers no final death but only change into increasingly better states until he becomes as Christ. All men will have this experience.

Unlike Christian Science, Unity recognizes the reality of matter, the world, sin, and sickness. Sin and sickness are real but may be overcome. Health is natural; sickness is unnatural. Anything that injures the body is to be avoided—such emotions, for instance, as strife, anger, hatred or self-interest, or the use of alcohol or tobacco, or indulgence in sex except for the purposes of procreation. But all this is strictly personal, and a matter of individual decision; Unity lays down no laws concerning health but concentrates on spiritual goals, knowing that healthful living habits will follow. Some Unity students are vegetarians, in the interests of health; many are not. Unity is personal; there are no social or health "programs" as such, no hospitals or relief agencies.

Solutions are suggested for every human want and illness. The follower is told to repeat over and over certain affirmations, which develop the all-powerful mind and bring to him from the Divine Mind whatever he needs. Mr. Fillmore once wrote a revised version of the twenty-third psalm calculated to help in the area of economic struggle and success:

The Lord is my banker; my credit is
  good . . . ;
He giveth me the key to His strongbox;
He restoreth my faith in riches;
He guideth me in the paths of prosperity
  for His name's sake.*

He does, however, stress the importance of giving above receiving and condemns the greed of mere money-getting as sinful and destructive.

The Bible is used constantly in Unity, but it is not considered the sole or final authority in faith and practice; man must be in direct, personal communion with God and not be dependent upon

* From *Prosperity*. Used by permission of Unity School of Christianity.

such secondary sources as the Scriptures. The sacred books of other faiths are also used in Unity.

Established on a huge estate near Kansas City (Lee's Summit, Missouri), Unity insists that it is not a church. "The true church is a state of consciousness in man." Ecclesiastical organization is distrusted, but Unity does have a national conference and annual conferences, a statement of faith, pulpits supplied with ministers who must be approved by Unity headquarters, and rituals for baptism, Communion, weddings, and funerals. Local groups are organized into centers, which are linked to headquarters by a field department. Fifty radio stations broadcast 250 Unity programs per week.

The real work of Unity School is done through what is called Silent Unity. A large staff of workers in the Kansas City building is available for consultation day and night, answering telephone calls, telegrams, and letters—an average of 10,000 calls a week. It is a service of counsel, prayer, and affirmation, offering help on every conceivable problem. Each case or call is assigned to one of this staff, who suggests the proper affirmations. The whole staff joins in group prayer and meditation several times a day. All calls and requests are answered. There is no charge for this service, but love offerings are accepted. In one year Unity answered 600,000 such calls for help, most of them coming from members of various Christian churches. No correspondent is ever asked to leave the church to which he belongs.

This is a growing movement; it is said to have at least 5,000,000 followers, although no official statistics are available. In addition to the services of Silent Unity some 4,000,000 books, booklets, tracts, and magazines are published and undoubtedly used by many who never contact headquarters at all and never in any sense become members of the school.

VEDANTA SOCIETY

The members of the Vedanta Society are followers of the Vedas, the scriptures of the Indo-Aryans, the oldest religious writings which exist in the world. This Indian philosophy, explaining the nature and end of all wisdom, harmonizes the findings of modern science and offers a scientific and philosophical basis for religion. It was first expounded in America by Swami Vivekananda at the World's Parliament of Religions held in Chicago in 1893. This society was founded by Swami Vivekananda in 1894.

There are eleven Vedanta centers in America. All belong to and are under the management of the Remakrishna Math and Mission founded by Swami Vivekananda with headquarters in Belur Math, near Calcutta. Each center is an independent, self-supporting unit with its own board of trustees, made up of American citizens. The Swamis are ordained monks and come as guest-teachers. There are approximately 1,200 members in the 11 societies.

VOLUNTEERS OF AMERICA

The Volunteers of America is a religious social welfare organization founded in 1896 by the late Ballington and Maud Booth and incorporated in the same year under the laws of the state of New York; 28,146 members were reported in 1958, but this figure hardly tells the whole story of services rendered to hundreds of thousands of people in the principal cities of the United States.

Religious services are offered in missions, Volunteer churches, Sunday schools, companionship leagues, prisons, and on the streets; the organization has its own rituals for baptism, the Lord's Supper, and marriage. Doctrine is evangelical, with strong emphasis on the saving grace of God, the Trinity, the atonement of Christ, regeneration through the Holy Spirit, the necessity of repentance and conversion, immortality, and future rewards and punishments.

The social welfare programs include departments of family welfare, salvage, health camps, day nurseries, hospices for working girls, maternity homes, homes for mothers and children, adoptive placements, clubs and homes for the aged, rehabilitation workshops, family counseling centers, transient men's homes, and boys' and girls' clubs. There is an excellent prison department, assisting discharged and paroled prisoners, men and women in prison, and their families; 300,000 prisoners are enrolled in the Volunteer Prison League.

Operation of the Volunteers is based on a semimilitary plan modeled on that of the United States Army. All officers bear military titles and wear uniforms. The chief governing body is called the Grand Field Council and is composed of those officers bearing the rank of lieutenant major or above. There is a board of 10 members known as the National Executive Board, which functions when the Grand Field Council is not in session. The incorporation has a directorate of 9, who are responsible financial officers and who act as trustees and custodians of all property. Military regulations do not apply in the selection of these top officers; they are chosen by democratic election. The commander in chief is elected for 5 years and is also president of the corporate body. There are 4 administrative areas known as eastern, central, midwestern, and western areas; national officers and staff are located in New York City.

The Volunteer statistical report for 1958 showed a total of more than 3,000,-000 people receiving material assistance through its various departments exclusive of religious services; 3,871,014 meals and 901,110 lodgings were furnished; 4,226 children were taken under the care of the organization; 14,301 elderly persons participated in the Sunset Club program; 17,007 interviews were held in prisons; 149,838 prisoners attended Volunteer religious services; 1,420 released prisoners were paroled in custody of the Volunteers; 21,921 persons were employed in the industrial department. Over 17,000,-000 articles such as furniture and clothing were distributed free or at nominal cost; positions were found for 17,012 unemployed. The organization is maintained through the voluntary contributions of the public.

HEADQUARTERS OF
DENOMINATIONS

(Addresses of denominational headquarters are given wherever possible; otherwise, names and addresses of chief, and preferably permanent, officials are listed.)

Adventists
   Seventh-day Adventists: Takoma Park, Washington 12, D. C.
   Advent Christian Church: Rev. J. Howard Shaw, Sec., 917 Hardin Street, Aurora, Ill.
   Primitive Advent Christian Church: Rev. C. D. Jones, Pres., 1036 Red Oak St., Charleston, W. Va.
   Church of God (Abrahamic Faith): National Bible Institution, Oregon, Ill.
   Life and Advent Union: Miss Mildred A. Hooper, Pres., 98 Grove Hill, Kensington, Conn.
The African Orthodox Church: Archbishop William E. Robertson, 122 W. 129th St., New York 27, N. Y.
Amana Church Society: Henry G. Moerschel, Pres., Homestead, Iowa.
American Ethical Union: 2 West 64th St., New York 23, N. Y.
American Evangelical Christian Churches: 192 N. Clark St., Chicago 1, Ill.
American Ministerial Association: P. O. Box 1252, York, Pa.
American Rescue Workers: 2827 Frankford Ave., Philadelphia 34, Pa.
Apostolic Overcoming Holy Church of God: Bishop W. T. Phillips, 1070 Congress St., Mobile, Ala.
Assemblies of God, General Council: 434 W. Pacific St., Springfield 1, Mo.
Bahá'í: 536 Sheridan Road, Wilmette, Ill.
Baptists
   American Baptist Convention: 152 Madison Ave., New York 16, N. Y.
   Southern Baptist Convention: 127 9th Ave., N., Nashville 3, Tenn.
   National Baptist Convention, U.S.A., Inc.: 412 4th Ave., N., Nashville, Tenn.
   National Baptist Convention of America: 523 2nd Ave., N., Nashville 3, Tenn.
   American Baptist Association: 214 E. Broad St., Texarkana, Ark.-Tex.
   Baptist Gen'l Conference of America: 5750 North Ashland Ave., Chicago 26, Ill.
   Bethel Baptist Assembly: 701-707 Main St., Evansville 8, Ind.
   Christian Unity Baptist Association: Elder D. O. Miller, Mod., Mountain City, Tenn.
   Conservative Baptist Association of America: Dr. B. Myron Cedarholm, Gen. Dir., 2561 N. Clark St., Chicago 14, Ill.
   Duck River (and Kindred) Associations of Baptists (Baptist Church of Christ): Elder S. P. Arnold, Mod., R. 3, Readyville, Tenn.
   Free Will Baptists: 3801 Richland Ave., Nashville 5, Tenn.
   General Baptists: Rev. Vern Whitten, Clerk, 1629 Stinson, Evansville 12, Ind.
   General Association of Regular Baptist Churches: 608 So. Dearborn St., Suite 848, Transportation Bldg., Chicago 5, Ill.
   General Conference of the Evangelical Baptist Church: 1601 East Rose St., Goldsboro, N. C.
   General Six-Principle Baptists: Erving D. Matteson, Clerk, RFD 1, Coventry, R. I.
   Independent Baptist Church of America: Rev. Elmer Erickson, Pres., 6370 Able St., N.E., Minneapolis 21, Minn.

National Baptist Evangelical Life and Soul Saving Assembly of the U.S.A.: 441 Monroe Ave., Detroit 26, Mich.

National Primitive Baptist Convention of the U.S.A.: 834 West Clinton St., Huntsville, Ala.

North American Baptist Association: 716 Main St., Little Rock, Ark.

North American Baptist General Conference: 7308 Madison St., Forest Park, Ill.

Primitive Baptists: W. H. Cayce, Thornton, Ark.

Regular Baptists: *Regular Baptist Magazine*, H. M. Flinn, Ed., Kensington, Md.

Separate Baptists: Rev. Russell Peterson, Clerk, Box 43, St. Paul, Ind.

Seventh Day Baptists: 510 Watchung Ave., Plainfield, N. J.

Seventh Day Baptists (German): Rev. Crist M. King, Pres., 238 So. Aiken St., Pittsburgh, Pa.

United Baptists: Omer E. Baker, Correspondent, Whispering Pines Retreat, Route 2, Box 260B, Wilmington, N. C.

The United Free Will Baptist Church: Kinston College, 1000 University St., Kinston, N. C.

Bible Protestant Church: Rev. F. Leon Taggart, Pres., 125 Walnut St., Audubon 6, N. J.

Brethren (Dunkers):

Brethren Church (Ashland, Ohio): Ashland, Ohio.

Church of the Brethren: 1451 Dundee Ave., Elgin, Ill.

Brethren Church (Progressive): Clyde K. Landrum, Sec., Box 245, Winona Lake, Ind.

Church of God (New Dunkards): Rev. W. H. Patterson, Mod., 613 Park Ave., Anderson, Ind.

Old German Baptist Brethren (Old Order Dunkers): Elder O. A. Custer, Foreman, North Manchester, Ind.

Plymouth Brethren: A. S. Loizeau, Correspondent, 430 Woodbine Ave., Towson 4, Md.

River Brethren:

Brethren in Christ: Bishop H. H. Brybaker, Gen. Conf. Sec., 2001 Paxton St., Harrisburg, Pa.

Old Order, or Yorker, Brethren: Rev. Jacob L. Horst, Elizabethtown, Pa.

United Zion Church: Rev. Wesley P. Martin, Gen. Conf. Sec., 711 Oak Ave., Akron, Ohio.

Buddhist Churches of America: 1881 Pine St., San Francisco 9, Calif.

Catholic Apostolic Church: 417 W. 57th St., New York 19, N. Y.

Christadelphians: Edwin A. Zilmer, Sec.-Treas., 507 Mitchell Ave., Waterloo, Iowa.

The Christian and Missionary Alliance: 260 W. 44th St., New York 36, N. Y.

Christian Catholic Church: 2700-14 Enoch Ave., Zion, Ill.

Christian Churches (Disciples of Christ) International Convention: 221 Ohmer Ave., P. O. Box 19136, Indianapolis 19, Ind.

Christian Church of North America: Rev. Alfred Palmer, Gen. Sec., 705 Hamilton St., Syracuse 4, N. Y.

Christian Congregation: Rev. O. J. Read, Correspondent, Augusta, Tex.

Christian Nation Church: Rev. R. E. Brockman, Gen. Overseer, 2319 Wythe Ave., Bluefield, W. Va.

Christian Union: Rev. Wayne Caulkins Sec., Grover Hill, R. R. 1, Ohio.

Christ's Sanctified Holy Church: S. Cutting Ave. and East Spencer St., Jennings, La.

Church of Christ (Holiness) U.S.A.: 329 East Monument St., Jackson, Miss.

Church of Christ, Scientist: 107 Falmouth St., Boston 15, Mass.

Church of God (Cleveland, Tenn.): 922-1080 Montgomery Ave., Cleveland, Tenn.

Church of God (Anderson, Ind.): Box 1004, Anderson, Ind.

Church of God (Seventh Day, Denver, Colo.): 1510 Cook St., Denver, Colo.

Church of God (Seventh Day, Salem, W. Va.): Box 328, Salem, W. Va.

Church of God (Tomlinson): 9305 224th St., Queens Village 28, N. Y.

The (Original) Church of God: 1611 S. Lyerly St., Chattanooga 4, Tenn.

Church of God of Prophecy: Bible Place, Cleveland, Tenn.

The Church of God and Saints in Christ: Belleville, Portsmouth, Va.

The Church of God in Christ: 958 Mason St., Memphis, Tenn.

The Church of Illumination: Beverly Hall, Clymer Rd., Quakertown, Pa.

Church of Our Lord Jesus Christ of the Apostolic Faith, Inc.: 112-118 East 125th St., New York 35, N. Y.

Church of the Nazarene: 6401 The Paseo, Kansas City 10, Mo.

Churches of Christ: *Gospel Advocate,* B. C. Goodpasture, Ed., 110 7th Ave., Nashville 1, Tenn.

Churches of Christ in Christian Union: Circleville Bible College, 459 E. Ogio St., Circleville, Ohio.

Churches of God, Holiness: Bishop K. H. Burruss, 170 Ashby St., Atlanta, Ga.

Churches of God in North America (General Eldership): 13th and Walnut Sts., Harrisburg, Pa.

Churches of the Living God:

Church of the Living God (Christian Workers for Fellowship): 4355 Washington Blvd., St. Louis 8, Mo.

House of God, Which is the Church of the Living God, The Pillar and Ground of the Truth, Inc.: Bishop A. H. White, 741 N. 40th St., Philadelphia 4, Pa.

Churches of the New Jerusalem:

General Church of the New Jerusalem: Bryn Athyn, Pa.

General Convention of the New Jerusalem in the USA: Rev. Horace C. Blackmer, Recd. Sec., 134 Bowdoin St., Boston 8, Mass.

Disciples of Christ: See Christian Churches (Disciples of Christ).

Divine Science Church and College: 1400 Williams St., Denver 18, Colo.

Eastern Churches:

Albanian Orthodox Church in America: Archbishop Fan Stylian Noli, 26 Blagden St., Boston 16, Mass.

The American Carpatho-Russian Orthodox Greek Catholic Church: The Very Rev. John Yurcisin, Chancellor, 249 Butler Ave., Johnstown, Pa.

The American Catholic Church (Syro-Antiochean): The Most Rev. Archbishop Metropolitan Ernest L. Petersen, Pres., 1811 N.W. 4th Court, Miami 36, Florida.

The American Holy Orthodox Catholic Apostolic Eastern Church: The Most Rev. Clement J. C. Sherwood, Archbishop Pres., 126 E. 128th St., New York 35, N. Y.

The American Orthodox Church: 52 Kingsbridge Road West, Mount Vernon, N. Y.

Assyrian Orthodox Church: Rev. Elias Sugar, Statistical Officer, 701 87th St., North Bergen, N. J.

Bulgarian Eastern Orthodox Church: The Very Rev. Kiril Antonoff, Administrator, 13th and G. Streets, Madison, Ill.

Diocese of the Armenian Church of North America: 314 East 35th St., New York 16, N. Y.

Greek Archdiocese of North and South America: 10 E. 79th St., N. Y. 21, N. Y.

Holy Apostolic and Catholic Church of the East (Assyrian): The Patriarchate, 1520 Sycamore St., Turlock, Calif.

Holy Orthodox Church in America (Eastern Catholic and Apostolic): See House, 321 W. 101st Street, New York 25, N. Y.

Romanian Orthodox Episcopate of America: 2522 Grey Tower Road, RFD No. 7, Jackson, Mich.

Russian Orthodox Catholic Church, Archdiocese of the Aleutian Islands and North America: 15 East 97th St., New York 29, N. Y.

Russian Orthodox Church Outside Russia: 75 East 93rd St., New York 28, N. Y.

Russian Orthodox Greek Catholic Church of America: 59 East 2nd St., New York 3, N. Y.

Serbian Eastern Orthodox Church: St. Sava Monastery, Libertyville, Ill.

Syrian Antiochian Orthodox Church: 239 85th Street, Brooklyn 9, N. Y.

Ukranian Orthodox Church of America (Ecumenical Patriarchate): St. Mary's Church, 1410 Vyse Ave., New York 59, N. Y.

Ukranian Orthodox Church of U.S.A.: Box 595, South Bound Brook, N. J.

Evangelical and Reformed Church: 1505 Race St., Philadelphia 2, Pa,

Evangelical Congregational Church: Myerstown, Pa.

Evangelical Covenant Church of America: 5101 N. Francisco, Chicago 25, Ill.

The Evangelical Free Church of America: 2950 Nicollet Ave., Minneapolis 8, Minn.
The Evangelical United Brethren Church: Evangelical Press Bldg., Harrisburg, Pa., and
 Knott Bldg., Dayton 2, Ohio.
Evangelistic Associations:
 Apostolic Christian Church (Nazarean): Elder Stephen Babin, 1466 Park Haven Road,
  Cleveland, Ohio.
 Apostolic Christian Churches of America: Elder Joe A. Getz., Corr., 410 E. Jefferson
  St., Morton, Ill.
 Church of Daniel's Band: Rev. Wesley Hoggard, Pres., RFD 2, Midland, Mich.
 Church of God (Apostolic): St. Peter's Church of God (Apostolic), 11th and Hickory
  Sts., Winston-Salem, N. C.
 Church of God as Organized by Christ: Information not available.
 Hepzibah Faith Missionary Assn.: No information available.
 Metropolitan Church Assn.: Box 156, Dundee, Ill.
 Missionary Church Assn.: 3901 South Wayne Ave., Fort Wayne, 6, Ind.
 Pillar of Fire: Zarepath, N. J.
 Fire Baptized Holiness Church: 556 Houston St., Atlanta, Ga.
 Fire Baptized Holiness Church (Wesleyan): Independence, Kansas.
Free Christian Zion Church of Christ: Nashville, Ark.
Friends:
 Religious Society of Friends (General Conference): Clarence E. Pickett, Chairman,
  510 Panmure Rd., Haverford, Pa.
 Five Years Meeting of Friends: 101 Quaker Hill Drive, Richmond, Ind.
 Religious Society of Friends (Conservative): John P. Williams, Clerk, Springville, Iowa.
House of David: Box 477, Benton Harbor, Mich.
Independent Assemblies of God: Information not available.
Independent Churches: No headquarters.
Independent Fundamental Churches of America: 542 South Dearborn St., Chicago 5, Ill.
International Church of the Foursquare Gospel: Angelus Temple, 1100 Glendale Blvd.,
 Los Angeles 26, Calif.
Jehovah's Witnesses: 124 Columbia Heights, Brooklyn 1, N. Y.
Jewish Congregations: Synagogue Council of America, 110 W. 42nd St., New York 36, N. Y.
Kodesh Church of Immanuel: Rev. F. R. Killingsworth, Sup. Elder, 1509 S. St., N. W.,
 Washington, D. C.
Latter-Day Saints, or Mormons:
 Church of Jesus Christ of Latter-Day Saints, or Mormons: 47 E. South Temple St.,
  Salt Lake City 1, Utah.
 Reorganized Church of Jesus Christ of Latter-Day Saints: Independence, Mo.
 Church of Christ, Temple Lot: Temple Lot, Independence, Mo.
 Church of Jesus Christ: P. O. Box 72, Monongahela City, Pa.
 Church of Jesus Christ (Cutlerites): Mrs. Amy L. Whiting, Sec., Clitherall, Minn.
 Church of Jesus Christ of Latter-day Saints (Strangites): Elder Vernon D. Swift, P. O.
  Box 522, Artesia, N. M.
Liberal Catholic Church: 2041 N. Argyle Ave., Los Angeles 28, Calif.
Life Messengers: 3530 Bagley Ave., Seattle 3, Wash.
Lithuanian National Catholic Church: Oak & Summer Sts., Scranton, Pa.
Lutherans:
 The American Lutheran Church: 422 So. 5th St., Minneapolis 15, Minn.
 Augustana Evangelical Lutheran Church: 2445 Park Ave., Minneapolis 4, Minn.
 American Evangelical Lutheran Church: Rev. Alfred Jensen, Pres., 1232 Pennsylvania
  Ave., Des Moines 16, Iowa.
 Evangelical Lutheran Church in America (Eielsen Synod): Rev. J. H. Stensether, Sec.,
  3032 17th Ave., S., Minneapolis 7, Minn.
 Evangelical Lutheran Synod: Rev. M. E. Tweit, Pres., Lawler, Iowa.
 Evangelical Lutheran Synodical Conference of N. A. : Rev. Herbert J. A. Bouman, Sec.,
  20 Seminary Terrace, St. Louis 2, Mo. Finnish Apostolic Lutheran Church of America:
  Rev. Andrew Mickelsen, Pres., Hancock, Mich.

Finnish Evangelical Lutheran Church (Suomi Synod): Dr. Raymond Wargelin, Pres., 403 Cooper Ave., Hancock, Mich.

Lutheran Brethren of America: Fergus Falls, Minn.

Lutheran Church—Missouri Synod: Lutheran Bldg., 210 N. Broadway, St. Louis 2, Mo.

Lutheran Free Church: 2122 Riverside Ave., Minneapolis 4, Minn.

National Evangelical Lutheran Church: Rev. R. W. Heikkinen, Pres., Box 93, Sebeka, Minn.

Negro Missions of the Lutheran Synodical Conference: Dr. H. J. A. Bouman, Sec., 20 Seminary Terrace, St. Louis 5, Mo.

Protestant Conference (Lutheran): Rev. W. I. Beitz, Sec., 2217 Wood Street, La Crosse, Wis.

Slovak Evangelical Lutheran Church: Rev. Paul Rafaj, Pres., 25 Hillcrest Drive, Olyphant, Pa.

United Lutheran Church in America: 231 Madison Ave., New York 16, N. Y.

Wisconsin Evangelical Lutheran Synod: 3624 West North Ave., Milwaukee 8, Wis.

Mayan Temple: No information available.

Mennonites:

Beachy Amish Mennonite Churches: Information, Ellrose D. Zook, Ed. Mennonite Yearbook, Scottdale, Pa.

Church of God in Christ (Mennonite): Goltry, Okla.

Conference of the Evangelical Mennonite Church: 1615 Vance Ave., Fort Wayne, Ind.

Conservative Mennonite Conference: David Showalter, Sec., Gays Creek, Ky.

Evangelical Mennonite Brethren: Sam J. Schmidt, Gen. Sec., Marion, S. D.

The General Conference Mennonite Church: 722 Main, Newton, Kan.

Hutterian Brethren: Rev. Daniel S. Wipf, Cor., Alexandria, S. D.

Krimmer Mennonite Brethren Conference: Arnold Holm, Sec., 659 11th St., Huron, S. D.

Mennonite Brethren Church of North America: Joel Wiebe, Sec., 2149 Toulumne, Fresno, Calif.

Mennonite Church: Dr. John C. Wegner, Mod., Goshen, Ind.

Old Order Amish Mennonite Church: Information, Ellrose D. Zook, Ed. Mennonite Yearbook, Scottdale, Pa.

Old Order (Wisler) Mennonite Church: Information, Ellrose D. Zook, Ed. Mennonite Yearbook, Scottdale, Pa.

Reformed Mennonite Church: Bishop J. Henry Fisher, 30 College Ave., Lancaster, Pa.

Stauffer Mennonite Church: Bishop Jacob S. Stauffer, Route 3, Ephrata, Pa.

Unaffiliated Mennonites: Information, Ellrose D. Zook, Ed. Mennonite Yearbook, Scottdale, Pa.

Methodists:

African Methodist Episcopal Church: 414 8th Ave., S., Nashville, Tenn.

African M. E. Zion Church: Rev. Claude Spurgeon, Gen. Sec., 1326-28 U Street, N. W., Washington 9, D. C

African Union First Colored Methodist Protestant Church, Inc.: 602 Spruce St., Wilmington, Del.

Apostolic Methodist Church: No information available.

Christian Methodist Episcopal Church: Rev. A. R. Davis, Sec., 2412 Emmitt St., Omaha, Neb.

Colored Methodist Protestant Church: No information available.

Congregational Methodist Church: 906 West Jefferson Blvd., Dallas 8, Texas.

Congregational Methodist Church of the USA: Decatur, Miss.

Cumberland Methodist Church: Rev. Carl A. Shadrick, Pres., Whitwell, Tenn.

Evangelical Methodist Church: 301 Palm St., Abilene, Texas.

Free Methodist Church of N. A.: Winona Lake, Ind.

Fundamental Methodist Church, Inc.: Rev. Onas Biellier, Chm., Route 8, Springfield, Mo.

Holiness Methodist Church: Rev. Henry C. Kurtz, Gen. Supt., 2823 Newton Ave., N., Minneapolis 11, Minn.

Independent African M. E. Church: Information unavailable.

Lumber River Annual Conference of the Holiness Methodist Church: Bishop M. L. Lowry, P. O. Box 81, Pembroke, N. C.
The Methodist Church: 475 Riverside Drive, New York 27, N. Y.
New Congregational Methodist Church: Bishop Joseph E. Kelly, 354 E. 9th St., Jacksonville 6, Fla.
People's Methodist Church: No information available.
Primitive Methodist Church, USA: Rev. Richard E. Owens, 313 E. Juniper St., Hazleton, Pa.
People's Methodist Church: No information available.
Primitive Methodist Church, USA: Rev. Richard E. Owens, 313 E. Juniper St., Hazleton, Pa.
Reformed Methodist Church: No information available.
Reformed Methodist Union Episcopal Church: Charleston, S. C.
Reformed New Congregational Methodist Church: No information available.
Reformed Zion Union Apostolic Church: Bishop G. W. Taylor, High Street, South Hill, Va.
Southern Methodist Church: Rev. Lynn Corbett, Pres., 2728 Preston St., Columbia, S. C.
Union American M. E. Church: Bishop David McClellan Harmon, 774 Pine St., Camden 3, N. J.
Wesleyan Methodist Church of America: P. O. Box 548, Marion, Ind.
Moravians:
Moravian Church (Unitas Fratrum): 69 W. Church St., Bethlehem, Pa.
Bohemian and Moravian Brethren: Rev. Francis R. Larew, RFD., No. 2, Cedar Rapids, Iowa.
Evangelical Unity of Czech-Moravian Brethren in North America: John A. Hegar, Corr. Sec., Route 2, West, Texas.
National David Spiritual Temple of Christ Church Union: Archbishop David William Short, Pres., 2812 Prospect Ave., Kansas City 28, Mo.
New Apostolic Church of North America: 3753 N. Troy St., Chicago 18, Ill.
Old Catholic Churches:
American Catholic Church: 218 Mira Mar, Long Beach 3, Calif.
The American Catholic Church, Archdiocese of New York: Most Rev. James Francis Lashley, Primate, 457 W. 144th St., New York 31, N. Y.
North American Catholic Church: Most Rev. Archbishop Hubert A. Rogers, 954 Gates Ave., Brooklyn 21, N. Y.
The Old Catholic Church in America: Archdiocesan Chancery, Box 433, Woodstock, N. Y.
Reformed Catholic Church (Utrecht Confession) Province of North America: Most Rev. W. W. Flynn, P. O. Box 2421, Los Angeles 28, Calif.
Open Bible Standard Churches, Inc.: 851 Nineteenth St., Des Moines 14, Ia.
Pentecostal Bodies:
Calvary Pentecostal Church, Inc., 416 S. 12th Ave., Seattle, Wash.
Emmanuel Holiness Church: Rev. Clark Sorrow, Gen. Overseer, Social Circle, Ga.
Church of God in Christ (Pentecostal): Bluefield, W. Va.
International Pentecostal Assemblies: 892 Berne St., S. E., Atlanta 16, Ga.
Pentecostal Church of Christ: Box 263, London, Ohio.
Pentecostal Assemblies of the World: 3040 North Illinois St., Indianapolis, Ind.
Pentecostal Church of God of America, Inc.: 1601 Maiden Lane, Joplin, Mo.
Pentecostal Fire-Baptized Holiness Church: Toccoa, Ga.
Pentecostal Holiness Church: Franklin Springs, Ga.
United Pentecostal Church, Inc.: 3645 S. Grand Blvd., St. Louis 18, Mo. Pilgrim Holiness Church: 230 East Ohio Street, Indianapolis 4, Ind.
Polish National Catholic Church of America: 529 E. Locust St., Scranton 5, Pa.
Presbyterians:
Associate Presbyterian Church of North America: Rev. Paul J. Hindman, Clerk, Box 349, Minneola, Kansas.

Associate Reformed Presbyterian Church: Rev. A. M. Rogers, Principal Clerk, P. O. Box 47, Chester, N. C.

Bible Presbyterian Church: Stated Clerk, 1347 Andrews Ave., Lakewood 7, Ohio.

Colored Cumberland Presbyterian Church: Rev. J. I. Hill, Stat. Clk., 905 Crim Street, Henderson 4, Texas.

Cumberland Presbyterian Church: Rev. H. Shaw Scates, Stat. Clk., Box 5535, Memphis 4, Tenn.

Orthodox Presbyterian Church: Schaff Bldg., 15th and Race Sts., Philadelphia 2, Pa.

Presbyterian Church in the U. S.: 341-A Ponce de Leon Ave., N. E., Atlanta 8, Ga.

Reformed Presbyterian Church in North America, Gen'l Synod: Rev. Harry H. Meiners, Gen'l Sec., 1818 Missouri Ave., Las Cruces, N. M.

Reformed Presbyterian Church of North America., Old School: Rev. D. Howard Elliott, Clerk, 207 Darlington Rd., Beaver Falls, Pa.

United Presbyterian Church in the USA: 510 Witherspoon Bldg., Walnut at Juniper St., Philadelphia 7, Pa.

Protestant Episcopal Church: 281 Fourth Ave., New York 10, N. Y.

Reformed Bodies:

Christian Reformed Church: R. J. Danhof, Stat. Clk., 2850 Kalamazoo Ave., S. E., Grand Rapids, Mich.

Hungarian Reformed Church in America: Bishop Zoltan Beky, 180 Home Ave., Trenton 10, N. J.

Netherlands Reformed Congregations: Rev. W. C. Lamain, 1935 Plainfield Ave., Grand Rapids, Mich.

Protestant Reformed Churches of America: Rev. G. Vanden Berg, Stat. Clk., 9402 South 53rd Court, Oak Lawn, Ill.

Reformed Church in America: 475 Riverside Drive, New York 27, N, Y.

Reformed Episcopal Church: Rev. Theophilus J. Herter, Sec., 232 Wendover Drive, Havertown, Pa.

The Roman Catholic Church: Apostolic Delegation, 3339 Massachusetts Ave., N. W., Washington, D. C.

The Salvation Army: 120-130 West 14th St., New York 11, N. Y.

The Schwenkfelder Church: Pennsburg, Pa.

Servants of Yah: P. O. Box 175, Levittown, L. I., N. Y.

Social Brethren: Rev. J. Roy Carr, Mod., Golconda, Ill.

Spiritualists:

International General Assembly of Spiritualists: 1915 Omohundro Ave., Norfolk, Va.

National Spiritual Alliance of the USA: RFD 1, Keene, N. H.

National Spiritualist Assn. of Churches: Emil C. Reichel, Sec., 11811 Watertown Plank Rd., Milwaukee 13, Wis.

Progressive Spiritual Church: No information available.

Triumph the Church and Kingdom of God in Christ: Bishop D. H. Harris, 7122 Campania Ave., Pittsburgh 6, Pa.

Unitarian Churches: 25 Beacon St., Boston 8, Mass.

United Brethren:

United Brethren in Christ: United Brethren Bldg., Huntington, Ind.

United Christian Church: Elder Henry C. Heagy, Mod., Lebanon R.D. 4, Lebanon County, Pa.

United Church of Christ: 257 Fourth Ave., New York 10, N. Y.

United Holy Church of America, Inc.: 500 Gulley St. Goldsboro, N. C.

United Missionary Church: 1819 So. Main St., Elkhart, Ind.

Unity School of Christianity: Lee's Summit, Mo.

Universalist Church of America: 16 Beacon St., Boston, Mass.

Vedanta Society: 34 West 71st Street, New York 23, N. Y.

Volunteers of America: 340 West 85th Street, New York 24, N. Y.

CHURCH MEMBERSHIP IN THE
UNITED STATES

The term "membership" seems to have various connotations and different bases of reckoning among the churches of the United States. The Roman Catholic Church and the Protestant Episcopal Church, and some Lutheran bodies, now report all baptized persons as members. The Jews regard as members all Jews in communities having congregations. The Eastern Orthodox churches include all persons in their nationality or cultural groups. Most Protestant bodies, however, count only those persons who have attained full membership, all but a small minority of whom are over thirteen years of age.

These statistics are quoted from the annual survey of churches and church membership taken by the Bureau of Research and Survey of the National Council of the Churches of Christ in the U.S.A., and are mainly for the calendar year 1959, or a fiscal year ending in 1959. Many of them will be different from statistics quoted in the body of this book, due to the fact that in many cases our information and statistics were secured after the National Council survey had been taken. We are indebted to Dr. Benson Y. Landis of the National Council for permission to reproduce these tables from the Council's *Yearbook of American Churches* for 1961.

Name of Religious Body	Year	No. of Churches Reported	Inclusive Church Membership
Adventist Bodies:			
Advent Christian Church	1959	412	30,586('58)
Church of God (Abrahamic Faith)	1959	107	5,400
Life and Advent Union	1959	3	363
Primitive Advent Christian Church	1959	12	586
Seventh-day Adventists	1959	3,002	311,535
African Orthodox Church	1957	24	6,000
Amana Church Society	1959	7	780
American Evangelical Christian Churches	1959	40	Not available
American Rescue Workers	1959	33	2,310
Apostolic Overcoming Holy Church of God	1956	300	75,000
Armenian Church, Diocese of N. A. and Diocese of Calif..	1959	51	125,000
Assemblies of God	1959	8,149	505,703
Associated Gospel Churches	No report		
Bahá'í Faith	No statistics available		
Baptist Bodies:			
American Baptist Association	1959	3,073	647,800
American Baptist Convention	1957	6,362	1,555,360
Baptist General Conference	1959	516	68,930

Name of Religious Body	Year	No. of Churches Reported	Inclusive Church Membership
Christian Unity Baptist Association	1959	12	643
Conservative Baptist Association of America	1959	1,300	275,000
Duck River (and Kindred) Associations of Baptists	1959	28	3,139
Evangelical Baptist Church, Inc., Gen. Conf.	1952	31	2,200
Free Will Baptists	1959	2,500	200,000
General Association of Regular Baptist Churches	1959	887	130,612
General Baptists	1959	738	55,637
General Six-Principle Baptists	1959	2	58
Independent Baptist Church of America	1959	2	30
National Baptist Convention of America	1956	11,398	2,668,799
National Baptist Convention, U.S.A., Inc.	1958	26,000	5,000,000
National Baptist Evangelical Life and Soul Saving Assembly of U.S.A.	1951	264	57,674
National Primitive Baptist Convention of the U.S.A.	1957	1,100	80,983
North America Baptist Association	1959	1,980	330,265
North American Baptist General Conference	1959	292	50,455
Primitive Baptists	1950	1,000	72,000
Regular Baptists	1936	266	17,186
Separate Baptists in Christ	1959	85	7,209
Seventh Day Baptist General Conference	1957	60	5,963
Seventh Day Baptists (German, 1728)	1951	3	150
Southern Baptist Convention	1959	31,906	9,485,276
Two-Seed-In-The-Spirit Predestinarian Baptists	1945	16	201
United Baptists	1955	586	63,641
United Free Will Baptist Church	1958	836('52)	100,000
Bible Protestant Church	1959	37	2,477
Bible Way Churches of Our Lord Jesus Christ World Wide, Inc.	1959	130	25,000
Brethren (German Baptists):			
Brethren Church (Ashland, Ohio)	1958	108	19,474
Brethren Church (Progressive)	1959	172	25,198
Church of the Brethren	1959	1,070	201,219
Church of God (New Dunkards)	1958	8	667
Old German Baptist Brethren	1959	56	4,002
Plymouth Brethren	1944	664('36)	25,000
Brethren (River):			
Brethren in Christ	1959	151	6,698
Old Order, or Yorker, River Brethren	1936	7	291
United Zion Church	1958	23	910
Buddhist Churches of America	1959	52	20,000
Catholic Apostolic Church	1936	7	2,577
Christadelphians	1957	500	15,000
Christian and Missionary Alliance	1959	1,014	59,644
Christian Catholic Church	1959	4	7,000
Christian Churches (Disciples of Christ), International Convention	1959	8,060	1,801,414
Christian Nation Church	1959	35	800
Christian Union	1959	122	7,300

NAME OF RELIGIOUS BODY	YEAR	No. OF CHURCHES REPORTED	INCLUSIVE CHURCH MEMBERSHIP
Christ's Sanctified Holy Church	1957	30	600
Church of Christ (Holiness), U.S.A.	1956	151	9,018
Church of Christ, Scientist	No statistics furnished		
Church of Eternal Life	1940	2	113
Churches of God:			
Church of God (Cleveland, Tenn.)	1959	3,183	162,794
Church of God (Anderson, Ind.)	1959	2,244	135,294
Church of God (Greenville, S. C.)	1959	5	100
Church of God (Seventh Day)	1959	15	1,500
The (Original) Church of God, Inc.	1959	50	7,000
The Church of God	1959	1,901	74,209
The Church of God (Seventh Day), Denver, Colo.	1959	124	3,800
The Church of God by Faith	1959	96	2,300
The Church of God of Prophecy	1959	1,243	32,673
Church of God and Saints of Christ	1959	217	38,127
Church of God in Christ	1959	3,800	382,679
Church of Illumination	1945	7	5,000
Church of Our Lord Jesus Christ of the Apostolic Faith, Inc.	1954	155	45,000
Church of the Gospel	1959	3	40
Church of the Nazarene	1959	4,418	300,771
The Church of Revelation	1959	7	1,360
Churches of Christ	1959	17,850	2,007,650
Churches of Christ in Christian Union	1957	205	11,500
Churches of God, Holiness	1957	42	25,600
Churches of God in N.A. (General Eldership)	1959	385	37,304
Churches of the Living God:			
Church of the Living God (Motto: Christian Workers for Fellowship)	1959	244	27,562
House of God, Which is the Church of the Living God, the Pillar and the Ground of Truth, Inc.	1956	107	2,350
Churches of the New Jerusalem:			
General Convention of the New Jerusalem in the U.S.A.	1959	60	3,941
General Church of the New Jerusalem	1959	7	1,832
Congregational Christian Churches	1959	5,447	1,414,595
Congregational Holiness Church	1959	147	4,664
Divine Science Church and College, Inc.	No report		
Eastern Churches:			
Albanian Orthodox Diocese in America	1959	15	14,000
American Carpatho-Russian Orthodox Greek Catholic Church	1959	61	100,000
American Catholic Church (Syro-Antiochean)	1958	40	4,563
The American Holy Orthodox Catholic Apostolic Eastern Church	1959	27	3,100
The American Orthodox Church	No report		
Apostolic Episcopal Church	1947	46	7,086
Assyrian Orthodox Church	1951	4	3,300
Bulgarian Eastern Orthodox Church	1959	21	80,000

Name of Religious Body	Year	No. of Churches Reported	Inclusive Church Membership
Church of the East and of the Assyrians	1952	10	3,200
Eastern Orthodox Catholic Church in America	Membership dispersed, 1959, to other Orthodox churches		
Greek Archdiocese of North and South America	1959	380	1,200,000
Holy Orthodox Church in America (Eastern Catholic and Apostolic)	1959	3	213
Holy Ukrainian Autocephalic Orthodox Church in Exile	1959	16	5,000
Romanian Orthodox Episcopate of America	1959	52	50,000
The Russian Orthodox Catholic Church, Archdiocese of the Aleutian Islands and North America	No statistics available		
The Russian Orthodox Church Outside Russia	1955	81	55,000('51)
The Russian Orthodox Greek Catholic Church of America	1957	352	755,000
Serbian Eastern Orthodox Church	1959	73	250,000
Syrian Antiochian Orthodox Church	1959	81	115,000
Syrian Orthodox Church of Antioch (Jacobite)	1959	23	50,000
Ukrainian Orthodox Church of America	1959	37	40,250
Ukrainian Orthodox Church of U.S.A.	1959	92	84,500
Ethical Culture Movement	1960	28	6,600
Evangelical and Reformed Church	1959	2,742	809,137
Evangelical Congregational Church	1959	163	29,676
Evangelical Covenant Church of America	1959	514	59,396
Evangelical Free Church of America	1958	368	31,192
Evangelical United Brethren Church	1959	4,317	749,788

Evangelistic Associations:

Apostolic Christian Church (Nazarean)	1959	37	1,960
Apostolic Christian Church of America	1959	65	8,400
The Christian Congregation	1959	167	26,240
Church of Daniel's Band	1951	4	200
Church of God (Apostolic)	1954	22	600
Church of God as Organized by Christ	1938	14	2,192
Metropolitan Church Association	1958	15	443
Missionary Bands of the World, Inc.	Merged, 1958, with Wesleyan Methodist Church		
Missionary Church Association	1958	118	7,577
Pillar of Fire	1948	61	5,100
Federated Churches	1936	508	88,411
Fire-Baptized Holiness Church	1958	53	988
Fire-Baptized Holiness Church (Wesleyan)	1957	53	1,007
Free Christian Zion Church of Christ	1957	728	18,989

Friends:

Central Yearly Meeting of Friends	1959	11	515
Five Years Meeting of Friends	1959	494	68,399
Ohio Yearly Meeting of Friends Church (Independent)..	1959	90	6,540
Oregon Yearly Meeting of Friends Church	1959	62	5,398
Pacific Yearly Meeting of Friends	1959	25	1,055
Philadelphia Yearly Meeting of the Religious Society of Friends	Included in statistics for the Religious Society of Friends (General Conference)		

NAME OF RELIGIOUS BODY	YEAR	No. of Churches Reported	Inclusive Church Membership
Religious Society of Friends (Conservative)	1957	21	1,894
Religious Society of Friends (General Conference)	1958	279	31,473
Religious Society of Friends (Kansas Yearly Meeting)..	1959	89	8,580
Holiness Church of God, Inc.	1959	29	652
House of David	No statistics available		
Independent Churches	1936	384	40,276
Independent Fundamental Churches of America	1959	400	90,000
Independent Negro Churches	1936	50	12,337
International Church of the Foursquare Gospel	1958	697	79,012

Italian:

Christian Church of North America	1958	217	20,200
Jehovah's witnesses	1959	4,020	239,418
Jewish Congregations	1954	4,079	5,500,000
Kodesh Church of Immanuel	1936	9	562

Latter-Day Saints:

Church of Christ, Temple Lot	1956	12	3,000
Church of Jesus Christ (Bickertonites)	1959	38	2,500
Church of Jesus Christ (Cutlerites)	1957	1	22
Church of Jesus Christ of Latter-Day Saints	1959	3,290	1,457,735
Reorganized Church of Jesus Christ of Later Day Saints	1959	927	152,408
Liberal Catholic Church	1956	8	4,000
Lithuanian National Catholic Church	1959	4	3,950

Lutherans:
The Evangelical Lutheran Synodical
Conference of North America:

Lutheran Church—Missouri Synod	1959	5,109	2,304,962
Wisconsin Evangelical Lutheran Synod (formerly Evangelical Lutheran Joint Synod of Wisconsin and Other States)	1957	841	342,993
Evangelical Lutheran Synod	1959	77	14,302
Norwegian Synod of the American Evangelical Lutheran Church	Name changed to Evangelical Lutheran Synod, 1958		
Synod of Evangelical Lutheran Churches (formerly Slovak Evangelical Lutheran Church)	1958	59	19,931
Negro Missions of the Synodical Conference	1959	53	7,999

National Lutheran Council Constituents:

American Evangelical Lutheran Church	1959	79	23,800
American Lutheran Church	1959	1,961	1,002,015
Augustana Evangelical Lutheran Church	1959	1,200	596,147
The Evangelical Lutheran Church	1959	2,482	1,125,867
Finnish Evangelical Lutheran Church (Suomi Synod)	1959	155	36,264
Lutheran Free Church	1959	329	82,595
United Evangelical Lutheran Church	1959	164	66,623
The United Lutheran Church in America	1959	4,260	2,369,263

CHURCH MEMBERSHIP IN THE UNITED STATES

Name of Religious Body	Year	No. of Churches Reported	Inclusive Church Membership
Church of the Lutheran Brethren of America	1958	50	4,771
Evangelical Lutheran Church in America			
(Eielson Synod)	1957	44	4,220
Finnish Apostolic Lutheran Church of America	1957	60	6,567 ('53)
National Evangelical Lutheran Church	1959	54	9,772
Protestant Conference (Lutheran)	1959	8	3,000 ('58)

Mennonite Bodies:

Name of Religious Body	Year	No. of Churches Reported	Inclusive Church Membership
Beachy Amish Mennonite Churches	1959	25	2,217
Church of God in Christ (Mennonite)	1957	33	4,156
Conference of the Evangelical Mennonite Church	1959	22	2,303
Conservative Mennonite Conference		Included with statistics of the Mennonite Church	
Evangelical Mennonite Brethren	1959	26	2,536
General Conference, Mennonite Church	1959	208	35,531
Hutterian Brethren	1959	26 ('57)	2,005
Krimmer Mennonite Brethren Conference	1959	21	1,578
Mennonite Brethren Church of N. A.	1959	72	11,582
Mennonite Church	1959	853	72,138
Old Order Amish Mennonite Church	1959	244	17,321
Old Order (Wisler) Mennonite Church	1959	28	4,391
Reformed Mennonite Church	1958	17	615
Unaffiliated Conservative and Amish Mennonite Churches	1958	13	882

Methodist Bodies:

Name of Religious Body	Year	No. of Churches Reported	Inclusive Church Membership
African Methodist Episcopal Church	1951	5,878	1,166,301
African Methodist Episcopal Zion Church	1959	3,090	780,000
African Union First Colored Methodist			
Protestant Church, Inc.	1953	33	5,000
Christian Methodist Episcopal Church	1951	2,469	392,167
Congregational Methodist Church	1957	223	14,274
Congregational Methodist Church of U.S.A.	1954	100	7,500
Cumberland Methodist Church	1954	4	65
Evangelical Methodist Church	1959	99	5,779
Free Methodist Church of N. A.	1959	1,203	55,568
Fundamental Methodist Church, Inc.	1959	15	696
Holiness Methodist Church	1959	30	1,000
Independent A.M.E. Denomination	1940	12	1,000
Lumber River Annual Conference of the Holiness			
Methodist Church	1959	7	360
The Methodist Church	1959	39,236	9,815,460
New Congregational Methodist Church	1958	11	518
Primitive Methodist Church, U.S.A.	1959	90	14,613
Reformed Methodist Union Episcopal Church	1954	33	11,000
Reformed Zion Union Apostolic Church	1956	52	12,000
Southern Methodist Church	1959	48	4,608
Union American Methodist Episcopal Church	1957	256	27,560
Wesleyan Methodist Church of America	1959	1,051	43,392

Moravian Bodies:

Name of Religious Body	Year	No. of Churches Reported	Inclusive Church Membership
Moravian Church in America (Unitas Fratrum)	1959	156	60,470
Unity of the Brethren (formerly Evangelical Unity of the Czech-Moravian Brethren in N. A.)	1959	32	6,103

NAME OF RELIGIOUS BODY	YEAR	NO. OF CHURCHES REPORTED	INCLUSIVE CHURCH MEMBERSHIP
Muslims	No report		
National David Spiritual Temple of Christ Church Union (Inc.). U.S.A.	1959	69	40,715
New Apostolic Church of N. A., Inc.	1959	155	13,595
Old Catholic Churches:			
American Catholic Church, Archdiocese of N. Y.	1947	20	8,435
North American Old Roman Catholic Church	1959	52	71,521
Old Catholic Archdiocese of America and Europe	No statistics available		
Old Catholic Church in America	1958	22	6,000
The Reformed Catholic Church (Utrecht Confession), Province of North America	1957	20	2,217
Open Bible Standard Churches, Inc.	1959	265	25,000
Pentecostal Assemblies:			
Calvary Pentecostal Church, Inc.	1944	35	20,000
Emmanuel Holiness Church	1955	56	1,200
International Pentecostal Assemblies	1957	43	5,000
Pentecostal Assemblies of the World, Inc.	1958	600	50,000
Pentecostal Church of Christ	1959	42	1,199
Pentecostal Church of God of America, Inc.	1958	900	103,500
Pentecostal Fire-Baptized Holiness Church	1958	42	615
Pentecostal Free-Will Baptist Church, Inc.	No statistics available		
Pentecostal Holiness Church, Inc.	1959	1,214	51,688
United Pentecostal Church, Inc.	1958	1,595	160,000
Pilgrim Holiness Church	1959	1,042	32,558
Polish National Catholic Church of America	1958	157	271,316
Presbyterian Bodies:			
Associate Presbyterian Church of N. A.	1959	6	475
Associate Reformed Presbyterian Church (General Synod)	1958	148	27,561
Bible Presbyterian Church, Inc.	1959	69	5,956
Cumberland Presbyterian Church	1959	984	87,263
Cumberland Presbyterian Church in the U.S. and Africa (formerly Colored Cumberland Presb. Church)	1959	121('44)	30,000('49)
Orthodox Presbyterian Church	1957	80	9,352
Presbyterian Church in the U.S.	1959	3,978	889,196
Reformed Presbyterian Church in N. A. (General Synod)	1957	11	1,206
Reformed Presbyterian Church of N.A. (Old School)	1959	72	6,214
The United Presbyterian Church in the U.S.A.	1959	9,145	3,145,733
Protestant Episcopal Church	1958	7,011	3,126,662
Reformed Bodies:			
Christian Reformed Church	1959	541	236,145
Hungarian Reformed Church in America	1959	40	11,110
Netherlands Reformed Congregations	1959	14	2,300
Protestant Reformed Churches of America	1959	19	2,754
Reformed Church in America	1959	867	219,770
Reformed Episcopal Church	1957	70	8,928

CHURCH MEMBERSHIP IN THE UNITED STATES

NAME OF RELIGIOUS BODY	YEAR	NO. OF CHURCHES REPORTED	INCLUSIVE CHURCH MEMBERSHIP
Roman Catholic Church	1959	23,346	40,871,302
Salvation Army	1959	1,259	253,061
The Schwenkfelder Church	1958	5	2,500
Social Brethren	1959	28	1,548
Spiritualists:			
International General Assembly of Spiritualists	1956	209	164,072
National Spiritual Alliance of the U.S.A.	1959	33	3,145
National Spiritualist Association of Churches	1959	245	8,825
Triumph the Church and Kingdom of God in Christ	1959	700	71,089
Unitarian Churches	1959	384	109,508
United Brethren Bodies:			
United Brethren in Christ	1959	328	20,896
United Christian Church	1959	14	530
United Holy Church of America, Inc.	1959	453	28,300
United Missionary Church	1959	208	10,357
United Seventh Day Brethren	1959	5	70
Universalist Church of America	1958	334	68,949
Vedanta Society	1959	11	1,000
Volunteers of America	1959	202	28,234
Totals: (254 bodies reporting)		314,345	112,226,905

An arrangement of the *latest information* by six major groups reveals the following:

Number of Churches and of Members by Religious Groups

RELIGIOUS GROUP	NO. OF BODIES REPORTING	NO. OF CHURCHES	NO. OF MEMBERS
Buddhist	1	52	20,000
Old Catholic, Polish National Catholic, and Armenian Church of North America, Diocese	6	322	484,489
Eastern Churches	19	1,414	2,807,612
Jewish Congregations*	1	4,079	5,500,000
Roman Catholic	1	23,346	40,871,302
Protestant	226	285,132	62,543,502
Totals	254	314,345	112,226,905

* Includes Orthodox, Conservative, and Reform.

GLOSSARY OF TERMS

THE DEFINITIONS HERE depend largely upon four sources: *The Dictionary of Religion and Ethics,* by Matthews and Smith (Macmillan); *Funk and Wagnalls College Standard Dictionary; Webster's Dictionary* (Merriam); and the new *Comprehensive Desk Dictionary,* by Thorndike and Barnhart (Doubleday).

ABSOLUTION: The remission of guilt and penalty for sin, by a priest, following confession.

ADOPTION: A legal term appropriated by theology, originating in Paul and signifying the act by which the privileges of a child of God are conferred upon the believer in Christ.

ADVENTIST: A believer in the incarnation of God in Christ, at the time of Christ's birth, or in the Second Coming or Advent.

AFFUSION: The pouring or sprinkling of water in baptism.

ANNUNCIATION: The announcement by the angel Gabriel to the Virgin Mary that she was to be the mother of Christ.

ANOINTING: The act of consecrating by the application of oil, used in consecrating sacred objects or persons, as preparation for death, or in completing the efficacy of baptism.

ANTINOMIANISM: The doctrine that the gospel or the Christian faith does away with the old moral law, so that the Christian is not bound by it.

APOSTOLIC: Of or pertaining to an apostle or according to the belief or practices of the apostles.

APOSTOLIC SUCCESSION: The doctrine of an unbroken line of succession in the episcopacy from the apostles to the present time, maintained in Greek, Roman, and Anglican churches.

ARMINIAN: The follower of Arminius (1560-1609), a Dutch Protestant theologian. Arminius denied Calvin's doctrine of unconditional predestination, limited atonement, and irresistible grace, and stood for universal salvation for all.

ATHANASIAN: The belief of Athanasius (293-373), who was a defender of the orthodox view of the divinity of Christ. He opposed and won over Arius at the Council of Nicea; Arius held that Christ was created by but was essentially different from the Father.

ATONEMENT: The reconciliation of the sinner with God through the sufferings of Jesus Christ.

AUTOCEPHALOUS: Ecclesiastically self-controlling, or having jurisdiction as an independent head. "Autocephali" was a term applied to bishops in early Christian times who recognized no ecclesiastical superior.

AUTONOMOUS: Self-governing, or independent.

BAN, THE: A sentence which amounts to excommunication or outlawry by the church upon those guilty of an act or speech forbidden by the church.

BAPTISM: The ceremonial application of water to a person by either sprinkling, immersion, or affusion as a sign of the washing away of sin and of admission into the church as commanded by Christ in Matt. 28:19. Spirit baptism in some sects is a baptism by the Holy Ghost, not with water.

CALVINISTS: Those holding the faith of John Calvin (1509-64). (For a summary of the five points of Calvinism see p. 176.)

Catholicos: An Oriental primate or head of a sect. "Catholikos" was a term assumed by the spiritual head of the Armenian Church and later applied to several prelates under him.

Celibacy: The state of being unmarried.

Chastity: The state of refraining from sexual relations in order to obtain religious or moral purity.

Chrism: An ungent, usually olive oil or balm, used in the Greek and Roman Catholic churches for anointing at baptism, confirmation, ordination, and consecration services, and sometimes for extreme unction. Chrismation is the act of anointing.

Christocentric: With Christ as the center.

Classis: In some Reformed churches a court made up of ministers and ruling elders with a status between a consistory and a synod, corresponding to the presbytery in Presbyterian churches. It may also mean the district it represents.

Communion: The Lord's Supper. "Open" communion is a sacrament open to all Christians; "close" communion is closed to all except those of a particular faith or belief. The word is also used occasionally as a synonym for denomination.

Confession: A statement of the religious beliefs of a religious body, or an admission of sin upon conversion.

Confirmation: The initiatory rite by which persons are inducted into the church, or the approval of authorities by which the election of bishops is ratified by the church.

Congregational: The church polity which makes the authority of the local congregation supreme within its own area.

Consecrate: To set apart as sacred certain persons, animals, places, objects, or times.

Consistory: An ecclesiastical court. The papal (Roman Catholic) consistory is composed of the college of cardinals, over whom the pope presides, and meets to ratify various measures. (2) The Dutch Reformed consistory corresponds to the Presbyterian session. (3) The French Reformed consistory is similar to the presbytery in Presbyterian polity. (4) The Lutheran consistory (abroad) is appointed by the state. (5) The consistory of the Anglicans has diocesan jurisdiction.

Consubstantiation: The theory that, following the words of institution in the Lord's Supper, the substantial body and blood of Christ join sacramentally with the bread and wine (which remains unchanged), the union remaining only until the purpose of the consecration is fulfilled. Applied often to Lutheran doctrine, it is denied by the Lutherans.

Conversion: Religiously, a radical spiritual and moral change, commonly attending a change of belief, and involving profoundly altered spirit and conduct—"a change of heart."

Creed: A statement of belief including the fundamentals considered necessary to salvation; a creed differs from a confession in that it may be held by Christians generally and recited in public worship.

Deacon: A minor church officer; its origin is often identified with the appointment of the seven in Acts 6:1-6.

Diocese: The territory of a church under the jurisdiction of a bishop.

Doctrine: That which is taught as the belief of a church.

Ecclesiastical: Pertaining to the church or the clergy.

Ecumenical or Oecumenical: General, universal, representing the whole Christian Church.

Election: Selection of an individual by God for salvation.

Episcopal: Having to do with bishops, or governed by bishops.

Eucharist: Holy Communion, the Lord's Supper.

Evangelical: A word used to denote primary loyalty to the gospel of Christ in contrast to ecclesiastical or rationalistic types of Christianity, spiritual-mindedness and zeal for Christian living as distinguished from ritualism, and so on.

Extreme unction: *See* Unction.

FASTING: Going without food or certain foods for a specified period.

FOOT WASHING: The practice of washing the feet of fellow church members, sometimes as a ceremonial cleansing from defilement preparatory to worship, sometimes as an ordinance, by Mennonites, Dunkards, the Church of God, and so on.

FREE WILL: Man's power to choose between good and evil without compulsion or necessity.

FUNDAMENTALIST: One who believes in the infallibility of the Bible as inspired by God and that it should be accepted literally, as distinguished from the modernist, who interprets the Bible in accordance with more modern scholarship or scientific knowledge, and who accepts the conservative orthodox position in all matters of doctrine and theology.

FUTURE PUNISHMENT: The punishment inflicted upon sinners *after death.*

GENERAL CONFESSION: A public, congregational confession of sins; among Roman Catholics, a confession in which the individual sums up past sins; among Protestants, a section of the ritual recited in unison by pastor and congregation, modeled on historic Roman Catholic and Anglican forms.

GENERATIONISM: The belief that the soul as well as the body is procreated by the parents of the child, in the act of propagation. Similar to traducianism, but different from creationism and pre-existence.

GENUFLECTION: The act of bending the knee in worship, or in entering the sanctuary or approaching the altar, as an indication of reverence and humility—a custom dating from the early church, still prevalent in many liturgical churches.

GIFT OF TONGUES: Ecstatic speech induced by religious excitement or emotion.

GRACE: The gift of God to man of the divine favor and inner power necessary to salvation.

HIERARCHY: Government by priests or prelates, as in the Roman Catholic Church.

HOLINESS: A state of moral and spiritual purity and sinlessness, or designating persons set apart for religious service.

IMMACULATE CONCEPTION, THE: The dogma that the Virgin Mary was conceived free of original sin.

IMMERSION: Baptism by complete submersion in water.

IMPANATION: The doctrine that the body and blood of Christ are present in one substance in the bread and wine of the Eucharist after consecration, but without transubstantiation; held to be heretical by the Roman Catholic Church.

IMMORTALITY: Life after death, life imperishable.

INFALLIBILITY: The authority of the Scriptures as incapable of error, or a term applied to the pope of Rome.

INSPIRATION, VERBAL: Signifying the supernatural influence upon the writers of the Scriptures by which divine authority was given their work and which places the Bible beyond error.

JUSTIFICATION: Freeing or being freed from the guilt or penalty of sin and restored to divine favor.

JUDGMENT, JUDGMENT DAY: The act of judging by God on the last "judgment day," when rewards and punishments are to be declared.

KISS OF PEACE, OR HOLY KISS: A religious greeting or ceremony, a kiss of welcome.

LITURGY, LITURGICAL: A liturgy is a prescribed form or collection of forms for public worship; in liturgical churches rite and ceremony are more prominent than the emphasis upon preaching or evangelism.

LAYING ON OF HANDS: A rite of consecration and confirmation.

LOVE FEAST: A common devotional meal partaken of by the early Christians, culminating in the Eucharist; sometimes called agape.

MASS, THE: The central worship service of the Roman Catholic Church, consisting of prayers and ceremonies; sometimes the Holy Eucharist as a sacrifice.

MODERNIST: *See* Fundamentalist.

MEDIUM: A person through whom supposed messages from the spirit world are sent, as in Spiritualism.

MONOPHYSITISM: The doctrine that Christ had but one composite divine-human nature.

NESTORIAN: Member of a Christian sect named after Nestorius, a fifth-century Syrian patriarch of Constantinople condemned as a heretic; still found in Turkey and Persia.

NICENE: Pertaining to Nicaea, where the Nicene Creed was adopted at the famous council of 325, settling the controversy concerning the persons of the Trinity; properly called the Niceno-Constantinopolitan Creed.

ORDERS, HOLY: The clerical office, or the spiritual power distinguishing the ecclesiastical hierarchy from the laity.

ORDINANCE: A religious rite or ceremony not considered as a sacrament.

ORTHODOXY: Belief in doctrine considered correct and sound, or holding the commonly accepted faith.

PACIFISM: Opposition to all military ideals, preparedness, war, and so on.

PATRIARCH: A bishop of highest rank, standing above metropolitans and ruling patriarchates.

POLITY: A particular form or system of government.

PENANCE: An ecclesiastical punishment inflicted for sin, or a sacrament of the Christian Church.

PENTECOSTAL: The religious experience of conversion based upon the descent of the Holy Ghost upon the apostles at the Jewish Pentecost.

PERFECTION: The complete realization of moral or spiritual possibilities in personal experience.

PLENARY: Full, complete; a plenary council is attended by all its qualified members.

PREDESTINARIAN: A believer in predestinarianism—that all events are predetermined by God and that each person's eternal destiny is fixed by divine decree.

PREMILLENARIANISM: Belief that the personal visible return of Christ will precede his reign for a thousand years on earth; postmillenarians believe that the return will come at the end of the millennium.

PRESBYTERY: A church court or assembly having the ecclesiastical or spiritual rule and oversight of a district, or the district itself.

REGENERATION: A new birth, re-creation, a radical renewal of life, or conversion.

REMISSION OF SIN: Pardon or forgiveness for sin.

REPENTANCE: Turning from a sinful to a godly life.

REPROBATION: Eternal condemnation, the fate of those not included in God's election.

SABBATARIAN: One who believes that the seventh day should be observed as the Christian Sabbath.

SACERDOTAL: A term denoting a religious system in which everything is valued in relation to the ministrations of the priestly order.

SACRAMENT: A religious rite composed of two elements, a physical sign and a spiritual good.

SALVATION: The rescue of man from evil or guilt by God's power, that he may obtain blessedness.

SANCTIFICATION: The work of the Holy Spirit by which the believer is set free from sin and exalted to holiness of life.

SECOND COMING: The second advent of Jesus. *See* Premillenarianism.

SEE: The local seat from which a bishop, archbishop, or the pope exercises jurisdiction.

SYNOD: An ecclesiastical council either of regular standing or appointed as needed; in Presbyterian churches a body between the presbyteries and the general assembly.

TOTAL DEPRAVITY: The equivalent of original sin, every human faculty having an innate evil taint.

TONSURED: The shaved head of a person admitted to a monastic order or to holy orders.

TONGUES, GIFT OF: An ecstatic utterance induced by religious excitement.

TRANSFIGURATION: Change in form or appearance, such as the transfiguration of Jesus (Mark 9:2-10).

TRANSMUTATION: The change from one nature, substance, or form to another.

TRANSUBSTANTIATION: The doctrine that there is present in the Eucharist after consecration of the elements the substantial body and blood of Christ, with his whole soul and divinity.

TRINE IMMERSION: A form of baptism in which the candidate is immersed three successive times, in the name of the Father, Son, and Holy Ghost.

TRINITARIAN: A believer in the Trinity—that there is a union of Father, Son, and Holy Ghost in one divine nature.

UNCTION: A ceremonial anointing with oil, as in extreme unction in case of death or imminent death.

UNIAT: Persons or churches acknowledging the supremacy of the pope but maintaining their own liturgies or rites.

UNITARIAN: The theology which insists upon the unity of God, denying the doctrine of the Trinity.

UNIVERSALISM: The universal fatherhood of God, and the final harmony of all souls with God.

BIBLIOGRAPHY

Included in this listing are books recommended by scholars and leaders within the various denominations, as they appeared in the first revised edition of the *Handbook*, and books added by the editor as he prepared this second edition. They are selected on the basis of accuracy and authority, and the list includes volumes published as recently as 1959-60.

Books are listed in two classifications: "General," covering the whole field of the church in the United States; and "Denominational," covering the separate groups.

Beyond this there are of course innumerable treatises, tracts, memorials, disciplines, theological outlines, confessions, and other statements of belief and organization obtainable from the headquarters of the churches, listed on pp. 229-35.

GENERAL

Religious Bodies: 1936. 2 vols. Washington, D.C.: U. S. Dept. of Commerce, Bureau of the Census.

Yearbook of American Churches. New York: National Council of the Churches of Christ in the U.S.A. Publ. annually.

Anderson, W. K. (ed.). *Protestantism: A Symposium.* Nashville: Commission on Ministerial Training, The Methodist Church, 1944.

Bach, Marcus. *Faith and My Friends.* Indianapolis: Bobbs-Merrill Co., Inc., 1951.

————. *Report to Protestants.* Indianapolis: Bobbs-Merrill Co., Inc., 1953.

Bilheimer, R. S. *The Quest for Christian Unity.* New York: Association Press, 1952.

Braden, C. S. *These Also Believe.* New York: The Macmillan Co., 1949.

Brauer, J. C. *Protestantism in America.* Philadelphia: Westminster Press, 1953.

Carroll, H. K. (ed.). *American Church History Series.* 12 vols. New York: Christian Literature Co., 1893.

Clark, Elmer T. *The Small Sects in America.* Nashville: Abingdon Press, 1949.

Dorchester, Daniel. *Christianity in the United States.* New York: 1888.

Eckardt, Arthur Roy. *The Surge of Piety in America.* New York: Association Press, 1958.

Engelder, Theodore, *et al. Popular Symbolics.* St. Louis: Concordia Publishing House, 1934.

Ferm, Vergilius (ed.). *The American Church of the Protestant Heritage.* New York: Philosophical Library, 1953.

Garrison, W. E. *The March of Faith.* New York: Harper & Bros., 1933.

Mayer, F. E. *The Religious Bodies of America.* St. Louis: Concordia Publishing House, 1954.

Mead, Frank S. *See These Banners Go.* Indianapolis: Bobbs-Merrill Co., Inc., 1936.

Neve, J. L. *Churches and Sects of Christendom.* Rev. ed. Blair, Nebr.: Lutheran Publishing House, 1952.

Rowe, H. K. *The History of Religion in the United States.* New York: The Macmillan Co., 1924.

Schaff, Philip. *The Creeds of Christendom.* New York: Harper & Bros.

Sperry, W. L. *Religion in America.* New York: The Macmillan Co., 1946.

Stuber, Stanley I. *How We Got Our Denominations*. Rev. ed.; New York: Association Press, 1948.

Sweet, Wm. W. *The American Churches: An Interpretation*. New York: Abingdon Press, 1948.

_____. *Religion in the Development of American Culture*. New York: Chas. Scribner's Sons, 1952.

_____. *The Story of Religions in America*. New York: Harper & Bros., 1930.

Williams, J. Paul. *What Americans Believe and How They Worship*. New York: Harper & Bros., 1952.

DENOMINATIONAL

ADVENTISM

Froom, Le Roy E. *The Prophetic Faith of Our Fathers*. 3 vols. Washington, D.C.: Review & Herald Publishing Assn., 1946-54.

Loughborough, J. N. *Rise and Progress of Seventh-Day Adventists*. Nashville: Southern Publishing Assn., 1892.

Olsen, M. E. *A History of the Origin and Progress of Seventh-Day Adventists*. Washington, D.C.: Review & Herald Publishing Assn., 1925.

White, Ellen G. *The Desire of Ages*. Mountain View, Cal.: Pacific Press Publishing Assn., 1940.

_____. *The Great Controversy Between Christ and Satan*. Mountain View, Cal.: Pacific Press Publishing Assn., 1927.

_____. *The Ministry of Healing*. Washington, D.C.: Review & Herald Publishing Assn., 1909.

_____. *Steps to Christ*. Washington, D.C.: Review & Herald Publishing Assn., 1908.

BAHÁ'Í

Esslemont, J. E. *Bahá'u'lláh and the New Era*. Rev. ed.; Wilmette, Ill.: Bahá'í Publishing Committee, 1952.

White, Ruth. *Bahá'í Leads Out of the Labyrinth*. New York: Universal Publishing Co., 1944.

BAPTISTS

Barnes, W. W. *The Southern Baptist Convention: 1845-1953*. Nashville: Broadman Press, 1954.

_____. *These Glorious Years* (German Baptists, 1843-1943). Cleveland: Roger Williams Press.

Campbell, Alexander. *Christian Baptism with Its Antecedents and Consequences*. Bethany, Va.: A Campbell, 1852.

Carroll, B. H. *Baptists and Their Doctrines*. Westwood, N.J.: Fleming H. Revell Co., 1913.

Cox, Norman W. *Encyclopedia of Southern Baptists*. 2 vols. Nashville: Broadman Press, 1958.

Mead, Frank S. *The Baptists*. Nashville: Broadman Press, 1954.

Newman, A. H. *History of the Baptist Churches in the United States*. Rev. and enl. ed.; Philadelphia: American Baptist Publication Society, 1913.

Newton, Louis De Votie. *Why I Am a Baptist*. New York: Thomas Nelson & Sons, 1957.

Olson, Adolf. *A Centenary History* (Baptist General Conference of America). Chicago: Baptist Conference Press, 1952.

Schwartz, E. M. *A Compendium of Baptist History*. Boston: Meador Publishing Co., 1939.

Straton, H. H. *Baptists: Their Message and Mission*. Philadelphia: American Baptist Publication Society, 1941.

Sweet, Wm. W. *Religion on the American Frontier: The Baptists, 1783-1830.* New York: Henry Holt & Co., Inc., 1931.

Torbet, R. G. *A History of the Baptists.* Philadelphia: Judson Press, 1950.

Ramaker, A. J. *The German Baptists in North America.* Cleveland: German Baptist Publication Society, 1924.

Vedder, H. C. *A Short History of the Baptists.* Philadelphia: Judson Press, 1907.

BRETHREN

Brumbaugh, M. G. *A History of German Baptist Brethren in America.* Elgin, Ill.: Brethren Publishing House, 1899.

Frantz, Edward. *Basic Belief.* Elgin, Ill.: Brethren Publishing House, 1943.

Mallott, Floyd E. *Studies in Brethren History.* Elgin, Ill.: Brethren Publishing House, 1954.

Winger, O. *History and Doctrine of the Church of the Brethren.* Elgin, Ill.: Brethren Publishing House, 1920.

CHRISTIAN SCIENCE

Bates, Ernest S., and Dittemore, John V. *Mary Baker Eddy.* New York: Alfred A. Knopf, Inc., 1932.

Beasley, Norman. *The Cross and the Crown: the History of Christian Science.* New York: Duell, Sloan & Pearce, 1952.

Eddy, Mary Baker. *Retrospection and Introspection.* Boston: Christian Science Publishing Society.

————. *Science and Health with Key to the Scriptures.* Boston: Christian Science Publishing Society.

————. *Truth vs. Error.* Boston: Christian Science Publishing Society.

Powell, Lyman P. *Mary Baker Eddy.* Boston: Christian Science Publishing Society, 1930.

Wilbur, Sibyl. *The Life of Mary Baker Eddy.* Boston: Christian Science Publishing Society, 1938.

CHURCH OF GOD

Brown, C. E. *When the Trumpet Sounded* (History of the Church of God of Anderson, Ind.). Anderson, Ind.: Warner Press, 1951.

Ferguson, C. W. *The New Book of Revelations.* New York: Doubleday, Doran & Co., Inc., 1929.

Forney, C. H. *History of the Churches of God.* Harrisburg, Pa.: 1914.

Frodsham, S. H. *With Signs Following.* Rev. ed. Springfield, Mo.: Gospel Publishing House, 1941.

Riggs, R. M. *The Spirit Himself.* Springfield, Mo.: Gospel Publishing House, 1949.

CHURCH OF THE NAZARENE

Redford, M. E. *The Rise of the Church of the Nazarene.* Kansas City: Nazarene Publishing House, 1951.

CHURCHES OF CHRIST

MacClenny, W. E. *Life of James O'Kelly.* Indianapolis, Ind.: United Christian Missionary Society, 1950.

Stone, B. W. *Biography of Elder Barton Warren Stone.* Cincinnati, Ohio: Standard Publishing Co., 1847.

West, E. *Search for the Ancient Order.* Indianapolis, Ind.: 1951.

CHURCHES OF THE NEW JERUSALEM (SWEDENBORGIANS)

Barrett, B. F. *The Question, What Are the Doctrines of the New Church? answered.* Germantown, Pa.: Swedenborg Publication Association, 1909.

Smyth, J. K. *Gist of Swedenborg*. Philadelphia: J. B. Lippincott Co., 1920.

Swedenborg, Emanuel. *Complete Works*. Boston: Houghton Mifflin Co., 1907.

CONGREGATIONAL CHRISTIAN CHURCHES

Atkins, G. G., and Fagley, F. L. *History of American Congregationalism*. Boston: Pilgrim Press, 1942.

Burton, C. E. *Manual of the Congregational and Christian Churches*. Boston: Pilgrim Press, 1936.

Dale, R. W. *History of English Congregationalism*. New York: Doubleday, Doran & Co., Inc., 1907.

Horton, W. M. *Our Christian Faith (Congregationalism Today and Tomorrow)*. Boston: Pilgrim Press, 1945.

DISCIPLES OF CHRIST

Abbott, B. A. *The Disciples, an Interpretation*. St. Louis: Bethany Press, 1924.

Campbell, Alexander. *Debate with N. L. Rice*. Cincinnati: Standard Publishing Co., 1917.

Campbell, Thomas. *Declaration and Address*. Cincinnati: American Christian Missionary Society, 1908.

Garrison, W. E. *An American Religious Movement*. St. Louis: Bethany Press, 1945.

————, and DeGroot, Alfred. *The Disciples of Christ: A History*. St. Louis: Bethany Press, 1948.

Tyler, B. B. *History of the Disciples of Christ* (American Church History Series, Vol. XII). New York: Christian Literature Co., 1893.

EASTERN ORTHODOX CHURCHES

Attwater, Donald. *The Catholic Eastern Churches*. Milwaukee: Bruce Publishing Co., 1935.

Bulgakov, S., *et al. Revelation*. Ed. John Baillie and Hugh Martin. New York: The Macmillan Co., 1937.

————. *The Wisdom of God*. New York: Paisley Press, Inc., 1937.

Fortescue, Adrian. *The Orthodox Eastern Church*. London: Catholic Truth Society, 1929.

Gavin, Frank S. B. *Some Aspects of Contemporary Greek Orthodox Thought*. New York: Morehouse-Gorham Co., 1923.

Horton, W. M. *Continental and European Theology (The Rediscovery of Orthodox Theology*, ch. 4). New York: Harper & Bros., 1938.

Janin, Raymond. *The Separated Eastern Churches*. Tr. P. Boylan. St. Louis: B. Herder Book Co., 1933.

Kephala, E. *The Church of the Greek People*. New York: The Macmillan Co., 1930.

Spinka, Matthew. *The Church and the Russian Revolution*. New York: The Macmillan Co., 1927.

EVANGELICAL AND REFORMED CHURCH

Evangelical Catechism. St. Louis: Eden Publishing House, 1929.

Bruning, D., *et al. Evangelical Fundamentals*. St. Louis: 1916.

Horstmann, J. H. E., and Wernecke, H. H. *Through Four Centuries*. St. Louis: Eden Publishing House, 1938

Schneider, C. E. *The German Church on the American Frontier*. St. Louis: Eden Publishing House, 1939.

EVANGELICAL UNITED BRETHREN

Albright, R. W. *History of the Evangelical Church*. Harrisburg, Pa.: Evangelical Press, 1942.

Breyfogel, S. C. *Landmarks of the Evangelical Association.* Reading, Pa.: 1888.

Drury, A. W. *History of the Church of the United Brethren in Christ.* Dayton, Ohio: Otterbein Press, 1924.

Eller, P. H. *These Evangelical United Brethren.* Dayton, Ohio: Otterbein Press, 1950.

FRIENDS

Barclay, Robert. *An Apology for the True Christian Divinity.*

Braithwaite, W. C. *The Beginnings of Quakerism.* New York: The Macmillan Co., 1912.

————. *The Second Period of Quakerism.* New York: The Macmillan Co., 1919.

Comfort, W. W. *Quakers in the Modern World.* New York: The Macmillan Co., 1949.

Grubb, Edward. *Quaker Thought and History.* New York: The Macmillan Co., 1925.

Jones, Rufus M. *The Faith and Practice of the Quakers.* New York: Harper & Bros., 1927.

————. *The Flowering of Mysticism.* New York: The Macmillan Co., 1939.

————. *The Later Periods of Quakerism.* New York: St. Martin's Press, Inc.

————. *The Quakers in Action.* New York: The Macmillan Co., 1929.

Lucas, Sidney. *The Quaker Story.* New York: Harper & Bros., 1949.

Russell, Elbert. *The History of Quakerism.* New York: The Macmillan Co., 1942.

Sykes, John. *The Quakers, A New Look at Their Place in Society.* Philadelphia: J. B. Lippincott Co., 1959.

Thomas, A. C. and R. H. *A History of the Friends in America.* 6th ed., rev. and enl.; Philadelphia: John C. Winston Co., 1930.

See also *Principles of Quakerism,* 1909, and *Faith and Practice,* 1926, published by the Philadelphia Book Store, and *The Book of Discipline* (Hicksites), 1927, published by the Race Street Meeting, Philadelphia, Pa.

JEHOVAH'S WITNESSES

New World Translation of the Christian Greek Scriptures. Brooklyn, N. Y.: Watch Tower Bible & Tract Society, 1950.

The Yearbook of Jehovah's Witnesses. Publ. annually since 1933. Brooklyn, N. Y.: Watch Tower Bible & Tract Society.

Russell, Charles Taze. *The Divine Plan of the Ages.* Brooklyn, N. Y.: Watch Tower Bible & Tract Society, 1908.

————. *Studies in the Scriptures.* Brooklyn, N. Y.: Watch Tower Bible & Tract Society, 1905-9.

Rutherford, J. F. *The Harp of Gold,* 1921; *Deliverance,* 1926; *Creation,* 1927; *Light,* 1929; *Prophecy,* 1929; *Riches,* 1936; *Salvation,* 1939; *Religion,* 1939. Brooklyn, N.Y.: Watch Tower Bible & Tract Society.

JEWISH CONGREGATIONS

Agus, Jacob Bernard. *Guideposts in Modern Judaism.* New York: Bloch Publishing Co., 1954.

Finkelstein, Louis. *The Jews: Their History, Culture, and Religion.* New York: Harper & Bros., 1949.

Gaer, Joseph. *Our Jewish Heritage.* New York: Holt, Rinehart and Winston, 1957.

Gordon, A. I. *Jews in Transition.* Minneapolis: University of Minnesota Press, 1949.

Janowsky, Oscar I. (ed.). *The American Jew.* New York: Harper & Bros., 1942.

Levinger, Lee J. *A History of the Jews in the United States.* New York: Union of American Hebrew Congregations, 1935.

Pool, David de Sola. *Why I Am a Jew.* New York: Thomas Nelson & Sons, 1957.

Steinberg, Milton. *Basic Judaism*. New York: Harcourt, Brace & Co., 1947.

Wouk, Herman. *This Is My God*. Garden City, N. Y.: Doubleday & Co., Inc., 1959.

LATTER DAY SAINTS (MORMONS)

Hinckley, G. B. *What of the Mormons?* Salt Lake City: Deseret Book Co., 1947.

Richards, F. D., and Little, J. A. *A Compendium of the Doctrines of the Gospel*. Salt Lake City: Deseret Book Co., 1925.

Smith, Joseph. *The Book of Mormon*. Ed. John A. Widtsoe. Salt Lake City: Deseret Book Co., 1925.

_____. *The Doctrines and Covenants*. Ed. John A. Widtsoe. Salt Lake City: Deseret Book Co., 1925.

_____. *The Pearl of Great Price*. Salt Lake City: Deseret Book Co., 1921.

Smith, J. F. *Essentials in Church History*. Salt Lake City: Deseret Book Co., 1928.

Talmage, James E. *Articles of Faith*. Salt Lake City: Deseret Book Co., 1925.

LUTHERANS

Allbeck, W. D. *Studies in the Lutheran Confessions*. Philadelphia: Muhlenberg Press, 1952.

Bainton, Roland. *Here I Stand* (Biography of Luther). Nashville: Abingdon Press, 1950.

Beck, Victor Emanuel. *Why I Am a Lutheran*. New York: Thomas Nelson & Sons, 1956.

Bente, Frederick. *American Lutheranism*. St. Louis: Concordia Publishing House, 1919.

Carnarius, Stanley E. *What Lutherans Believe*. Philadelphia: United Lutheran Publishing House, 1951.

Fendt, E. C. (ed.). *What Lutherans Are Thinking*. Columbus, Ohio: Wartburg Press, 1947.

Ferm, Vergilius. *Crisis in American Lutheran Theology*. New York: Century Co., 1927.

_____, (ed.). *What Is Lutheranism?* New York: The Macmillan Co., 1930.

Kerr, H. T., Jr. (ed.). *A Compend of Luther's Theology*. Philadelphia: The Westminster Press, 1943.

Neve, J. L. *History of the Lutheran Church in America*. Burlington, Iowa: Lutheran Literary Board, Inc., 1934.

_____. *Introduction to the Symbolical Books of the Lutheran Church*. Columbus, Ohio: Lutheran Book Concern, 1926.

Richard, J. W. *The Confessional History of the Lutheran Church*. 1909.

Sasse, Hermann. *Here We Stand*. Tr. T. G. Tappert. New York: Harper & Bros., 1938.

Wentz, A. R. *The Lutheran Church in American History*. Philadelphia: United Lutheran Publication House, 1933.

Wentz, A. R. *A Basic History of Lutheranism in America*. Rev. ed.; Philadelphia: Muhlenberg Press, 1955.

MENNONITES

Bender, H. S. *Conrad Grebel, 1498-1526. The Founder of the Swiss Brethren, Sometimes Called Anabaptists*. Scottdale, Pa.: Herald Press, 1950.

Hershberger, G. F. *War, Peace, and Nonresistance*. Scottdale, Pa.: Herald Press, 1953.

Smith, C. H. *The Story of the Mennonites*. 3rd ed., rev. and enl. Newton, Kan.: Mennonite Publication Office, 1950.

Wenger, John C. *Glimpses of Mennonite History and Doctrine*. Scottdale, Pa.: Herald Press, 1949.

_____. *Introduction to Theology: An Interpretation of the Doctrinal Content of Scripture. Written to Strengthen a Childlike Faith in Christ*. Scottdale, Pa.: Herald Press, 1954.

_____. *Separated Unto God: A Plea for Christian Simplicity of Life and for a Scriptural Nonconformity to the World*. Scottdale, Pa.: Herald Press, 1951.

BIBLIOGRAPHY

METHODISTS

The Journal of John Wesley. 8 vols. Ed. N. Curnock.

Anderson, W. K. (ed.). *Methodism.* New York: Methodist Publishing House, 1947.

Carter, Henry. *The Methodist Heritage.* Nashville: Abingdon Press, 1951.

Clark, Elmer T., Potts, J. Manning and Payton, Jacob S. *The Journals and Letters of Francis Asbury.* Nashville: Abingdon Press, 1960.

Faulkner, J. A. *The Methodists.* Rev. ed.; New York: Methodist Book Concern, 1925.

History of Methodist Missions. New York: Board of Missions and Church Extension of the Methodist Church, 1949-1957.

Harmon, Nolan B. *The Organization of the Methodist Church.* Rev. ed.; Nashville: Methodist Publishing House, 1953.

————. *Understanding the Methodist Church.* Nashville: Methodist Publishing House, 1955.

Kennedy, Gerald Hamilton. *The Methodist Way of Life.* Englewood Cliffs, N. J.: Prentice-Hall, 1958.

Lee, Umphrey. *The Lord's Horseman.* New York and Nashville: Abingdon Press, 1954.

Luccock, Halford E., and Hutchinson, Paul. *The Story of Methodism.* Rev. ed.; New York and Nashville: Abingdon Press, 1950.

Rowe, G. T. *The Meaning of Methodism.* Nashville: Cokesbury Press, 1926.

Stokes, Mack B. *Major Methodist Beliefs.* Nashville: The Methodist Publishing House, 1956.

Sweet, W. W. *Methodism in American History.* Rev. and enl. ed.; New York and Nashville: Abingdon Press, 1954.

Tipple, E. S. (ed.). *The Heart of Asbury's Journal.* New York: Methodist Book Concern, 1904.

MORAVIANS

The Moravian Manual. Bethlehem, Pa.: Moravian Book Store, 1901.

Allen, W. H. *The Moravians, a World-Wide Fellowship.* Bethlehem, Pa.: Moravian Book Store, 1940.

Hamilton, J. T. *A History of the Church Known as the Moravian Church or the Unitas Fratrum.* Bethlehem, Pa.: Moravian Book Store, 1900.

Schweinitz, E. A. *The History of Unitas Fratrum.* Bethlehem, Pa.: Moravian Book Store, 1885.

————— and Schultze, A. *The Moravians and Their Faith.* Bethlehem, Pa.: Moravian Book Store, 1930.

PENTECOSTAL BODIES

Clark, E. T. *The Small Sects in America.* Rev. ed.; New York and Nashville: Abingdon Press, 1949.

Ferguson, C. W. *The New Book of Revelations.* New York: Doubleday, Doran & Co., Inc., 1929.

Frodsham, S. H. *With Signs Following.* Rev. ed.; Springfield, Mo.: Gospel Publishing House, 1941.

Riggs, R. M. *The Spirit Himself.* Springfield, ·Mo.: Gospel Publishing House, 1949.

Stolee, H. J. *Pentecostalism.* Minneapolis: Augsburg Publishing House, 1936.

PRESBYTERIANS

Briggs, C. A. *American Presbyterianism.* New York: Chas. Scribner's Sons, 1885.

Drury, C. M. *Presbyterian Panorama.* Philadelphia: Westminster Press, 1952.

Gillet, E. H. *History of the Presbyterian Church in the United States of America*. Philadelphia: Westminster Press, 1864.

Loetscher, Lefferts A. *A Brief History of the Presbyterians*. Rev. ed.; Philadelphia: Westminster Press, 1958.

Miller, Park Hays. *Why I Am A Presbyterian*. New York: Thomas Nelson & Sons, 1956.

Reed, R. C. *History of the Presbyterian Churches of the World*. Philadelphia: Westminster Press, 1905.

Roberts, W. H. *A Concise History of the Presbyterian Church in the United States of America*. Philadelphia: Westminster Press, 1920.

Thompson, R. E. *A History of the Presbyterian Churches in the United States* (American Church History Series, Vol. VI). New York: Chas. Scribner's Sons.

Zenos, Andrew C. *Presbyterianism in America*. New York: Thomas Nelson & Sons, 1937.

PROTESTANT EPISCOPAL CHURCH

Addison, J. T. *The Episcopal Church in the United States: 1789-1931*. New York: Chas. Scribner's Sons, 1951.

Chorley, E. C. *Men and Movements in the American Episcopal Church*. New York: Chas. Scribner's Sons, 1946.

Damrosch, Frank, Jr. *The Faith of the Episcopal Church*. New York: Morehouse-Gorham Co., 1946.

Manross, W. W. *A History of the American Episcopal Church*. New York: Morehouse-Gorham Co., 1950.

McConnell, S. D. *History of the American Episcopal Church*. Milwaukee: Morehouse Publishing Co., 1916.

Tiffany, C. C. *A History of the Episcopal Church* (American Church History Series). New York: Chas. Scribner's Sons, 1895.

Will, Theodore. *The Episcopal Church*. New York: Morehouse-Gorham Co., 1934.

Wilson, Frank E. *Faith and Practice*. New York: Morehouse-Gorham Co., 1941.

REFORMED BODIES

The Word of God and the Reformed Faith. American Calvinistic Conference. Grand Rapids, Mich.: Baker Book House, 1942.

Berts, H. *The Christian Reformed Church in North America*. Grand Rapids, Mich.: Eastern Avenue Book Store, 1923.

Boettner, Loraine. *Studies in Theology*. Grand Rapids, Mich.: Wm. B. Eerdmans Publishing Co., 1941.

Brown, W. D. *History of the Reformed Church in America* New York: Board of Publication & Bible School Work of the Reformed Church in America, 1928.

Corwin, E. T., *et al*. *A History of the Reformed Church, Dutch, the Reformed Church, German, and the Moravian Church in the United States* (American Church History Series, Vol. VIII). New York: Chas. Scribner's Sons.

Demerast, D. D. *The Reformed Church in America*. New York: Board of Publication of the Reformed Dutch Church, 1884.

ROMAN CATHOLIC CHURCH

Catholic Dictionary. Ed. Donald Attwater. 2nd rev. ed.; New York: The Macmillan Co., 1955.

The Catholic Encyclopedia. 15 vols. New York: Robert Appleton Co., 1907.

Hughes, Philip. *A History of the Church*. New York: Sheed & Ward, Ltd., 1934-47.

Maynard, Theodore. *The Story of American Catholicism* (by a convert). New York: The Macmillan Co., 1941.

BIBLIOGRAPHY

McSorley, Joseph. *An Outline History of the Church by Centuries.* St. Louis: B. Herder Book Co., 1948.

O'Gorman, Thomas. *History of the Roman Catholic Church in the United States* (American Church History Series). New York: Christian Literature Co., 1895.

Sheehan, Michael. *Apologetics and Catholic Doctrine.* Philadelphia: Peter Reilly Co.

Smith, G. D. (ed.). *The Teaching of the Catholic Church, a Summary of Catholic Doctrine.* New York: The Macmillan Co., 1949.

Stuber, S. I. *Primer on Roman Catholicism for Protestants.* New York: Association Press, 1953.

SPIRITUALISTS

The Spiritualist Manual. Washington, D.C.: National Spiritualist Assn. of the United States of America.

Bach, Marcus. *They Have Found a Faith.* Indianapolis: Bobbs-Merrill Co., Inc., 1946.

Braden, Chas. S. *These Also Believe.* New York: The Macmillan Co., 1949.

Graebner, Theodore T. *Spiritism.* St Louis: Concordia Publishing House, 1919.

Hill, J. A. *Spiritualism: Its History, Phenomena and Doctrine.* New York: Doubleday, Doran & Co., Inc., 1919.

Leaf, H. *What Is This Spiritualism?* New York: Doubleday, Doran & Co., Inc., 1919.

UNITARIANS

Scholefield, H. B. *Unitarianism—Some Past History and Present Meanings.* Boston: Beacon Press, 1950.

Wilbur, E. M. *A History of Unitarianism.* Cambridge, Mass.: Harvard University Press, 1952.

————. *Our Unitarian Heritage.* Boston: Beacon Press, 1925.

UNIVERSALISTS

Ballou, Hosea. *The Ancient History of Universalism.* Boston: Marsh & Capen, 1829.

Brotherson, B. W. *A Philosophy of Liberalism.* Boston: Universalist Publishing House, 1934.

Cole, A. S. *Our Liberal Heritage.* Boston: Beacon Press, 1951.

Kapp, M. A. *These Universalists.* Boston: Universalist Publishing House.

Perkins, F. W. *Beliefs Commonly Held Among Us.* Boston: Universalist Publishing House.

Thayer, T. B. *The Theology of Universalism.* Boston: Universalist Publishing House, 1862.

INDEX

280
M
MEAD, FRANK S.
   Handbook of denominations
in the United States

7064

DATE DUE		
OCT 1	JAN 24	
FEB 17	APR 18 1994	
MAY 11	APR 01 1990	
OCT 31		
JAN 10		
MAY 12		
FEB 10		
MAY 8,'84		
Long term		
JAN 5 1988		